Artificial Intelligence f Robotics

Build intelligent robots that perform human tasks using
AI techniques

Francis X. Govers

Packt>

BIRMINGHAM - MUMBAI

Artificial Intelligence for Robotics

Commissioning Editor: Vijin Boricha
Acquisition Editor: Namrata Patil
Content Development Editor: Sharon Raj
Technical Editor: Mohit Hassija
Copy Editor: Safis Editing
Project Coordinator: Drashti Panchal
Proofreader: Safis Editing
Indexer: Pratik Shirodkar
Graphics: Tom Scaria
Production Coordinator: Arvindkumar Gupta

First published: August 2018

Production reference: 1290818

Published by Packt Publishing Ltd.
Livery Place
35 Livery Street
Birmingham
B3 2PB, UK.

ISBN 978-1-78883-544-2

www.packtpub.com

I would like to dedicate this book to the memory of my father, Francis X. Govers II, who taught me from a young age to dream big and never stop reading and learning.

Mapt

Mapt is an online digital library that gives you full access to over 5,000 books and videos, as well as industry leading tools to help you plan your personal development and advance your career. For more information, please visit our website.

Why subscribe?

- Spend less time learning and more time coding with practical eBooks and Videos from over 4,000 industry professionals

- Improve your learning with Skill Plans built especially for you

- Get a free eBook or video every month

- Mapt is fully searchable

- Copy and paste, print, and bookmark content

PacktPub.com

Did you know that Packt offers eBook versions of every book published, with PDF and ePub files available? You can upgrade to the eBook version at www.PacktPub.com and as a print book customer, you are entitled to a discount on the eBook copy. Get in touch with us at service@packtpub.com for more details.

At www.PacktPub.com, you can also read a collection of free technical articles, sign up for a range of free newsletters, and receive exclusive discounts and offers on Packt books and eBooks.

Contributors

About the author

Francis X. Govers is an autonomous vehicle designer at Bell Helicopter Textron. He is the designer of 28 unmanned vehicles or robots for land, sea, air, and space, including RAMSEE, the autonomous security guard robot. Francis helped design the International Space Station, the F-35 JSF Fighter, the US Army Future Combat Systems, and systems for NASCAR and IndyCar. He is an engineer, pilot, author, musician, artist, and maker. He received five outstanding achievement awards from NASA and recognition from Scientific American for *World Changing Ideas*.

I want to thank everyone who supported me in the writing of this book, starting with my wife, Carol, who cheered me on; our adult children, Jessica, Peter, Corbin, and Ammie, for their encouragement. To my grandchildren, William, Oliver, Amelia, and Henry, for their inspiration. To my editors at Packt Publishing, Namrata Patil and Sharon Raj, for encouragement and tireless dedication. I also have to thank Dr. Bob Finkelstein, my robotics guru and mentor. Finally, to Jay Blanchard, my oldest and dearest friend and fellow author.

About the reviewers

Nikhil Borkar holds a CQF designation and a post-graduate degree in quantitative finance. He also holds the Certified Financial Crime examiner and Certified Anti-Money Laundering Professional qualifications. He is a registered research analyst with the **Securities and Exchange Board of India** (**SEBI**) and has a keen grasp of the Indian regulatory landscape pertaining to securities and investments. He is currently working as an independent FinTech and legal consultant. Prior to this, the worked with Morgan Stanley Capital International (MSCI) as a global RFP project manager.

Lentin Joseph is an author and robotics entrepreneur from India. He runs a robotics software company called Qbotics Labs in India. He has 8 years of experience in the robotics domain, primarily in ROS, OpenCV, and PCL. He has authored seven books on ROS, which include *Learning Robotics Using Python*, both the first and second edition, *Mastering ROS for Robotics Programming*, first and second edition. He has a master's in Robotics and Automation and also did research at Robotics Institute, CMU, USA.

Packt is searching for authors like you

If you're interested in becoming an author for Packt, please visit `authors.packtpub.com` and apply today. We have worked with thousands of developers and tech professionals, just like you, to help them share their insight with the global tech community. You can make a general application, apply for a specific hot topic that we are recruiting an author for, or submit your own idea.

Table of Contents

Preface

The objective of this book is to deliver exactly what is on the cover – *Artificial Intelligence for Robotics*. The emphasis is on machine learning techniques applied to ground mobile robots. The book starts with professional robot design principles that have been scaled down for smaller robot projects. The AI section begins with convolutional neural networks for object recognition and continues with reinforcement learning and genetic algorithms. The robot gets a voice and learns to tell jokes using AI-based voice recognition that can discern user intent. The book introduces a novel way to navigate without a map using a literal divide and conquer program that uses the upper part of the room to remember paths, and the lower part of avoid obstacles. The book demonstrates how path planning, decision trees, object classification, and navigation are all part of the same problem set. We finish by giving the robot an artificial personality. The final chapter concludes with thoughts on the future of robots and gives advice on robotics as a career.

The entire book is built around a single fun example task, which is to design and build a robot that can pick up toys in an indoor, unstructured environment. As you will learn, this project is anything but easy.

Who this book is for

This book is designed for intermediate to advanced robotics researchers, professionals, and hobbyists, as well as students who have worked past the basics of robotics and are looking for the next step in their education and skill set.

Readers should be familiar with Python and the **Robotics Operating System** (**ROS**), as well as Linux. Advanced math is most definitely not required to get a lot out of this book.

What this book covers

Chapter 1, *Foundation for Robotics and AI*, introduces artificial intelligence (AI) and covers the basics of robotics as applied in this book. The chapter also introduces the AI framework used, which is the **Observe-Orient-Decide-Act** (**OODA**) model, and soft real-time control.

Chapter 2, *Setting Up Your Robot*, covers the robot architecture, ROS, and setting up the software and hardware, including the construction of the robot example for the book.

Chapter 3, *A Concept for a Practical Robot Design Process*, introduces a simplified systems approach to robot design that combines use cases (from systems engineering) and storyboards (from Agile development) to give the reader a structure and a process to use when solving problems with robots and AI.

Chapter 4, *Object Recognition Using Neural Networks and Supervised Learning*, teaches how to build an artificial neural network. Readers will learn the basics of image recognition as well as the training and evaluation of neural networks using Keras and Python.

Chapter 5, *Picking Up the Toys*, introduces techniques that allow the robot to learn for itself how to user its robot arm. The key technique is to have a mechanism for the robot to score how well it does. We explore reinforcement learning and dive into Genetic Algorithms.

Chapter 6, *Teaching the Robot to Listen*, We develop on top of a voice-based command system, a type of digital assistant that uses AI techniques to understand words and divine the intent of the speaker. Basic concepts of speech recognition and natural language processing are introduced, such as context, knowledge bases, intent recognition, and sentence reconstruction. We teach the robot to both tell and understand knock-knock jokes.

Chapter 7, *Avoiding the Stairs*, helps the readers understand robot navigation, including SLAM. It will help you navigate the robot using a combination of two techniques: Floor Finding for obstacle avoidance, and Neural Network Image recognition for learned navigation without a map.

Chapter 8, *Putting Things Away*, covers path planning, decision trees, classification techniques, wave front, the A* (A star) and D* (D star) algorithms, and node-based planners.

Chapter 9, *Giving the Robot an Artificial Personality*, describes simulation and Monte Carlo modeling, the Robot Emotion Engine, the Human Emotion Model, and integrating personality rules into a chatbot-based conversation engine.

Chapter 10, *Conclusions and Remarks*, has some words about the future of AI and robotics, as well as advice about robotics as a career.

To get the most out of this book

The reader should have a good grasp of programming with Python, either 2.7 or 3.6. Most of the examples are written in 2.7, but conversion to 3.6 or above is fairly simple – it is mostly changing the `print` statements. The ROS works only in Linux. The reader can use a virtual machine to emulate Linux on a Windows computer. This was done by the author when writing this book. Packt Publishing has several excellent books that explain how to use ROS, if you need more detailed instruction. No special math skills are required past high-school level. If you want to follow the robot's construction, then basic hand tools (screwdrivers, wrenches, Allen keys, and a soldering iron) will be required.

All the other installation instructions are in the appropriate chapters as the book progresses.

Download the example code files

You can download the example code files for this book from your account at `www.packtpub.com`. If you purchased this book elsewhere, you can visit `www.packtpub.com/support` and register to have the files emailed directly to you.

You can download the code files by following these steps:

1. Log in or register at `www.packtpub.com`.
2. Select the **SUPPORT** tab.
3. Click on **Code Downloads & Errata**.
4. Enter the name of the book in the **Search** box and follow the onscreen instructions.

Once the file is downloaded, please make sure that you unzip or extract the folder using the latest version of:

- WinRAR/7-Zip for Windows
- Zipeg/iZip/UnRarX for Mac
- 7-Zip/PeaZip for Linux

The code bundle for the book is also hosted on GitHub at `https://github.com/PacktPublishing/Artificial-Intelligence-for-Robotics`. In case there's an update to the code, it will be updated on the existing GitHub repository.

We also have other code bundles from our rich catalog of books and videos available at `https://github.com/PacktPublishing/`. Check them out!

Download the color images

We also provide a PDF file that has color images of the screenshots/diagrams used in this book. You can download it here: `https://www.packtpub.com/sites/default/files/downloads/ArtificialIntelligenceforRobotics_ColorImages.pdf`

Code in Action

Visit the following link to check out videos of the code being run:
`http://bit.ly/2ohcbLg`

Conventions used

There are a number of text conventions used throughout this book.

`CodeInText`: Indicates code words in text, database table names, folder names, filenames, file extensions, pathnames, dummy URLs, user input, and Twitter handles. Here is an example: "We are writing our control loop in Python, so we will use the `time.time()` function."

A block of code is set as follows:

```
# set our frame rate - how many cycles per second to run our loop?
FRAMERATE = 30
# how long does each frame take in seconds?
FRAME = 1.0/FRAMERATE
# initialize myTimer
# This is one of our timer variables where we will store the clock time
from the operating system.
myTimer = 0.0
```

Any command-line input or output is written as follows:

```
Sudo apt-get install python-pip python-dev build-essential
Sudo pip install -upgrade pip
```

Bold: Indicates a new term, an important word, or words that you see onscreen. For example, words in menus or dialog boxes appear in the text like this. Here is an example: "One concept you will hear around AI circles is the **Turing test**."

Warnings or important notes appear like this.

Tips and tricks appear like this.

Get in touch

Feedback from our readers is always welcome.

General feedback: Email `feedback@packtpub.com` and mention the book title in the subject of your message. If you have questions about any aspect of this book, please email us at `questions@packtpub.com`.

Errata: Although we have taken every care to ensure the accuracy of our content, mistakes do happen. If you have found a mistake in this book, we would be grateful if you would report this to us. Please visit `www.packtpub.com/submit-errata`, selecting your book, clicking on the Errata Submission Form link, and entering the details.

Piracy: If you come across any illegal copies of our works in any form on the Internet, we would be grateful if you would provide us with the location address or website name. Please contact us at `copyright@packtpub.com` with a link to the material.

If you are interested in becoming an author: If there is a topic that you have expertise in and you are interested in either writing or contributing to a book, please visit `authors.packtpub.com`.

Reviews

Please leave a review. Once you have read and used this book, why not leave a review on the site that you purchased it from? Potential readers can then see and use your unbiased opinion to make purchase decisions, we at Packt can understand what you think about our products, and our authors can see your feedback on their book. Thank you!

For more information about Packt, please visit `packtpub.com`.

1
Foundation for Advanced Robotics and AI

This book is for readers who have already begun a journey learning about robotics and wish to progress to a more advanced level of capability by adding AI behaviors to your robot, unmanned vehicle, or self-driving car. You may have already made a robot for yourself out of standard parts, and have a robot that can drive around, perhaps make a map, and avoid obstacles with some basic sensors. The question then is: what comes next?

The basic difference between what we will call an AI robot and a more normal robot is the ability of the robot and its software to make decisions, and learn and adapt to its environment based on data from its sensors. To be a bit more specific, we are leaving the world of deterministic behaviors behind. When we call a system deterministic, we mean that for a set of inputs, the robot will always produce the same output. If faced with the same situation, such as encountering an obstacle, then the robot will always do the same thing, such as go around the obstacle to the left. An AI robot, however, can do two things the standard robot cannot: make decisions and learn from experience. The AI robot will change and adapt to circumstances, and may do something different each time a situation is encountered. It may try to push the obstacle out of the way, or make up a new route, or change goals.

The following topics will be covered in this chapter:

- What is Artificial Intelligence (AI)?
- Modern AI – nothing new
- Our example problem
- What you will learn in this book – AI techniques covered
- Introduction to TinMan, our robot
- Keeping control – soft real-time control
- The OODA loop – basis for decision making

Technical requirements

- Python 2.7 or 3.5 with numpy, scipy, matplotlib, and scikit-learn installed.
- **Robotics Operating System (ROS)** Kinetic Kame.
- A computer running Linux for development or a virtual machine running Linux under Windows. Ubuntu 16.04 is used for the examples and illustrations.
- Raspberry Pi 3 or a similar single board computer (BeagleBone Black, Odroid, or similar). We are not using the GPIO or special interfaces on the Pi3.
- An Arduino Mega 2560 microcontroller.

The repository for the source code in this chapter on GitHub is: `https://github.com/FGovers/AI_and_Robotics_source_code/chapter_1`

Check out the following video to see the Code in Action: `http://bit.ly/2BT0Met`

The basic principle of robotics and AI

Artificial intelligence applied to robotics development requires a different set of skills from you, the robot designer or developer. You may have made robots before. You probably have a quadcopter or a 3D printer (which is, in fact, a robot). The familiar world of **Proportional Integral Derivative (PID)** controllers, sensor loops, and state machines must give way to artificial neural networks, expert systems, genetic algorithms, and searching path planners. We want a robot that does not just react to its environment as a reflex action, but has goals and intent—and can learn and adapt to the environment. We want to solve problems that would be intractable or impossible otherwise.

What we are going to do in this book is introduce a problem – picking up toys in a playroom—that we will use as our example throughout the book as we learn a series of techniques for applying AI techniques to our robot. It is important to understand that in this book, the journey is far more important than the destination. At the end of the book, you should gain some important skills with broad applicability, not just learn how to pick up toys.

One of the difficult decisions I had to make about writing this book was deciding if this is an AI book about robotics or a robotics approach to AI—that is, is the focus learning about robotics or learning about AI? The answer is that this is a book about how to apply AI tools to robotics problems, and thus is primarily an AI book using robotics as an example. The tools and techniques learned will have applicability even if you don't do robotics, but just apply AI to decision making to trade on the stock market.

What we are going to do is first provide some tools and background to match the infrastructure that was used to develop the examples in the book. This is both to provide an even playing field and to not assume any knowledge on the reader's part. We will use the Python programming language, the ROS for our data infrastructure, and be running under the Linux operating system. I developed the examples in the book with Oracle's VirtualBox software running Ubuntu Linux in a virtual machine on a Windows Vista computer. Our robot hardware will be a Raspberry Pi 3 as the robot's on-board brain, and an Arduino Mega2560 as the hardware interface microcontroller.

In the rest of this chapter, we will discuss some basics about AI, and then proceed to develop two important tools that we will use in all of the examples in the rest of the book. We will introduce the concept of soft real-time control, and then provide a framework, or model, for interfacing AI to our robot called the **Observe-Orient-Decide-Act** (**OODA**) loop.

What is AI (and what is it not)?

What would be a definition of AI? In general, it means a machine that exhibits some characteristics of intelligence—thinking, reasoning, planning, learning, and adapting. It can also mean a software program that can simulate thinking or reasoning. Let's try some examples: a robot that avoids obstacles by simple rules (if the obstacle is to the right, go left) is not an AI. A program that learns by example to recognize a cat in a video, is an AI. A mechanical arm that is operated by a joystick is not AI, but a robot arm that adapts to different objects in order to pick them up is AI.

There are two defining characteristics of artificial intelligence robots that you must be aware of. First of all, AI robots learn and adapt to their environments, which means that they change behaviors over time. The second characteristic is **emergent behavior**, where the robot exhibits developing actions that we did not program into it explicitly. We are giving the robot controlling software that is inherently non-linear and self-organizing. The robot may suddenly exhibit some bizarre or unusual reaction to an event or situation that seems to be odd, or quirky, or even emotional. I worked with a self-driving car that we swore had delicate sensibilities and moved very daintily, earning it the nickname *Ferdinand* after the sensitive, flower loving bull from the cartoon, which was appropriate in a nine-ton truck that appeared to like plants. These behaviors are just caused by interactions of the various software components and control algorithms, and do not represent anything more than that.

One concept you will hear around AI circles is the **Turing test**. The Turing test was proposed by Alan Turing in 1950, in a paper entitled *Computing Machinery and Intelligence*. He postulated that a human interrogator would question an hidden, unseen AI system, along with another human. If the human posing the questions was unable to tell which person was the computer and which the human was, then that AI computer would pass the test. This test supposes that the AI would be fully capable of listening to a conversation, understanding the content, and giving the same sort of answers a person will. I don't believe that AI has progressed to this point yet, but chat bots and automated answering services have done a good job of making you believe that you are talking to a human and not a robot.

Our objective in this book is not to pass the Turing test, but rather to take some novel approaches to solving problems using techniques in machine learning, planning, goal seeking, pattern recognition, grouping, and clustering. Many of these problems would be very difficult to solve any other way. A software AI that could pass the Turing test would be an example of a **general artificial intelligence**, or a full, working intelligent artificial brain, and just like you, a general AI does not need to be specifically trained to solve any particular problem. To date, a general AI has not been created, but what we do have is **narrow AI**, or software that simulates thinking in a very narrow application, such as recognizing objects, or picking good stocks to buy.

What we are *not* building in this book is a general AI, and we are not going to be worried about our creations developing a mind of their own or getting out of control. That comes from the realm of science fiction and bad movies, rather than the reality of computers today. I am firmly of the mind that anyone preaching about the *evils* of AI or predicting that robots will take over the world has not worked or practiced in this area, and has not seen the dismal state of AI research in respect of solving general problems or creating anything resembling an actual intelligence.

There is nothing new under the sun

Most of AI as practiced today is not new. Most of these techniques were developed in the 1960s and 1970s and fell out of favor because the computing machinery of the day was insufficient for the complexity of the software or number of calculations required, and only waited for computers to get bigger, and for another very significant event – the invention of the internet. In previous decades, if you needed 10,000 digitized pictures of cats to compile a database to train a neural network, the task would be almost impossible—you could take a lot of cat pictures, or scan images from books. Today, a Google search for cat pictures returns 126,000,000 results in 0.44 seconds. Finding cat pictures, or anything else, is just a search away, and you have your training set for your neural network—unless you need to train on a very specific set of objects that don't happen to be on the internet, as we will see in this book, in which case we will once again be taking a lot of pictures with another modern aid not found in the 1960s, a digital camera. The happy combination of very fast computers; cheap, plentiful storage; and access to almost unlimited data of every sort has produced a renaissance in AI.

Another modern development has occurred on the other end of the computer spectrum. While anyone can now have a supercomputer on their desk at home, the development of the smartphone has driven a whole series of innovations that are just being felt in technology. Your wonder of a smartphone has accelerometers and gyroscopes made of tiny silicon chips called **microelectromechanical systems** (**MEMS**). It also has a high resolution but very small digital camera, and a multi-core computer processor that takes very little power to run. It also contains (probably) three radios: a WiFi wireless network, a cellular phone, and a Bluetooth transceiver. As good as these parts are at making your iPhone™ fun to use, they have also found their way into parts available for robots. That is fun for us because what used to be only available for research labs and universities are now for sale to individual users. If you happen to have a university or research lab, or work for a technology company with multi-million dollar development budgets, you will also learn something from this book, and find tools and ideas that hopefully will inspire your robotics creations or power new products with exciting capabilities.

What is a **robot**? For the purposes of this book, a robot is a machine that is capable of sensing and reacting to its environment, and that has some human or animal-like function. We generally think of a robot as some sort of automated, self-directing mobile machine that can interact with the environment.

The example problem – clean up this room!

In the course of this book, we will be using a single problem set that I feel most people can relate to easily, while still representing a real challenge for the most seasoned roboticist. We will be using AI and robotics techniques to pick up toys in my upstairs game room after my grandchildren have visited. That sound you just heard was the gasp from the professional robotics engineers and researchers in the audience. Why is this a tough problem, and why is it ideal for this book?

This problem is a close analog to the problem Amazon has in picking items off of shelves and putting them in a box to send to you. For the last several years, Amazon has sponsored the *Amazon Robotics Challenge* where they invited teams to try and pick items off shelves and put them into a box for cash prizes. They thought the program difficult enough to invite teams from around the world. The contest was won in 2017 by a team from Australia.

Let's discuss the problem and break it down a bit. Later, in Chapter 2, we will do a full task analysis, use cases, and storyboards to develop our approach, but we can start here with some general observations.

Robotics designers first start with the environment – where does the robot work? We divide environments into two categories: structured and unstructured. A **structured environment**, such as the playing field for a *first* robotics competition, an assembly line, or lab bench, has everything in an organized space. You have heard the saying *A place for everything and everything in its place*—that is a structured environment. Another way to think about it, is that we know in advance where everything is or is going to be. We know what color things are, where they are placed in space, and what shape they are. A name for this type of information is *a prior* knowledge – things we know in advance. Having advanced knowledge of the environment in robotics is sometimes absolutely essential. Assembly line robots are expecting parts to arrive in exactly the position and orientation to be grasped and placed into position. In other words, we have arranged the world to suit the robot.

In the world of our game room, this is simply not an option. If I could get my grandchildren to put their toys in exactly the same spot each time, then we would not need a robot for this task. We have a set of objects that is fairly fixed – we only have so many toys for them to play with. We occasionally add things or lose toys, or something falls down the stairs, but the toys are a elements of a set of fixed objects. What they are not is positioned or oriented in any particular manner – they are just where they were left when the kids finished playing with them and went home. We also have a fixed set of furniture, but some parts move – the footstool or chairs can be moved around. This is an **unstructured environment**, where the robot and the software have to adapt, not the toys or furniture.

The problem is to have the robot drive around the room, and pick up toys. Let's break this task down into a series of steps:

1. We want the user to **interact** with the robot **by talking** to it. We want the robot to understand what we want it to do, which is to say, what our intent is for the commands we are giving it.

2. Once commanded to start, the robot will have to **identify an object** as being a toy, and not a wall, a piece of furniture, or a door.

3. The robot must **avoid hazards**, the most important being the stairs going down to the first floor. Robots have a particular problem with negative obstacles (dropoffs, curbs, cliffs, stairs, and so on), and that is exactly what we have here.

4. Once the robot finds a toy, it has to determine how to **pick the toy up** with its robot arm. Can it grasp the object directly, or must it scoop the item up, or push it along? We expect that the robot will try different ways to pick up toys and may need several trial and error attempts.

5. Once the toy is acquired by the robot arm, the robot needs to **carry the toy to a toy box**. The robot must recognize the toy box in the room, remember where it is for repeat trips, and then position itself to place the toy in the box. Again, more than one attempt may be required.

6. After the toy is dropped off, the robot returns to **patrolling the room looking for more toys.** At some point, hopefully, all of the toys are retrieved. It may have to ask us, the human, if the room is acceptable, or if it needs to **continue cleaning**.

What will we be learning from this problem? We will be using this backdrop to examine a variety of AI techniques and tools. The purpose of the book is to teach you how to develop AI solutions with robots. It is the process and the approach that is the critical information here, not the problem and not the robot I developed so that we have something to take pictures of for the book. We will be demonstrating techniques for making a moving machine that can learn and adapt to its environment. I would expect that you will pick and choose which chapters to read and in which order according to your interests and you needs, and as such, each of the chapters will be standalone lessons.

The first three chapters are foundation material that support all of the rest of the book by setting up the problem and providing a firm framework to attach all of the rest of the material.

What you will learn

Not all of the chapters or topic in this book are considered *classical* AI approaches, but they do represent different ways of approaching machine learning and decision-making problems.

Building a firm foundation for robot control by understanding control theory and timing. We will be using a soft real-time control scheme with what I call a frame-based control loop. This technique has a fancy technical name – rate monotonic scheduling—but I think you will find the concept fairly intuitive and easy to understand.

At the most basic level, AI is a way for the robot to make decisions about its actions. We will introduce a model for decision making that comes from the US Air Force, called the OODA (Observe- Orient-Decide- Act) loop. Our robot will have two of these loops: an inner loop or introspective loop, and an outward looking environment sensor loop. The lower, inner loop takes priority over the slower, outer loop, just as the autonomic parts of your body (heartbeat, breathing, eating) take precedence over your task functions (going to work, paying bills, mowing the lawn). This makes our system a type of subsumption architecture in Chapter 2, *Setting Up Your Robot*, a biologically inspired control paradigm named by Rodney Brooks of MIT, one of the founders of iRobot and designer of a robot named Baxter.

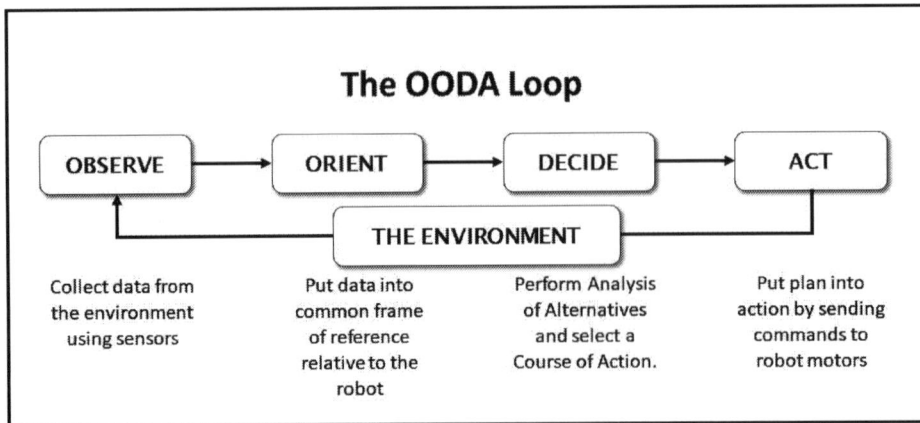

The OODA Loop

OBSERVE	→	ORIENT	→	DECIDE	→	ACT

THE ENVIRONMENT

Collect data from the environment using sensors	Put data into common frame of reference relative to the robot	Perform Analysis of Alternatives and select a Course of Action.	Put plan into action by sending commands to robot motors

The OODA Loop

The **OODA loop** was invented by Col. John Boyd, a man also called *The Father of the F-16*. Col. Boyd's ideas are still widely quoted today, and his OODA loop is used to describe robot artificial intelligence, military planning, or marketing strategies with equal utility. The OODA provides a model for how a thinking machine that interacts with its environment might work.

Our robot works not by simply doing commands or following instructions step by step, but by setting goals and then working to achieve these goals. The robot is free to set its own path or determine how to get to its goal. We will tell the robot to *pick up that toy* and the robot will decide which toy, how to get in range, and how to pick up the toy. If we, the human robot owner, instead tried to treat the robot as a teleoperated hand, we would have to give the robot many individual instructions, such as move forward, move right, extend arm, open hand, each individually and without giving the robot any idea of why we were making those motions.

Before designing the specifics of our robot and its software, we have to match its capabilities to the environment and the problem it must solve. The book will introduce some tools for designing the robot and managing the development of the software. We will use two tools from the discipline of systems engineering to accomplish this – use cases and storyboards. I will make this process as streamlined as possible. More advanced types of systems engineering are used by NASA and aerospace companies to design rockets and aircraft – this gives you a taste of those types of structured processes.

Artificial intelligence and advanced robotics techniques

The next sections will each detail a step-by-step example of the application of a different AI approach.

We start with object recognition. We need our robot to recognize objects, and then classify them as either *toys* to be picked up or *not toys* to be left alone. We will use a trained **artificial neural network (ANN)** to recognize objects from a video camera from various angles and lighting conditions.

The next task, once a toy is identified, is to pick it up. Writing a general purpose *pick up anything* program for a robot arm is a difficult task involving a lot of higher mathematics (google `inverse kinematics` to see what I mean). What if we let the robot sort this out for itself? We use **genetic algorithms** that permit the robot to invent its own behaviors and learn to use its arm on its own.

Our robot needs to understand commands and instructions from its owner (us). We use **natural language processing** to not just recognize speech, but understand intent for the robot to create goals consistent to what we want it to do. We use a neat technique called the "fill in the blank" method to allow the robot to reason from the context of a command. This process is useful for a lot of robot planning tasks.

The robot's next problem is avoiding the stairs and other hazards. We will use **operant conditioning** to have the robot learn through positive and negative reinforcement where it is safe to move.

The robot will need to be able to find the toy box to put items away, as well as have a general framework for planning moves into the future. We will use **decision trees** for path planning, as well as discuss **pruning** for quickly rejecting bad plans. We will also introduce **forward and backwards chaining** as a means to quickly plan to reach a goal. If you imagine what a computer chess program algorithm must do, looking several moves ahead and scoring good moves versus bad moves before selecting a strategy, that will give you an idea of the power of this technique. This type of decision tree has many uses and can handle many dimensions of strategies. We'll be using it to find a path to our toy box to put toys away.

Our final practical chapter brings a different set of tools not normally used in robotics, or at least not in the way we are going to employ them.

I have four wonderful, talented, and delightful grandchildren who love to come and visit. You'll be hearing a lot about them throughout the book. The oldest grandson is six years old, and autistic, as is my grandaughter, the third child. I introduced the grandson, William, to the robot , and he immediately wanted to have a conversation with it. He asked *What's your name?* and *What do you do?* He was disappointed when the robot made no reply. So for the grandkids, we will be developing an engine for the robot to carry on a small conversation. We will be creating a robot personality to interact with children. William had one more request of this robot: he wants it to tell and respond to *knock, knock* jokes.

While developing a robot with actual feelings is far beyond the state of the art in robotics or AI today, we can simulate having a personality with a finite state machine and some Monte-Carlo modeling. We will also give the robot a model for human interaction so that the robot will take into account the child's mood as well. I like to call this type of software an **artificial personality** to distinguish it from our *artificial intelligence*. AI builds a model of thinking, and AP builds a model of emotion for our robot.

Introducing the robot and our development environment

This is a book about robots and artificial intelligence, so we really need to have a robot to use for all of our practical examples. As we will discuss in Chapter 2 at some length, I have selected robot hardware and software that would be accessible to the average reader, and readily available for mail order. In the Appendix, I go through all of the setup of all of the hardware and software required and show you how I put together this robot and wired up his brain and control system. The base and robot arm were purchased as a unit from AliExpress, but you can buy them separately. All of the electronics were purchased from Amazon.

As shown in the photo, our robot has tracks, a mechanical six degree-of-freedom arm, and a computer. Let's call him TinMan, since, like the storybook character in *The Wizard of Oz*, he has a metal body and all he wants for is a brain.

Our tasks in this book center around picking up toys in an interior space, so our robot has a solid base with two motors and tracks for driving over a carpet. Our steering method is the tank-type, or differential drive where we steer by sending different commands to the track motors. If we want to go straight ahead, we set both motors to the same forward speed. If we want to travel backward, we reverse both motors the same amount. Turns are accomplished by moving one motor forward and the other backward (which makes the robot turn in place) or by giving one motor more forward drive than the other. We can make any sort of turn this way. In order to pick up toys we need some sort of manipulator, so I've included a six-axis robot arm that imitates a shoulder – elbow – wrist- hand combination that is quite dexterous, and since it is made out of standard digital servos, quite easy to wire and program.

You will note that the entire robot runs on one battery. You may want to split that and have a separate battery for the computer and the motors. This is a common practice, and many of my robots have had separate power for each. Make sure if you do to connect the ground wires of the two systems together. I've tested my power supply carefully and have not had problems with temperature or noise, although I don't run the arm and drive motors at the same time. If you have noise from the motors upsetting the Arduino (and you will tell because the Arduino will keep resetting itself), you can add a small filter capacitor of 10 μf across the motor wires.

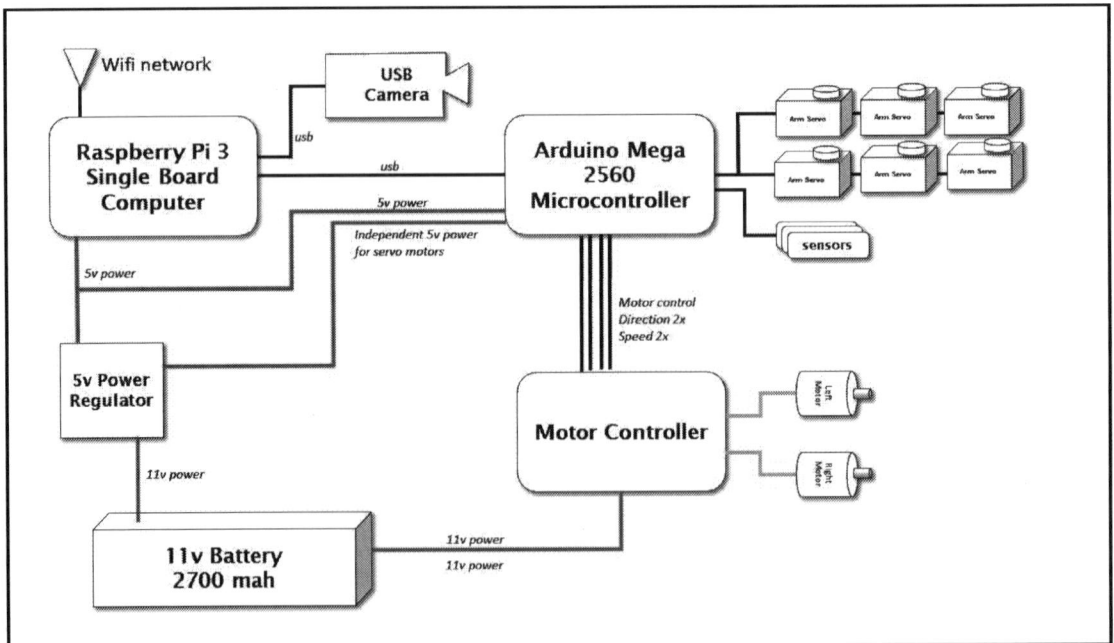

The main control of the TinMan robot is the Raspberry Pi 3 single board computer (SBC), that talks to the operator via a built-in Wi-Fi network. An Arduino Mega 2560 controller based on the Atmel architecture provides the interface to the robot's hardware components, such as motors and sensors.

You can refer to the preceding diagram on the internal components of the robot. We will be primarily concerned with the Raspberry Pi3 **single board computer** (**SBC**), which is the brains of our robot. The rest of the components we will set up once and not change for the entire book.

The Raspberry Pi 3 acts as the main interface between our control station, which is a PC running Linux in a virtual machine, and the robot itself via a Wi-Fi network. Just about any low power, Linux-based SBC can perform this job, such as a BeagleBone Black, Oodroid XU4, or an Intel Edison.

Connected to the SBC is an Arduino 2560 Mega microcontroller board that will serve as our hardware interface. We can do much of the hardware interface with the PI if we so desired, but by separating out the Arduino we don't have to worry about the advanced AI software running in the Pi 3 disrupting the timing of sending PWM (pulse width modulated) controls to the motors, or the PPM (pulse position modulation) signals that control our six servos in the robot arm. Since our motors draw more current than the Arduino can handle itself, we need a motor controller to amplify our commands into enough power to move the robot's tracks. The servos are plugged directly into the Arduino, but have their own connection to the robot's power supply. We also need a 5v regulator to provide the proper power from the 11.1v rechargeable lithium battery power pack into the robot. My power pack is a rechargeable 3S1P (three cells in series and one in parallel) 2,700 ah battery normally used for quadcopter drones, and came with the appropriate charger. As with any lithium battery, follow all of the directions that came with the battery pack and recharge it in a metal box or container in case of fire.

Software components (ROS, Python, and Linux)

I am going to direct you once again to the Appendix to see all of the software that runs the robot, but I'll cover the basics here to remind you. The base operating system for the robot is Linux running on a Raspberry Pi 3 SBC, as we said. We are using the ROS to connect all of our various software components together, and it also does a wonderful job of taking care of all of the finicky networking tasks, such as setting up sockets and establishing connections. It also comes with a great library of already prepared functions that we can just take advantage of, such as a joystick interface.

The ROS is not a true operating system that controls the whole computer like Linux or Windows does, but rather it is a backbone of communications and interface standards and utilities that make putting together a robot a lot simpler. The ROS uses a *publish/subscribe* technique to move data from one place to another that truly decouples the programs that produce data (such as sensors and cameras) from those programs that use the data, such as controls and displays. We'll be making a lot of our own stuff and only using a few ROS functions. Packt Publishing has several great books for learning ROS. My favorite is *Learning ROS for Robotics* by *Aaron Martinez* and *Enrique Fernandez.*

The programming language we will use throughout this book, with a couple of minor exceptions, will be Python. Python is a great language for this purpose for two great reasons: it is widely used in the robotics community in conjunction with ROS, and it is also widely accepted in the machine learning and AI community. This double whammy makes using Python irresistible. Python is an interpreted language, which has three amazing advantages for us:

- **Portability**: Python is very portable between Windows, Mac, and Linux. Usually the only time you have to worry about porting is if you use a function out of the operating system, such as opening a file that has a directory name.
- As an interpreted language, Python does **not require a compile step**. Some of the programs we are developing in this book are pretty involved, and if we write them in C or C++, would take 10 or 20 minutes of build time each time we made a change. You can do a lot with that much time, which you can spend getting your program to run and not waiting for **make** to finish.
- **Isolation**. This is a benefit that does not get talked about much, but having had a lot of experience with crashing operating systems with robots, I can tell you that the fact that Python's interpreter is isolated from the core operating system means that having one of your Python ROS programs crash the computer is very rare. A computer crash means rebooting the computer and also probably losing all of your data you need to diagnose the crash. I had a professional robot project that we moved from Python to C++, and immediately the operating system crashes began, which shot the reliability of our robot. If a Python program crashes, another program can monitor that and restart it. If the operating system is gone, there is not much you can do without some extra hardware that can push the *reset button* for you. (For further information, refer to *Python Success Stories* https://www.python.org/about/success/devil/).

Robot control systems and a decision-making framework

Before we dive into the coding of our base control system, let's talk about the theory we will use to create a robust, modular, and flexible control system for robotics. As I mentioned previously, we are going to use two sets of tools in the sections: soft real-time control and the OODA loop. One gives us a base for controlling the robot easily and consistently, and the other provides a basis for all of the robot's autonomy.

Soft real-time control

The basic concept of how a robot works, especially one that drives, is fairly simple. There is a master control loop that does the same thing over and over; it reads data from the sensors and motor controller, looks for commands from the operator (or the robot's autonomy functions), makes any changes to the state of the robot based on those commands, and then sends instructions to the motors or effectors to make the robot move:

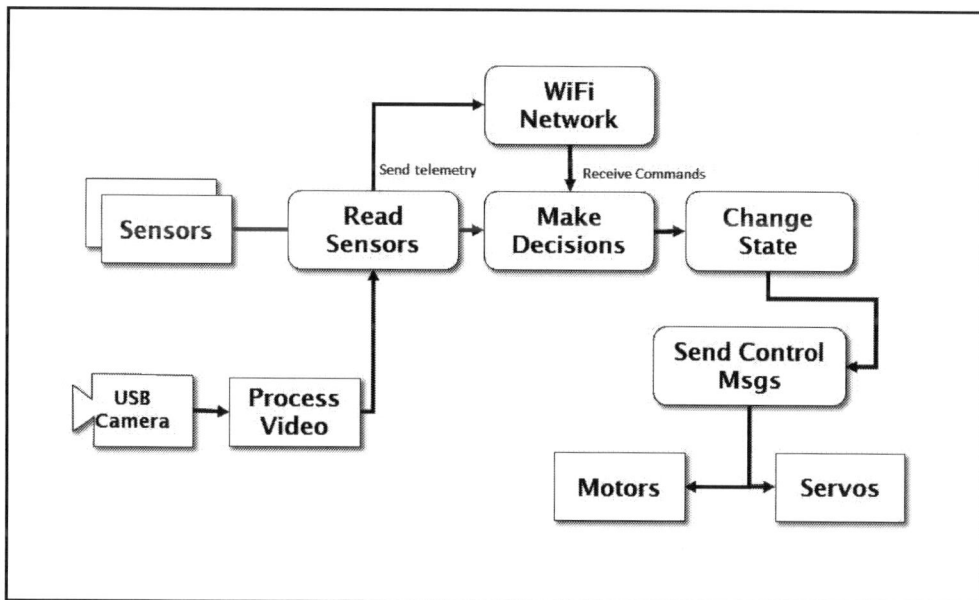

The preceding diagram illustrates how we have instantiated the OODA loop into the software and hardware of our robot. The robot can either act autonomously, or accept commands from a control station connected via a wireless network.

What we need to do is perform this control loop in a consistent manner all of the time. We need to set a base frame rate, or basic update frequency, in our control loop. This makes all of the systems of the robot perform better. Without some sort of time manager, each control cycle of the robot takes a different amount of time to complete, and any sort of path planning, position estimate, or arm movement becomes more complicated.

If you have used a PID controller before to perform a process, such as driving the robot at a consistent speed, or aiming a camera at a moving target, then you will understand that having even-time steps is important to getting good results.

Control loops

In order to have control of our robot, we have to establish some sort of control or feedback loop. Let's say that we tell the robot to move 12 inches (30 cm) forward. The robot has to send a command to the motors to start moving forward, and then have some sort of mechanism to measure 12 inches of travel. We can use several means to accomplish this, but let's just use a clock. The robot moves 3 inches (7.5 cm) per second. We need the control loop to start the movement, and then at each update cycle, or time through the loop, check the time, and see if 4 seconds has elapsed. If it has, then it sends a stop command to the motors. The timer is the control, 4 seconds is the set point, and the motor is the system that is controlled. The process also generates an error signal that tells us what control to apply (in this case, to stop). The following diagram shows a simple control loop. What we want is a constant temperature in the pot of water:

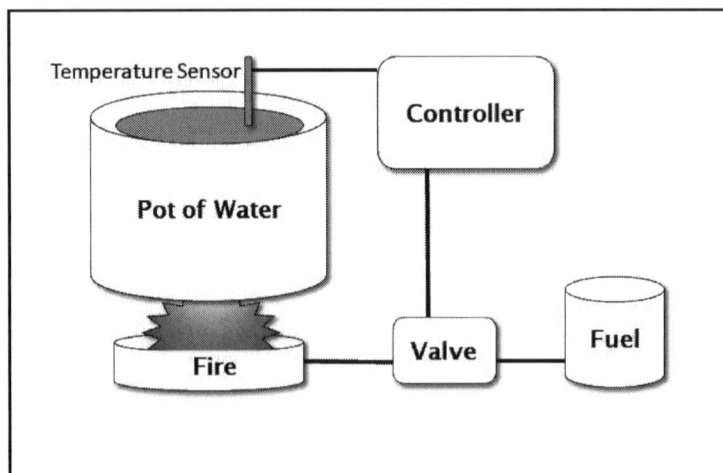

The **Valve** controls the heat produced by the fire, which warms the pot of water. The **Temperature Sensor** detects if the water is too cold, too hot, or just right. The **Controller** uses this information to control the valve for more heat. This type of schema is called a **closed loop control system**.

You can think of this also in terms of a process. We start the process, and then get feedback to show our progress, so that we know when to stop or modify the process. We could be doing speed control, where we need the robot to move at a specific speed, or pointing control, where the robot aims or turns in a specific direction.

Let's look at another example. We have a robot with a self-charging docking station, with a set of **light emitting diodes** (**LEDs**) on the top as an optical target. We want the robot to drive straight into the docking station. We use the camera to see the target LEDs on the docking station. The camera generates an error, which is the direction that the LEDs are seen in the camera. The distance between the LEDs also gives us a rough range to the dock. Let's say that the LEDs in the image are off to the left of center 50% and the distance is 3 feet (1 m) We send that information to a control loop to the motors – turn right (opposite the image) a bit and drive forward a bit. We then check again, and the LEDs are closer to the center (40%) and the distance is a bit less (2.9 feet or 90 cm). Our error signal is a bit less, and the distance is a bit less, so we send a slower turn and a slower movement to the motors at this update cycle. We end up exactly in the center and come to zero speed just as we touch the docking station. For those people currently saying "But if you use a PID controller …", yes, you are correct, I've just described a "P" or proportional control scheme. We can add more bells and whistles to help prevent the robot from overshooting or undershooting the target due to its own weight and inertia, and to damp out oscillations caused by those overshoots.

The point of these examples is to point out the concept of control in a system. Doing this consistently is the concept of **real-time control.**

In order to perform our control loop at a consistent time interval (or to use the proper term, deterministically), we have two ways of controlling our program execution: **soft real time** and **hard real time**.

A hard real-time system places requirements that a process executes inside a time window that is enforced by the operating system, which provides deterministic performance – the process always takes exactly the same amount of time.

The problem we are faced with is that a computer running an operating system is constantly getting interrupted by other processes, running threads, switching contexts, and performing tasks. Your experience with desktop computers, or even smart phones, is that the same process, like starting up a word processor program, always seems to take a different amount of time whenever you start it up, because the operating system is interrupting the task to do other things in your computer.

This sort of behavior is intolerable in a real-time system where we need to know in advance exactly how long a process will take down to the microsecond. You can easily imagine the problems if we created an autopilot for an airliner that, instead of managing the aircraft's direction and altitude, was constantly getting interrupted by disk drive access or network calls that played havoc with the control loops giving you a smooth ride or making a touchdown on the runway.

A **real-time operating system** (**RTOS**) allows the programmers and developers to have complete control over when and how the processes are executing, and which routines are allowed to interrupt and for how long. Control loops in RTOS systems always take the exact same number of computer cycles (and thus time) every loop, which makes them reliable and dependable when the output is critical. It is important to know that in a hard real-time system, the hardware is enforcing timing constraints and making sure that the computer resources are available when they are needed.

We can actually do hard real time in an Arduino microcontroller, because it has no operating system and can only do one task at a time, or run only one program at a time. We have complete control over the timing of any executing program. Our robot will also have a more capable processor in the form of a Raspberry Pi 3 running Linux. This computer, which has some real power, does quite a number of tasks simultaneously to support the operating system, run the network interface, send graphics to the output HDMI port, provide a user interface, and even support multiple users.

Soft real time is a bit more of a relaxed approach. The software keeps track of task execution, usually in the form of **frames**, which are set time intervals, like the frames in a movie film. Each frame is a fixed time interval, like 1/20 of a second, and the program divides its tasks into parts it can execute in those frames. Soft real time is more appropriate to our playroom cleaning robot than a safety-critical hard real-time system – plus, RTOSs are expensive and require special training. What we are going to do is treat the timing of our control loop as a feedback system. We will leave extra "room" at the end of each cycle to allow the operating system to do its work, which should leave us with a consistent control loop that executes at a constant time interval. Just like our control loop example, we will make a measurement, determine the error, and apply a correction each cycle.

We are not just worried about our update rate. We also have to worry about "jitter", or random variability in the timing loop caused by the operating system getting interrupted and doing other things. An interrupt will cause our timing loop to take longer, causing a random jump in our cycle time. We have to design our control loops to handle a certain amount of jitter for soft real time, but these are comparatively infrequent events.

The process is actually fairly simple in practice. We start by initializing our timer, which needs to be as high a resolution as we can get. We are writing our control loop in Python, so we will use the `time.time()` function, which is specifically designed to measure our internal program timing performance (set frame rate, do loop, measure time, generate error, sleep for error, loop). Each time we call `time.time()`, we get a floating point number, which is the number of seconds from the Unix clock.

The concept for this process is to divide our processing into a set of fixed time **frames**. Everything we do will fit within an integral number of frames. Our basic running speed will process 30 frames per second. That is how fast we will be updating the robot's position estimate, reading sensors, and sending commands to motors. We have other functions that run slower than the 30 frames, so we can divide them between frames in even multiples. Some functions run every frame (30 fps), and are called and executed every frame. Let's say that we have a sonar sensor that can only update 10 times a second. We call the `read sonar` function every third frame. We assign all our functions to be some multiple of our basic 30 fps frame rate, so we have 30, 15, 10, 7.5, 6,5,4.28,2, and 1 frames per second if we call the functions every frame, every second frame, every third frame, and so on. We can even do less that one frame per second – a function called every 60 frames executes once every 2 seconds.

The tricky bit is we need to make sure that each process fits into one frame time, which is 1/30 of a second or 0.033 seconds or 33 milliseconds. If the process takes longer than that, we have to ether divide it up into parts, or run it in a separate thread or program where we can start the process in one frame and get the result in another. It is also important to try and balance the frames so that not all processing lands in the same frame. The following diagram shows a task scheduling system based on a 30 frames per second basic rate.

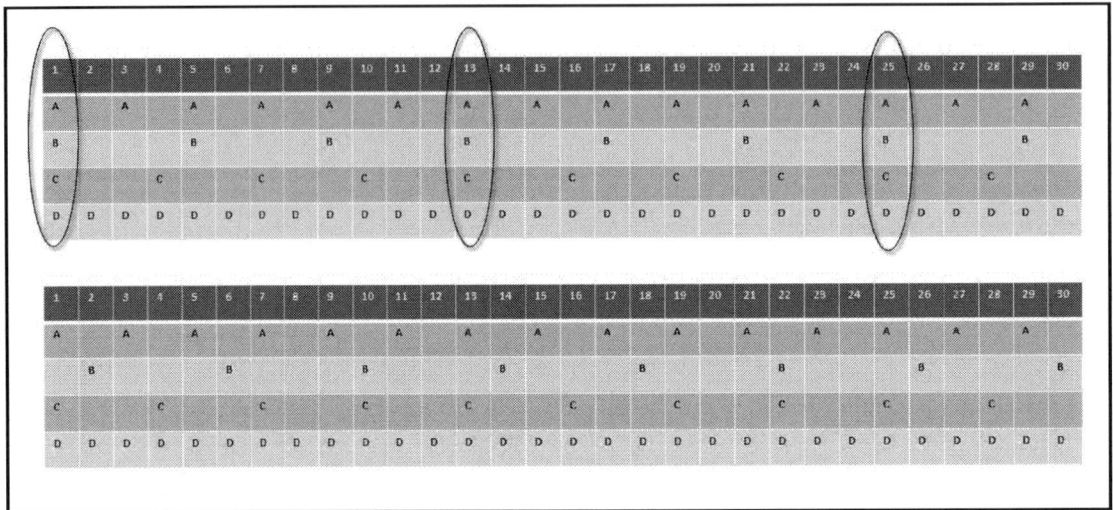

We have four tasks to take care of: **Task A** runs at 15 fps, **Task B** runs at 6 fps (every five frames), **Task C** runs at 10 fps (every three frames), and **Task D** runs at 30 fps, every frame. Our first pass (the top diagram) at the schedule has all four tasks landing on the same frame at frames 1, 13, and 25. We can improve the balance of the load on the control program if we delay the start of Task B on the second frame, as shown in the bottom diagram.

This is very akin to how measures in music work, where a measure is a certain amount of time, and different notes have different intervals – one whole note can only appear once per measure, a half note can appear twice, all the way down to 64th notes. Just as a composer makes sure that each measure has the right number of beats, we can make sure that our control loop has a balanced measure of processes to execute each frame.

Let's start by writing a little program to control our timing loop and to let you play with these principles.

This is exciting; our first bit of coding together. This program just demonstrates the timing control loop we are going to use in the main robot control program, and is here to let you play around with some parameters and see the results. This is the simplest version I think is possible of a soft-time controlled loop, so feel free to improve and embellish.

The following diagram show what we are doing with this program:

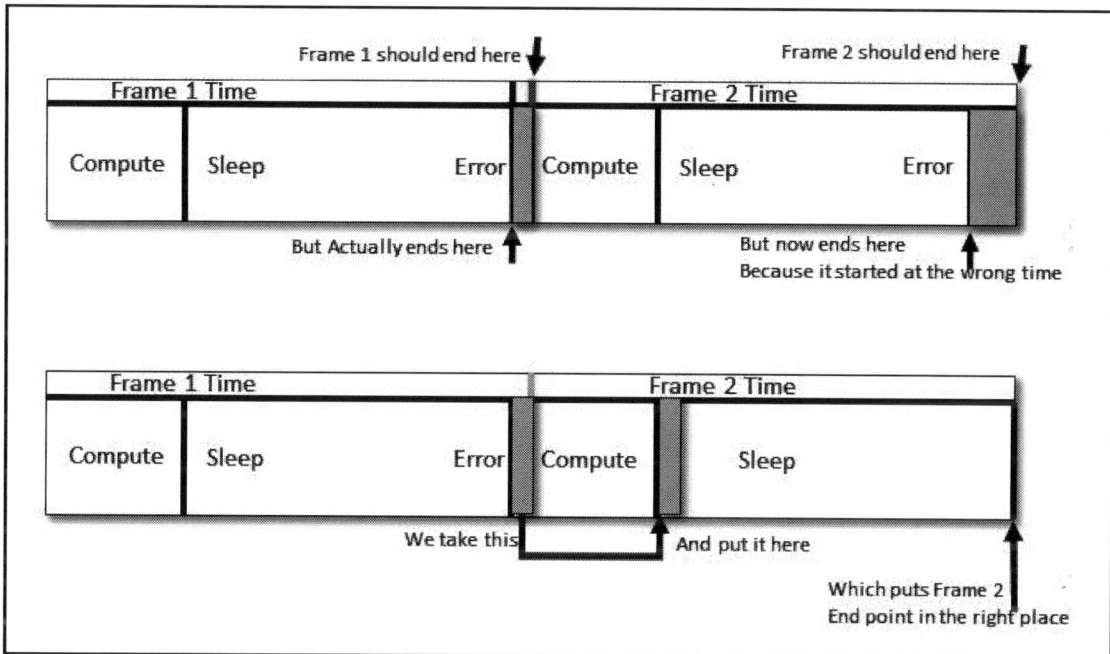

Now we begin with coding. This is pretty straightforward Python code; we won't get fancy until later. We start by importing our libraries. It is not surprising that we start with the time module. We also will use the mean function from numpy (Python numerical analysis) and matplotlib to draw our graph at the end. We will also be doing some math calculations to simulate our processing and create a load on the frame rate.

```
import time
from numpy import mean
import matplotlib.pyplot as plt
import math
#
```

Now we have some parameters to control our test. This is where you can experiment with different timings. Our basic control is the FRAMERATE – how many updates per second do we want to try? Let's start with 30, as we did before:

```
# set our frame rate - how many cycles per second to run our loop?
FRAMERATE = 30
# how long does each frame take in seconds?
FRAME = 1.0/FRAMERATE
# initialize myTimer
# This is one of our timer variables where we will store the clock time
from the operating system.
myTimer = 0.0
```

The duration of the test is set by the counter variable. The time the test will take is the FRAME time times the number of cycles in the counter. In our example, 2000 frames divided by 30 frames per second is 66.6 seconds, or a bit over a minute to run the test:

```
# how many cycles to test?  counter*FRAME = runtime in seconds
counter = 2000
```

We will be controlling our timing loop in two ways. We will first measure the amount of time it takes to perform the calculations for this frame. We have a stub of a program with some trig functions we will call to put a load on the computer. Robot control functions, such as computing the angles needed in a robot arm, need lots of trig math to work.

We will measure the time for our control function to run, which will take some part of our frame. We then compute how much of our frame remains, and tell the computer to sleep this process for the rest of the time. Using the sleep function releases the computer to go take care of other business in the operating system, and is a better way to mark time rather that running a tight loop of some sort to waste the rest of our frame time. The second way we control our loop is by measuring the complete frame – compute time plus rest time – and looking to see if we are over or under our frame time. We use TIME_CORRECTION for this function to trim our sleep time to account for variability in the sleep function and any delays getting back from the operating system:

```
# factor for our timing loop computations
TIME_CORRECTION= 0.0
# place to store data
```

We will collect some data to draw a "jitter" graph at the end of the program. We use the `dataStore` structure for this. Let's put a header on the screen to tell the you the program has begun, since it takes a while to finish:

```
dataStore = []
# Operator information   ready to go
# We create a heading to show that the program is starting its test
print "START COUNTING: FRAME TIME", FRAME, "RUN TIME:",FRAME*counter
# initialize the precision clock
```

In this step, we are going to set up some variables to measure our timing. As we mentioned, the objective is to have a bunch of compute frames, each the same length. Each frame has two parts: a compute part, where we are doing work, and a sleep period, when we are allowing the computer to do other things. `myTime` is the "top of frame" time, when the frame begins. `newTime` is the end of the work period timer. We use `masterTime` to compute the total time the program is running:

```
myTime = newTime = time.time()
# save the starting time for later
masterTime=myTime
# begin our timing loop
for ii in range(counter):
```

This section is our "payload", the section of the code doing the work. This might be an arm angle calculation, a state estimate, or a command interpreter. We'll stick in some trig functions and some math to get the CPU to do some work for us. Normally, this "working" section is the majority of our frame, so let's repeat these math terms 1,000 times:

```
    # we start our frame - this represents doing some detailed math
calculations
    # this is just to burn up some CPU cycles
    for jj in range(1000):
    x = 100
    y = 23 + ii
    z = math.cos(x)
    z1 = math.sin(y)
    #
    # read the clock after all compute is done
    # this is our working frame time
    #
```

Now we read the clock to find the working time. We can now compute how long we need to sleep the process before the next frame. The important part is that *working time + sleep time = frame time*. I'll call this `timeError`:

```
newTime = time.time()
# how much time has elapsed so far in this frame
# time = UNIX clock in seconds
# so we have to subract our starting time to get the elapsed time
myTimer = newTime-myTime
# what is the time left to go in the frame?
timeError = FRAME-myTimer
```

We carry forward some information from the previous frame here. `TIME_CORRECTION` is our adjustment for any timing errors in the previous frame time. We initialized it earlier to zero before we started our loop so we don't get an undefined variable error here. We also do some range checking because we can get some large "jitters" in our timing caused by the operating system that can cause our sleep timer to crash if we try to sleep a negative amount of time:

> We use the Python `max` function as a quick way to clamp the value of sleep time to be zero or greater. Max returns the greater of two arguments. The alternative is something like `if a< 0 : a=0`.

```
# OK time to sleep
# the TIME CORRECTION helps account for all of this clock reading
# this also corrects for sleep timer errors
# we are using a porpotional control to get the system to converge
# if you leave the divisor out, then the system oscillates out of control
sleepTime = timeError + (TIME_CORRECTION/1.5)
# quick way to eliminate any negative numbers
# which are possible due to jitter
# and will cause the program to crash
sleepTime=max(sleepTime,0.0)
```

So here is our actual `sleep` command. The `sleep` command does not always provide a precise time interval, so we will be checking for errors:

```
# put this process to sleep
time.sleep(sleepTime)
```

This is the time correction section. We figure out how long our frame time was in total (working and sleeping) and subtract it from what we want the frame time to be (`FrameTime`). Then we set our time correction to that value. I'm also going to save the measured frame time into a data store so we can graph how we did later, using `matplotlib`. This technique is one of Python's more useful features:

```
#print timeError,TIME_CORRECTION
# set our timer up for the next frame
time2=time.time()
measuredFrameTime = time2-myTime
##print measuredFrameTime,
TIME_CORRECTION=FRAME-(measuredFrameTime)
dataStore.append(measuredFrameTime*1000)
#TIME_CORRECTION=max(-FRAME,TIME_CORRECTION)
#print TIME_CORRECTION
myTime = time.time()
```

This completes the looping section of the program. This example does 2,000 cycles of 30 frames a second and finishes in 66.6 seconds. You can experiment with different cycle times and frame rates.

Now that we have completed the program, we can make a little report and a graph. We print out the frame time and total runtime, compute the average frame time (total time/counter), and display the average error we encountered, which we can get by averaging the data in the `dataStore`:

```
# Timing loop test is over - print the results
#
# get the total time for the program
endTime = time.time() - masterTime
# compute the average frame time by dividing total time by our number of
frames
avgTime = endTime / counter
#print report
 print "FINISHED COUNTING"
 print "REQUESTED FRAME TIME:",FRAME,"AVG FRAME TIME:",avgTime
 print "REQUESTED TOTAL TIME:",FRAME*counter,"ACTUAL TOTAL TIME:", endTime
 print "AVERAGE ERROR",FRAME-avgTime, "TOTAL_ERROR:",(FRAME*counter) -
endTime
 print "AVERAGE SLEEP TIME: ",mean(dataStore),"AVERAGE RUN
TIME",(FRAME*1000)-mean(dataStore)
 # loop is over, plot result
 # this let's us see the "jitter" in the result
 plt.plot(dataStore)
 plt.show()
```

Results from our program are shown in the following code. Note that the average error is just 0.00018 of a second, or .18 milliseconds out of a frame of 33 milliseconds:

```
START COUNTING: FRAME TIME 0.0333333333333 RUN TIME: 66.6666666667
FINISHED COUNTING
REQUESTED FRAME TIME: 0.0333333333333 AVG FRAME TIME: 0.0331549999714
REQUESTED TOTAL TIME: 66.6666666667 ACTUAL TOTAL TIME: 66.3099999428
AVERAGE ERROR 0.000178333361944 TOTAL_ERROR: 0.356666723887
AVERAGE SLEEP TIME:  33.1549999714 AVERAGE RUN TIME 0.178333361944
```

The following diagram shows the timing graph from our program. The "spikes" in the image are **jitter** caused by operating system interrupts. You can see the program controls the frame time in a fairly narrow range. If we did not provide control, the frame time would get greater and greater as the program executed. The diagram shows that the frame time stays in a narrow range that keeps returning to the correct value:

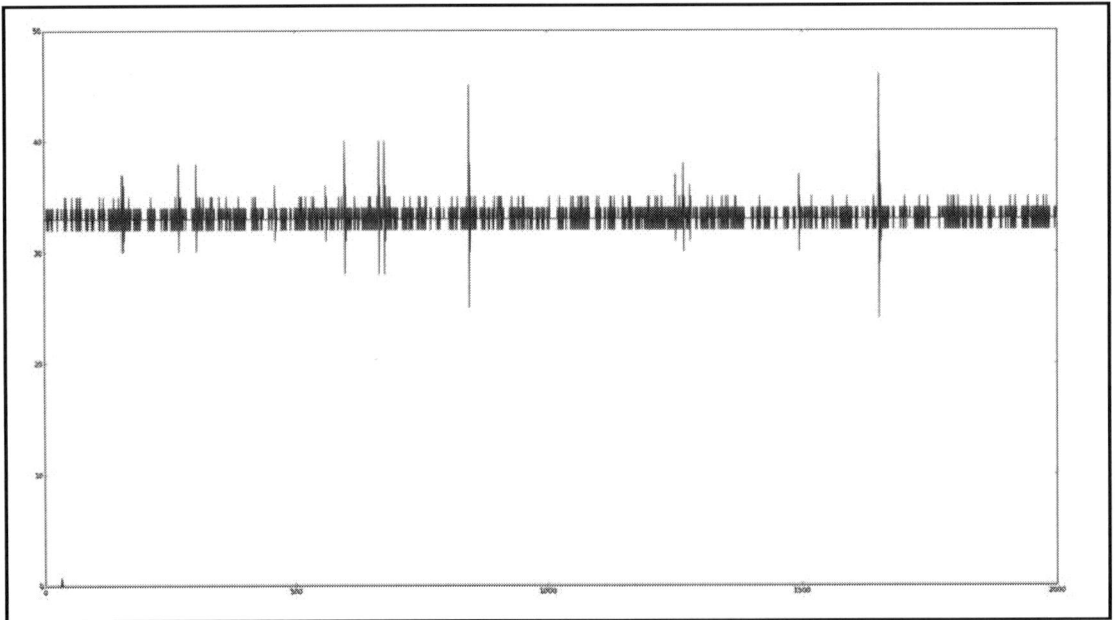

The robot control system – a control loop with soft real-time control

Now that we have exercised our programming muscles, we can apply this knowledge into the main control loop for our robot. The control loop has two primary functions:

- To respond to commands from the control station
- To interface to the robot's motors and sensors in the Arduino Mega

We will use a standard format for sending commands around the robot. All robot commands will have a three letter identifier, which is just a three letter code that identifies the command. We will use "DRV" for motor drive commands to the tracks, "ARM" for commands to the robot arm, and "TLn" for telemetry data (where "n" is a number or letter, allowing us to create various telemetry lists for different purposes). Error messages will start with "ERR", and general commands will start with "COM". A motor telemetry message might look like this:

```
TL11500,1438\n
```

Here `TL1` is the identifier (telemetry list 1) and the data is separated by commas. In this case, the two values are the motor states of the left and right drive motors. The \n is the *end of line* character escape character in Python, which designates the end of that message.

We will also be adding a feature that I always include in all of my robots and unmanned vehicles. It is always good to maintain "positive control" over the robot at all times. We don't want a hardware fault or a software error to result in the robot being stuck in a loop or run out of control. One of the means we can use to detect faults is to use end-to-end heartbeats. A **heartbeat** is a regular message that is periodically passed from the control station, to the robot's brain, and down to the microcontroller, and then back again. One of the tricks I use is to put a time tag on the heartbeat message so that it also acts as a latency measurement. **Latency** is the delay time that it takes from the time a command is generated until the robot acts on that command. If we have a heartbeat failure, we can detect that a process is stuck and stop the robot from moving, as well as send an error message to the operator.

This robot, like most of my creations, is designed to run autonomously a majority of the time, so it does not require communications with a control station full time. You can log onto the robot, send some commands, or operate it as a teleoperated unit, and then put it back into autonomous mode. So we have to design the heartbeat to not require a control station, but allow for heartbeats to and from a control station if one is connected.

Twice a second the main computer, the Raspberry Pi3, will send a message with a header of HBB, along with the clock time. The Arduino will simply repeat the HBB message back to the Pi3 with the same time information; that is, it just repeats the message back as soon as it can. This allows the Pi3 to measure the route trip delay time by looking at its clock. Repeating the clock eliminates the problem of synchronizing the clocks on the two systems. When a control program running on my PC is connected to the robot, a separate HBB message comes via the ROS message interface on a special topic called `robotCommand`, which is just a string message type. The command station puts a time tag on the heartbeat message, which allows the network latency along the wireless (Wi-Fi) network to be measured. Once a command station connects to the robot, it sends a HBB message once a second to the Pi 3 using ROS. The robot just repeats the message back as fast as it can. This tells the control station that the robot is being responsive, and tells the robot that someone is connected via Wi-Fi and is monitoring and can send commands.

Here is a diagram explaining the process:

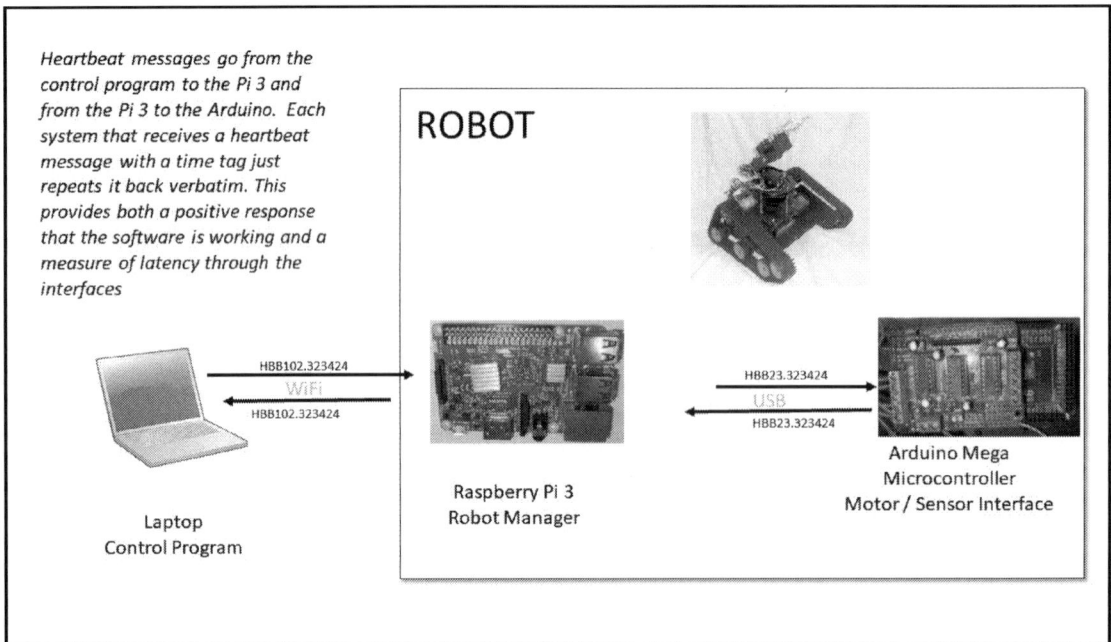

Heartbeat messages go from the control program to the Pi 3 and from the Pi 3 to the Arduino. Each system that receives a heartbeat message with a time tag just repeats it back verbatim. This provides both a positive response that the software is working and a measure of latency through the interfaces

ROBOT

HBB102.323424
WiFi
HBB102.323424

HBB23.323424
USB
HBB23.323424

Arduino Mega
Microcontroller
Motor / Sensor Interface

Raspberry Pi 3
Robot Manager

Laptop
Control Program

OK, now let's start into our main robot control program that runs on the Raspberry Pi3 and handles the main controls of the robot, including accepting commands, sending instructions to the motors, receiving telemetry from the Arduino, and keeping the robot's update rate managed:

```python
import rospy
import tf.transformations
from geometry_msgs.msg import Twist
from std_msgs.msg import String
import time
import serial
#GLOBAL VARIABLES
# set our frame rate - how many cycles per second to run our loop?
FRAMERATE = 30
# how long does each frame take in seconds?
FRAME = 1.0/FRAMERATE
# initialize myTimer
topOfFrame = 0.0
endOfWork = 0.0
endOfFrame=0.0
# how many cycles to test? counter*FRAME = runtime in seconds
counter = 2000
# fudge factor for our timing loop computations
TIME_CORRECTION= 0.0
class RosIF():
 def __init__(self):
 self.speed = 0.0
 self.turn = 0.0
 self.lastUpdate = 0.0
 rospy.init_node('robotControl', anonymous=True)
 rospy.Subscribe("cmd_vel",Twist,self.cmd_vel_callback)
 rospy.Subscribe("robotCommand",String,self.robCom_callback)
 self.telem_pub = rospy.Publish("telemetry",String,queue_size=10)
 self.robotCommand=rospy.Publish("robotCommand",String,queue_size=10)

 def cmd_vel_callback(self,data):
 self.speed = data.linear.x
 self.turn = data.angular.z
 self.lastUpdate = time.time()

 def command(self,cmd):
 rospy.loginfo(cmd)
 self.robotCommand.Publish(cmd)
 def robCom_callback(self,cmd):
 rospy.loginfo(cmd)
 robot_command = cmd.data
 # received command for robot - process
 if robot_command == "STOP":
```

```
 robot.stop()
 if robot_command == "GO":
 robot.go()
# This object encapsulates our robot
class Robot():
 def __init__(self):
 # position x,y
 # velocity vx, vy
 # accelleration ax, ay
 # angular position (yaw), angular velocity, angular acceleration
<< CODE SNIPPED - SEE APPENDIX>>
```

We will cover the design of the robot object in the *Appendix*. The full code is available in the repository on GitHub. Since we are not using this part of the program for the example in this chapter, I'm going to snip this bit out. See the Appendix; we will be using this section in great detail in later chapters.

Reading serial ports in a real-time manner

One of our functions for the robot control program is to communicate with the Arduino microcontroller over a serial port. How do we do that and maintain our timing loop we have worked so hard for? Let's put down another very important rule about controlling robots that will be illustrated in the next bit of code. Let's make this a tip:

> In real-time systems (hard or soft) *never* use blocking calls . Always poll to get your data.

Let's have a quick review. A blocking call suspends execution of our program to wait for some event to happen. In this case, we would be waiting for the serial port to receive data ending in a new line character. If the system on the other end of the serial port never sends data, we can be blocked forever, and our program will freeze. So how do we talk to our serial port? We poll the port (examine the port to see if data is available), rather than wait for data to arrive, which would the be standard manner to talk to a serial port. That means we use read instead of readline commands, since readline blocks (suspends our execution) until a newline character is received. That means we can't count on the data in the receive buffer to consist only of complete lines of data. We need to pull the data until we hit a newline character (\n in Python), then put that data into our dataline output buffer (see the following code), and process it. Any leftover partial lines we will save for later, when more data is available. It's a bit more work, but the result is that we can keep our timing.

For advanced students, it is possible to put the read serial function into a separate thread and pass the data back and still use a blocking call, but I think this is just as much work as what we are doing here, and the polling technique is less overhead for the processor and more control for us, because we are never blocked:

```
def readBuffer(buff):
# the data we get is a series of lines separated by EOL symbols
# we read to a EOL character (0x10) that is a line
# process complete lines and save partial lines for later
#
EOL = '\n'
if len(buff)==0:
    return
dataLine = ""
lines=[]
for inChar in buff:
    if inChar != EOL:
    dataLine +=inChar
else:
    lines.append(dataLine)
    dataLine=""
for telemetryData in lines:
    processData(telemetryData)
return dataLine
```

This part of the code processes the complete lines of data we get from the Arduino. We have three types of message we can get from the microcontroller. Each message starts with a three letter identifier followed by data. The types are HBB for heartbeat, TLn for telemetry, and ERR for error messages. Right now we just have one telemetry message, TL1 (telemetry list 1). Later we will add more telemetry lists as we add sensors to the robot. The HBB message is just the Arduino repeating back the heartbeat message we send it twice a second. We'll use ERR to send messages back to the control program from the microcontroller, and these will be things like illegal motor command:

```
def processData(dataLine):
  #
  # take the information from the arduino and process telemetry into
  # status information
  # we recieve either heartbeat (HBB), TL1 (telemtry List 1), or ERR (Error
messages)
  # we are saving room for other telemetry lists later
  dataType = dataLine[:3]
  payload = dataLine[3:] # rest of the line is data
  if dataType == 'HBB':
  # process heartbeat
```

```
# we'll fill this in later
pass
if dataType == "TL1": # telemetry list 1
# we'll add this later
pass
if dataType == "ERR": # error message
print "ARUDUINO ERROR MESSAGE ",payload
# log the error
rospy.loginfo(payload)
return
```

This section starts our main program. We start by instantiating our objects for the ROS interface and the robot. I like to put the ROS interface stuff in an object because it makes it easier to keep track of and make changes. Then, we open the serial port to the Arduino on /dev/ttyUSB0. Note that we set the timeout to zero. I don't think this is relevant since we are not using blocking calls on the serial port, but it can't hurt to double check that no blocking takes place. We do some error checking with the try...except block to catch any errors. Since the lack of a connection to the robot motors means we can't operate at all, I've had the program raise the error and stop the program run:

```
# main program starts here
# ****************************************************
rosif = RosIF() # create a ROS interface instance
robot = Robot() # define our robot instance
serialPort = "/dev/ttyUSB0"
# open serial port to arduino
ser = serial.Serial(serialPort,38400,timeout=0) #
# serial port with setting 38,400 baud, 8 bits, No parity, 1 stop bit
try:
 ser.open()
except:
 print "SERIAL PORT FOR ARDIONO DID NOT OPEN ", serialPort
 raise
```

Now, we start the ROS loop. not rospy.is_shutdown() controls the program and allows us to use the ROS shutdown command to terminate the program. We also initialize our frame counter we use to schedule tasks. I count the frames in each second (frameKnt) and then can set tasks to run at some divisor of the frame rate, as we discussed earlier in the chapter:

```
frameKnt = 0 # counter used to time processes
while not rospy.is_shutdown():
# main loop
topOfFrame=time.time()
# do our work
# read data from the seral port if there is any
```

```
serData = ser.read(1024)
# process the data from the arduino
# we don't want any blocking, so we use read and parse the lines ourselves
holdBuffer = readBuffer(serData)
#drive command
com = ',' # comma symbol we use as a separator
EOL = '\n'
if robot.newCommand:
ardCmd = "DRV"+str(robot.leftMotorCmd)+com+str(robot.rightMotorCmd)+EOL
serial.write(ardCmd)
serial.flush() # output Now
```

Here is an example of scheduling a task. We want the heartbeat message to go to the Arduino twice a second, so we compute how many frames that is (15 in this case) and then use the modulo operator to determine when that occurs. We use the formula in case we want to change the frame rate later, and we probably will.:

```
if frameKnt % (FRAMERATE/2)==0: # twice per second
hbMessage = "HBB"+com+str(time.time())+EOL
serial.write(hbMessage)
serial.flush() # output Now
```

We manage the frame counter, resetting it each second back to zero. We could let it just run, but let's keep it tidy. We'll reset the frame counter each second so we don't have to worry about overflow later:

```
frameKnt +=1
if frameKnt > FRAMERATE: frameKnt = 0 # just count number of frames in a
second

# done with work, now we make timing to get our frame rate to come out
right
#
endOfWork = time.time()
workTime = endOfWork - topOfFrame
sleepTime = (FRAME-workTime)+ timeError
time.sleep(sleepTime)
endOfFrame = time.time()
actualFrameTime = endOfFrame-topOfFrame
timeError = FRAME-actualFrameTime
# clamp the time error to the size of the frame
timeError = min(timeError,FRAME)
timeError = max(timeError,-FRAME)
```

Finally, when we fall out of the loop and end the program, we need to close the serial port to prevent the port from being locked the next time we start up:

```
# end of the main loop
#
ser.close()
```

Summary

In this chapter, we introduced the subject of artificial intelligence, and discussed that this is an artificial intelligence book applied to robotics, so our emphasis will be on AI. The main difference between an AI robot and a "regular" robot is that an AI robot may behave non-deterministically, which is to say it may have a different response to the same stimulus, due to learning. We introduced the problem we will use throughout the book, which is picking up toys in a playroom and putting them into a toy box. Next, we discussed two critical tools for AI robotics: the OODA loop (Observe-Orient-Decide-Act), which provides a model for how our robot makes decisions, and the soft real-time control loop, which manages and controls the speed of execution of our program. We applied these techniques in a timing loop demonstration and began to develop our main robot control program. The *Appendix* provides detailed instructions on setting up the various environments and software we will use to develop our AI-based robot, which I call TinMan.

Questions

1. What does the acronym PID stand for? Is this considered an AI software method?
2. What is the Turing test? Do you feel this is a valid method of assessing an artificial intelligence system?
3. Why do you think robots have a problem in general with negative obstacles, such as stairs and potholes?
4. In the OODA loop, what does the "orient" step do?
5. From the discussion of Python advantages, compute the following. You have a program that needs 50 changes tested. Assuming each change requires one run and a recompile step to test. A "C" Make step takes 450 seconds and a Python "run" command takes 3 seconds. How much time do you sit idle waiting for the C compiler?
6. What does RTOS stand for?

7. Your robot has the following scheduled tasks: telemetry: 10 Hz GPS 5 Hz Inertial 50 Hz Motors 20 Hz. What base frame rate would you use to schedule these tasks? (Hz or hertz means times per second. 3 Hz = three times per second)

8. Given that a frame rate scheduler has the fastest task at 20 frames per second, how would you schedule a task that needs to run at seven frames per second? How about one that runs at 3.5 frames per second?

9. What is a blocking call function? Why is it bad to use blocking calls in a real-time system like a robot?

Further reading

- Coram, R. (2004). *Boyd: The Fighter Pilot Who Changed the Art of War*. New York, NY: Back Bay Books/Little, Brown. (History of the OODA Loop)
- Fernández, E., Crespo, L. S., Mahtani, A., and Martinez, A. (2015). *Learning ROS for Robotics Programming: Your One-Stop Guide to the Robot Operating System*. Birmingham, UK: Packt Publishing.
- Joshi, P. (2017). *Artificial Intelligence with Python: A Comprehensive Guide to Building Intelligent Apps for Python Beginners and Developers*. Birmingham, UK: Packt Publishing Ltd.
- Brooks, R. (1986). `"A robust layered control system for a mobile robot"`. Robotics and Automation, IEEE Journal of . 2 (1): 14–23. `doi:10.1109/JRA.1986.1087032`.

Setting Up Your Robot 2

This chapter begins with some background on my thoughts as to what a robot is, and what robots are made of – a fairly standard list of parts and components. This chapter is designed to allow you to duplicate the exercises and use the source code that is found throughout the book. I thought you would appreciate information on how I set up my environments for development, what tools I use to create my code, and how I install the **Robotic Operating System** (**ROS**). We will also cover the assembly of TinMan, our robot hardware that I used for the development and testing of the code in this book. There are many types and configurations of robots that can work with our concepts and source code, with some minor modifications.

Topics covered in this chapter include the following:

- What is a robot?
- Robot anatomy – what are little robots made of?
- Software – Linux, ROS, Raspberry Pi 3, Arduino
- Software installation and configuration
- Hardware – assembling the TinMan robot

Technical requirements

The hardware and software requirements for this chapter are as follows:

- Python 2.7 or 3.5, with NumPy, SciPy, Matplotlib, and scikit-learn installed.
- ROS Kinetic Kame.
- A computer running Linux for development or a virtual machine running Linux under Windows. Ubuntu 16.04 is used for the examples and illustrations.

- A Raspberry Pi 3 or similar single board computer (BeagleBone Black, Odroid, or similar). We are not using the GPIO or special interfaces on the Pi 3, so there is not a lot of RasPi-specific code.
- An Arduino Mega 2560 microcontroller.
- A Pololu Micro Maestro Servo Controller x6.
- An Arduino development environment. This can be installed either on the control station (a laptop running Windows or a Linux laptop), or on the Raspberry Pi.
- The TinMan robot hardware was purchased from AliExpress and was called *Track Cars Creeper Truck Crawler Kits with 6DOF Robot Arm and 6PCS MG1501 Servos Robo-Soul TK-6A*. It came with no instructions and a lot of extra hardware.

What is a robot?

The word **robot** entered the modern language from the play **R.U.R.** by the Czech author, Karel Capek, which was published back in 1920. Roboti is supposed to be a Czech word meaning **forced servitude**. In the play, an industrialist learns how to build artificial people – not mechanical, metal men, but made of flesh and blood, who emerge from a factory fully grown. The English translation of the name as **Rossum's Universal Robots** (**R.U.R.**) introduced the word "robot" to the world.

Robot anatomy – what are robots made of?

In our limited definition of **robots** as meaning mobile machines that have sensors and interact with their environment, there is a fairly standard collection of components and parts that make up the vast majority of robots. Even robots as outwardly different as a self-driving car, the welding robot that built the car, and a Roomba vacuum cleaner, are actually composed of some version of the same parts. Some will have more components, others less, but pretty much all robots will have the following categories of parts
(*Reference: Murphy, Robin R. **Introduction to AI Robotics**, MIT Press, 2000, Chapter 1*):

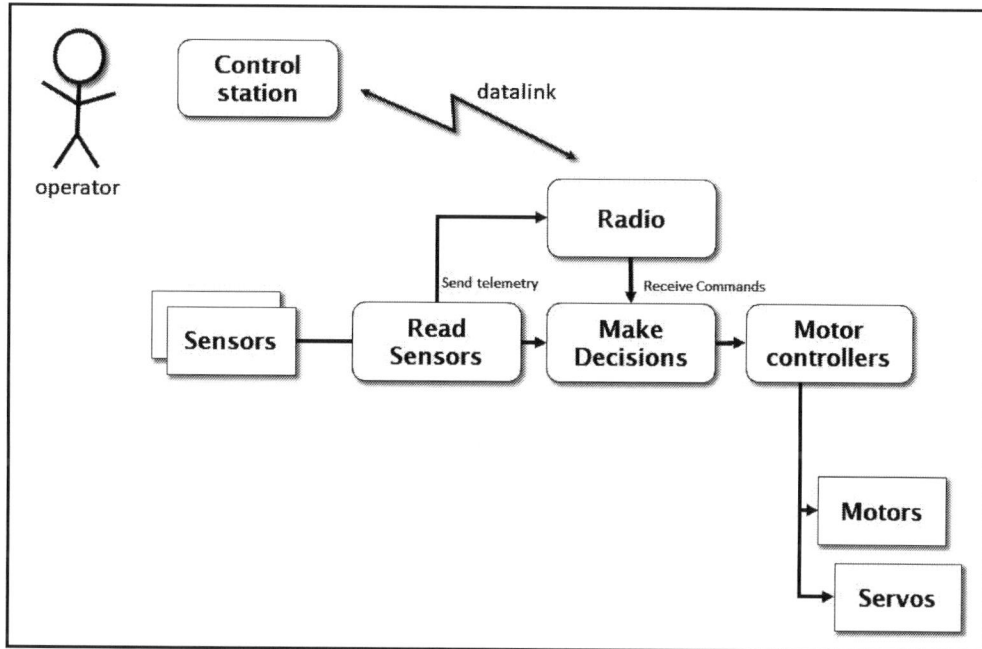

- **Controller**: A unit that runs the programming that controls the robot. This can be a traditional computer, a microcontroller, a **single board computer** (**SBC**), like the one we have, or some other sort of processor that sends and receives commands. Robot arms and some types of industrial robots will use a **programmable logic controller** (**PLC**), which mimics the way robots were programmed before digital computers with relays.
- **Control station** or **human/robot interface** (**HRI**): Robots are designed to perform tasks, which require that humans must have some means of sending instructions to the robot and supervising that the robot is behaving correctly. We will be using a laptop or desktop computer for this function, and will talk to the robot via a network. Control stations send commands to the robot, and receive **telemetry** from the robot in the form of **data**, **video**, or **audio**.
- **Radio** or **datalink**: Mobile robots, like the one we are designing in this book, are capable of moving and exploring their environment. While it is possible to send commands to a robot over a tether or wire, a preferred way is to use a radio link. The ubiquitous availability of wireless networks, such as Wi-Fi and cellular data services, has made creating data links a lot easier. I have had a lot of robot projects where a network link was unavailable or impractical, and a custom radio solution needed to be devised. Other types of radio used in robots may include Bluetooth, Zigbee, and various mesh network systems, such as Flutter.

- **Motors** or **effectors**: Our definition of a robot included the ability for self-propulsion – in other words, the robot is able to move. In order to move, the robot needs one or more motors. Our robot, TinMan, has eight motors, two for driving, and six for controlling the robot arm and hand. Motors, in general, convert electricity into motion. There are many, many different types, and picking the correct motor is difficult. You must match the torque (how hard the motor can pull), the speed in revolutions per minute, and voltage. Many robot motors also feature gearboxes to slow the speed of the motor down, basically exchanging speed for torque. TinMan's electric motors have reduction gear boxes.

  There are other ways to provide motion to a robot, in fact, many other ways. We call these things that make the robot move **effectors**. Effectors are only limited by your imagination, and include pneumatics (systems actuated by compressed air), hydraulics (things actuated by incompressible fluid), linear actuators that go back and forth rather than round and round, and even exotic effectors, such as Shape Memory Alloy or piezoelectric crystals, which change shape when electricity is applied. There are robot fish, robot octopi, squishy robots that fit under doors, robots that roll, robots that jump, and robots that walk.

- **Servos**: Some of the motors in our robot are a special category of motors called **Servos**. Servo motors feature a feedback mechanism and a control loop, so that they behave in a particular manner, either to maintain a position or a speed. The feedback is provided by a sensor. The servos we are using consist of a small electric motor that drives a gearbox made up of a whole series of gears that reduce the speed and increase the torque of the motor. The sensor is a potentiometer (variable resistor) that can measure the angle of the output gear shaft. When we send a command to the servo, it tells the motor to set to a particular angle. The angle is measured by the sensor, and any difference between the motor's position and the sensor creates an error signal that moves the motor in the correct direction. You can hear the motor making a lot of noise, because the motor turns many times through seven reduction gears to make the arm move. The gearbox lets us get a lot of torque without drawing a lot of current.

- **Motor controller**: Motors are not very useful by themselves – you need some capability to convert commands from the control computer into motion from the motors. Since motors require more voltage and current than the control computer (our Raspberry Pi) can provide, we need a device to turn small digital signals into large analog voltage and current. This device is called a **motor controller**, or sometimes an **electronic speed control**. Since we have a tank-drive robot, we also need the motors to be able to run in forward or reverse. The motor controller takes a special input signal called a **pulse width modulation (PWM)**. PWM is a repeating signal where the voltage turns on and off. The motor throttle (how fast the motor turns) is proportional to the amount of time the PWM signal stays in the **ON** position:

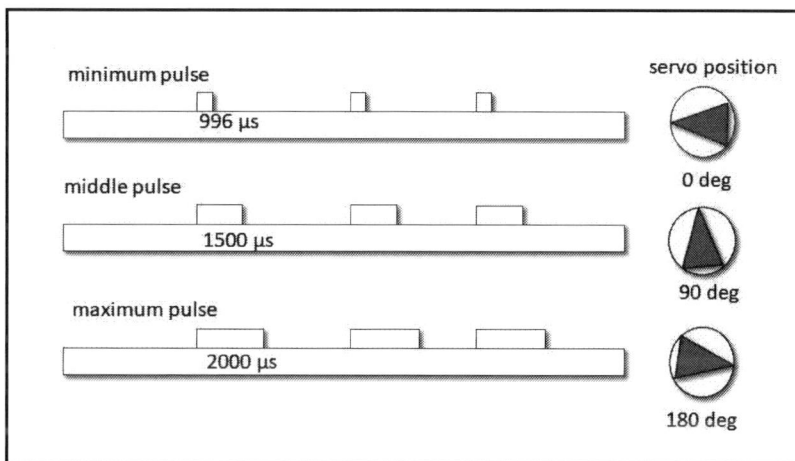

The motor controller has several kinds of connections, and has to be wired carefully due to the higher voltages and currents provided. There are two control wire inputs – one for speed (the PWM signal), while the other is a direction signal. We put the motor in reverse by changing the direction signal – 1 is forward, and 0 is backward. The next thing we need is a ground – it is very important that the controller sending the PWM signal (in our case, the Arduino Mega) and the motor control have their ground lines connected together. We'll cover this in the *wiring* section later in the chapter. Next, the motor controller needs the motor voltage and current, which we get directly from our battery. Finally, we connect two wires from each motor to the controller. It is interesting that we don't care which wire goes to which side of the motor, since we can run both forward and backward. If the motor is turning the wrong way, just switch the two wires. This is the only time you get to say *just reverse the polarity* outside of a science fiction movie!

- **Sensors**: A robot can be described as a machine that can move and react to its environment. In order for the robot to be able to see its surroundings, it needs **sensors.** Sensors take information from the outside or inside of the robot and convert it into a digital or electronic format. If we use a camera sensor, it takes light information and turns it into digital pixels recorded as an array of numbers. A sonar sensor would measure the distance to an object, such as a wall, by sending a pulse of energy (sound waves) and listening for the time delay before hearing an echo. Measuring the time delay gives us the distance to an object. For our TinMan project, the robot has several types of sensor, some more obvious than others. Our primary sensor is a wide-angle video camera, which we will use for avoiding obstacles and detecting objects. We will also use a microphone to listen for sounds and perform speech recognition. We mentioned servo motors in a previous paragraph – each servo motor contains an angle sensor that detects the amount of rotation, and allows us to direct the robot arm and hand. We have our Emergency Stop button, which is wired to the Arduino, and is a type of tactile (touch) sensor. When the button is pressed, the digital signal line to the Arduino is connected to ground, which we can detect as a 0 value on that pin. The Arduino can also perform an **analog-to-digital** (**A2D**) conversion. This means we can put a voltage on an Arduino pin from 0 to 5 volts and measure the amount of that voltage. We could use that to monitor our power supply, or to measure temperature via a thermistor. A **thermistor** is just a device that changes resistance with temperature. If we put a voltage through the thermistor, we can measure changes in that voltage on the thermistor's output.

Subsumption architecture

At this point, I want to spend a bit more time on the idea behind the **subsumption architecture**, and point out some specifics of how we will be using this concept in the design of our robot project. Many of you will be familiar with the concept from school or from study, and so you can look at my diagram and then move on. For the rest of us, let's talk a bit about this biologically inspired robot concept.

Subsumption architecture was originally described by Dr. Rodney Brooks, a professor at MIT, who would later help found iRobot Corporation and invent the Baxter Robot. Rodney was trying to develop analogues of insect brains in order to understand how to program intelligent robots. Robots before this time (1986) were very much single-threaded machines that pretty much only did one thing at a time. They read sensors, made decisions and then acted – and only had one goal at any one time. Creatures such as flies or ants have very simple brains but still manage to function in the real world. Brooks reasoned that there were several layers of closed-loop feedback processes going simultaneously.

The basic concept of subsumption has been around for some time, and it has been adapted, reused, refined, and simplified in the years since it was first introduced. What I am presenting here is my take, or my interpretation, of how to apply the concept of subsumption to a robot in the context of what we are trying to accomplish.

The first aspect to understand is that we want our robot to act on a series of goals. The robot is not simply reacting to each stimulus in total isolation, but is rather carrying out some sort of goal-oriented behavior. The goal may be to pick up a toy, or navigate the room, avoiding obstacles. The paradigm we are creating has the user set goals for the robot and the robot determine how to carry those goals out, even if the goal is simply to move one meter forward.

The problem begins when the robot has to keep more than one goal in mind at a time. The robot is not just driving around, but driving around avoiding obstacles and looking for toys to pick up. How do we arbitrate between different goals, to determine which one has precedence? The answer is found in the following diagram:

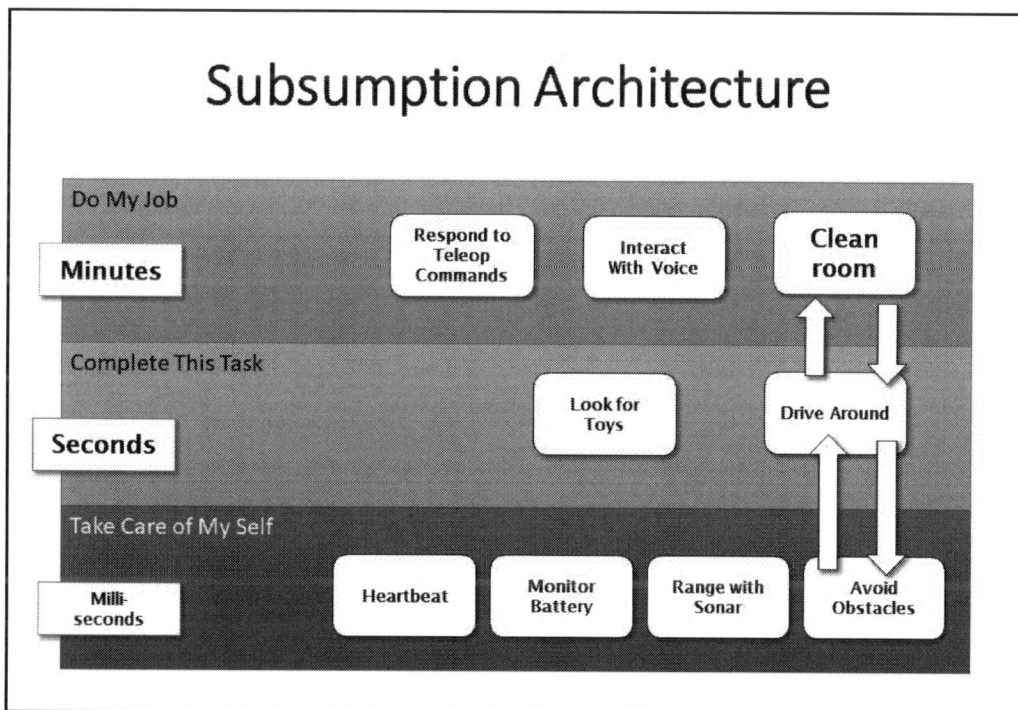

Subsumption Architecture

Do My Job			
Minutes	**Respond to Teleop Commands**	**Interact With Voice**	**Clean room**

Complete This Task		
Seconds	**Look for Toys**	**Drive Around**

Take Care of My Self				
Milli-seconds	**Heartbeat**	**Monitor Battery**	**Range with Sonar**	**Avoid Obstacles**

We will divide the robot's decision-making systems into three layers. Each layer has a different level of responsibility and operates on a different time scale. At the lowest levels are what we might call the robot's autonomic nervous system – it contains the robot's internal health-keeping and monitoring functions. These processes run very fast – 20 times a second or so, and only deal with what is inside the robot. This would include reading internal sensors, checking battery levels, and reading and responding to heartbeat messages. I've labeled this level *take care of myself.*

The next level handles individual tasks, such as driving around, or looking for toys. These tasks are short term and deal with what the sensors can see. The time period for decisions is in the second range, so these tasks might have one or two hertz update rates, but slower than the internal checks. I call this level *complete the task* – you might call it *drive the vehicle* or *operate the payload.*

The final and top level is the section devoted to *completing the mission*, and it deals with the overall purpose of the robot. This level has the overall state machine for finding toys, picking them up, and then putting them away, which is the mission of this robot. This level also deals with interacting with humans and responding to commands. The top level works on tasks that take minutes, or even hours, to complete.

The rules of the subsumption architecture – and even where it gets its name – have to do with the priority and interaction of the processes in these layers. The rules are as follows (and these are my version):

- Each layer can only talk to the layers next to it. The top layer talks only to the middle layer, and the bottom layer also talks only to the middle layer. The middle layer can communicate with either.
- The layer with the lower level has the highest priority. The lower level has the ability to interrupt or override the commands from higher layers.

Think about this for a minute. I've given you the example of driving our robot in a room. The lowest level detects obstacles. The middle level is driving the robot in a particular direction, and the top layer is directing the mission. From the top down, the uppermost layer is commanded to *clean up the room*, the middle layer is commanded to *drive around*, and the bottom layer gets the command *left motor and right motor forward 60% throttle*. Now, the bottom level detects an obstacle. It interrupts the *drive around* function and overrides the command from the top layer to turn the robot away from the obstacle. Once the obstacle is cleared, the lowest layer returns control to the middle layer for the driving direction.

Another example could be if the lowest layer loses the heartbeat signal, which indicates that something has gone wrong in the software. The lowest layer causes the motors to halt, overriding any commands from the upper layers. It does not matter what they want; the robot has a fault and needs to stop. This *priority inversion* of the lowest layers having the highest priority is the reason we call this a subsumption architecture, since the lower layers can subsume – or take precedence over – the higher layers.

The major benefit of this type of organization is that it keeps procedures clear as to which events, faults, or commands take precedence over others, and prevents the robot from getting stuck in an indecision loop.

Each type of robot may have different numbers of layers in their architecture. You could even have a supervisory layer that controls a number of other robots and has goals for the robots as a team. The most I have had so far has been five, for one of my self-driving car projects.

Software setup

To match the examples in this book, and to have access to the same tools that are used in the code samples, you will have to set up three environments:

- **A laptop or desktop computer**: This will run our control panel, and also be used to train neural networks. I used a Windows 10 computer with Oracle VirtualBox supporting a virtual machine running Ubuntu 16.14. You may run a computer running Ubuntu or another Linux operating system by itself (without Windows) if you want. Several of the AI packages we will use in the tutorial sections of the book will require Ubuntu 16 or later to run. We will load ROS on this computer. I will also be using a PlayStation-type game controller on this computer for teleoperation (remote control) of the robot.
- **Raspberry Pi 3**: Also running Ubuntu Linux (you can also run other Linux versions, but you will have to make any adjustments between those OS versions yourself). The Pi 3 also runs ROS. We will cover the additional libraries we need in each section of the text.
- **Arduino Mega 256**: We need to be able to create code for the Arduino. I'm using the regular Arduino IDE from the Arduino website. It can be run in Windows or in Linux. Installation will be covered regardless.

Laptop preparation

I will just cover creating the Ubuntu Linux virtual machine under VirtualBox, since that is my setup. You can find instructions for installing Ubuntu 16.04 LTS without VirtualBox at `https://tutorials.ubuntu.com/tutorial/tutorial-install-ubuntu-desktop#0`:

1. Download and install VirtualBox from `https://www.virtualbox.org/wiki/Downloads`. Pick the version that matches your computer setup (Windows).

2. Download the Ubuntu system image from `https://www.ubuntu.com/download/desktop`. It will be an `.iso` file that is quite large (almost 2 GB). An `.iso` is a disk image file that is a byte-for-byte copy of another filesystem.

3. Open VirtualBox and select **New.**

4. Make up a descriptive name for this virtual machine and select **Linux** and **Ubuntu (64-bit)** in the **Type** and **Version** fields. Select **Next.**

5. Set a **Base Memory size**. I picked **3** GB.

6. Select a size for your virtual machine partition. I made a **40** GB virtual drive.

7. Click **Next.**

8. Select **Start** (green arrow) and pick your **Media Source** as the `.iso` we downloaded in Step 2.

9. Finish the installation by following the prompts.

10. Restart the virtual machine once you are finished.

Installing Python

The Linux Ubuntu system will come with a version of Python. I am going to assume that you are familiar with Python, as we will be using it throughout the book. If you need help with Python, *Packt Publishing* has several fine books on the subject.

Once you log on to your Virtual Machine, check which version of Python you have by opening up a terminal window and typing `python` at the command prompt. You should see the Python version as follows:

```
Python 2.7.12 (default, Dec  4 2017, 14:50:18)
[GCC 5.4.0 20160609] on linux2
Type "help", "copyright", "credits" or "license" for more information.
>>>
```

You can see that I have version 2.7.12.

We are going to need several add-on libraries that augment Python and extend its capability. The first thing to check is to see whether you have `pip` installed. **Pip** is a **Python Installation Package** that helps to load other packages from the internet to extend Python. Check to see whether you have `pip` by typing the following:

```
pip
```

If you get `No command 'pip' found,` then you need to install `pip`. Enter the following:

```
Sudo apt-get install python-pip python-dev build-essential
Sudo pip install -upgrade pip
```

Now we can install the rest of the packages that we need. To begin with, we need the python math packages `numpy`, the scientific python libraries `scipy`, and the math plotting libraries `matplotlib`. I will direct you to install other packages as required in the relevant chapters.

Let's install our other libraries. We need the numerical python library (`numpy`), the scientific python library (`scipy`), and `matplotlib` for making graphs:

```
>>sudo apt-get install python-numpy python-scipy python-matplotlib python-sympy
```

If you want to use the iPython (interactive Python) and Jupyter Notebook process to test your code (and document it at the same time), you can install those as well. I will not be using them in this book, but I do admit that they are quite useful.

```
>>sudo apt-get install ipython ipython-notebook
```

I'll cover the other Python libraries that we will use later (Open CV, Scikit-Learn, Keras, and so on) as we need them in the appropriate chapters.

Installing ROS on the laptop

We need a copy of ROS to talk to our robot and to execute development. You can find directions on how to do this at the ROS website repository at `http://wiki.ros.org/kinetic/Installation/Ubuntu`.

I'll give you the quick and dirty method here:

Get on your Linux laptop/desktop computer – virtual or otherwise – and get to a command prompt. We need to establish the source of the software. We do this as follows:

```
sudo sh -c 'echo "deb http://packages.ros.org/ros/ubuntu $(lsb_release -sc)
main" > /etc/apt/sources.list.d/ros-latest.list'
```

We need to set up our key to get access to the software with this command. Remember that you can cut and paste this from the ROS website as well:

```
sudo apt-key adv --keyserver hkp://ha.pool.sks-keyservers.net:80 --recv-key
421C365BD9FF1F717815A3895523BAEEB01FA116
```

At this point, it is recommended that you check that your Linux installation is up to date. We can do this by entering the following command:

```
sudo apt-get update
```

This is going to take a bit of time depending on your internet connection and computer.

Now, we are finally ready to install the main ROS distribution. Since we are on a desktop or laptop computer, we can get the whole thing, so that we have all of the tools and user interfaces. Note that we are using ROS Kinetic, the latest full release as at the time of publication of this book:

```
sudo apt-get install ros-kinetic-desktop-full
```

Expect that this step can take quite a while – it was about 30 minutes on my computer. Once it finally finishes, we can proceed to setting up the ROS on our computer. We need to set up the ROS dependency manager using these commands:

```
sudo rosdep init
rosdep update
```

rosdep keeps up with which other packages your program depends on, and will download them automatically if they are missing. This is a good feature to have, and we won't be needing it very often – just when we install a new package.

This next part is really important. ROS uses several environment variables to configure some important parts of the system, such as keeping up with which computer is in charge. The default configuration is set by doing the following:

```
echo "source /opt/ros/kinetic/setup.bash" >> ~/.bashrc
source ~/.bashrc
```

The first setup appends the `/opt/ros/kinetic/setup.bash` to our default `.bashrc` file so that those environment variables will get automatically created each time we start a new terminal window. The `.bashrc` script is executed when a new bash shell program is started.

We can check the default setup by looking at the environment variables. Let's get only the ones with the string ROS inside them by using a pipe (|) symbol and the `grep` command:

```
>>:~$ env | grep ROS
ROS_ROOT=/opt/ros/kinetic/share/ros
ROS_PACKAGE_PATH=/opt/ros/kinetic/share
ROS_MASTER_URI=http://localhost:11311
SESSION_MANAGER=local/BookROS:@/tmp/.ICE-unix/1847,unix/BookROS:/tmp/.ICE-
unix/1847
ROS_DISTRO=kinetic
ROS_ETC_DIR=/opt/ros/kinetic/etc/ros
```

The most important variable in this set is the `ROS_MASTER_URI`. This points to the place where the ROSCORE program is running. Normally, this will be on the robot. Let's say the robot's IP address is `192.168.1.15`. Then, we set the `ROS_MASTER_URI` to be `http://192.168.1.15:11311`. You can also set up an entry in the `/etc/hosts` file with the name of the robot and the IP address as follows:

```
>>:sudo nano /etc/hosts

192.168.1.15          tinman
```

Then you can use the hostname `tinman` in place of the IP address:

```
env ROS_MASTER_URI=http://tinman:11311.
```

Remember to change this in the `.bashrc` script as well (`nano .bashrc`).

Setup of Raspberry Pi 3

I ended up doing two different operating systems on the Raspberry Pi 3, depending on whether or not I wanted to use the Google Voice interface. In the chapter on Artificial Personality, we will be using the Google Voice Assistant as one option for providing the robot with the ability to listen and respond to commands, as well as adding some personality and additional conversation capability. The easiest way to perform this is to use the Raspbian operating system image that Google provides with the DIY Voice Kit. You can see `https://aiyprojects.withgoogle.com/voice` to look at the kit. This very inexpensive piece of hardware ($24.95) includes a very nice speaker, a pair of sensitive microphones, and even a cool LED light-up button. We will cover the use of this hardware add-on in the chapter on Artificial Personality. It is much easier to use the operating system image provided with that kit than try and transplant all that capability onto an already built Raspberry Pi operating system. So, if you want to do the voice part of the robot project, go to that chapter and we will cover the setup of the Raspberry Pi 3 image and the Raspbian operating system there.

Otherwise, if you don't want to use the Google Voice Assistant, you can build up a Raspberry Pi 3 with another operating system image. I happen to prefer to run Ubuntu on my Pi 3 to match my virtual machine.

For this setup, we will use an image provided by Ubuntu. Go to the Ubuntu Wiki website concerning the Raspberry Pi 3 (`https://wiki.ubuntu.com/ARM/RaspberryPi`).

The basic step, which you can follow on the website, is to prepare an SD card with the operating system image on it. I used Win32DiskImager, but there are several programs available that will do the job. You need an SD card with at least 8 GB of space –and keep in mind you are erasing the SD card in doing this.

Download the disk image from (`https://downloads.ubiquityrobotics.com/`) and pick the version for the Raspberry Pi 3. It is 1.2 GB of data, so it may take a bit. This image already has the ROS on it, so it will save a lot of time later.

Follow the directions with your SD card – the website advises using a Class 10 memory card of at least 8 GB, or preferably 16 GB. Put the SD card in your reader and start up your disk imager program. Double (and triple) check that you are picking the right drive letter – you are erasing the disk in that drive. Select the disk image you downloaded – I used the 16.04.2 version. Hit the **write** button and let the formatter create your Pi 3 disk image on the SD card.

You can follow the usual setup for setting your language and keyboard, as well as setting up the network. I like to use a static IP address for the robot, since we will be using this a lot. Use the same instructions from the preceding section on setting up ROS environment variables. Put your robot's name in the `/etc/hosts` file and set the `ROS_MASTER_URI` to the Pi 3's host name – `tinman` in my case.

> It is always a good idea to set a new user ID and change out the default passwords for your own security.

The operating system comes with Python already installed, as before when we set up the laptop/desktop virtual machine, so we follow the same procedures as previously to load the python libraries NumPy, SciPy, and a new package, Pyserial. We need this for talking to the serial port:

```
>>: pip install pyserial
```

VNC

One tool that I have added to my Raspberry Pi 3 is Virtual Network Computing, or VNC. This utility, if you are not familiar with it, allows you to see and work with the Pi 3 desktop as if you were connected to it using a keyboard, a mouse, and a montor. Since the Pi 3 is physically installed inside a robot that travels by itself, attaching a keyboard, mouse, and monitor is not often convenient (or possible). There are many different versions of VNC, which is a standard protocol used among many Unix-type – and non-Unix type - operating systems. The one I used is called RealVNC. You need two parts – the server and the client. The server side runs on the Pi 3 and basically copies all of the pixels appearing on the screen and sends them out the Ethernet port. The client catches all of this data and displays it to you on another computer. Let's install the VNC server on the Pi 3 using this command:

```
>>: sudo apt-get install realvnc-vnc-server
```

You can reference the RealVNC website at `https://www.realvnc.com/en/raspberrypi/`. This will cover configuration items and how to set up the software. The VNC software is generally included in most Pi 3 Raspbian releases.

Load the viewer on your Windows PC, Linux virtual machine, or do like I did, and load VNC on your Apple iPad. You will find the ability to log directly into the robot and use the desktop tools to be very helpful.

Setting up catkin workspaces

We will need a catkin workspace on your development machine –laptop or desktop – as well as on the Raspberry Pi. Follow the instructions at `http://wiki.ros.org/catkin/Tutorials/create_a_workspace`.

If you are already a user of ROS, then you know what a catkin workspace is, and how it is used to create packages that can be used and deployed as a unit. We are going to keep all of our programs in a package we will call `tinman`. Let's go ahead and put this package together. It takes just a few steps.

Start in the home directory:

```
mkdir -p catkin_ws/src
cd catkin_ws/src
catkin_make
source devel/setup.bash
catkin_create_pkg tinman
catkin_make
cd src/tinman/src
mkdir script
mkdir launch
```

You'll be left with a directory structure that looks something like this:

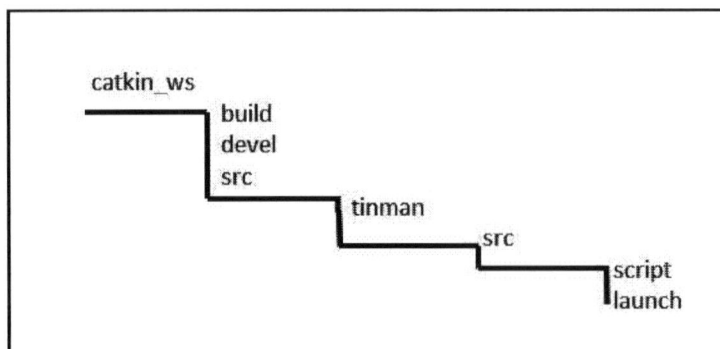

Hardware

The TinMan robot is based on a kit I found from a Chinese company named **Robo-Soul**. It is called the TK-6A Robot base with a 6-DOF Robot arm. The kit arrived in a timely fashion via post, but arrived with no instructions whatsoever. Also, the pictures on the website did not match the kit, either, so I have basically no guide to putting this thing together, other than trial and error. I will provide an abbreviated version here in the book that will get you through the rough parts. A complete version will be on the website for the book at `http://github.com/fgovers/ai_and_robots`.

Beginning at the beginning – knolling

The best way to start with a kit this complex, particularly when you don't have instructions, is by knolling. What is knolling, you ask? **Knolling** is the process of laying out all of the parts in an orderly fashion, all at right angles, so that you can see what you are working with, as demonstrated in the following image:

Knolling was – discovered – by a janitor by the name of Andrew Kromelow, who worked at Frank Gehry's furniture factory. The factory designed and made chairs for Knoll, a company started by Florence Knoll, who designed furniture with simple geometric forms. Each night, Andrew would arrange all of the tools and workbenches in careful arrays of rectangular forms, which he called *knolling* in honor of the furniture. We use knolling to figure out just what we have and what order to put it together in.

> **ⓘ** I can thank Adam Savage, of Mythbusters, for introducing me to knolling in his podcast on Tested.com. See the video at `https://www.youtube.com/watch?v=U46Yo_6z_F4`.

Assembling the tracks

We start by assembling the track components. Grab the big triangular plates. The cut-out part goes in the back at the top, since that is where the motor and drive wheel goes. You will have one of two track configurations – one with either five small metal wheels, or, like me, a setup with four large plastic bogie wheels. I believe that the plastic wheels will be the default going forward. Each wheel goes into the smaller holes on the triangle piece – ignore the big holes. The wheels are held in place by the black hex bolts with bare shafts, and fastened with the nylon lock nuts provided. Leave the frontmost wheel off (or remove it later when we mount the tracks):

Next, we construct the drive wheels. Each drive wheel is made up of two sprocket wheels (with the rectangular teeth, a motor coupler (thick brass cylinder), three brass spacers (thin hexagonal hollow parts) and a triangular cap with four holes. Note that one of the sprocket wheels has a round opening and one has a hexagonal opening. The brass motor coupler likewise has a hexagonal end and a round end. The motor coupler runs down the center of the drive wheel assembly. Attach the three brass spacers and the triangular end cap to the sprocket wheel with the hexagon opening using small round-head screws and lock washers. Put the motor coupler into the hexagonal hole and attach with a larger round head screw. Put the other sprocket wheel on the spacers and attach with small screws. Repeat for the other drive wheel. You will notice the small holes in the motor coupler for set screws to be added later – make sure you can get to these holes. There are sets of holes on either side of the motor coupler. I had to disassemble one of my drive wheels to reposition the set-screw holes:

Attach the motor mounts (L-shaped bracket) to one of the robot base plates (largest plate with clipped corners) – both plates are identical. Use four longer screws and lock washers. Next, attach the motor to the motor mount using three screws. Now it gets exciting, as we can attach the two triangular track units at the side of the base plate to the upper pair of holes in the triangular drive plates, leaving the round corner for the motor to poke through. Attach the drive wheels to the motors by sliding the motor shaft into the coupler and attach with set screws (use the regular small round head screws).

Mounting the tracks

The most difficult part of the base assembly is getting the tracks onto the bogie wheels. First, you must assemble the tracks into continuous loops. The tracks are composed of a bunch of small plastic tread units that are connected to each other with small metal pins. If you look at your tracks, one end will have a pin, and the other will not. You have to remove the pin by pulling or pushing it out using a thumbtack (which was helpfully provided in the kit). You want to push the pin away from the side with the small cylinders – it needs to come out the other side. You can see this in the following image. Pull the pin out far enough to engage the two ends of the track, and carefully push it back in to connect the track. I did not need the extra track sections that were provided. Now we have a loop of track. If you put the frontmost bogie wheel on the drive section, remove it now. Loop the track around the bogie wheels and over the drive wheel. You will have to adjust the drive wheel in or out to engage the sprockets with the tracks. Now you have to lever the front drive bogie wheel into place by angling the long screw into its hole and tightening the nut until it all drops into place. This took a fair amount of effort and about an hour of careful wiggling to get it all to line up. You must keep at it until you can move the tracks easily around the bogie wheels and the drive wheel. If one of the bogie wheels is stuck, loosen up the lock nut just a tiny bit to allow it to turn without binding. There is no track tension adjustment on this kit, which can be a problem. You can make the front bogie wheel a slot rather than a hole to get some tension adjustment. I did not have to do this on my version of the robot kit:

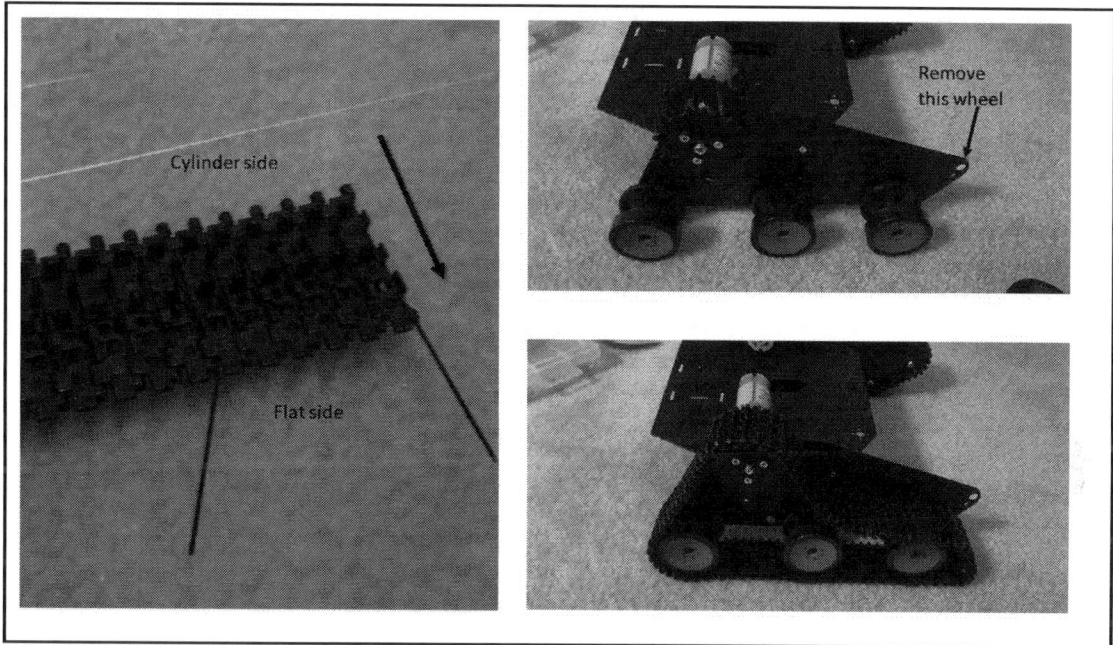

Now we can assemble the other large base plate on the bottom two holes in the track plates and our drive base is complete. The second base plate goes upside down relative to the first plate – the bent outer section goes up. I staggered the two plates by rotating the bottom plate 180 degrees, but they can also go exactly parallel if you want. I liked the staggered arrangement for later placement of sensors.

You will need to solder wires onto the drive motors before installing the robot arm. Some very nice *spaghetti* wire was included in the kit for this purpose.

Spaghetti wire has a high strand count, and is very flexible, making it ideal for use with motors or anywhere where you are expecting a lot of movement or vibration. We call it spaghetti wire because it is limp, like cooked spaghetti, not stiff like most wire.

Now I have some good news and some bad news: We are done with the base (good news!) but we still have to do the arm, and it is much more difficult to assemble (bad news!).

An important note regarding Servo installation: you need to install the servos in the arm at the middle of their travel. Each servo can turn its gears through 170 degrees of angle. You need to assemble the arm with the servos in the middle. I ran the servos all the way to the left by turning the gear by hand, and then all the way to the right, and then picked a point half-way before putting them into the arm. I tried to visualize each arm joint in the middle of its travel, and assemble the arm that way.

Arm base assembly (turntable)

The turntable is the rotating assembly that forms the base of the robot arm, and will create the robot shoulder rotate axis. This is a fairly involved part that I approached with a great deal of skepticism. However, we will see that the result is most satisfactory and appears to be a very solid design. We start with two critical steps. You must do the following first, or you will have to disassemble everything and start over. You can guess how I know this. First, pick one of the two smaller circular plates with the small holes in their center. Into one of these, you will attach one of the servo couplers, the aluminum disks that attach to the servos. To the other one you will bolt one of the "universal servo brackets", the U-shaped arm part that has two small arms and one large arm, along with a large number of holes. This will form the shoulder elevate joint later. You have to bolt these on first because you can't do it later:

Now we sandwich the large bearing between the two small circular plates and attach them with four long screws and nuts. The servo attaches to the bottom (silver disk) and the arm servo bracket is on the top. The screws must go down so that we don't have anything poking up to interfere with the arm. After taking a moment to admire our work, we now attach to two larger circles with the big cutouts. These are secured with four of the very long screws. Next, we grab the large circle with the servo-shaped hole in the middle, and install one of our servos in that rectangular spot with four screws and nuts. Then, we need to secure the bottom of the larger turntable assembly by putting four of the brass spacers all the way down on the very long screws until they touch the bottom of the metal plate. Now, mate the servo's spline output to the silver disk-shaped servo adapter you placed on the bottom of the turntable. We can now add four nuts to the long screws to secure the bottom plate. Be sure to get them all even and do not tilt the plate with the servo to one side or the other. Our turntable is done, and you can mount it to the robot mobile base if you wish, or keep the arm assembly all together and mount the turntable later after you have assembled the entire arm:

Arm assembly

The robot arm is made out of what is generally called the **servo construction kit** components. You will note that there are several standard parts used over and over. There is what I call the **universal servo bracket**, which is the U-shaped bracket with all of the holes. Most of the arm servos will fit into these brackets. There are three C-shaped brackets with rounded corners. We have one right angle bracket, one robot hand (which is pretty obvious), the five remaining servo motors, and a plastic bag with the servo couplers, which are aluminum disks with four holes around the outside and one hole in the middle. We also have three bearings in that same bag.

Our first step in the arm assembly is to take two of the large C brackets and fasten them back to back to make one long bracket with the curved sections on either end. I used four screws for this, but there are six holes. I picked the two outer and inner holes:

Now, all of the servos that attach to the C-shaped arms will go together the same way. We grab one of the small bearings and a short screw and fasten the bearing into the side of the rounded part of the C bracket away from the side of the servo. Now attach the bearing and the screw to the universal servo bracket (which I will just call a *US bracket* from now on) and fasten with a nut. If you think about how the servo goes in, you will see which side to attach the bracket. You now install the servo in the US bracket with four screws. Now, you have two pivot points on either side of the servo. Install the servo coupler (silver disk) to the servo and attach the servo coupler to the C bracket to complete the shoulder elevate joint.

Now for the elbow joint: we take one of the loose US brackets and also get the L-shaped bracket. We want to fasten these two together at right angles which is how the servo goes in. The image should explain how this works. Now, we repeat the technique we used to assemble the shoulder joint – we mount the bearing in the other end of the long C bracket, attach the universal bracket to it with a nut, and then install the servo. That completes the elbow, so now we work our way to the wrist. We attach the other C bracket to the end of the L bracket that we just attached to the elbow joint:

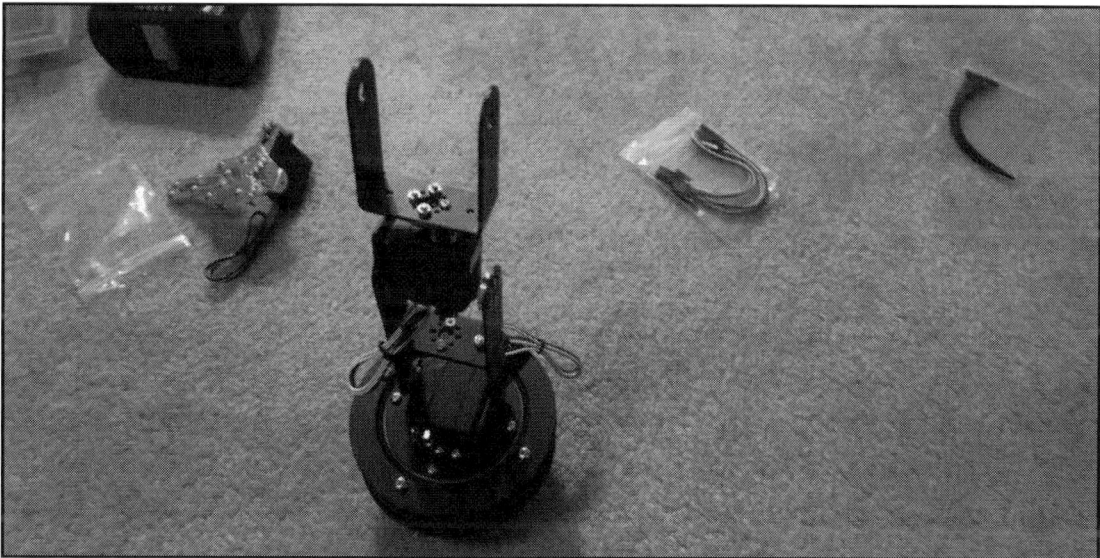

This next bit is a bit tricky. We need to fasten two of the US brackets together in the middle and at right angles to one another. We will be making a wrist joint that can both tilt and rotate, and that takes two servo motors perpendicular to each other. Once that is done, we can grab our remaining bearing and mount it in the C bracket that we attached to the elbow. Now use a screw and nut to attach one of the universal brackets to the C bracket, just as we did before, and then install the servo and servo coupler to the wrist tilt joint:

This is as good a time as any to take a break and think through the next steps. Grab the robot hand, and you can directly attach one of your servos. Make sure you first put the servo in the middle, and then incorporate the hand grip into the middle of its travel as well. Then, line things up and install the servo. That was not too bad. Now install the wrist rotate servo to the US bracket on top of the wrist joint. Our final assembly step should be pretty obvious. We put the servo coupler on the wrist with a screw in the center hole, then line up the hand, and put two screws into the matching holes in the hand and the wrist.

Our erector-set construction is complete and we have the mechanical form of the robot.

Take some time now and tidy up all of the servo cables. There are four sets of servo extension cables in the kit, so attach these to the four top servos in the arm. I used cable ties to attach the cables to the side of the arm. There is also a spiral cable organizer – at least I think that is what it is called – in the kit. You can use this to also clean up the arm cables, and it makes everything all the same color.

Wiring

The power wiring diagram is included by way of illustration. We have four main electronic components: the Raspberry Pi 3, our robot's brain; the Arduino Mega; the motor shield; and the servo controller. We will be needing two sets of power – the Pi and servo controller need 5v, while the motor controller needs the full 11 volts from the battery pack. I purchased a 5v power supply to convert the battery to 11v. The motor controller needs power on the screw terminals labeled "EXT_PWR". Hence, we need to create a power harness with two splits – one split that puts 11v into the power supply board and the motor controller. We can then wire 5v from the power supply board to the Pi 3. A second 5v goes to the "servo power" connection on the servo controller board. This is the two-pin connector that is aligned with the six servo three-pin connectors, as can be seen in the following diagram:

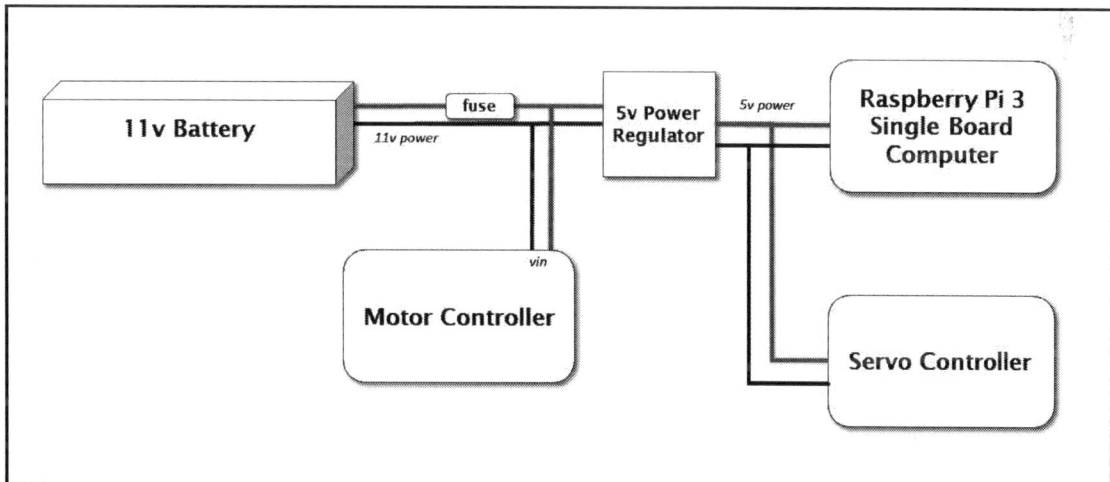

The Pi 3 has sufficient power on its USB interface to power the Arduino (that has almost no load on it) and on the servo controller logic circuit, which also takes very little power. We run USB cables from Pi 3 to Arduino, and from Pi 3 to the servo controller. Later, we will plug a USB camera into the Pi 3 as well. If we need to, we can run a separate 5 v to the Arduino at a later date if we are having power problems. The USB lines also take care of control signals to the Arduino and the servo controller. The motor shield is plugged directly onto the top of the Arduino Mega and needs no further connections.

My plan of attack was to put together the battery and power converter and test them for the proper voltages and polarity using a voltmeter before connecting any of the sensitive components. I also loaded the drivers and control software to the Arduino and Raspberry Pi 3 before plugging them into the battery power supply and connecting with USB cables. All of the servo cables can be installed in the servo controller, being careful to put the black wires, which are the ground wires (or negative wires), all on the same side. They go to the outside of the servo controller. You will want to double check that all of the black wires on the servos are lined up on the "-" or negative pins.

I've provided connections for teleoperations using a PlayStation/Xbox-type joystick, which is useful for establishing that all motors are running the right way. We'll cover calibration in the software section. If one or other of the drive motors are running backward, you just have to switch the motor wires.

Summary

This chapter covered several important topics. It started with some of the basics of robotics, for readers who needed a bit more background. We talked about common robot parts, such as sensors, computers, and motors/actuators. We discussed the subsumption architecture in more depth and showed how it helped the robot arbitrate between responding to different events and commands.

The next section covered the software setup for running the robot, including the offboard development environment and the onboard Raspberry Pi 3 computer environments. We set up the ROS and installed the Python tools.

The final section covered the hardware construction of the example robot, TinMan, with its tank-tread base and robot arm composed of servo motors. We showed how to wire the power supply up and connect all of the components to the Raspberry Pi 3 controller. We installed the ROS software that we will be using to control the robot.

In the next chapter, we will discuss how to go from a concept to a working plan for developing complex robot AI-based software using systems engineering practices such as use cases and storyboards.

Questions

1. Name three types of robot sensors.
2. What does the acronym PWM stand for?
3. What is analog-to-digital conversion? What goes in and what comes out?
4. Who invented the subsumption architecture?
5. Compare my diagram of the three-layer subsumption architecture to the Three Laws of Robotics postulated by Isaac Asimov. Is there a correlation? Why is there one, or why not?
6. Do you think I should have given our robot project – TinMan – a name? Do you name your robots individually, or by model?
7. What is the most important environment variable in ROS?

Further reading

Brooks, Rodney. **Cambrian Intelligence: The Early History of the New AI**. MIT Press, 1999. Boston, MA

A Concept for a Practical Robot Design Process

3

This chapter represents a bridge between the preceding sections on general theory, introduction, and setup, and the following chapters, where we will apply problem-solving methods that use artificial intelligence techniques to robotics. The first step is to clearly state our problem, from the perspective of the use of the robot, as compared to our view as the designer/builder of the robot. Then, we need to decide how to approach each of the physical and mental challenges that we and the robot will attempt.

This chapter will cover the following topics:

- A systems engineering-based approach to robotics
- How to state the problem using use cases
- How to approach solving problems with storyboards
- How to decompose use cases and storyboards into requirements

A systems engineering-based approach to robotics

When you set out to create a complex robot, with artificial intelligence-based software, you can't just jump in and start slinging code and throwing things together without some sort of game plan as to how the robot goes together and how all the parts communicate with one another. We will discuss a systematic approach to robot design based on **systems engineering** principles. We will be learning about **use cases** and **storyboards** as a technique to understand what we are building and what parts are needed.

Our task – cleaning up the playroom

We have already talked a bit about our main task for Tinman, our robot example for this book, which is to clean up the playroom in my house after my grandchildren come to visit. We need to provide a more formal definition of our problem, and then to turn that into a list of tasks for the robot to perform along with a plan of action on how we might accomplish those tasks.

Why are we doing this? Well, consider this quote:

"If you don't know where you are going, how do you know when you get there? – Me.

I guess I am going to have to attribute this quote to myself, since I can't find any reference to someone else saying it. What I am saying is that if you don't know where the finish line is, how do you know when you are done?

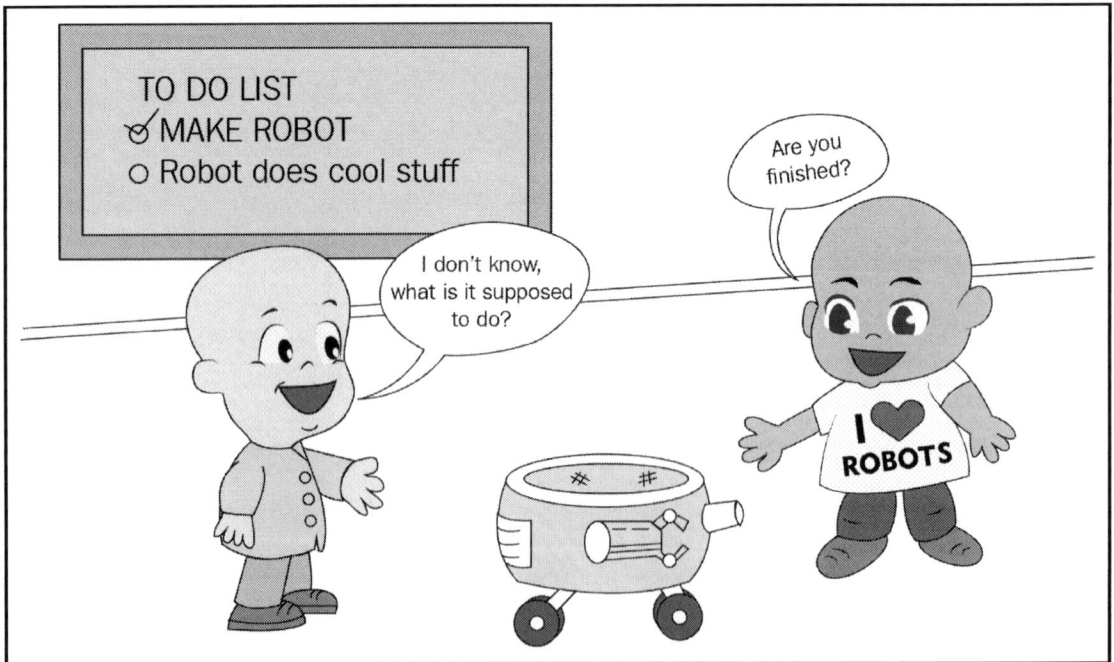

The internet and various robot websites are littered with dozens of robots that share one fatal character flaw: the robot and its software was designed first and then they went out to look for a job for it. In the robot business, this is called the **ready, fire, aim problem**. The task, the customer, the purpose, the use, the job of the robot comes first.

Another way of saying this is: in order to create an effective tool, the first step is to decide what you do with it.

I could have written this book as a set of theories and exercises that would have worked well in a classroom setting, and would have introduced you to a whole lot of new tools you would not know how to apply.

This chapter is here to provide you with tools and methods to provide a path from having good idea to having a good robot, with as little misdirection, pain, suffering, tears, and torn hair as I can provide. You are on your own on burns; please be careful with the soldering iron.

The process we will use is straightforward. The first step is to look at the robot from the user's perspective and then describe what is does. We will call these descriptions **use cases**– examples of how the robot will be used. Next we will break each use case down into **storyboards** (step-by-step illustrations), which can be word pictures or actual pictures. From the storyboards, we can extract tasks – a to-do list for our robot to accomplish. The final step for this part of the process is to separate the to-do list into things we can do with software and things we will need hardware for. This will give us the detailed information for designing our robot and its AI-based software. Keep in mind that one of the robot's uses is to be a good example for this book.

Use cases

Let's start with a statement of the problem.

The problem – part 1

About once or twice a month, my four delightful, intelligent, and playful grandchildren come to visit my wife and me. Like most grandparents, we keep a box full of toys in our upstairs game room for them to play with during their visits. The first thing they do upon arrival – at least the bigger grandkids– is to take every single toy out of the toy box and start playing. This results in the the following photo – basically toys randomly and uniformly distributed throughout the playroom. Honestly, you could not get a better random distribution. They are really good at this. Since, as grandparents, our desire is to maximize the amount of time that our grandchildren have fun at our house and we want them to associate Granddad and Grandmother's house with having fun, we don't make them pick up the toys when they go home. You can see where this is heading.

By the way, if you are a parent, let me apologize to you in advance; this is indeed an evil plot on we, the grandparents, part, and you'll understand when you get grandkids of your own—and you will do this, too.

The problem: actual, unretouched photo of game room in the immediate aftermath of grandchildren

Where were we...? Yes, a room full of randomly and uniformly distributed foreign objects – toys – scattered about an otherwise serviceable game room, which need to be removed. Normally, I'd just have to sigh heavily, and pick up all this stuff myself, but I am a robot designer, so what I want to do is to have a robot that does the following:

1. Pick up the toys – and not the furniture, lights, books, speakers, or other items in the room that are *not toys*
2. Put them in the toy box
3. Continue to do this until there are no more toys to be found and then stop

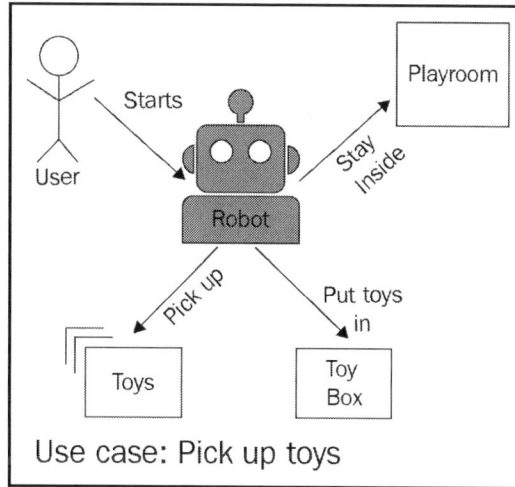

Use case: Pick up toys

Now we can ask some pertinent questions. I took a lot of journalism classes in school and I was taught the usefulness of the *5 Ws and an H – Who, What, When, Where, Why,* and *How*? These are just as useful for examining use cases. I've got one firm rule here in this section: no implementation details. Don't worry about how you are going to do this. Just worry about defining the results. So we leave out the *H* for now and just do *Ws*. Let's give this a try.

Who – the robot

That was easy. We want the robot to do something; as in the robot does this and not me. What do we want the robot to do?

What – pick up toys and put them in the toy box

What does this answer tell us? It says we are going to be grasping and lifting something – toys. What are toys? We could rephrase this as a negative:

What – pick up and put away in the toy box the items that were not previously in the room

The toys were not in the room before the grandkids pulled them all out. So we either want to classify items as toys, or as things that were not in the room before. *Not in the room* implies that the robot somehow knows what belongs in the room, possibly by making a survey prior to the children's arrival. However, *toys* implies that the robot can classify objects at least as *toys* and *not toys*. Let's stick with that for now. We may have some items in the room that are not toys, but are out of place, and thus don't belong in the toy box. You can already see these questions shaping what comes later in this process.

When – after the grandchildren have visited and they have left, continue to pick up toys until there are none left

That gives us two conditions for the *when*: a start and a stop. In this case, start is defined as the grandkids have visited, and they have left. Now it is perfectly fair for me to state in the use case that I'll tell the robot when these conditions are met, since that is not putting me out. I'll be here, and I know when the room needs to be cleaned. So let's change *when* to the following.

When – when I (the user) tell you to, and don't stop until there are no more toys to be found

Now we could have decided that the robot needs to figure this out for itself, and turn itself on after the grandchildren leave, but what is the return on investment for that? That would be a lot of work, for not a lot of gain. The *pain point* for me, the user, is picking up toys, not deciding when to do it. This is a lot simpler.

Note that my *when* statement has a start and an end. Anyone who watched Mickey Mouse in the *Sorcerer's Apprentice* segment of *Fantasia* understands that when you have a robot, telling it when to stop can be important. Another important concept is defining the end condition. I did not say *stop when all of the toys are picked up* because that would imply the robot needed to know all of the toys, either by sight or number. It is easier as a task definition to say *stop when you see no more toys* instead, which accomplishes what we want without adding additional requirements to our robot.

It is perfectly normal to have to revisit use cases as the robot designer understands more about the problem – sometimes you can be working hard to solve a problem that is not relevant to solving the user's task. You can image some robot engineer in a team being given the task of *pick up all the toys* as meaning all toys ever invented, in all cultures, in all parts of the world! Then you get a request for a $500,000 database software license and a server farm to house it. We just want to pick up the toys found in the game room. That is the beauty of use cases – we don't worry about *how* until later.

Where – the game room upstairs

OK now we have some tricky parts. The area to be cleaned is a specific area of the house, but it is not really bound by walls. And it is upstairs – there is a stairway going down in the game room that we don't want our robot tumbling down. How would you have known this? You won't unless you ask these kind of questions! The environment the robot operates in is just as important as what it does. In this case, let's got back and ask the user. I'll stick in a floorplan for you here to define what I mean by *game room*. On the bright side, we don't need to climb or descend stairs in this task. But we do need to look out for the staircase as a hazard:

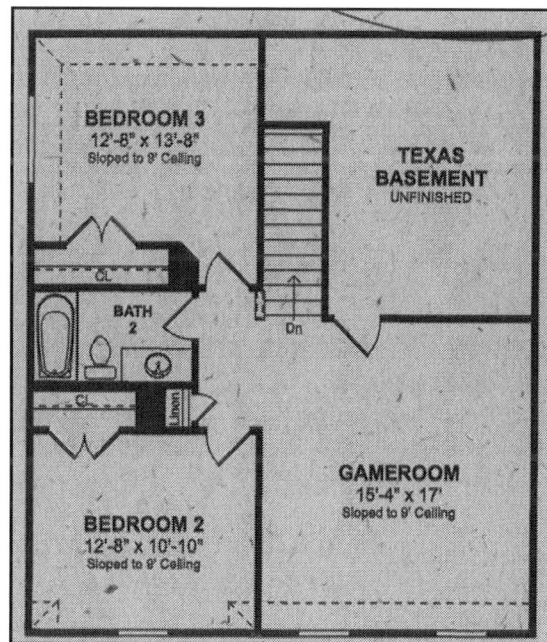

Our robot has more than one use case – it has more than one function to perform.

The problem – part 2

The robot needs to interact with my grandchildren. Why is this here? As I told you in Chapter 1, the grandchildren were introduced to some of my other robots, and one of the grandkids, William, always tries to talk to the robots. I have two grandchildren who are on the autistic spectrum, so this is not an idle desire – I've read research, such as *Robots for Autism* (https://robots4autism.com/) that state that robots can be helpful. While I'm not trying to do therapy, I'd like my robot to interact with my grandchildren verbally. I also have one specific request – the robot must be able to tell and respond to knock-knock jokes, a favorite of William.

So, here is a diagram of this use case:

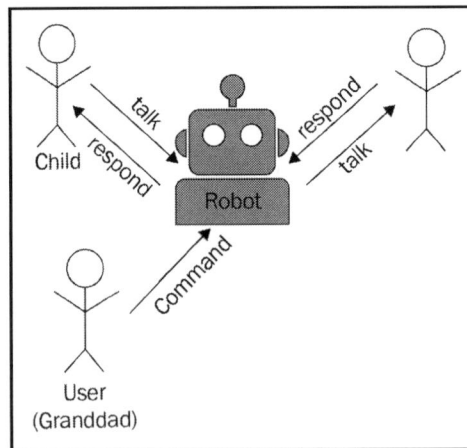

So let's go through our same exercise with this use case. We ask the pertinent questions: *who, what, when, where,* and *why*?

Who – the robot, the user (granddad), and the grandchildren

In this case, user interaction is part of the task. Who are we interacting with? I need to be able to command the robot to begin to interact. Then we want the robot to both talk to and listen to the children.

What – receive commands and verbally interact (hold a conversation) with children, which must include knock-knock jokes

We keep the two kinds of functions: receive commands from – let's call me the robot controller, to make this more generic. The other function is to have a conversation with the children, including telling knock-knock jokes. We'll define *conversation* further on in our breakdown, so we'll be setting some limits on that function, but to introduce the topic we will be spending an entire chapter on, we are referring to "small talk" or phatic conversation. Klaus Schneider in his PhD thesis ,*"Small Talk: Analyzing Phatic Discourse"*, compared these short conversations we all have to moves in a game – which means we can model them and create strategies for them like a game as well. Oh, dear, I've violated my one and only rule for use cases: I talked about "how" in the "what" section. Let that be a lesson to you. it Is quite easy to violate this rule and you have to catch yourself and stop. Delete everything from your memory after "moves in a game".

Schneider, K. (1988), *Small Talk: Analysing Phatic Discourse*, PhD thesis, Philipps Universität, Marburg, W. Germany

Fortunately for us, the `knock=knock` joke has a very structured form based on puns and a call-and-response format that goes like this:

```
Robot: Knock Knock
Child: Who's There?
Robot: Lettuce
Child: Lettuce Who?
Robot: lettuce(let us) in, we're freezing out here!
```

I'll leave diagramming the opposite form – responding to a knock-knock joke—to you, but you can see that the joke is pretty easy even for a robot.

When – as requested by the robot controller, then when the child speaks to the robot

I think this is fairly self-explanatory: the robot interacts when sent a command to do so. It then waits for someone to talk to it. One thing we can extrapolate from this information: when we are picking up toys, we are not expecting the robot to talk – the two activities are exclusive. We only pick up toys after the kids are gone, ergo no one to talk to.

Where – in the game room, within about six feet of the robot

We have to set some limits on how far we can hear – there is a limit on how sensitive our microphone can be. I'm suggesting six feet as a maximum distance. We may revisit this later. When you come to a requirement like this, you can ask the customer "Why six feet?". They may say, "Well, that sounds like a reasonable distance". You can ask, "Well, if it was five feet, would that be a failure of this function?". And the user might respond, "No, but it would not be as comfortable". You can continue to ask questions on distances until you get a feeling for the required distance (how far away to not fail), which might be three feet in this case (so that the child does not have to bend over the robot to be heard), and the desired distance, which is how far the user wants the function to work. These are important distinctions when we get around to testing. Where is the pass-fail line for this requirement?

What is our robot to do?

Now we are going to do some detailed analysis of what the robot needs to do by using the storyboard process. This works like this: We take each of our two tasks and break them down as completely as we can based on the answers to all of our *W* questions. Then we make a picture of each step. The pictures can be either a drawing or a word picture (a paragraph) describing what happens in that step.

I like to start the decomposition process by describing the robot in terms of a state machine, which for the first problem may be a good approach to understanding what is going on. You are probably familiar with state machine diagrams, but just in case: a state machine diagram describes the robot's behavior as a series of discrete states, or sets of conditions that define what actions are available to the robot:

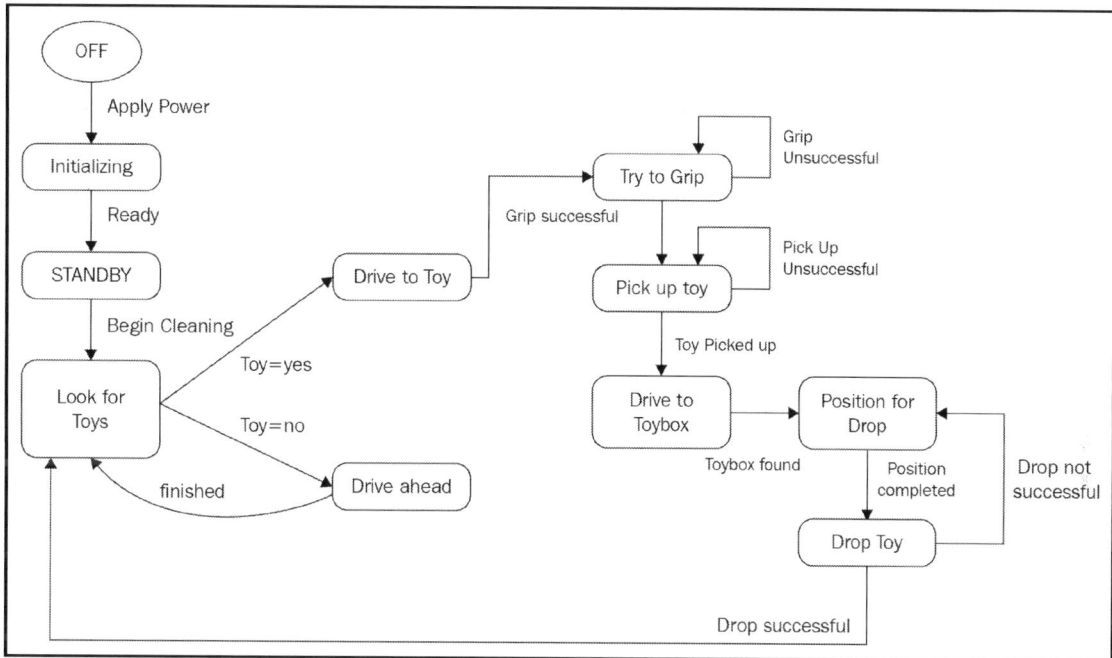

Our first state is simply **OFF** – the robot has no power turned on.

Each state is an event or events that cause the state to change. These are called **transitions**. To get from the off state to whatever is next, some event has to occur – like the human operator turning on the power. We'll call that transition event **power applied**. Now what state are we in? There is some amount of time to get the computer booted and the programs loaded (**Initializing**). Once everything boots up and initializes, the robot will be ready to accept commands. Let's call this state **STANDBY**. The robot is just sitting waiting for instructions. Now we want to start cleaning the room. I send a command to the robot to **Begin Cleaning**, which changes the state to – what? What do we need to happen next? We could define a state called **cleaning**, but that would encompass a lot of complex functions and we would not learn much from that. We need the robot to look around itself for toys. If it does not find a toy, it needs to drive forward – avoiding obstacles – and then look again. If it does find a toy, then it needs to position itself within reach of the robot arm to grab the toy. So in the state machine diagram we add the transition **Begin Cleaning**, which changes the state from **STANDBY** to **Looking for Toys**. Now we can add two more transitions: one called **Toy=no** and one called **Toy=yes**. The **Toy=no** branch goes to a state called drive ahead, where the robot moves forward – while avoiding obstacles – and then goes back to the **Look for Toys** state and tries again to find a toy.

So now we have found a toy, what do we do now? We need to drive to the toy, which puts it in range of our robot arm. We try to grip the toy with the robot's arm and hand. We may not be successful in the first try, in which case we simply try again. The loop transition, which is labeled **Grip Unsuccessful** says go back and try again if you don't succeed the first time. Where have I heard that before? You can see the same with **Pick up toy**. Why are there two parts? We need to first get a hold on the toy before we can lift it. So I thought it needed two states, since we may fail to "get a grip"— the toy falls out of the hand, separately from picking the toy up, where the toy is too heavy or awkward to lift.

OK, we found a toy and picked it up. What is next? We need to put it in the toy box. The next state is **Drive to Toybox**. Don't worry about *how* at this stage; this is just what we need to do. Later we can further decompose this state into a more detailed version. We drive until we get to the event **Toybox Found**. That means we see the toy box. Then we go to the **Position for Drop** state, which moves the robot to a place where it can drop the toy in the box. The final state, **Drop Toy**, is self-explanatory. We've dropped the toy, the robot has nothing in its gripper, and guess what? We start over by returning to the **Look for Toys** state. If the robot decides that the drop was not successful (the toy is still in the gripper), then we have it try that step again also.

This is all well and good, and our little robot goes around forever looking for toys, right? We've left out two important transitions. We need a **No More Toys** event, and we need a way to get back to the **OFF** state. Getting to **OFF** is easy – the user turns off the power. I use the shorthand method of having a block labeled **any state** since we can hit the off button at any time, no matter what else the robot is doing, and there is nothing the robot can or should do about it. It may be more proper to draw a line from each state back to OFF, but that clutters the diagram, and this notation still gets the meaning across.

The new state machine diagram looks like this:

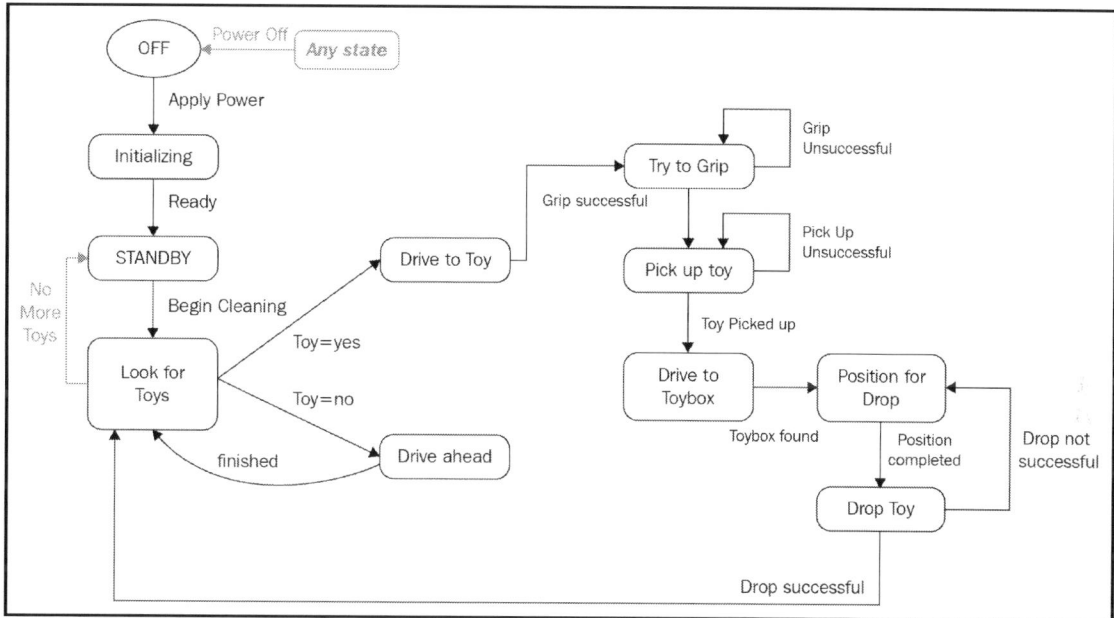

Let's take a minute and talk about the concept of **No More Toys**. How do we define this? This may take some experimentation, but for now, we'll say if we have not found a toy after 10 minutes of trying, then we are satisfied that there are no more toys to be found. Later, we can adjust that time as necessary. It is possible that 5 minutes is totally adequate for a room our size. Note that the **No More Toys** event can only come from the **Look for Toys** state, which should make sense.

We mentioned that the robot needs to avoid obstacles. But we don't have a state called **Avoid Obstacles**. Why is that? That is because several of the states include driving, and each of those includes avoiding obstacles. It would not be appropriate to have a state for avoiding obstacles, since it is not unique to one state. What we need is a separate state machine that describes the robot's driving. As I mentioned in the section in the last chapter on the subsumption architecture, we can have more than one goal operational at a time. The goal of "zz is the mission, which is the overall goal of the robot. **Avoid Obstacles** is a goal of the driving engine, the mid-level manager of our robot.

Storyboards

We've done our use cases and a state machine diagram, so now let's move on to the next step, which is to create our storyboards. We are going to decompose our use cases further in order to understand the various tasks our robot must undertake on our behalf in the course of its two missions. I've created some quick little drawings to illustrate each point.

The concept of storyboards is borrowed from the movie industry, where a comic-strip like narration is used to translate words on a page in the script into a series of pictures or cartoons that convey additional information not found in the script, such as framing, context, movement, props, sets, and camera moves. The practice of storyboarding goes all the way back to silent movies, and is still used today.

We can use storyboards in robotics design for the same reasons: to convey additional information not found in the words of the use cases. Storyboards should be simple, quick, and just convey enough information to help you understand what is going on.

Let's get started. We are not going to create storyboards for "apply power", "initialize", or "ready" because they are not really needed for those simple concepts. We will jump ahead to the "begin cleaning" event in our state diagram.

Storyboard – put away the toys

The first step in our process after "begin cleaning" is "look for toys". This storyboard frame is what the robot sees as it is commanded to start cleaning. It sees the room, which has three kinds of objects visible: toys, things that are not toys (the green ottoman and the red fireplace), and the room itself, the walls, and the floor:

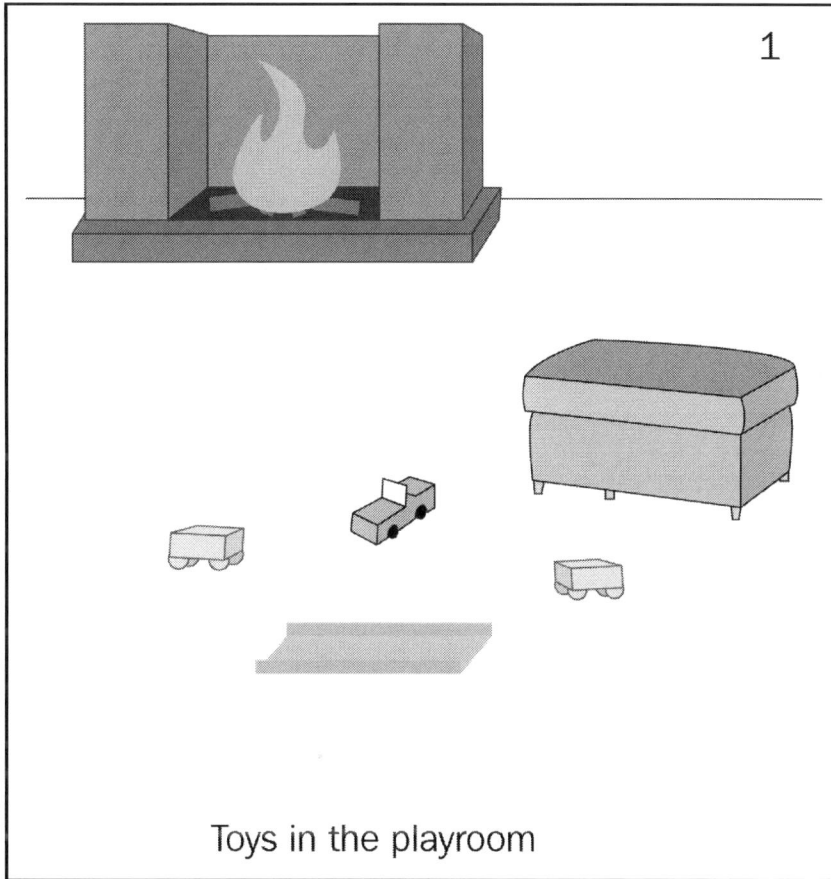

Toys in the playroom

We could select any sort of sensor to detect our toys and direct our robot. We could have a Lidar, or a thermal scanner, or sonar. Let's make an hypothesis that the best sensor tool for this task is a regular USB camera. We have control of the lighting, the toys are not particularly warmer or cooler than the surroundings, and we need enough information to identify objects by type. Video it is. We will work later to determine exactly what kind of camera we need, so add that to our "to do" list.

Our next storyboard is to look for toys:

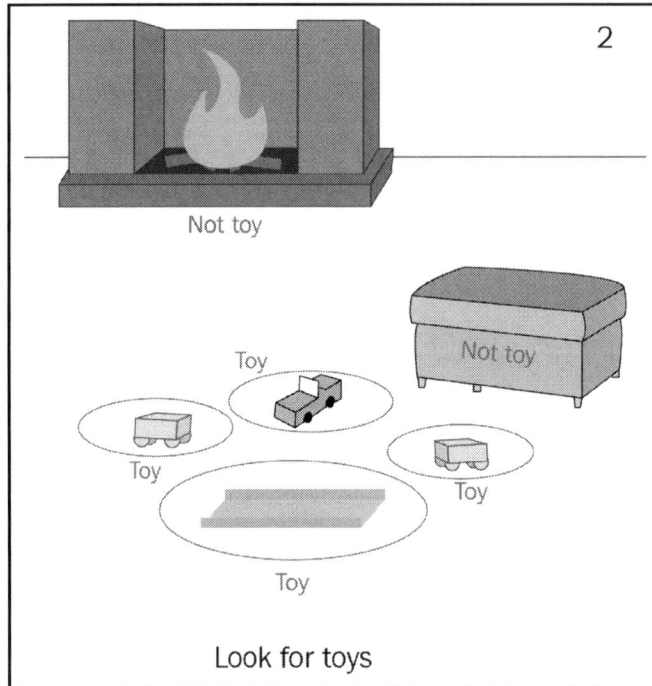

Look for toys

We need to run some sort of algorithm or technique to classify objects by type. The results of that algorithm is to both find the objects - separate them from the background of the floor - and then to classify each object as a toy or not a toy. We don't really care to have any more breakdown than that - we leave all **Not toy** objects alone, and pick up all **Toy** objects. Note that we draw circles around the objects that are toys, which is another way of saying that we must locate them in the camera frame. So what does this simple picture tell us we did not know before? It tells us that:

- We need to segment the camera image by objects
- We need to locate the objects in the camera frame
- We need to classify the objects as either **Toy** or **Not Toy**
- We need to be able to store and remember this information

We really only can pick up and move one toy at a time - we only have one hand, and no-one said in the use cases that we need to pick up more than one at a time. So we only care about one toy - and let's arbitrarily say its the closest one to the robot:

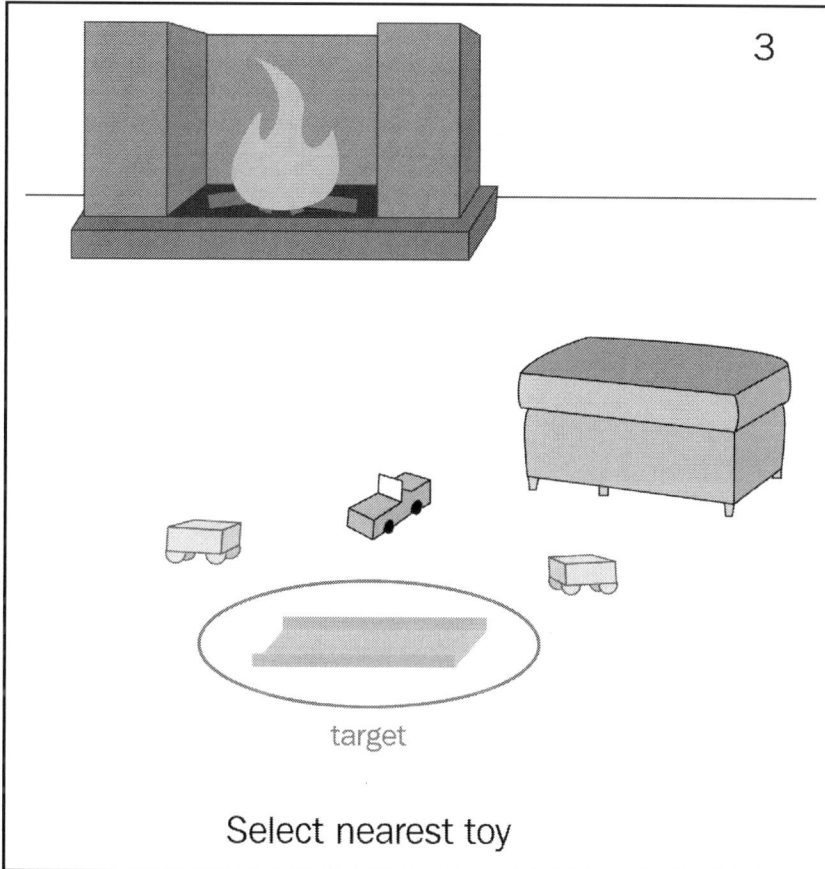

target

Select nearest toy

We might also say that it's the toy that is easiest to get to, which might be a slightly different process than choosing the closest one. We set that toy to be the target for our next action, which is what?

If you said to drive to the toy, you would be correct. However, we must not just drive to the toy, but to put the toy in a position where the robot arm can get to it. By the way, that means the robot arm must be able to reach to the ground or very close to the ground, as we have some small toys:

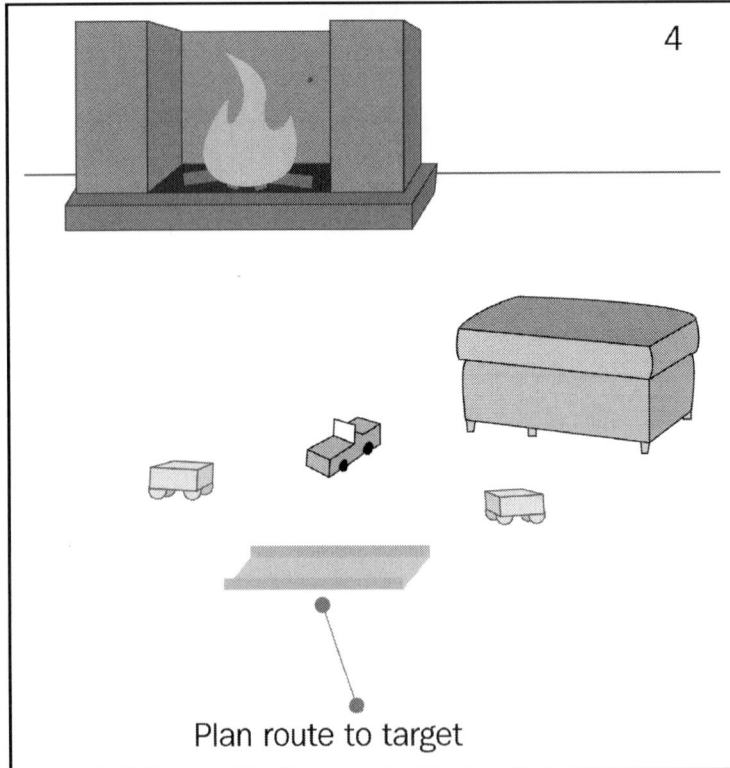

Plan route to target

Our robot must plan a route from its current position to a spot where it can attempt to pick up the toy. We set a target goal an arms-length away from the center of the toy:

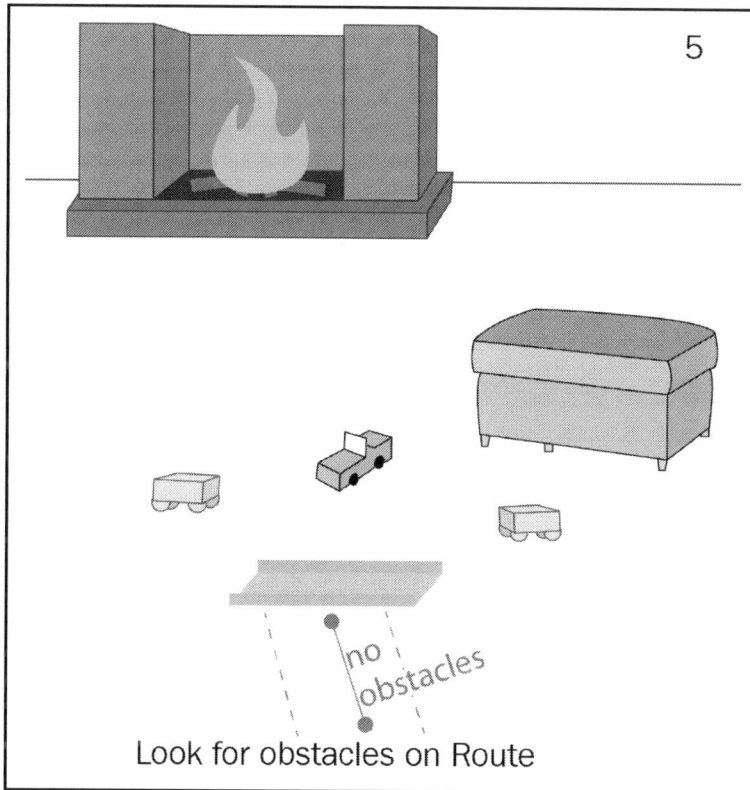

The robot needs to make sure that there are no obstacles enroute. There are two ways of doing this. As illustrated, you can clear the path that the robot is traveling on by adding the width of the robot (plus a bit of extra) and see if any obstacles are in that area, or we can add a border around obstacles and see if our path goes into those boundaries. Regardless, we need to have a path free of obstacles:

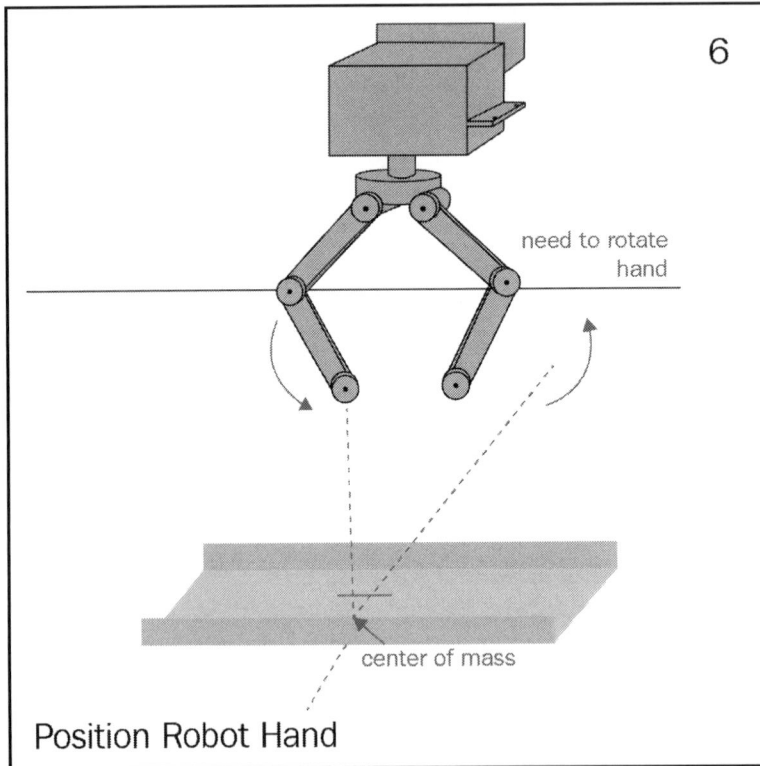

Position Robot Hand

The robot determines for itself the proper alignment to prepare to pick up the toy.

Now that the robot has completed its drive, the robot can move the robot hand to a position to pick up the toy. We need to put the robot hand over the center of mass of the toy, and then rotate the hand to match a narrow part of the toy so we can pick it up. One of our goals of this project is to not dictate how the robot does this, but rather to let it learn for itself. So we can say for this storyboard panel that the robot uses its training and machine learning to use an appropriate hand pose to prepare to grasp the object. We can surmise that that includes lining the hand up:

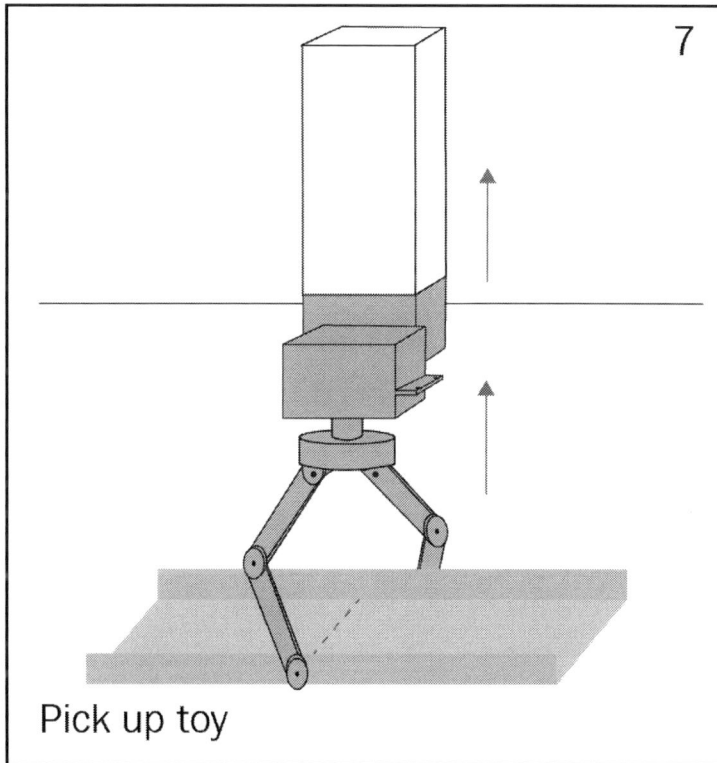

Pick up toy

Probably step 6 is the hard part, and in step 7 the robot completes the grasp of the object and picks it up. The robot has to be able to determine if the pick up was successful, and if not, try again. That was in our state machine diagram we did before. We have now picked up the toy. What's next? Find the toy box!

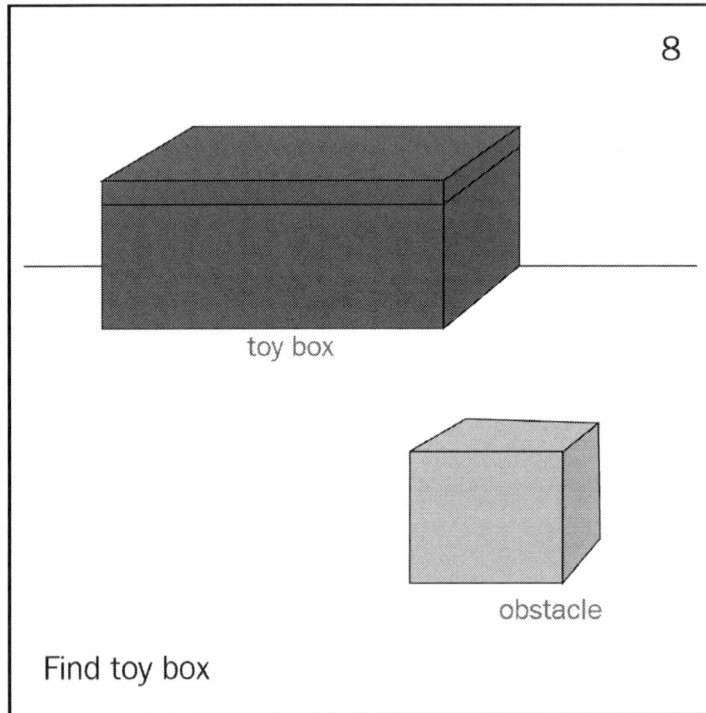

8

toy box

obstacle

Find toy box

Now we need the robot to find the toy box. Again, we don't care how at this point. We are still worried about "what" and not "how". Somehow the robot looks around and finds the toy box, which in this case is large, against the wall, and a distinctive color. Regardless, the robot has to find the toy box on its own. The labels in the picture indicate that the robot can distinguish the toy box and considers all other objects it perceives as obstacles. We can see we don't need to have the "toy/not toy" capability active at the same time, only the "toy box / not toy box" decision-making process. This does ease some of our processing and will make machine learning easier:

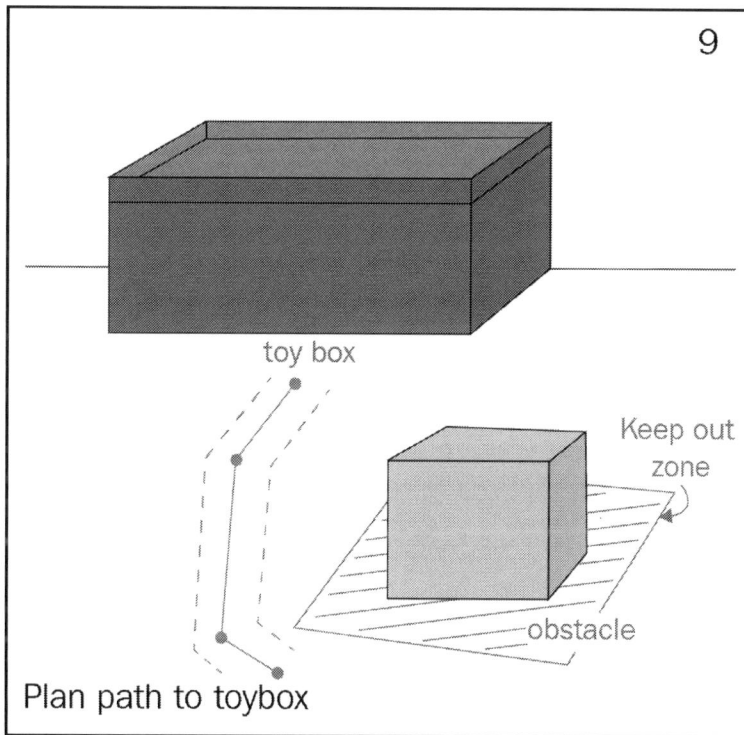

toy box

Keep out zone

obstacle

Plan path to toybox

Now that we have found the toy box, we illustrate a slightly more complex task of navigating around an obstacle to get there. In this example, we show the purple outline of the robot's base, compared to a red outline around the obstacle, which I labeled **Keep out zone**. This gives us more guidance on how to avoid obstacles. Wee want to keep the center of the robot out of the keep out zone. We need to get close enough to the toy box to drop in our toy:

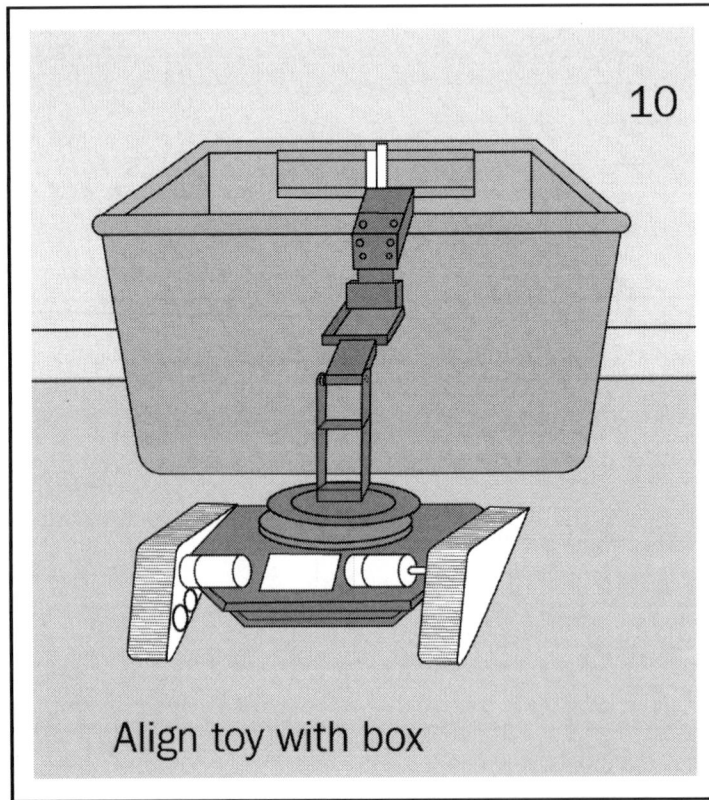

Align toy with box

In storyboard 10, we lift the toy high above the top of the toybox, and position our toy to fall inside the toybox when we let go of it. Make a note that we have to have the toy lifted before the final few inches to the toybox. We put the robot hand over the top of the opening of the toybox, just as far forward as we can and in the middle of the toybox.

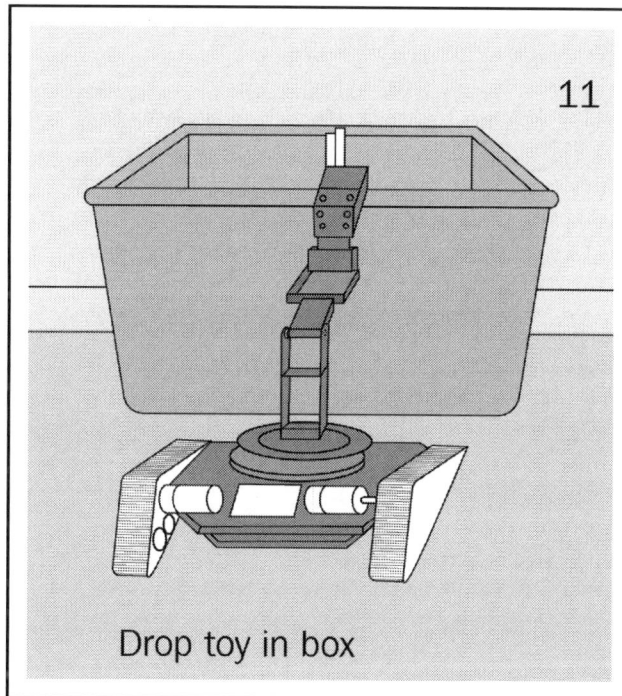

11

Drop toy in box

Our final step in the toy saga is to open the robot hand and let the toy hopefully fall in to the toy box. I will predict that we will have to spend some trial and error time getting this right. We may have to tilt the open hand right and left to get the toy to drop. If the toy falls outside of the box, then it is not put away and we have to start all over and try to put it away again. We don't need a new state for this because it returns to being a toy on the floor and we already have a state for that.

I hope that you have seen in the storyboard process how this provides insight into visualizing the robot's tasks. I would say the more important benefit is that it forces you to think about what the robot is doing and to break down each step into smaller and smaller parts. Don't hesitate to take this storyboard and break an individual panel down into its own storyboard, if that is what you feel you need to do.

Project goals

Since this is an AI/machine learning project, we have to add to our project goals not just putting away toys, but using machine learning, adaptive systems, neural networks, and other tools to provide a new approach to solving these sorts of problems. You may think, "why bother? You can do this better with a standard programming approach". I would say that you are wrong, and you can do your own research to see where companies, large and small, have tried to solve this sort of problem and failed -or at least not succeeded. This problem is not easily solved by any means, and using an AI-based approach has a far greater chance of success than standard programming techniques. Now, I'm not saying we are going to succeed beyond our wildest dreams at this task in this book, but our objective is to learn a whole lot along the way!

So we pause at this point in defining our project to say that we are deliberately choosing to use artificial intelligence and machine learning as an approach to solve a problem that has proven to be difficult with other means.

Since we are going to be teaching the robot various tasks, it will be more effective if we can teleoperate the robot and drive it around like a radio controlled car, in order to collect data and take pictures we will use for object recognition later. We will add this required operation to our "to do" list.

In our next step, we are going to extract from all of our hard work the **hardware** and **software** tasks that our robot will have to accomplish. Then we can talk about how to write a **component specification**, and finally, we can discuss **performance measurement and testing**.

Decomposing hardware needs

Based on our storyboards, I extracted or derived the following hardware tasks:

- Drive the robot base
- Carry the robot arm
- Lift toys
- Put toys in toy box (arm length)
- Sensors:
  - Arm location
  - Hand status (open/close)

- Robot vision (camera)
- Obstacle avoidance:
    - Camera
    - Sonar (optional)
    - Detect stairs

- Provide power for all systems:
    - 5V for Raspberry Pi3
    - 5V for Arduino
    - Arm power
    - Motor power sensors
- Onboard computers:
    - Computer that can receive commands remotely (Wi-Fi- Raspberry Pi 3)
        - Runs ROS
        - Ru
        - ns Python
    - Computer that can interface to a camera (also Raspberry Pi 3)
    - Computer that can control motors (Arduino)
    - Interface that can drive servo motors for the robot arm (servo controller)

Breaking down software needs

This list of software tasks was composed by reviewing the state machine diagram, the use cases, and the storyboards. I've highlighted the steps that will require AI and will be covered in detail in the coming chapters:

1. Power on self-test (POST):
    - Start up robot programs
    - Check that the Pi 3 can talk to the Arduino and back
    - Try to establish communications with the control station
    - Report POST success or failure as appropriate and enter in the log

2. Receive commands via Wi-Fi:
    * Teleoperate:
        * Drive motor base (right/left/forward/back)
        * Move hand up/down/right/left/in/out/twist
        * Record video or record pictures as image files

3. Send telemetry via Wi-Fi
4. Monitor progress (map?)
5. Send video
6. Navigate safely
    * Learn to avoid obstacles
    * Learn to not fall down stairs

7. Find toys:
    * Detect objects
    * Learn to classify objects (toy/not toys)
    * Determine which toy is closest

8. Pick up toys:
    * Move to the position where the arm can reach the toy
    * Devise a strategy for grasp
    * Attempt grasp
    * Determine whether grasping was successful
    * If not, try again with a different strategy
    * Reweight grasp technique score based on success

9. Put toys in the toy box:
    1. Learn to identify the toy box
    2. Find the toy box:
        * Navigate around the room
        * Search the camera image for the toy box
        * Report whether the toy box is in image with a range and direction
    3. Move to the dump location:
        * Avoid obstacles
        * Lift the toy above the toy box lid
    4. Drop the toy
    5. Check to see whether the toy drop was successful
    6. If not, reposition and try again

7. If the toy misses the toy box, we treat it as a toy on the floor again

10. Determine whether there are no more toys

11. Stand by for instructions

12. Teleoperate:
    - Move base forward/backward/left/right
    - Move arm up/down/right/left
    - Move hand in/out/twist/open/close
    - Record video/take pictures

13. Simulate personality:
    - Have moods
    - Have feelings
    - Show empathy
    - Interact with people
    - Talk
    - Listen/recognize words
    - Understand some commands
    - Tell knock-knock jokes
    - Understand knock-knock jokes

14. Voice commands:
    - Clean-up room
    - Put this away
    - Come here
    - Stop
    - Wait
    - Resume
    - Go home
    - Turn left/ right
    - Forward/ back
    - Hand up/hand down
    - Hand left/hand right
    - Open hand/close hand

In this list, where did I get "teleoperate"? We don't remember discussing that in the use cases and storyboards.

Writing a specification

Our next task is to write specifications for our various components. I'll go through an example here that we must do as part of our toy-grasping robot project: we need to select a camera. Just any old camera will not do – we need one that meets our needs. But what are those needs? We need to write a camera specification, so that we can tell when we are looking at cameras to buy which one will do the job.

We've created our storyboard and our use cases, so we have the information we need to figure out what our camera needs to do. We can "reverse engineer" this process somewhat: let's discuss what things make one camera different from another. First of all is the interface: this camera goes on board the robot, so it has to interface with the robot's computer, which has USB, Ethernet, and the special Raspberry Pi camera bus. What other things about cameras do we care about? We certainly care about cost. W e don't want (or need) to use a $1,000 camera for our inexpensive robot. Cameras have resolution: the number of pixels in each image. That can vary from 320 x 240 to 4000 x 2000 (4K). Cameras also have a field of view, which is the number of angular degrees the camera can see. This can vary from 2.5 degrees (very narrow) to 180 degrees (very wide). There are also cameras that see in the dark, or have various types of infrared sensitivity. Finally, there is size and weight; we need a small camera that fits on our robot.

This makes our parameters that we need to decide the following:

- Field of view: [180 - > 2.5]
- Resolution: [320x280 -> 4000x2000]
- Cost: (low to high) – cheaper is better
- Sees in the dark: (yes / no)
- Size and weight: Smaller and lighter is much better; must fit on the robot.
- Interface: USB, Ethernet, or camera bus; power >11V

The reason for listing these parameters like this is that we can now concentrate on those features that we can select for, so we are not wasting time looking at other parameters that we don't care about. Let's see if we can knock off some of the parameters. If we use USB as the interface, the power is provided on the connector, and we don't need extra cables or routers. This is also the lowest cost method, so we choose USB as the interface. We also don't have any requirements in our use cases to see in the dark, so we don't need a special infrared camera. The next question is to determine the field of view. We need to see the entire area where the robot arm can move in as it picks up a toy. We also need enough field of view to see when we are driving to avoid obstacles.

We can take some measurements from the robot, but we can quickly see that we mostly need to see close to the robot, and we can't see past the tracks on either side. This sets the field of view required to be close to 90 degrees. More field of view than this is acceptable, less is not.

Our final problem is determining the resolution we need to perform our object recognition. For that we need an additional data point – how many pixels do we need to recognize an object as a toy? That is what we will do doing with this camera – recognizing toys and things that are not toys. We also have to pick a distance in which we can recognize the toy. We don't have a firm requirement out of the use cases, so we have to make an educated guess. We know that our room is 17 feet long, and it has furniture in it. Let's guess that we need eight feet of distance. How do we know this is correct? We do a thought experiment. If we can identify a toy eight feet away, can we accomplish our task? We can see the toy half a room away. That gives the robot plenty of space to go drive to the toy and it won't spend much time looking for toys. As a check, if the robot had to be four feet away to recognize a toy, would that be unusable? The answer is probably not – the robot would work OK. How about three feet? Now we are getting to the point where the robot has to drive right up to the toy to determine what it is, and that might result in more complicated logic to examine toys. So, we say that three feet is not enough, four feet is acceptable, and eight feet would be great.

What resolution is required in the camera to recognize a toy at eight feet with a 90 degree lens? I can tell you that the ImageNet database requires a sample 35 pixels wide to recognize an object, so we can use that as a benchmark. We assume at this point that we need an image at least 35 pixels across. Let's start with a camera with 1,024x768 pixels, which is 1,024 pixels wide. We divide by 90 degrees to get each degree has 11.3 pixels (1,024/90). How big is our smallest toy at eight feet? Our smallest toy is a Hot Wheels toy, which is approximately three inches long. At eight feet, this is 1.79 degrees or 20.23 pixels (1.79 degrees * 11.3 pixels/degree). That is not enough. Solving the distance equation for three inches, we get a maximum distance of 4.77 feet for a camera with 1,024x768. That is just barely acceptable. What if we had an HD sensor with 1,900x1200 pixels? Then at eight feet I get 75 pixels – more than enough to give us the best possible distance. If we use a sensor 1,200 wide, we have a recognition distance of 5.46, which is adequate but not great.

I walked through this process to show you how to write a specification, and show you the types of questions you should be asking yourself as you decide what sensors to acquire for your project.

Summary

This chapter outlines a suggested process for developing your "to do" list as you develop your robot project. This process is called **systems engineering**. Our first step was to create use cases, or descriptions of how the robot is to behave from a user's perspective. Then we created more detail behind the use cases by creating storyboards, where we went step by step through the use case. Our example followed the robot finding and recognizing toys, before picking them up and putting them in the toy box. We extracted our hardware and software needs, creating a to do list of what the robot will be able to do. Finally, we wrote a specification of one of our critical sensors, the camera.

Questions

1. Describe some of the differences between a storyboard for a movie or cartoon, and a storyboard for a software program.
2. What are the five *W* questions? Can you think of any more questions that would be relevant to examine a use case?
3. Complete this sentence: A use case shows what the robot does but not
   _____.
4. Take the storyboard in step 9, where the robot is driving to the toy box, and break it down into more sequenced steps in your own storyboard. Think about all that must happen between frames 9 and 10.
5. Complete the reply form of the *knock-knock* joke, where the robot answers the user telling the joke. What do you think is the last step?
6. Look at the teleoperate operations. Would you add any more, or does this look like a good list?
7. Write a specification for a sensor that uses distance measurement to prevent the robot from driving down stairs.
8. What is the distance a camera with 320x200 pixels and a 30 degree field of view (FOV) can see a six inch stuffed animal, still assuming we need 35 pixels for recognition?

Further reading

- Freidenthal, S., Moore, A., Steiner, R. A Practical Guide to SysML: The Systems Modeling Language (2014) MK/OMB Press.
- *The Standard Introduction to Model-Based Systems Engineering (MBSE).*
- Flewelling, Paul. The Agile Developer's Handbook. (Feb. 2018). Packt Publishing, Birmingham.

4
Object Recognition Using Neural Networks and Supervised Learning

This is the chapter where we start to combine robotics and artificial intelligence to accomplish some of the tasks we have laid out so carefully in the previous chapters. The subject of this chapter is image recognition – we will be teaching the robot to recognize what is a toy, and what is not a toy, so that it can then decide what to pick up and what to leave alone. We will be using convolutional neural networks as a machine learning tool to separate objects in images, recognize them, and locate them in the camera frame, so that the robot can then locate them.

In this chapter, we will cover the following topics:

- The basics of image recognition: what is an image?
- Artificial neural networks: what is a neuron, and how do they work?
- Training neural networks using stochastic gradient descent
- Image processing and dataset creation: training sets and test sets, multiplying data
- Convolution: image processing for robots
- The LeNet framework from Keras
- Training and testing the network
- Deploying our trained network on the Raspberry Pi 3 in the robot

Technical requirements

We will actually be able to accomplish all of these tasks without a robot, if yours cannot walk yet. We will, however, get better results if the camera is in the proper position on the robot. If you don't have a robot, you can still do all of these tasks with a laptop and a USB camera.

- Hardware: Laptop or portable computer, Raspberry Pi 3, USB camera
- Software:
  - Python
  - Open CV2
  - Keras (https://keras.io/)
  - Tensorflow (https://www.tensorflow.org/install/)
  - USB camera drivers installed on your laptop or Raspberry Pi

The source code for this chapter can be found at https://github.com/PacktPublishing/Artificial-Intelligence-for-Robotics/chapter4.

Check out the following video to see the Code in Action:
http://bit.ly/2wwM9Zl

The image recognition process

Having a computer or robot recognize an image is not as simple as taking two pictures and then saying "If picture A = picture B, then toy". We are actually going to have to do quite a bit of work to have the ability to recognize a variety of objects that are randomly rotated, strewn about, and at various distances. We could recognize simple shapes – hexagons, for instance, or simple color blobs, but nothing as complex as a toy stuffed dog. Writing a program that did some sort of analysis of an image and computed the pixels, colors, distributions, and ranges of every possible permutation would be extremely difficult, and the result very fragile – it would fail at the slightest change in lighting or color. I had a recent misadventure with a large robot that mistook an old, faded soft drink machine for its charging station – let's just say that I had to go and buy more fuses.

What we will do instead is teach the robot to recognize a set of images corresponding to toys that we will take from various angles, by using a special type of **artificial neural network** (**ANN**) that performs convolution encoding on images. We will discuss this in the following sections: how do we process images, what is "convolution", and how do you build a neural network? There are a lot of good books and good tutorials on generic neural network construction, so I'll be emphasizing the unique components we will use to accomplish our task of recognizing toys in an image. Do you remember from Chapter 3, what the storyboard said to do:

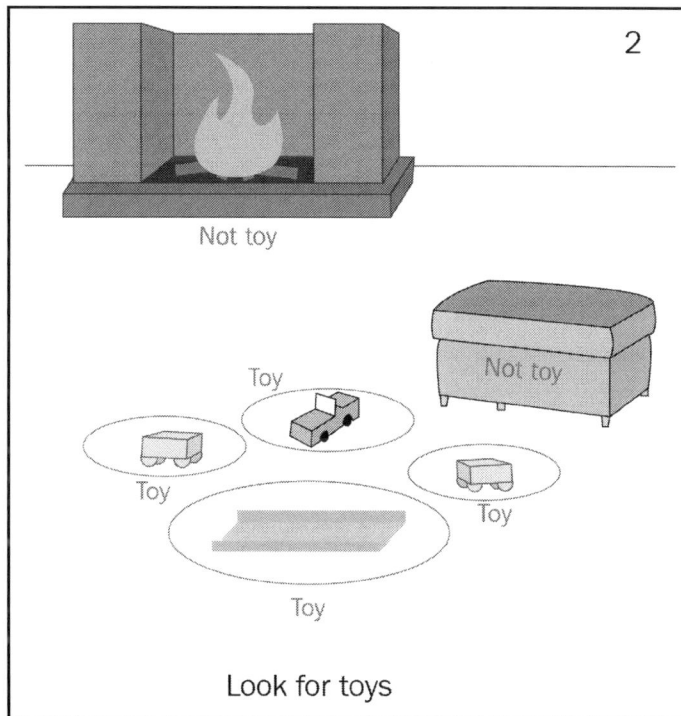

The result from our image recognizer is to figure out what objects are toys and then locate them in the image—illustrated in my sketch by drawing circles around them; not just *what* they are, but also *where* they are.

The image recognition training and deployment process – step by step

Most of you will be very familiar with computer images. Just like the safety belt demonstration on every commercial flight, just in case, I'll cover images, pixels, and depth. If you already know this, skip ahead.

Images are stored in a computer as a two-dimensional array of pixels, or picture elements. Each pixel is a tiny dot. Thousands or millions of tiny dots make up each image. Each individual pixel is a number or series of numbers that describe its color. If the image is only a gray-scale, or black and white image, then each pixel is represented by a single number that corresponds to how dark or light the tiny dot is. This is fairly straightforward so far.

If the image is a color picture, then each dot has three numbers that are combined to make its color. Usually, these numbers are intensity of Red, Green, and Blue (RGB) colors. The combination (0,0,0) is black (or the absence of all color), and (255,255,255) is white – the sum of all colors. This process is called the additive color model. If you work with watercolors instead of computer pixels, you know that adding all the colors in your watercolor box makes black – that is, a subtractive color model.

While RGB is one set of three numbers that can describe a pixel, there are other ways of describing the "color formula" that have various usages. We don't have to use RGB, for instance; we can also use CYM – Cyan, Yellow, and Magenta, which are the complementary colors to Red, Green, and Blue. We can also break down colors using the HSV (Hue, Saturation, and Value) model, which classifies color by Hue (type of color), Saturation (intensity of color), and Value, or brightness of color. HSV is a very useful color space for certain calculations, such as converting a color image to gray-scale (black and white). To turn an RGB to a gray-scale pixel, you have to do a bit of math – you can't just pull out one channel and keep it. The formula for RGB to gray-scale is *(0.3*Red + 0.58*Green + 0.11*Blue)*. This is because the different wavelengths of light behave differently in our eyes, which are more sensitive to green. If you have color in the HSV color model, then creating a grayscale image is just taking the V(value) number and throwing the Hue and Saturation away. You can see that is a lot simpler.

We will be doing quite a bit of image manipulation through this chapter.

An RGB pixel is represented by the three colors, which means the actual image is a three-dimensional array rather than two-dimensional, because each pixel has three numbers, making an array of (height, width, 3). So, a picture that is 800 by 600 would have an array of (800,600,3), or 1,440,000 numbers. That is a lot of numbers. We will be working very hard to minimize the numbers of pixels we are processing at any given time.

Image processing

So now that we have an image, what can we do with it? You have probably played with Photoshop, or some other image manipulation program such as GIMP, and you know that there are thousands of operations, filters, changes, and tricks you can play on images. What are a few of them? We can make an image brighter or darker by adjusting the brightness. We can increase the contrast between the white parts of the image and the dark parts. We can make an image blurry, usually by applying a Gaussian blur filter. We can also make an image sharper (somewhat) by using a filter such as unsharp mask. You may have also tried an **edge detector** filter, such as the Canny filter, to isolate the edges of an image, where color or value changes. We will be using all of these techniques to help the computer identify images.

What on earth is **unsharp mask**? This image enhancing process was invented in the 1930s in Germany, and was originally used with film. The original image is blurred slightly, and then inverted (black becomes white and vice-versa). This positive image is used as a mask to block where the negative image is combined. The net result is to amply the high frequency (in other words, fine detail) in the image. The effect in Photoshop or GIMP uses a threshold in the difference of the blurred and normal images to simulate the masking process.

What we are trying a achieve with all this manipulation for the computer is to not have the computer be sensitive to the size of the image – which is called **scale invariance**, the angle at which the photograph was taken – **angle invariance**, and the lighting available – illumination invariance. This is all very desirable in a computer vision system – we would not want an AI system that only recognized our toys from exactly the same angle and distance as the original image. Remember that we are going to train our vision system to recognize toys based on a training set of images we take in advance, and the robot will have to recognize objects based on what it learned from the training set.

What we are going to do is use features about the image that mostly don't change based on size, angle, distance, or lighting. What sorts of features might that be?

If we look at a common household object, such as a chair, and inspect if from several angles, what about the chair does not change? The easy answer is the edges and corners. The chair has the same number of corners all of the time, and we can see a consistent number of them from most angles. It also has a consistent number of edges.

Admittedly, that is a bit of an oversimplification of the approach. We will be training our ANN to example a whole host of image features that may or may not be unique to this object, and let it decide which ones work and which do not. We will accomplish this by means of a generic approach to image manipulation called **convolution**.

Convolution

Every once in a while, you come across some mathematical construction that turns a complex task into just a bunch of adding, subtracting, multiplying, and dividing. Vectors in geometry work like that, and, in image processing, we have the convolution kernel. It transpires that most of the common image processing techniques – edge detection, corner detection, blurring, sharpening, enhancing, and so on, can be accomplished with a simple array construct.

It is pretty easy to understand that in an image, the neighbors of a pixel are just as important to what a pixel is as the pixel itself. If you were going to try and find all the edge pixels of a box, you would look for a pixel that has one type of color on one side, and another type on the other. We need a function to find edges by comparing pixels on one side of a pixel to the other.

The convolution kernel is a matrix function that applies weights to the pixel neighbors – or pixels around the one pixel we are analyzing. The function is usually written like this, as a 3 x 3 matrix:

-1	0	1
-2	0	2
-1	0	1

This is the **sobel edge detector** in the Y direction. This detects edges going up and down. Each block represents a pixel. The pixel being processed is in the center. The neighbors of the pixels on each side are the other blocks – top, bottom, left, and right. To compute the convolution, you apply the weight to the value of each pixel by multiplying the value (intensity) of that pixel, and then adding all of the results. If this image is in color – RGB – then we compute the convolution for each color separately and then combine the result. Here is an example of a convolution being applied to a pixel:

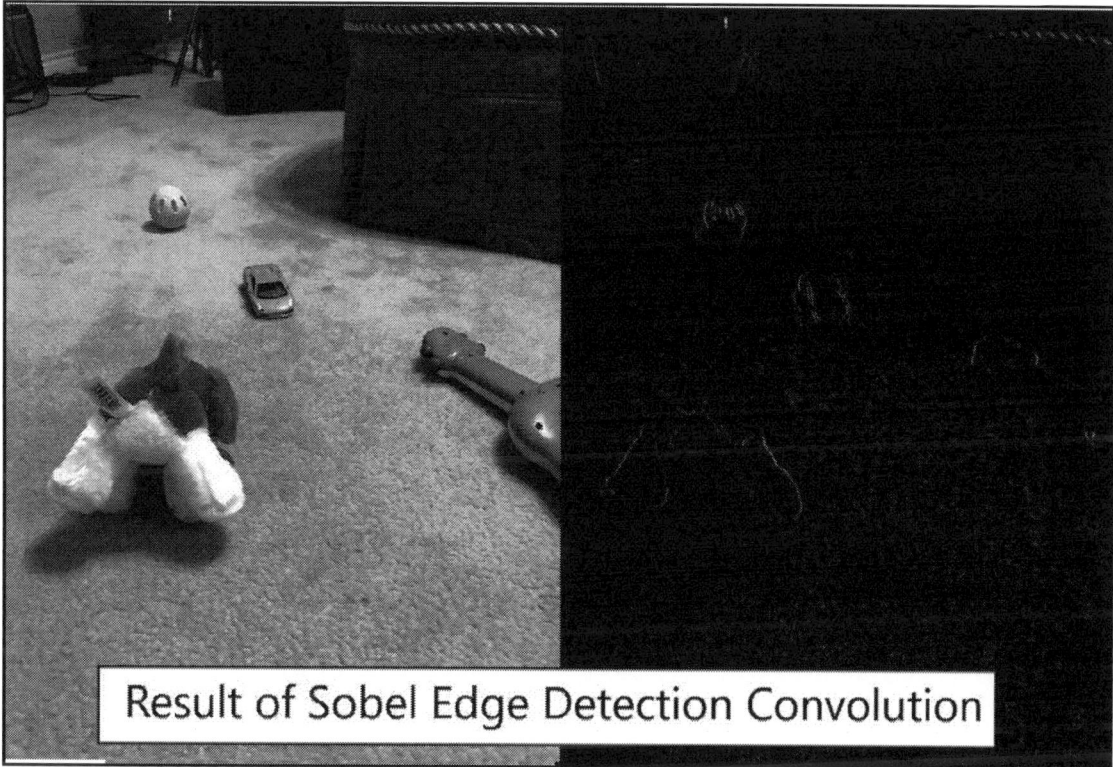

Result of Sobel Edge Detection Convolution

Add the final result to a sample image. Note that we only get the edge as the result – if the colors are the same on either side of the center pixel, they cancel each other out and we get zero, or black. If they are different, we get 255, or white, as the answer.

If we need a more complex result, we may also use a 5 x 5 convolution, which takes into account the two nearest pixels on each side, instead of just one.

The good news is that you don't have to choose the convolution to apply to the input images – the Keras AI frontend will set up all of the convolutions, and you only have to set the size as either 3 x 3 or 5 x 5. The neural network will determine which convolutions provide the most data and support the training output we want.

But wait, I hear you say. What if the pixel is on the edge of the image and we don't have neighbor pixels on one side? In that event, we have to add padding to the image – which is a border of extra pixels that permit us to consider the edge pixels as well.

Artificial neurons

Now, let's get into the guts of a neural network. What is a neuron? And how do we make a network out of them?

An artificial neuron is a software construction that approximates the workings of the neurons in your brain. If you can remember what you learned in biology, a biological or natural neuron has inputs, or dendrites, that connect it to other neurons or to sensor inputs. All of the inputs come to a central body, and then leave via the axion, or connection, to other neurons via other dendrites. The connection between neurons is called a synapse, which is a tiny gap that the signal from the nerve has to jump. A neuron takes inputs, processes them, and activates, or sends an output, after some level or threshold is reached:

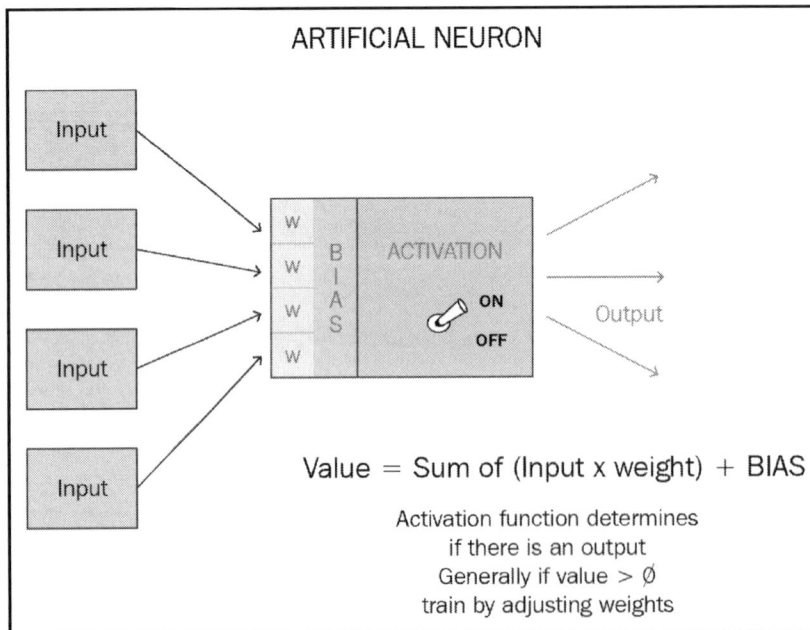

An artificial neuron is a very, very simplified version of this natural neuron. It has a number of inputs, a set of weights, a bias, an activation function, and then some number of outputs to other neurons or as a result of the network. The following section describes each component in detail:

- **Inputs**: A number or value received from other neurons or as an input to the network. In our image processing example, these are pixels. This number can be a float or an integer – but it must be just one number.

- **Weight**: To determine the value of a neuron, we sum up all of the inputs. As the neural network is trained, the weights are adjusted on each input that favors some inputs over others. We multiply the input by the weight and then total the inputs.
- **Bias**: A number added to the sum of the weights. Bias prevents the neuron from getting "stuck" on zero and improves training. This is usually a small number.
- **Activation function**: This determines the output of the neuron based on the inputs. The most common types are the **Rectifier Linear Unit**, or **ReLU** (if the value of the neuron is less than zero, the output is zero, otherwise, the output is the value) or the **SIGMOID** function (Sigmoid means "s-shaped"), which is a log function. The activation function propagates information across the network:

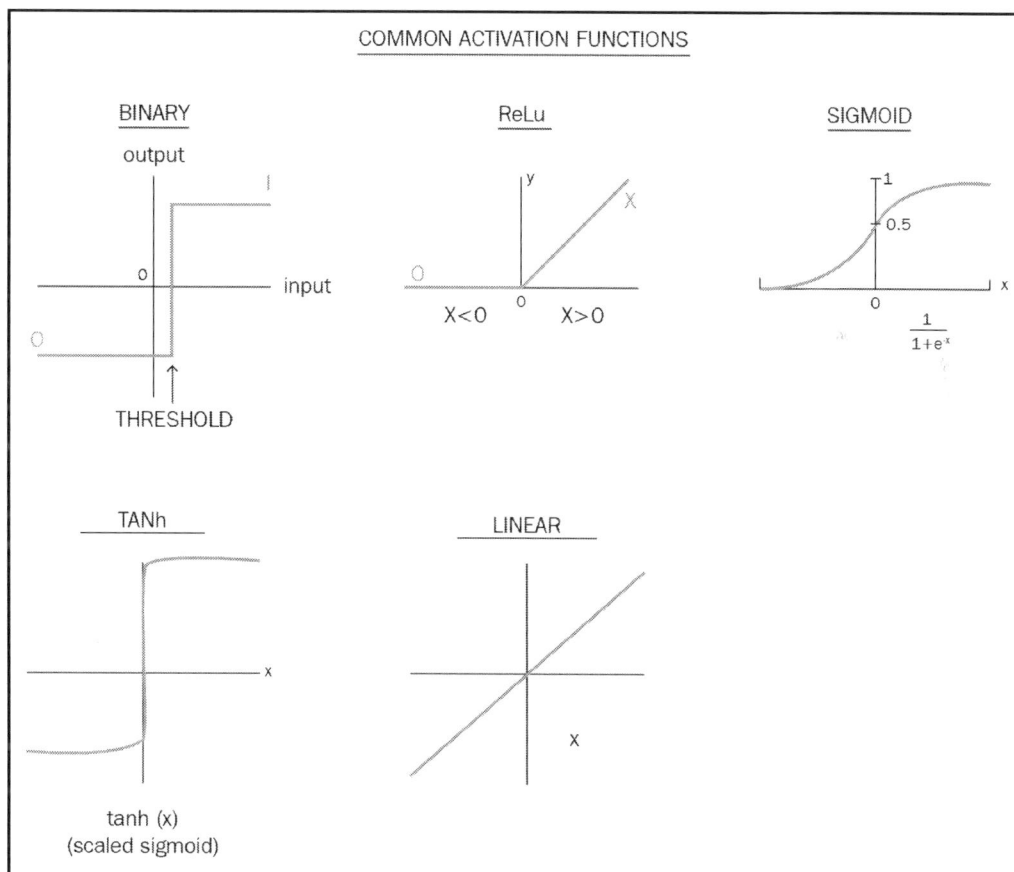

COMMON ACTIVATION FUNCTIONS

BINARY

output

0

input

0

THRESHOLD

ReLu

y

X

$X<0$ 0 $X>0$

SIGMOID

1

0.5

0

x

$\frac{1}{1+e^x}$

TANh

x

tanh (x)
(scaled sigmoid)

LINEAR

X

- **Outputs**: Each layer in the sequential neural network is connected to the next layer. Some layers are fully connected – with each neuron in the first layer connected to each neuron in the second layer. Others are sparsely connected. There is a common process in neural network training called **dropout**, where we randomly remove connections. This forces the network to have multiple paths for each bit of information it learns, which strengthens the network.

- **Max Pooling of outputs:** We will use a special type of output connection called **Max Pooling**, where groups of neurons corresponding to regions in our image – say a 5 x 5 block of pixels – go to one neuron in the next level. The maxpool neuron only takes the largest value from each of the 25 input neurons. This has the effect of downsampling the image (making it smaller). This allows the network to associate small features (such as the wheels in a Hot Wheels™ car) with larger features, such as the hood, or windshield, to identify a toy car:

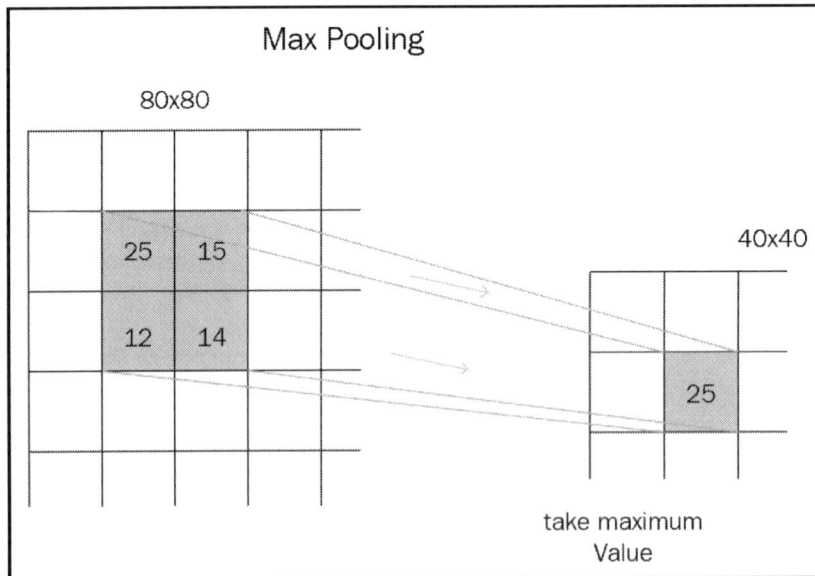

The convolution neural network process

I want to provide you with an end-to-end look at what we will be doing in the code for the rest of this chapter. Remember that we are building a **convolutional neural network** (**CNN**) that examines objects in a video frame and outputs if one or more toys are in the image, and where they are:

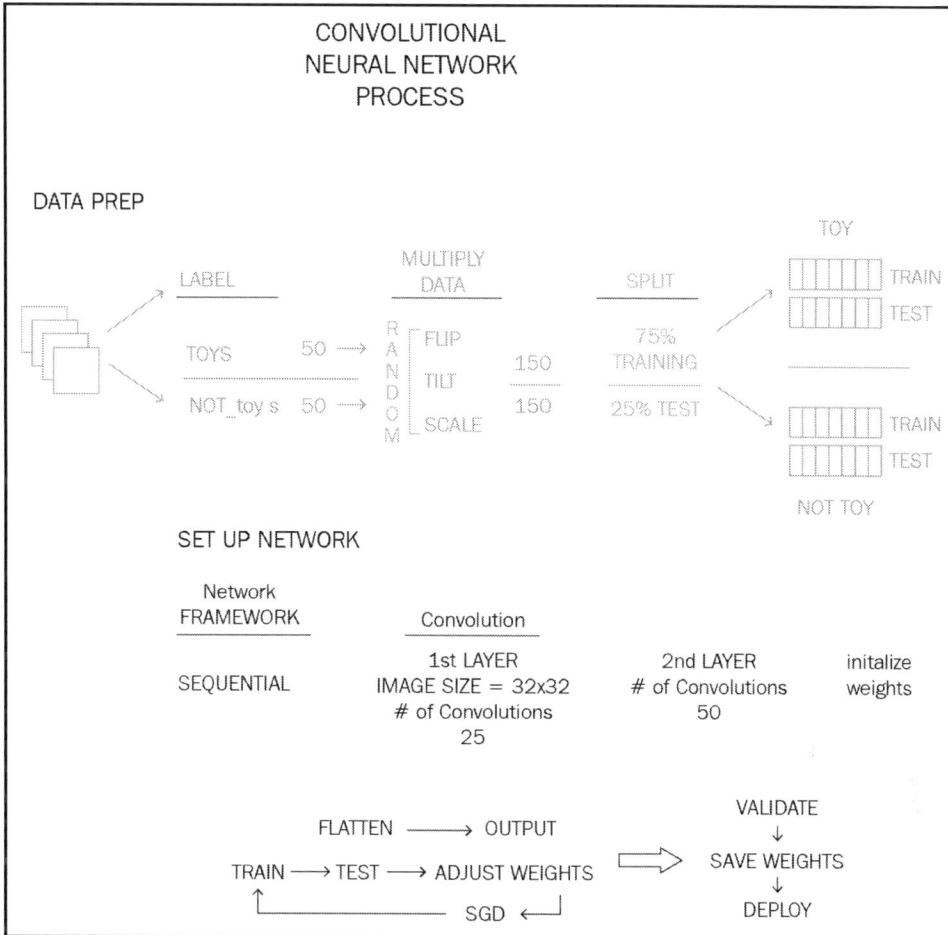

CONVOLUTIONAL
NEURAL NETWORK
PROCESS

DATA PREP

LABEL

MULTIPLY
DATA

SPLIT

TOY

TRAIN
TEST

TOYS   50 →

R
A
N
D
O
M

FLIP

TILT

SCALE

150

150

75%
TRAINING

25% TEST

NOT_toy s   50 →

TRAIN
TEST

NOT TOY

SET UP NETWORK

Network
FRAMEWORK

SEQUENTIAL

Convolution

1st LAYER
IMAGE SIZE = 32x32
# of Convolutions
25

2nd LAYER
# of Convolutions
50

initalize
weights

FLATTEN ——→ OUTPUT

TRAIN —→ TEST —→ ADJUST WEIGHTS

SGD ←⅃

VALIDATE
↓
SAVE WEIGHTS
↓
DEPLOY

Here is an overview of the process:

1. Prepare a training set of images of the room with and without toys.
2. Label the area of the images that contain toys – in a separate folder.
3. Label images that don't contain toys – in a separate folder.
4. Break the training set into two parts: a set we use to train the network, and a set we use to test the network.
5. We will be building two programs: the training program that runs on our desktop computer, and trains the network, and the working program that uses the trained network to find toys.
6. Program 1: Train the network (`toyTrainNetwork.py`).

7. We take each image and multiply its training value by randomly scaling, rotating, and flipping (mirroring) the images. This increases our training set 20 fold:

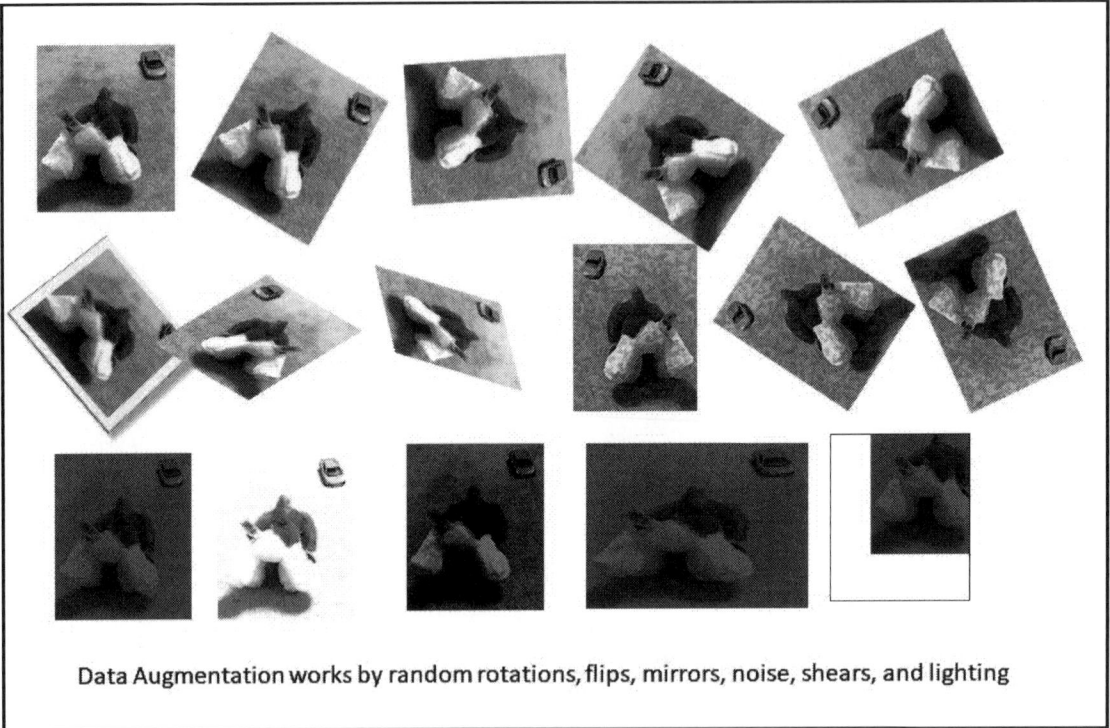

Data Augmentation works by random rotations, flips, mirrors, noise, shears, and lighting

8. We build our CNN network with a convolution layer, a maxpooling layer, another convolution layer, another maxpooling layer, then a fully connected layer, and an output layer. This type of CNN is call a **LeNet**.

9. Now, we scale all our images down to reduce the amount of processing.

10. The network is initialized with random weights.

11. We present a labeled image to the network. We get an answer that is either right or wrong. If it is right, we reinforce the weights on the inputs that contributed to this answer by incrementing them (the training value). If the answer is wrong, we reduce the weights instead. In neural networks, the error between the desired result and the actual result is called **loss**.

12. Repeat for each image.

13. Now, we test the network by running the testing set of images – which are pictures of the same toys, but that were not in the training set. We see what sort of output we get over this set (how many wrong, how many right). If this answer is above 90%, we stop. Otherwise, we go back and run all the training images again.

14. Once we are happy with the results – and we should need between 100 and 500 iterations to get there – we stop and store the weights that we ended up with in the training network. This is our *trained* CNN.

15. Program 2: Find the toys (`ToyFindNetwork.pyp`).

16. Now, we *deploy* the trained network by loading it and using our video images from the live robot to look for toys. We will get a probability of an image having a toy from 0 to 100%. We scan the input video image in sections and find which sections contain toys. If we are not happy with this network, we can reload this network into the training program and train it some more.

17. Done!

Now, let's cover this in detail, step by step. We have a bit more theory to cover before we start writing the code.

Our first task is to prepare a training set. We put the camera on the robot, and drive the robot around using the teleoperation interface (or just by pushing it around by hand), snapping still photos every foot or so. We need to do at least two passes of this: one with toys in the room, and one without toys in the room. We need about 200 pictures each way, and more is better. We also need to do a set of pictures in the daytime with natural light, and at night, if your room changes lighting between day and night. This affords us several advantages: we are using the same room and the same camera to find the toys, and under the same lighting conditions.

Now, we need to label the images. I used a small program called **LabelImg,** which is available at `github/tzutalin/labelImg`. This program creates boundaries of labeled objects in the ImageNet data format. ImageNet is a popular dataset used in competitions between image classifers, and has 1,000 types of objects labeled. We have to do this ourselves. Download the binary version of LabelImg and start it up. Use the `Open Dir` command to select the directory with your images of toys. It will present the first picture.

The process for us is fairly straightforward. We look at each picture in turn, and draw a box around any toy objects. Use the *W* shortcut key with each box. The label dialog box opens up. On the first occasion, you will have to type `toy` as the label. We label these – as you might guess – `toy`. We also draw boxes around objects that are not toys – and label them `not_toy`. This is going to take a while. We put the finished product, which is an XML file, into a file folder labeled `data`. We will need to convert the XML file into a CSV (comma separated values) file to input into our classifier training program.

In the next section, we will write our Keras/Tensorflow-based network training program, but, for the moment, let's talk about what we are going to do first. The program will read in the images one at a time, and then create additional images by randomly rotating, scaling, flipping, translating, and adding noise to the images. Now, our 200 pictures will do the work of 2,000 pictures.

We create our **convolutional neural network (CNN)** with an AI development package called **Keras**. The first step is to build a **sequential** network framework to incorporate the layers. Sequential networks are the most common topology used for neural networks, indicating that the network is composed of layers each connected to the layer above and the layer below, and nowhere else. We are building a five-layer network. The first network is a **convolution layer**. We'll use 20 convolutions and a 5 x 5 convolution matrix, which looks at the neighboring two pixels around each pixel to develop features. Keras will determine which convolution kernels to use. We specify the padding to match the convolution size, which adds two rows of pixels to all four sides of our image, so that we don't get *out of range* errors. Next, we have to add the **activation function** for this layer, which will be the **Rectifier Linear Unit**, or **ReLU** function, which just forwards all values greater than zero, and returns zero otherwise.

The next layer is a **maxpooling** layer, which we will set as 2 x 2 with a stride of 2 x 2. This converts blocks of four pixels into one pixel, and takes the maximum value out of the four pixels, which conserves features in the image. This layer reduces the image size to one-quarter of its original size, which increases the speed of our network, and lets the next layer work to recognize larger features in the image. If the first layer recognized tires on our toy cars, the second layer after maxpooling will look for windows, hoods, and car trunks.

The third layer is again a **convolution** using the reduced sized image as input. This convolution layer needs to have twice as many convolutions as the first layer, so it has 40 convolutions and again uses a 5 x 5 kernel size. We again use the ReLU activation function for this layer.

We add a 2 x 2 maxpooling layer after the second convolution, just like the first one.

Now, we are going to **flatten** our data into a single set of numbers in preparation for generating our output. We use the Keras flatten function and then add a **dense** or fully connected layer for layer five. We have to get from an image to a binary yes or no value, and so we flatten the data to convert the image data to a string of numbers.

The final layer is our output layer, which just has two neurons – one for **toy** and one for **not toy**, which are our two classes of objects we will be identifying. We give the network constructor our number of classes – two – and set its activation to SoftMax. **Softmax** converts the outputs of each of our classes to be a number between 0 and 1, and then divides the outputs so that the sum of all the outputs equals 1. Since we only have two classes, we could have used a sigmoid function, but the SoftMax activation function is more generic and lets us add more classes later if we want. Our output will be two numbers – the predicted probability that the image contains a toy, and the probability that the image does not contain a toy. The total will add up to 1, so if the toy probability is 0.9, then the not_toy probability will be 0.1.

The final two steps in building our network are to specify our loss, or error function, and to choose a **training optimizer.** The loss function is how we compute the error, or loss, from the network. Each pass, the network will be presented with an image that either contains a toy, or does not. We labeled the images so that the program knows which is which – I like to think of this as the "truth" value. The network analyzes the image and produces our two numbers – the "toy" and "not toy" values. Our error is the difference between the truth value and the predicted value. If the toy value is true, or 1.0, and the prediction is toy = 0.9, then our error is 0.1. If the image did not contain a toy, and we still got 0.9 as the result, then the error would be 0.9. Since we use a lot of data to come to that one number, we have to have a way of portioning the error out to the individual neurons. We will select the **binary cross entropy** loss calculation, which has been shown to work well with this sort of problem where there are only two classes.

How we use that information in our training is the role of the **training optimizer.** We will use the **ADAM** optimizer for this example, which is an improved version of **stochastic gradient descent (SGD)** training. SGD is another of those simple concepts with a fancy name. **Stochastic** just means **random.** What we want to do is tweek the weights of our neurons to give a better answer than we got the first time – this is what we are training, by adjusting the weights. We want to change the weights a small amount – but in which direction? We want to change the weights in the direction that improves the answer – it makes the prediction closer to the truth.

Let's do a little thought experiment. We have a neuron that we know is producing the wrong answer, and needs adjusting. We add a small amount to the weight and see how the answer changes. It gets slightly worse – the number is further away from the correct answer. So we subtract a small amount instead – and, as you might think, the answer gets better. We have reduced the amount of error slightly. If we made a graph of the error produced by the neuron, we are moving towards an error of zero, or we are descending the graph toward some minimum value. Another way of saying descending is that the slope of the line is negative – going toward zero. The amount of the slope can be called a **gradient** – just as you would refer to the slope or steepness of a hill as the gradient. We can calculate the partial derivative (in other words, the slope of the line near this point) and that tells us the slope of the line.

The way we go about adjusting the weights on the network as a whole is called **backpropogation**. That is because, as you might surmise, we have to start at the end of the network – where we know what the answer is supposed to be – and work our way toward the beginning. We have to calculate the contribution of each neuron to the answer we want, and adjust it a small amount (the learning rate) in the right direction to move toward the correct answer every time. We go back to the idea of a neuron – we have inputs, weights for each inputs, a bias, and then an activation function to produce an output. If we know what the output is, we can work backward through the neuron to adjust the weights. Let's take a simple example. Here is a neuron with three inputs, Y1, Y2, and Y3. We have three weights – W1, W2, and W3. We'll have the bias, B, and our activation function, D, which is the ReLU rectifier. Our inputs are 0.2, 0.7, and 0.02. The weights are 0.3, 0.2, and 0.5. Our bias is 0.3, and the desired output is 1.0. We calculate the sum of the inputs and weights and we get a value of 0.21. Adding our bias, we get 0.51. The ReLU function passes any value greater than zero, so the activated output of this neuron is 0.51. Our desired value is 1.0, which comes from the truth (label) data. So, our error is 0.49. If we add the training rate value to each weight, what happens? Observe the following diagram:

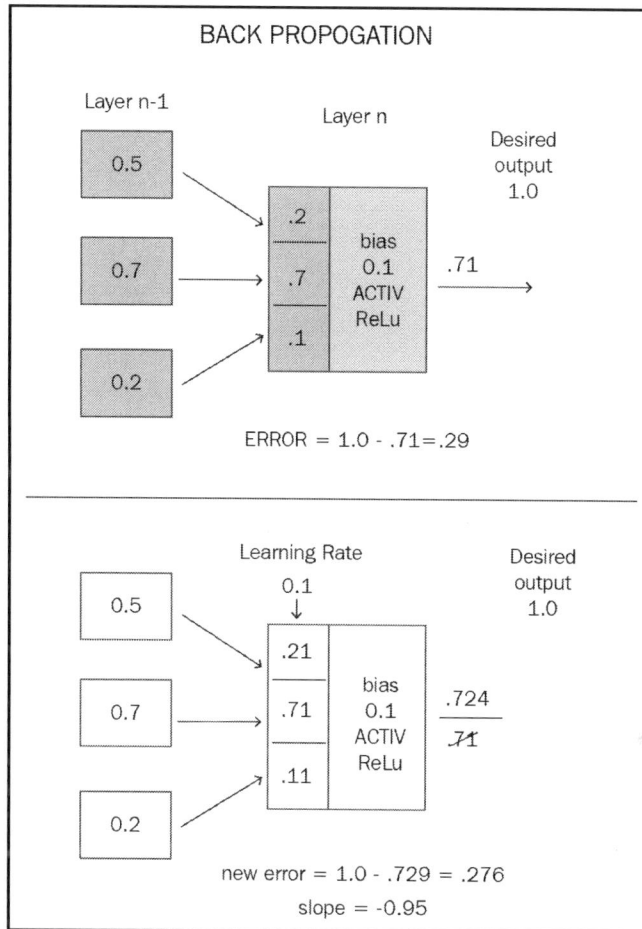

BACK PROPOGATION

Layer n-1   Layer n   Desired output 1.0

0.5

0.7

0.2

.2

bias 0.1 ACTIV ReLu

.7

.1

.71

ERROR = 1.0 - .71 = .29

Learning Rate 0.1   Desired output 1.0

0.5

0.7

0.2

.21

bias 0.1 ACTIV ReLu

.71

.11

.724
.71

new error = 1.0 - .729 = .276
slope = -0.95

The output value now goes up to 0.5192. Our error goes down to 0.4808. We are on the right trail! The gradient of our error slope is *(.4808-.49) / 1 = -0.97*. The 1 is because we just have one training sample so far. Where does the stocahastic part come from? Our recognition network may have 50 million neurons. We can't be doing all of this math for each one. So we take a random sampling of inputs rather than all of them to determine whether our training is positive or negative.

In math terms, the slope of an equation is provided by the derivative of that equation. So, in practice, backpropagation takes the partial derivative of the error between training epochs to determine the slope of the error, and thus determine whether we are training our network correctly. As the slope gets smaller, we reduce our training rate to a smaller number to get closer and closer to the correct answer:

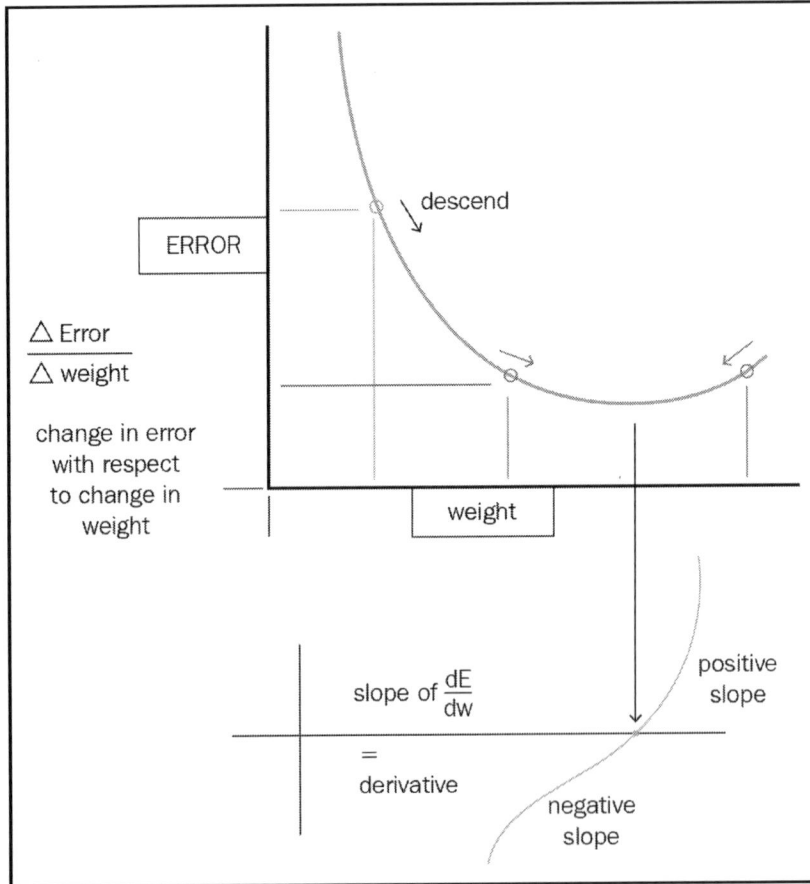

Our next problem is: how do we go up layers. We can see here at the output neuron how we determine error – just the label value minus the output of the network. How do we apply this information to the previous layer? Each neuron's contribution to the error is proportional to its weight. We divide the error by the weight of each input, and that value is now the applied error of the next neuron up the chain. Then, we can recompute their weights and so on. You start to see why neural networks take so much compute power:

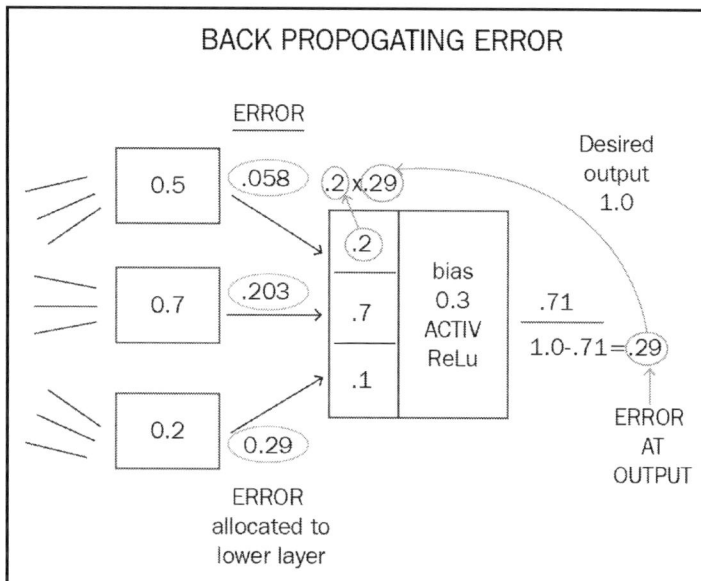

We backpropagate the error back up the network from the end back to the beginning. Then, we start all over again with the next cycle

Build the toy/not toy detector

The next section covers the training program for our CNN that will tell toys apart from *not toys*, that is to say, it will tell us whether there is a toy in the field of view of the camera.

We start by building our training sets. We divide our pictures of the playroom into pictures with toys and pictures taken without toys. We put the toy pictures in a directory under our program directory called `images/toys`. We put the pictures without toys in a directory called `images/not_toys`. We need about 200 examples of each. So far so good:

Examples of images without toys in them (top image) and with toys in them (bottom image). Thanks to the grandchildren for helpfully providing these examples. We can tell the difference, but can the robot?

Now, we can begin our program to train our neural network we have heard so much about. We will be using a CNN with the Keras framework. Keras (a cool word that is Greek for "Horn", and has a complicated backstory you can look up yourself) is a simplified frontend for several neural network packages, such as TensorFlow (what I'm using), CNTK, or Theano. Keras makes our work much easier and simpler, which is a boon given how complex neural network theory can be. I do have some good news – neural network practice is much easier than the theory.

This section has been inspired by the work of *Adrian Rosbrock* at PyimageSearch (`https://www.pyimagesearch.com/`), a great website, and *Adventures in Machine Learning* by *Andy Thomas* (`adventuresinmachinelearning.com`). The LeNet architecture comes from *Gradient-Based Learning Applied to Document Recognition*, written in 1998 by *Yann LeCun, Leon Bouttou, Yoshua Bengio,* and *Patrick Haffner*.

> **TIP**
>
> You can control whether or not you use CUDA, the Nvidia GPU neural network libary, to accelerate your program. The environment variable `CUDA_VISIBLE_DEVICES` turns CUDA on or off. Set this environment variable to -1 to disable CUDA and use 0 (zero) otherwise.

With that, let's dive right in. Open an editor and create a program called `trainTheCNN.py`.

We begin, as is customary for a Python program, by importing a bunch of libraries:

```
# program to train Convolution Neural Network to detect toys and not toys
# import the necessary packages
from keras.preprocessing.image import ImageDataGenerator
from keras.optimizers import Adam, SGD,Adadelta,Adagrad
from sklearn.model_selection import train_test_split
from keras.preprocessing.image import img_to_array
from keras.utils import to_categorical
from keras.models import Sequential
from keras.layers.convolutional import Conv2D
from keras.layers.convolutional import MaxPooling2D
from keras.layers.core import Activation
from keras.layers.core import Flatten
from keras.layers.core import Dense
from keras import backend as K
from imutils import paths
import numpy as np
import random
import cv2
import os, time
```

You'll observe that a lot of these imports are from Keras, as expected. We will use the `ImageDataGenerator` to magically multiply our image so that they provide more training data, test some training optimizers called `Adam`, a type of stochastic gradient descent that uses adaptive training rates, several image processing routines, and a bunch of layers from Keras.

Now, we create a class to build our neural network, which we will use later in the program. This is the fun part, so we can get this out of the way up front. We are going to build a generic LeNet object class. The input parameters are the width, height, and depth of our images (which are 126 x 126 pixels with a depth of three colors). We have two classes we will be looking for: `toys` and `not_toys`. We use the sequential type of neural network, which covers most neural networks. Keras also lets you define your own model architecture, but we won't go into that here. To begin with, we set the shape and size of our model:

```
class LeNet:
            @staticmethod
            def build(width, height, depth, classes):
                        # initialize the model
                        model = Sequential()
                        inputShape = (height, width, depth)
```

Some data files come `channels first` – so if that is the case, we set the shape to be 3 x height x width, instead of height x width x 3. The three channels are the Red, Green, and Blue color values:

```
                        # if we are using "channels first", update
the input shape
                        if K.image_data_format() ==
"channels_first":
                                    inputShape = (depth,
height, width)
```

Now, we add our first layer to the model. It is a convolution layer with 20 convolutions (operations), each of which will isolate some feature of the image. We set the convolution size to be 5 x 5, and add padding to the image to match. Our activation function is the ReLU, which is the value if value > 0, and 0 otherwise. It "rectifies" any below-zero value to be just zero. Remember a color less than zero is just black – our color values will run from 0 to 1. Since a color value less than zero has no sense – blacker than black?- we just make it 0.

```
                        model.add(Conv2D(20, (5, 5),
padding="same",
                                    input_shape=inputShape))
                        model.add(Activation("relu"))
```

Our second layer is a maxpooling layer. We use 2 x 2 cells (4 pixels) and skip (stride) 2 pixels for no overlap. This cuts the size of our image by ¼ (half the width and half the height= one quarter). Now, instead of 128 x 128, we are 64 x 64 pixels:

```
model.add(MaxPooling2D(pool_size=(2, 2),
strides=(2, 2)))
```

Now, we add another convolution layer that is twice as complex as the first – 40 convolutions instead of 20. This is a common practice in CNNs. This layer detects more details than the first layer. If the first layer can be said to detect eyes, toes, and fingers, the second layer would detect arms and legs. We use the same ReLU function as before, for the same reason. The activation determines the output of the neurons from this layer:

```
model.add(Conv2D(40, (5, 5),
padding="same"))
model.add(Activation("relu"))
```

Now, we add another maxpooling layer just as before. Our 64 x 64 pixels are now 32 x 32. We are seeing only the largest features of the images after this:

```
model.add(MaxPooling2D(pool_size=(2, 2),
strides=(2, 2)))
```

Now, we flatten the image in preparation of using the classifier later. We turn our 64 x 64 x 3 image into a one-dimensional array with 12,228 values:

```
model.add(Flatten())
```

After the flatten function, we add a dense (fully connected) layer – each neuron connects to each neuron in the layer below it. Its activation function is also still ReLU:

```
model.add(Dense(500))
model.add(Activation("relu"))
```

Our final layer has just the two classes to hold our output values. One is the probability from 0 to 1 that our image contains a toy, and the other is the probability that the image does not contain a toy. The `softmax classifier` takes the output from the network and normalizes them into values – one per class – that add up to one. Softmax is a more generic function that can handle multiple classes. We are just using two, but this makes the network more generic:

```
# softmax classifier
model.add(Dense(classes))
model.add(Activation("softmax"))


# return the completed network structure
return model
```

There we go – the LeNet is a simple CNN structure with just two convolution layers.

Now, we define some of our data files, including where our training images are located:

```
# data files
imageDirectory = "images/"
model_file = "toy_not_toy.model"
```

Here are the metaparameters for our training program. We set up the number of repetitions on which to train the network, the learning rate (how fast to change the values of the weights), and the batch size. The batch size is how many images we hold in memory at a time. If we run out of memory, we can reduce the batch size:

```
# Set up the number of training passes (epochs), learning rate, and batch
size
EPOCHS = 200
LEARNING_RATE = 1e-3
BATCH_SIZE = 32
```

This section sets up the training images and labels so that we can ingest them:

```
# initialize the data and labels
print("Loading training images set...")
data = []
labels = []
```

We load the images from the hard drive and shuffle them randomly, so there is no particular order that the network could learn accidentally:

```
# grab the images from the directories and randomly shuffle them
imagePaths = sorted(list(paths.list_images(imageDirectory)))
# use a random seed number from the time clock
random.seed(int(time.time()%1000))
random.shuffle(imagePaths)
```

We load all of the images one at a time, downsample them to 128 x 128 pixels, and add them to an array of numbers. We put this into an array called `data`:

```
# loop over the input images
for imagePath in imagePaths:
                # load the image, pre-process it, and store it in the data
    list
                image = cv2.imread(imagePath)
                image = cv2.resize(image, (128, 128))
                image = img_to_array(image)
                data.append(image)
```

To create the labels list, we have put the pictures with toys in one directory and the images without toys in the other. We use the directory name as the label for the image (`toy` or `not_toy`). We put this in an array called `labels`, where we can locate them again later:

```
extract the class label from the image path and update the labels list
label = imagePath.split(os.path.sep)[-2]
if label == "toy":
label = 1
else:
label = 0
labels.append(label)
```

Now, we convert the values of the colors in our image from being integer numbers from 0 to 255, to being real numbers from 0 to 1. This is called **normalization** and is a standard step in neural networks for obtaining all of the inputs in a common range:

```
# Normalize the values of the pixels to be between 0 and 1 instead of 0 to
255
data = np.array(data, dtype="float") / 255.0
labels = np.array(labels)
```

As we are training our neural network, we need to continually test whether the network is working properly. The training process tells us the errors in images that were used in the training set, but we will be using this network to classify new images it has never seen before. We split our supply of pictures into two groups – the training set, which has the majority (80%) of the pictures, and the testing set, which has the remaining 20%. We train the network with the bigger set of images, and then we test against the smaller set of pictures that are still on the same subject, but were not part of the training set. This gives us a basis for believing that the network will properly classify images it has not seen before:

```
# split the data between a testing set and a training set
(trainX, testX, trainY, testY) = train_test_split(data,
labels, test_size=0.20, random_state=time.time())
```

Now, we convert the labels from text (`toy` or `not_toy`) to numbers, - 0 and 1, so that the network can process them:

```
# convert the labels from integers to vectors
trainY = to_categorical(trainY, num_classes=2)
testY = to_categorical(testY, num_classes=2)
```

This is one of the fun parts. We are going to augment our data by randomly shifting, shearing, zooming, and flipping the images so that one image becomes 10. This gives our network a lot more information to work with:

```
# construct the image generator for data augmentation
aug = ImageDataGenerator(rotation_range=40, width_shift_range=0.2,
height_shift_range=0.2, shear_range=0.1, zoom_range=0.2,
horizontal_flip=True, fill_mode="nearest")
```

Now we are ready to build our network. We instantiate the LeNet object by using the `build` function to create our `cnNetwork` (CNN Network) data structure. We've already covered what that does – two convolutions, a flatten, and an output layer. We set our network size to 124 x 124 pixels, set our depth to three for a color image, and then set our classes to 2 – toy and not toy. The next step sets up our learning optimizer. I've selected ADAM, which is described to me as the *generic go-to* optimizer for CNNs. ADAM has the stochastic gradient descent model, which is fast, plus a bunch of modifications to enhance the learning curve, and adjust the learning rate as the model learns. The model slows down the learning rate as the network reaches its maximum level and the gradient flattens out. I've included the code for the regular SGD for you in case you want to compare these, as I did while building the model. ADAM worked slightly better for me. If I used the SGD optimizer, I had to add more training passes (epochs):

```
# initialize the weights of the network
print("Building CNN network...")
cnNetwork = LeNet.build(width=124, height=124, depth=3, classes=2)
```

```
#use adam optimizer. tried SGD for comparison - needs more epochs (>100)
opt = Adam(lr=LEARNING_RATE, decay=LEARNING_RATE / EPOCHS)
#opt = SGD(lr=LEARNING_RATE,decay=LEARNING_RATE / EPOCHS)
```

We compile the network and specify what our loss function will be. We use `binary_cross` entropy, which is appropriate for a network that has only two classes. If there were more than two classes, you can use categorical cross entropy instead. Cross entropy loss systems are used for networks where the final output is a probability number between 0 and 1, like the one we are building. Cross entropy loss is a log loss, where the error increases greatly as the expected output and the network's prediction diverge. This exaggeration helps to drive the network back toward the training goal. Generally, cross entropy loss is the negative log (-log) of the difference between the true result (the label on the image) and the output of the network (which is a probability number from 0 to 1):

```
cnNetwork.compile(loss="binary_crossentropy", optimizer=opt,
metrics=["accuracy"])
```

This code block actually trains the network. We can think of creating a neural network as making a stepwise approximation of a non-linear function, which math majors like to call **fitting the curve** – making a curve function that fits the input data. Hence, the function that trains the network is called **fit**. We input our training sets (`trainX` = toys and `trainY` = not toys), the batch size (which regulates the amount of memory used), our validation data that we will test with, and the number of epochs. Throw in a pinch of salt and stir vigorously:

```
# train the network - here is where the magic happens...
print("[INFO] training network...")
H = cnNetwork.fit_generator(aug.flow(trainX, trainY,
batch_size=BATCH_SIZE),
 validation_data=(testX, testY), steps_per_epoch=len(trainX) // BATCH_SIZE,
 epochs=EPOCHS, verbose=1)
```

The program will print status reports on how the training is going. If you want, you can collect this data and make a graph out of it, as I did below. The output looks like this – you can see the time each epoch takes – which is about nine seconds in this case. The loss, or error, is reported, and you can see that it decreases over time. The `acc` stands for accuracy of the trained model, and then the validation error and accuracy is reported:

```
3/3 [==============================] - 11s 4s/step - loss: 0.8696 - acc:
0.6264 - val_loss: 0.6710 - val_acc: 0.5806
Epoch 2/100
3/3 [==============================] - 10s 3s/step - loss: 0.6962 - acc:
0.5000 - val_loss: 0.7323 - val_acc: 0.2903
Epoch 3/100
3/3 [==============================] - 9s 3s/step - loss: 0.6913 - acc:
```

```
0.5818 - val_loss: 0.6469 - val_acc: 0.7097
Epoch 4/100
3/3 [==============================] - 9s 3s/step - loss: 0.7441 - acc:
0.6458 - val_loss: 0.6768 - val_acc: 0.7097
Epoch 5/100
3/3 [==============================] - 9s 3s/step - loss: 0.7307 - acc:
0.6169 - val_loss: 0.6315 - val_acc: 0.7097
Epoch 6/100
3/3 [==============================] - 9s 3s/step - loss: 0.6108 - acc:
0.7500 - val_loss: 0.6369 - val_acc: 0.7097
Epoch 7/100
3/3 [==============================] - 9s 3s/step - loss: 0.6635 - acc:
0.6530 - val_loss: 0.6354 - val_acc: 0.7097
Epoch 8/100
3/3 [==============================] - 9s 3s/step - loss: 0.6594 - acc:
0.6474 - val_loss: 0.6193 - val_acc: 0.7097
Epoch 9/100
3/3 [==============================] - 9s 3s/step - loss: 0.6551 - acc:
0.6458 - val_loss: 0.6085 - val_acc: 0.7097
```

If you collect all this data and make a graph, it looks like this:

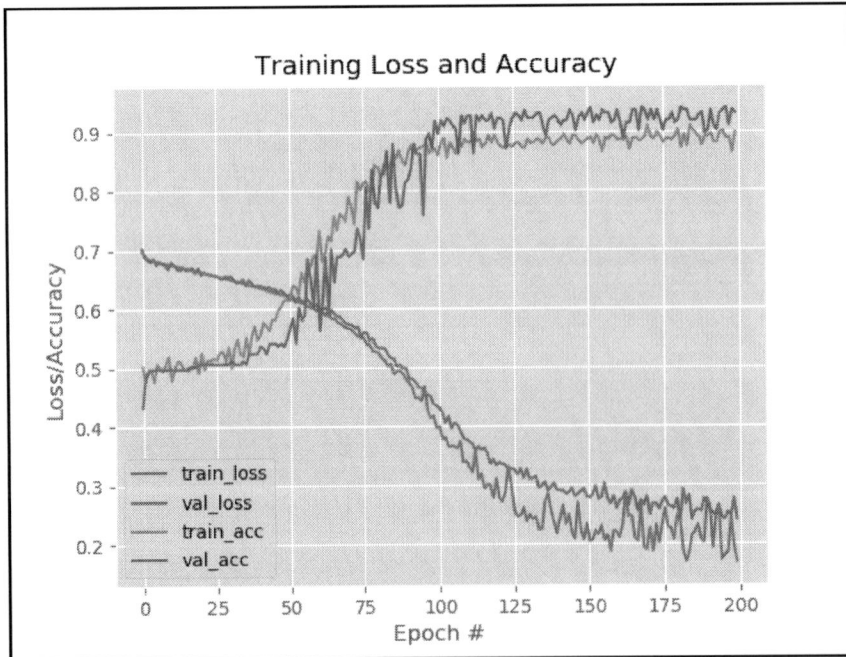

This is the result I obtained from training the network over 200 epochs, and with 100 toy and 100 "not toy" images to work with. That is actually a bit sparse for a CNN; 200 images would be better, so I'll be taking some more pictures. Regardless, the output results are quite good – we have a toy/not toy accuracy in the 90% range, which is more than good enough for our robot. We can also look at the training and validation loss curves – the training loss continues to decrease after the accuracy has leveled off. This means that the error values and weights can still be improved after the accuracy has maxed out. This gives the network more confidence. We can realistically stop the training after about epoch 150.

Our final step is to save the network weights and biases to a file so that we can reuse them in our next section, which is a program to test that our neural network is working properly:

```
# save the CNN network weights to file
print("Saving Network Weights to file...")
cnNetwork.save(model_file)
```

Using the neural network

Now that we have created our file and saved the results of our trained neural network, we can put this trained system to work by having it identify from images whether or not there is a toy in the image. We start a new Python program file and call it test_the_network.py.

We start with a header and import our libraries for Python. We use OpenCV (cv2) to perform our image manipulation, and Keras for the neural networks:

```
# Test Network Program
# part of the toy detector
# uses LeNet to detect if toys are in the image
#
# Francis X. Govers 2018
#
# references:
#
https://www.pyimagesearch.com/2017/12/18/keras-deep-learning-raspberry-pi/
#
# import the necessary packages
from keras.preprocessing.image import img_to_array
from keras.models import load_model
import numpy as np
import imutils
import cv2

load the image
```

```
image = cv2.imread("toy2.jpg")
orig = image.copy()
```

We load our image into memory – in this case, a picture that has a toy in it. We use OpenCV's image read function and keep a copy to display later.

Our next step is to pre-process our image to present to the neural network. We resize the image to 128 by 128, the original image size the network is expecting. We normalize the color values from 0 to 255 into a range from 0 to 1, as we did in the training. We convert the image format into a normal NumPy numerical array and make it a 2D array with the expand_dims function.

```
pre-process the image for classification
image = cv2.resize(image, (128, 128))
image = image.astype("float") / 255.0
image = img_to_array(image)
image = np.expand_dims(image, axis=0)
```

Now, we can load our pre-trained network we saved in the last program. I called it toy_not_toy.model. This creates a neural network with the weighs already set to the last configuration set during training:

```
load the trained convolutional neural network
print("loading network...")
model = load_model("toy_not_toy.model")
```

The actual predict function does all of the work for us in this case. It runs the image through the neural network and collects the results. We place these answers in two variables – not toy and toy – which each get a number from 0 to 1 of the probability that the neural network thinks that the image either does or does not contain a toy. The two numbers should add up to one. Now that we have our prediction, we take the larger number and declare the winner using the Python max function. We format the result so that we can display it over the image:

```
classify the input image
(nottoy, toy) = model.predict(image)[0]
print("toy = ",toy, " Not Toy = ",nottoy)
# build the label
label = "toy" if toy > nottoy else "Not toy"
probability = max(toy, nottoy)
label = "{}: {:.2f}%".format(label, probability * 100)

draw the label on the image
output = imutils.resize(orig, width=400)
cv2.putText(output, label, (200, 25), cv2.FONT_HERSHEY_SIMPLEX,
0.7, (200, 255, 40), 2)
```

Finally, we can show the output image on the screen, and write the answer out to disk so we have a record of it and can paste it into the book, which is very important:

```
# show the output image
cv2.imshow("Output", output)
cv2.imwrite("toy_classify2.jpg", output)
cv2.waitKey(0)
```

What we get out of the network are the following images:

So that gives us our toy detector program. In future chapters, we will be extending this toy detector to determine the toy location and provide navigation guidance to the robot.

Summary

We dived head first into the world of ANN. ANN are computer approximations of human nerve cell processes, and are composed of artificial neurons. Each neuron has several parts: inputs, weights, bias, and activation.

The ANN can be thought of as a stepwise non-linear approximation function that slowly adjusts itself to fit a curve that matches the desired input to the desired output. This process happens through the learning function. The learning process has several steps, including preparing data, labeling data, creating the network, initializing the weights, the forward pass that provides the output, and the calculation of loss (also called error). The weights of the individual neurons are adjusted by backpropogation, which starts at the output and works backward to apportion error to each neuron and each neuron input.

We created a CNN to examine images. The network was trained on two sets of images – one containing toys and one without toys. We trained the network to get a better than 90% accuracy in classifying images as either having toys, or not having toys. Finally, we tested the network to verify its output.

In the next chapter, we will look at training the robot arm with reinforcement learning and genetic algorithms.

Questions

1. We went through a lot in this chapter. You can use the framework provided to investigate the properties of neural networks. Try several activation functions, or different settings for convolutions to see what changes in the training process.
2. Draw a diagram of an artificial neuron and label the parts. Look up a natural, human biological neuron, and compare.
3. What features of a real neuron and an artificial neuron are the same?
4. What are different?
5. What relationship does the first layer of a neural network have to the input?
6. What relationship does the last layer of a neural network have to the output?
7. Look up three kinds of loss functions and describe how they work. Include mean square loss and the two kinds of cross entropy loss.
8. What would you change if your network trained to 40% and got "stuck", or was unable to learn anything further?

Further reading

- Bakker, Indra den, *Python Deep Learning Cookbook*, Packt Publishing, 2017.
- Joshi, Prateek, *Artificial Intelligence with Python*, Packt Publishing, 2017.
- Zocca, V, Spacagna, G, Slater, D, and Roelants, P, *Python Deep Learning*, Packt Publishing, 2017
- Rosebrock, Adrian, *PyImageSearch Blog*, Published at pyimagesearch.com. 2018.

5
Picking up the Toys

Our task in this chapter is one of the most daunting in the book. We are going to teach our robot, TinMan, to pick up a variety of toys with its robot arm. As shown in the illustrations, we are on steps 6 and 7 of our storyboard – positioning the arm and picking up the toy. We want to teach the robot how to perform this task, or we might say give the robot the tools and methods to do the task and then let it teach itself. How are we going to do this?

How would you teach a child to pick up toys from his or her room? You would use either the offer of a reward, or the threat of punishment. This is another way of saying you would use positive and negative reinforcement to get the behavior you want. This is the approach we will use – reinforcement learning. We will reward good behaviors by giving the robot points, and punish bad or useless behaviors by taking points away. We will write the software to have the robot want to maximize positive results and avoid negative results.

If you think this is something like a game, with points being added or removed from a score, with some concept of *winning* at the end, that is exactly what it is. We can treat this process just like playing a game, and indeed, that is what the robot will be doing – trying to win the game of picking up toys. That seems remarkably similar to the Mary Poppins concept of getting the children she was in charge of to do their chores:

> *"For every job that must be done,*
> *There is an element of fun,*
> *You find the fun and snap!*
> *The job's a game"*
> - *"A Spoonful of Sugar", Mary Poppins, 1964, Robert and Richard Sherman.*
>
> *So here we have Mary Poppins join the ranks of Ada Lovelace and Robin Murphy in showing us how to create robots.*

In this chapter, we will cover the following topics:

- Task analysis
- Teaching the robot arm
- Other robot arm machine-learning approaches

This chapter covers the use of two techniques for machine learning for robot arms. The first one is **reinforcement learning** (**RL**), which seek to train behaviors in a robot by maximizing rewards. RL is a balance between reward for individual actions and accumulation of value for completing a task.

The second technique uses genetic algorithms to simulate natural selection and evolution to craft a motion path out of smaller elements. The process creates a large number of individual **chromosomes** that represent possible paths the robot can take. Each chromosome is composed of small steps. Each chromosome is tested with a fitness function to determine whether it is kept or discarded. New chromosomes are created by mating, or crossing, two parent chromosomes together. Mutation is also simulated by randomly switching individual genes, or steps.

Technical requirements

This unit does not require new software from the previous chapter. We will be using **Python** with **NumPy**, the **matplotlib** library to make plots and graphs, and the **pickle** library to store data.

A robot and a robot arm would be helpful, but all of the functions we will learn in this chapter can also be performed via simulation and modeling, which are included in the examples.

Check out the following video to see the Code in Action:
`http://bit.ly/2wupSdD`

Task analysis

Let's talk a bit first about what we have to work with. We have a mobile base with a six degree-of-freedom arm attached to it. We are fortunate that TinMan's robot arm is constructed out of servo motors. We can tell where all of the parts of the arm are if we know where the servos are commanded to be, since we are commanding the angles of the servos. We can use forward kinematics, which is to sum up all the angles and levers of the arm in order to deduce where the hand is located at. We can use this hand location as our desired state – our reward criteria. We will give the robot points, or rewards, based on how close the hand is to the desired position and orientation we want. We want the robot to figure out what it takes to get to that position. We need to give the robot a way to test out different theories, or actions that will result in the arm moving. To start with, let's freeze the base of the arm at the shoulder so it can't rotate, thus eliminating one degree of freedom. We will just worry about in-plane motion down the center line of the robot. We will also do the hand rotating, and the fingers opening and closing later as part of a different process when we learn how to grasp objects.

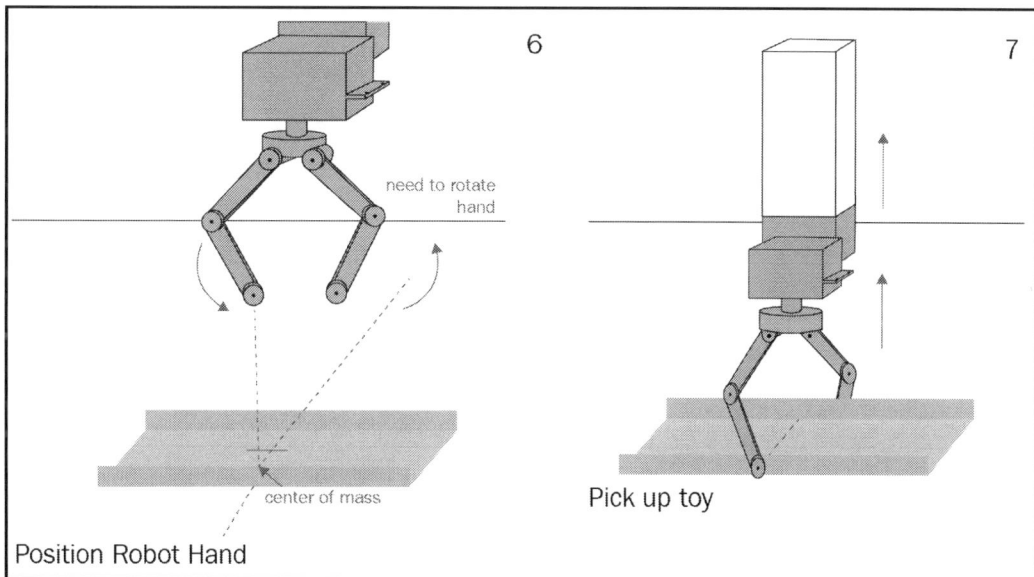

Position Robot Hand

Pick up toy

That leaves us with an action space with just three actions – setting the position of the three middle servomotors, which I will call shoulder pitch, elbow pitch, and wrist pitch. Our possible actions are shoulder pitch from 0 to 180, elbow pitch from 0 to 180, and wrist pitch from 0 to 180. This produces a large range of motion from just these three motors.

Setting up the solution

We will call the act of setting the motors to a different position an **action**, and we will call the resulting position of the robot hand the **state**. We are going to have the robot associate **states** (a beginning position of the hand) and an **action** (the motor commands used when at that state) with the probability of generating either a positive or negative **outcome** – we will be training the robot to figure out which sets of actions result in maximizing the **reward**. We will use some of the same tools we used before in our neural network to propagate a reward to each step in a chain of movements that result in the hand moving to some location. In reinforcement learning circles, this is called **discounting the reward** – distributing portions of rewards to the step in a multi-step process. Likewise, the combination of a state and an action is called a **policy** – because we are telling the robot, *when you are in this position, and want to go to that position, do this action.*

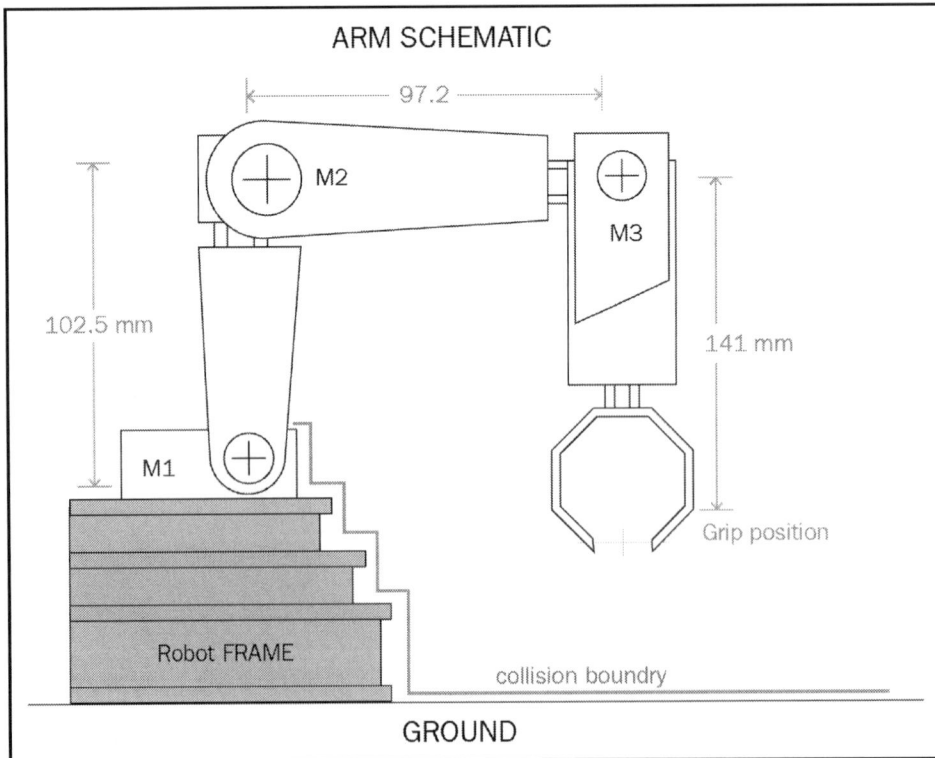

ARM SCHEMATIC

97.2

M2

M3

102.5 mm

141 mm

M1

Grip position

Robot FRAME

collision boundry

GROUND

Our process for learning with the robot arm will look like this – we will set a goal position for the robot arm. We can start by saying we have four arm positions we want – neutral carry (where the arm is above the ground and out of the way of the camera when we are driving around), pick up (in front of the robot where a toy would be), high carry (when we are carrying a toy), and drop off (similar to high carry but extended so we can put the toy in the toy box). These are our starting four positions. We can add more later if it looks like we need them:

Drop Off
At toy box

Pick Up ⇧

Neutral Carry –
normal arm
position

⇨
High Carry

We set our goal position of the robot hand, which is the position of the robot hand in x and y coordinates in millimeters from the rotational center of the arm. The robot will try a series of movements to try and get close to that goal. We will not be giving the robot what motor positions it needs to get to that goal – which the robot must learn. The movements at first will be totally randomly generated. We will restrict the delta movement (analogous to the learning rate from the previous chapter) to some small size so we don't get wild flailing of the arm. At each incremental movement, we will score the movement based on whether or not the arm moved closer to the goal position. The robot will remember these movements by associating the beginning state and the action (movement) with the reward score. Later, we will train a neural network to generate probabilities of positive outcomes based on inputs of starting state and movement action. This will allow the arm to learn which sequences of movement achieve positive results. Then we will be able to predict which movement will result in the arm moving correctly based on the starting position.

You can also surmise that we must add a reward for accomplishing the task quickly – we want the results to be efficient, and so we will add rewards for taking the shortest time to complete the task – or you can say we subtract a reward for each step needed to get to the goal so that the process with the fewest steps gets the most reward.

We calculate rewards using the **Q-function**. Q represents the reward the robot will be getting (or expecting to get) from a particular action.

Where $Q(s,a)$ is the final reward for an action given the starting state, reward(s,a) is the reward for that action, g is a discount function that rewards getting to the goal quicker, and $max(Q(s',a')$ selects the action that results in the largest reward out of the set of actions available at that state. In the equation, *s* and *a* represent the current state and action, and *s'* and *a'* represent the next state and next action.

How do we pick actions?

What actions can the robot arm perform? We have three motors, and we have three options for each motor. We can do nothing – that is, not move at all. We can move counterclockwise, which will make our motor angle smaller, and we can move clockwise, which makes our motor angle larger.

Note: most servo motors treat positive position changes as clockwise rotation. Thus, if we command the rotation to change from 200 to 250 degrees, the motor will turn clockwise 50 degrees.

Our action space for each motion of the robot arm is to move each motor either left, right, or not at all. This gives us 27 combinations with three motors (3 x 3 x 3 possible actions). We will note this with an action matrix. Each action will have three values. An action that reduces the angle of motor 1, holds motor 2 in place, and increases motor 3, noted by [-1, 0, 1]. We will just use 1 in the action matrix because we will set the magnitude of the motion in another way. The *x-y* coordinates of the hand can be computed from the sums of the joints.

These actions make up the state-space of our robot arm, which is the set of all possible actions. What we will be doing in this chapter is investigating various ways of picking which action to perform and when to accomplish our tasks, and using machine learning to do it.

Another way of looking at this process is that we are generating a decision tree. You are probably familiar with the concept. We have a bit of a unique application when applying this to a robot arm, because our arm is a series of joints connected together, and moving one moves all of the other joints farther out on the arm. When we move motor 1, motors 2 and 3 move position in space, and their angles and distances to the ground and to our goal change. Each possible motor move adds 27 new branches to our decision tree, and can generate 27 new arm positions. All we have to do is pick which one to keep.

The rest of this chapter will deal with just how we go about selecting our motions.

Summary of robot arm learning process

The result for our arm training is a combination of several AI techniques in one mashup process. We have reinforcement learning in the process of maximizing rewards. We are using Q-learning to compute rewards for successful completion or partial completion of a goal. We use a straight **artificial neural network** (**ANN**) to predict the outcomes of actions given a beginning state. And we introduced genetic algorithms to innovate and make movement patterns that we can teach to the robot arm:

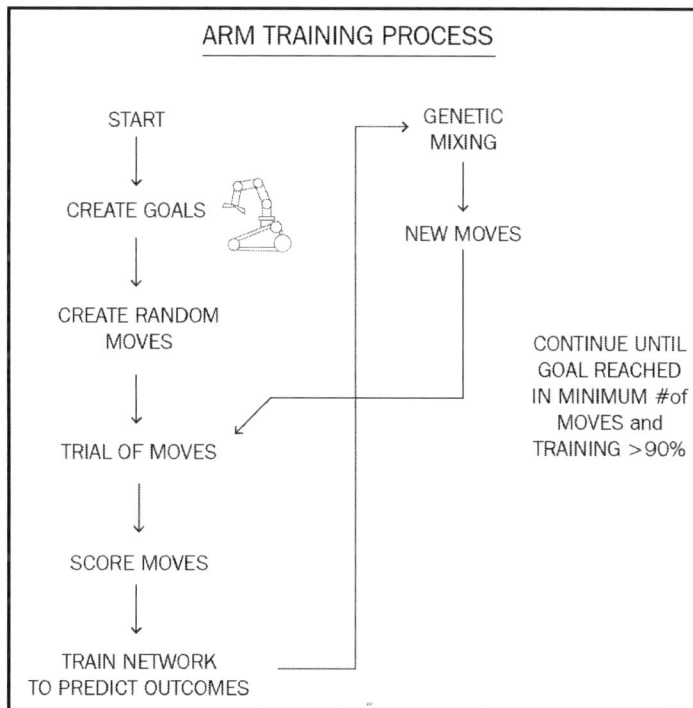

Our general process for teaching the arm how to move is based on a type of reinforcement learning called Q-Learning. Our concepts are summarized in the following equation:

$$Q(s,a) = R(s,a) + G \, max[Qs_{t+1}, a]$$

Here, $Q(s,a)$ is the value of an action done in a particular state. R is the reward given for that action. G is a discount factor that reduces rewards for longer sets of actions. G is normally set to a number less than 1, like .9. For example, a set of actions that reaches the goal in 10 steps (actions) gets a higher Q than a set of actions that takes 20 steps. This is very similar to how we distributed the changes in weights for neural networks in the last chapter. The function $max[Qs_{t+1}, a]$ says to look at the next state of the robot, and select the action that results in the highest Q value for the next state.

Teaching the robot arm

Now we jump off the deep end and start writing some code.

We can begin by talking about how we send commands to the arm. The motors I have selected for TinMan are stronger versions of standard hobby servo motors, with metal gears. Servo motors are commanded by setting an angle for the motor's output shaft to assume. The angles run from 0 to 180 degrees. However, the commands for the motor positions run from 1 to 255, so they fit into a single 8-bit value. We'll be converting these byte-based motor commands to and from angles in the program.

Version one – action state reinforcement learning

Our first version of the arm training program will introduce the basic framework, and use the most primitive form of machine learning, which is to just try random movements until the program finds something that works.

> **TIP**
>
> You must keep in mind that a particular arm position may have several valid solutions in our combination of three motors. For example, motor 1 may have slightly more angle, and motor 3 slightly less, to get to the same Cartesian coordinates.

```
import numpy as np
from math import *
import matplotlib.pyplot as mp
```

We start with setting up some global variables and objects we will be using. The action matrix is the set of all actions available in any state, and is a combination of three motors with three actions – rotation to the left, no motion, or rotation to the right. Three motors with three actions each gives us 27 combinations. Why do we include the combination [0,0,0], which represents no motion at all? We calculate the reward for each action and if every other action except [0,0,0] results in a lower reward score, then we have maximized our attainment of our goal:

```
# action matrix - all possible combinations of actions of the three motors
ACTIONMAT = np.array([[0,0,-1],[0,0,0],[0,0,1],
        [0,-1,-1],[0,-1,0],[0,-1,1],
        [0,1,-1],[0,1,0],[0,1,1],
        [-1,0,-1],[-1,0,0],[-1,0,1],
        [-1,-1,-1],[-1,-1,0],[-1,-1,1],
        [-1,1,-1],[-1,1,0],[-1,1,1],
        [1,0,-1],[1,0,0],[1,0,1],
        [1,-1,-1],[1,-1,0],[1,-1,1],
        [1,1,-1],[1,1,0],[1,1,1]])
```

Now we build a robot arm object so that we can provide a standard interface to arm functions and create a data structure to hang our information about the robot arm on. The arm has a state, which is the current set of the three motor positions. Motor positions are given in radians. The arm has a goal, which is a two-dimensional (*x* and *y*) coordinate of the goal to move the gripper position of the arm:

```
class RobotArm():
    def __init__(self):
        self.state = [0,0,0]
```

The setState method of RobotArm updates the current state of the arm motors. It also recalculates the *x-y* coordinates of the robot hand (which is measured from the tip of the gripper jaws):

```
def setState(self,st):
    self.state = st
    self.position = calHandPosition(st)
```

The setGoal method sets a new goal for the robot hand:

```
def setGoal(self,newGoal):
    self.goal = newGoal
```

The `Calculate Reward` method calculates the reward based on the current relationship between the robot hand, given by `self.position`, and the goal point, stored in `self.goal`. We want the reward to be proportional to the distance between the goal and the position. We award 100 points for being at the goal, and 0 points for being as far away as the hand can get, which happens to be 340 mm away. We calculate this by computing a percentage of the completed goal. We use Cartesian distance. Just remember –the closer to the goal, then more the reward:

> I am deliberately using a more straightforward use of Python that avoids some readability issues in order to convey clarity of purpose to the reader. I am aware that Python has some pretty cool tricks for efficiently combining vectors, tables, lists, and arrays, and you are welcome to post your suggestions for improvement on the GitHub site.

```
def calcReward(self):
    dx = self.goal[0] - self.position[0]
    dy = self.goal[1] - self.position[1]
    dist2goal = sqrt(dx*dx + dy*dy)
    self.dist2goal = dist2goal
    # we want the reward to be 100 if the goal is met
    # and proportional to the distance from goal otherwise
    # the arm is 340mm long, so that is as far away as we can get
    #
    self.reward = (340.0-dist2goal)/340.0 * 100.0
    return self.reward
```

The `step` method is really the heart of the learning process for this example program. We are going to input the new action to consider, and the learning rate, which is how far to move the motor at each increment. For this first program, we will set the learning rate to be `1.0`. We apply the action to the current state of the robot arm to get a new state.

Our next step is to do a range check of the application of the new action to see that we don't drive the motor out of bounds. Our angle values run from 0 to 255 integer units. We use the `max` and `min` functions to restrict our motors to these values:

```
def step(self,act,learningRate):
    newState = self.state + (act * learningRate)
    # range check
    for ii in range(3):
        newState[ii]=max(newState[ii],0)
        newState[ii]=min(newState[ii],255.0)
    self.setState(newState)
    reward = self.calcReward()
```

```
            return self.state,reward
# for a given action, return the new state
# just a utility to display the joint angle in degrees
def joint2deg(jointPos):
    return jointPos * (180.0 / 255.0)
def calHandPosition(stat):
    m1,m2,m3=stat
    # calculate hand position based on the position of the servo motors
    # m1, m2, m3 = motor command from 0 to 255
    # forward kinematics
    # we first convert each to an angle
    d1 = 102.5  # length of first joint (sholder to elbow) in mm
    d2 = 97.26  # length of second joint arm (elbow to wrist) in mm
    d3 = 141    # length of thrird joint arm (wrist to hand)
    right = pi/2.0 # right angle, 90 degrees or pi/2 radians
    m1Theta = pi - m1*(pi/255.0)
    m2Theta = pi - m2*(pi/255.0)
    m3Theta = pi - m3*(pi/255.0)
    m2Theta = m1Theta-right+m2Theta
    m3Theta = m2Theta-right+m3Theta
# begin main program
# starting state
 # our arm has states from 0 to 255 which map to degrees from 0 to 180
 # here is our beginning state
 state = [127,127,127]
 oldState = state
 learningRate = 2.0
 robotArm = RobotArm()
 robotArm.setState(state)
 goal=[14,251]
 robotArm.setGoal(goal)
 knt = 0 # counter
 reward=0.0 # no reward yet...
 d2g=0.0
 oldd2g = d2g
 curve = []
 # let's set the reward value for reaching the goal at 100 points
# 98% is good enough
while reward < 98:
    index = np.random.randint(0,ACTIONMAT.shape[0])
    action = ACTIONMAT[index]
    state,reward = robotArm.step(action,learningRate)
    d2g = robotArm.dist2goal
    if d2g > oldd2g:
        # if the new reward is worse than the old reward, throw this state
away
        #print("old state",oldState,state,d2g,oldd2g)
        state=oldState
```

```
robotArm.setState(state)
knt +=1
oldd2g=d2g
oldState=state
curve.append(reward)
if knt > 10000: reward = 101
#print ("NewState ",state, "reward ",reward)
# see how long doing this randomly takes
print ("Count",knt,"NewState ",state, "reward ",max(curve))
mp.plot(curve)
mp.show()
```

The results of our first program are summarized in the following output diagram, showing that the machine learning process can occur even in a very primitive program such as this one, that just tries random stuff until it finds something that works:

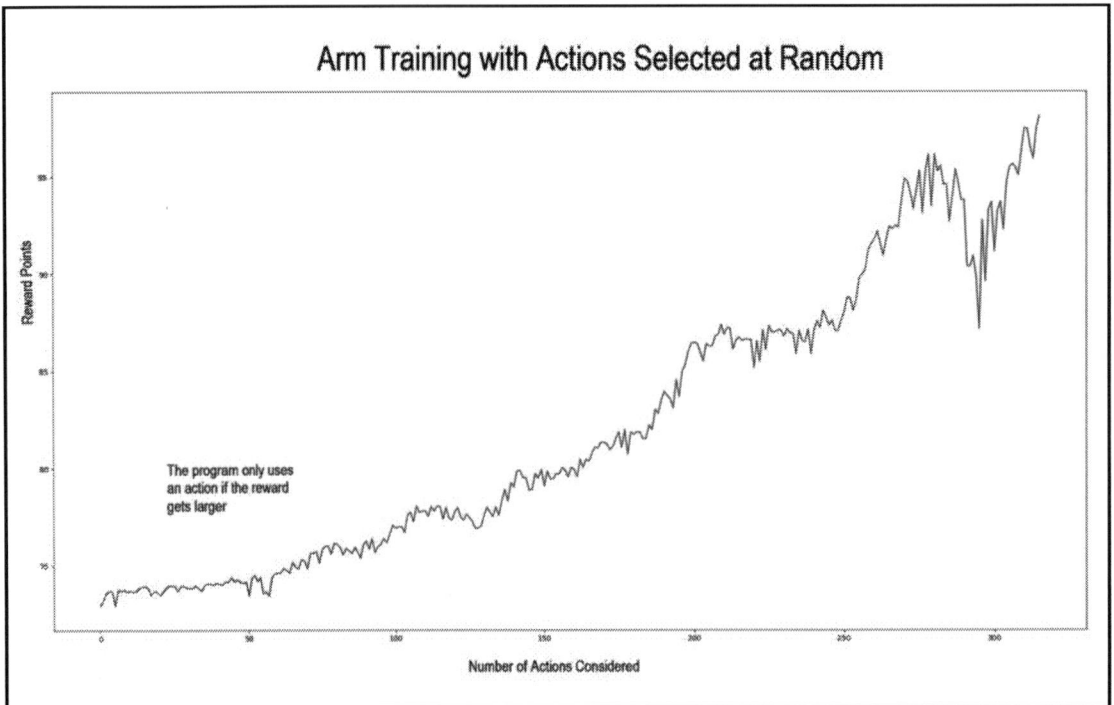

Number of iterations: 399, final state: [211. 57. 55.], and final reward: 98.32.

Adaptive learning rate

In our first example, we used a constant learning rate of three units to move our robot arm. This equates to about 2.1 degrees of movement from the motor. This step is the smallest and largest single step motion we took at each part of the learning process. What if we changed the learning rate adaptively? As we get closer to the goal, we can make the steps smaller, and if we get farther away, we can take bigger steps. We insert a line at each update just after where we calculate the reward, as shown here:

```
state,reward = robotArm.step(action,learningRate)
# insert this new line to try an adaptive learning rate
learningRate = (100-reward)/2.5
```

The maximum reward for reaching the goal is `100` points. We want the learning rate to be an inverse ratio to the reward. As the reward gets bigger, the `learningRate` gets smaller. I also added the learning rate to the data recording, and created the following diagram from the results. You can see that the training action converged much faster. After a number of trials, it averages about four times as fast as the random approach we used in the first example. You can see the learning rate approaching zero as the reward nears 100:

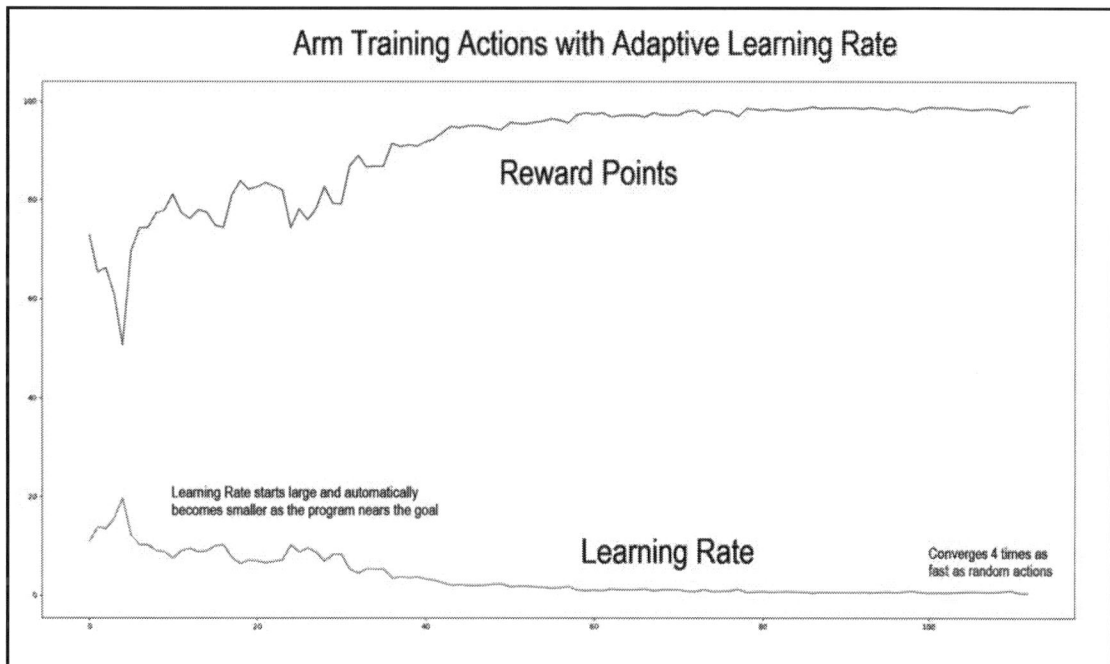

- Number of Iterations: 98; final state [51 199 198]
- Reward: 99.15
- Distance to Goal: 2.88 mm
- Learning Rate: Maximum: 14.17 Minimum: 0.34

Q-learning implementation

Now in this next part of the computer code, we will be *evolving* our arm learning code to include something that you may have noted was missing from the first program in the preceding section. It did not do any path planning; it just provided the combination of three motor positions that resulted in the the hand being in the proper position. It did not try to find a good path from the starting point to the ending point. Our next program will do just that, and will utilize the Q-learning technique we discussed.

I'm going to leave out the utility functions that we developed in the first program that are reused in the second program. The complete code will be available for download from the GitHub website. This lets us confine ourselves to the new sections in this block of code. Some quick notes: in a lot of Q-learning programs, the entire set of possible states are available from the beginning. The robot arm has a large volume it can explore, but we will only be using a small subset of its range to perform our tasks. I will let the program iterate on the possible states of the motors, and will add new states as they are reached to our Q-list.

As a quick review, in Q learning, we develop a overall value of a set of actions that together result in the robot reaching its goal. This total value of a valid path to the goal is called **Q**.

We add a discount factor that penalizes longer paths; a shorter path is better. This discount factor is usually called by the Greek letter **Gamma**. The discount is a number less than 1 (usually 0.9 or so), and it is one of our tunable parameters. Imagine that we are at the goal: we get the full reward, 100 points, and the discount is 0. Then we move back to the state before we get to the goal, that is one step away. We multiply it by 0.9, so it gets 9/10 of the reward (90 points). The next space, two steps back, gets the reward from the 1-step space (90 points) times the discount factor (Gamma), which is 0.9 x 90 or 81. So each step back from the goal gets a bit less of the reward. A path with 10 steps gets more points than a path with 20 steps.

Another important point in the Q-learning process is that the Q value is set for this state (the current position of the robot hand) by picking the next action that results in the highest reward. This is how a path is found. We are looking for the action that gets us closer to the goal, and we value this action at this state by how much the next action will improve our reward. Another way of explaining this concept is this: at each state, or position, we figure out our next move that will get us to a new position by picking the next move with the largest reward. For our program, we compute a reward as being inversely proportional to the distance to our goal: the closer to the goal, the bigger the reward.

Here is the main program for Q-learning.

We can begin by setting up our starting or beginning state. Our arm has states from 0 to 255, which map to degrees from 0 to 180. Here is our beginning state:

```
BEGIN MAIN PROGRAM
state = [127,127,127]

We initialize our "Q" matrix. Q is a matrix of the number of states by the
number of actions. We will add states as we go in this version of this
program, so Q starts out as an empty list:
  Q=[]
```

We use an initial learning rate for the arm. We start with three units per move, which is roughly 2 degrees of motion per motor:

```
learningRate = 3.0
```

We instantiate our RobotArm object and initialize it:

```
robotArm = RobotArm()
```

We set the robot arm's state to match our local variable that we set to the middle value of 127,127,127. You can also set the robot arm's initial state to some random point, but you need to do some checking to make sure you don't have an invalid position that hits the body of the robot. I checked that this middle position is acceptable:

```
robotArm.setState(state)
```

Next, we set the goal for this training session. This is the *grab* position of the arm, where the arm is poised to pick up an object:

```
goal=[14,251]
  robotArm.setGoal(goal)
```

We initialize some local variables. We need a counter to keep track of our iterations, and create our reward variable and set it to zero:

```
knt = 0 # counter
reward=0.0
```

Gamma is our discount rate that we use to penalize longer paths. Since it will take quite a few steps at our small step size, we need this number to be just less than 1. This will reduce the reward by five percent for each step taken:

```
gamma = 0.95 # discount for rewards that take more time
```

We use the stateReset value to reset the robot's state between runs so that we are starting in the same place each time:

```
stateReset = [127,127,127]
state = stateReset
robotArm.setState(state)
```

G is our total value of a path from start to finish. It is the sum of rewards for that path. Each step in the path gets an individual reward, and G is the sum of the reward for all those steps:

```
G=0
```

This section begins to perform training using Q learning. We set a number of training epochs, or episodes. We need the computer to fill in as many state-action pairs as we can to provide a complete matrix for training. Each entry has a state, the action selected, and the reward value for that action:

```
for epoch in range(1,100):
```

We set the done variable to False when the training reward passes some threshold:

```
done=False
```

Now reset the path value, reward, and counter for each run:

```
G,reward,knt = 0,0,0
  state = stateReset
  robotArm.setState(state)
```

This is the actual training loop. We run until we either find a valid path, or exceed our maximum number of tries. A path with 1,000 steps is not very valuable, so we set the maximum path length to 1,000.

The action sample function has two modes in this program. In Q mode, it looks up the next action with the highest possible value as determined by the Q function. If no Q value has been determined for this state/action pair, then we add a random move from our state table and evaluate this action. We store the actions in the Q matrix as an enumeration that we can look up using the `ACTIONMAT` matrix we created in the previous program. It has the 27 possible actions we can take from each state. This type of enumeration is common in machine learning programs:

```
while not done:
  action = action_sample("Q",state,Q)
  motorAction = ACTIONMAT[action]
```

The `step` function works just as before. It computes the reward and new state of the robot arm given the action selected by the `action_sample` function:

```
state2,reward = robotArm.step(motorAction,learningRate)
```

This is the Q learning function that determines the value of the previous action based on the reward of the next state:

```
newQ=reward + gamma * maxQ(Q, state2)
```

I had to create a function to insert this new Q value into the Q matrix at the appropriate location. The Q matrix is indexed by `state` and `action`. By the end of training, each possible state will have 27 values, one for each possible action, including taking no action at all:

```
setQ(Q,state,action,newQ)
```

G is the accumulated value of this path, so it is just the sum of all of the rewards:

```
G += reward
```

We increment our counter and check to see if our path is too long. If it has not reached a solution by 1,000 steps, we start over. Remember, our goal is to fill out the Q matrix, not to just compute a path:

```
knt +=1
  if knt > 1000 or reward > 90:
  done=True
```

These two lines of code update the state of the robot arm in the arm object now that we have completed our computations and selected the action and state to perform next in our path:

```
state = state2
robotArm.setState(state)
```

We print a little report to let the operator know how things are going:

```
if epoch % 2 == 0:
    print("Epoch ",epoch,"TotalReward:",G," counter:",knt,"Q Len ",len(Q))
```

The output of our program looks like this:

```
Epoch 2 TotalReward: 1408.5684481305104 counter: 101 Q Len 658
Epoch 4 TotalReward: 1967.41782263554 counter: 30 Q Len 1623
Epoch 6 TotalReward: 7268.7078233576185 counter: 154 Q Len 1841
Epoch 8 TotalReward: 2930.969165320549 counter: 39 Q Len 2023
Epoch 10 TotalReward: 3159.6160871381835 counter: 100 Q Len 2918
Epoch 12 TotalReward: 9189.000528212566 counter: 316 Q Len 3368
Epoch 14 TotalReward: 4293.976761223593 counter: 115 Q Len 3566
Epoch 16 TotalReward: 31415.15446438481 counter: 1001 Q Len 4686
Epoch 18 TotalReward: 2951.8615312851393 counter: 46 Q Len 4998
Epoch 20 TotalReward: 4863.635334567336 counter: 78 Q Len 5611
Epoch 22 TotalReward: 11702.393914624867 counter: 737 Q Len 6571
Epoch 24 TotalReward: 29049.025812767548 counter: 752 Q Len 7408
Epoch 26 TotalReward: 4359.228666547103 counter: 1001 Q Len 8945
Epoch 28 TotalReward: 8860.919025609743 counter: 191 Q Len 9625
Epoch 30 TotalReward: 17966.243729318052 counter: 312 Q Len 10157
Epoch 32 TotalReward: 4551.9521073138185 counter: 235 Q Len 11264
Epoch 34 TotalReward: 5491.852803948144 counter: 280 Q Len 11892
Epoch 36 TotalReward: 7456.222978066394 counter: 136 Q Len 12743
Epoch 38 TotalReward: 2796.5324272086796 counter: 62 Q Len 13387
Epoch 40 TotalReward: 21549.573621139356 counter: 516 Q Len 14871
Epoch 42 TotalReward: 3751.1177055281605 counter: 66 Q Len 15105
```

You can watch the counter to see that the paths generated are generally getting shorter, but keep in mind that this process is primarily exploring the space that the robot arm can reach and setting values to motor actions to move the arm.

Version 2 – indexed states and actions

I was not really happy with the performance of the first version of this program, so I looked around to make some improvements. The program took quite a while to run – over an hour for the first iteration. I was particularly annoyed by how I was storing the states. It would be quite a bit simpler to put the states into some list, and then refer to them by index or subscript. Remember that each state is represented by three numbers, showing the positions of each of our three arm motors – M1, M2, and M3. Let's create an index to those states and replace that with a single number which we will refer to as **stat** (state minus the "e"). Then any variable that has stat rather than state uses the index and not the full three values for the state. This both simplifies the code greatly, and lets us use the much faster numpy functions to manipulate the lists. I also created a `getStateIndex` function that does double duty . If the state is already in the table, we return the index number (pointer for you C fans). If it is not in the table, we add it. That keeps the logic simple. We use a global variable `MAXSTATE` to keep track of how many states we have in the table. These modest changes resulted in a 40x speed increase in the training program. I also added a `pickle` function at the end to save the Q table so we can use it again for deployment. The `pickle` function lets you store the contents of a variable, in this case our numpy array of Q values, to the hard drive so you can retrieve it later:

```
STATEINDEX = []
def getStateIndex(state):
    global MAXSTATE
    thisState = state.tolist()
    if thisState in STATEINDEX:
        return STATEINDEX.index(thisState)
    else:
        # not found in state index, we add it
        STATEINDEX.append(thisState)
        MAXSTATE +=1
```

I added a mode to the `action_sample` function that I call `maxreturn`. You will remember that we started by just randomly selecting an action and computing the reward, then keeping the action if the action resulted in the arm moving closer to the goal. If we already have a Q score computed for this action, we take that. If we do not have a Q value, we compute the reward for all 27 possible actions and take the one with the highest reward – rather than value (Q). This feature performs a maximum reward for (state,action) pair (usually annotated as max R(s,a)). This definitely speeds up the process of converging to a solution:

```
def action_sample(mode,stat,Qmatrix, learningRate, goal):
    state = STATEINDEX[stat]
    if mode=="random":
```

```
            index = np.random.randint(0,ACTIONMAT.shape[0])
            print("RAND ACTION",index)
            #action = ACTIONMAT[index]
            return index
    if mode=="maxreturn":
        state=STATEINDEX[stat]
        maxRew=-9990
        doAction=1
        for adex in range(len(ACTIONMAT)):
            act = ACTIONMAT[adex]
            thisReward = predictReward(state,goal,act,learningRate)
            if thisReward > maxRew:
                maxRew=thisReward
                doAction = adex
            if maxRew == -9990:
                doAction=
action_sample("random",stat,Qmatrix,learningRate,goal)
        return doAction
    if mode=="Q":
        try:
            # note this returns the number of the action with the highest Q
score!
            action = np.argmax(Q[statQ])
            return(action)
        except:
            # no action found
            action=
action_sample("maxreturn",stat,Qmatrix,learningRate,goal)
            return action
```

Begin the main program loop and create a starting state. Our arm has states from 0 to 255, which map to degrees from 0 to 180. Here is our beginning state of (127,127,127), the position of the three motors in the middle of their range. We initialize our Q matrix by creating a zero-filled array. Q is a matrix of the number of states multiplied by the number of actions. We will add states as we go in this version of this program, but we don't want a lot of thrashing of memory, so we create a large table to start with. We preallocate 15,000 spaces to put states and actions in the Q matrix and if we need to make it bigger, we use `np.resize` to expand it:

```
Q=np.zeros((150000,27))
state = np.array([127,127,127])
# initial learning rate for the arm - we start with 3 units
learningRate = 10
robotArm = RobotArm()
robotArm.setState(state)
goal=[14,251]
robotArm.setGoal(goal)
```

```
# Q learning phase
stateReset = np.array([127,127,127])
state = stateReset
robotArm.setState(state)
# discount function
gamma = 0.6
rewardData = []
# perform training on Q Learning
for epoch in range(1,1000):
    done=False
    G,reward,knt = 0,0,0
    state = randomState()
    #state = np.array([127,127,127])
    robotArm.setState(state)
    stat = getStateIndex(state)
    while not done:
        action = action_sample("Q",stat,Q, learningRate,robotArm.goal)
        motorAction = ACTIONMAT[action]
        state2,reward = robotArm.step(motorAction,learningRate)
        stat2 = getStateIndex(state2)
        Q[stat,action]=reward + gamma * np.max(Q[stat2])
        G += reward
        knt +=1
        if knt > 1000 or reward > 90:
            done=True
        stat = stat2
        robotArm.setState(STATEINDEX[stat])
        # see if we need more states...
        if len(STATEINDEX)> len(Q)-10:
            wid,hit = Q.shape
            wid += 1000
            print( "Adding 1,000 more Q values", wid)

            Q.append(np.zeros((1000,hit)))      if epoch % 2 == 0:
print("Epoch ",epoch,"TotalReward:",int(G)," counter:",knt,"Q Len
",MAXSTATE)
 # now that we are done, we save the Q array so we can reuse it
 output = open('q-arm-matrix.pkl', 'wb')
 # Pickle dictionary using protocol 0.
 pickle.dump(Q, output)
 output.close()
```

We finish our program by printing a report for you so you can see how things are going. We also save away the Q array so it can be used in deployment. We would use the Q learning by referencing the matrix in another program and selecting the state-action pair with the highest Q value from the matrix. If our state was 234,14, we would look in the matrix and see that action 13 had the highest reward. Then we would check our action table and see that action 13 is [-1, -1, -1], moving each motor one step counter-clockwise. We would then send that command to the robot.

Here is the output of our Q-learning program. In this particular case, Q learning is not very effective. The total reward should be going up and it is not. This is due to the fact that we have a huge number of states and we are only scoring a small number of state-action pairs in each epoch. We will need to run lots of epochs (over 1,000) to see Q learning start to work in this case:

```
Epoch 134 TotalReward: 894 counter: 12 Q Len 1003
Epoch 136 TotalReward: 568 counter: 7 Q Len 1008
Epoch 138 TotalReward: 572 counter: 9 Q Len 1010
Epoch 140 TotalReward: 479 counter: 9 Q Len 1023
Epoch 142 TotalReward: 443 counter: 8 Q Len 1029
Epoch 144 TotalReward: 406 counter: 9 Q Len 1047
Epoch 146 TotalReward: 444 counter: 11 Q Len 1049
Epoch 148 TotalReward: 460 counter: 9 Q Len 1067
Epoch 150 TotalReward: 270 counter: 18 Q Len 1076
Epoch 152 TotalReward: 681 counter: 9 Q Len 1082
Epoch 154 TotalReward: 689 counter: 11 Q Len 1092
Epoch 156 TotalReward: 553 counter: 10 Q Len 1102
Epoch 158 TotalReward: 467 counter: 7 Q Len 1107
Epoch 160 TotalReward: 552 counter: 8 Q Len 1116
Epoch 162 TotalReward: 588 counter: 8 Q Len 1124
Epoch 164 TotalReward: 907 counter: 15 Q Len 1139
Epoch 166 TotalReward: 314 counter: 14 Q Len 1141
Epoch 168 TotalReward: 263 counter: 7 Q Len 1153
Epoch 170 TotalReward: 527 counter: 7 Q Len 1153
Epoch 172 TotalReward: 654 counter: 10 Q Len 1161
```

Genetic algorithms

We have tried out Q-learning in a couple of different configurations, with a limited amount of success in training our robot. The main problem with Q-learning is that we have a very large number of possible states, or positions, that the robot arm can be in. This means that gaining a lot of knowledge about any one position by repeated trials is very difficult. We are going to introduce a different approach using **genetic algorithms** to generate our movement actions.

Moving the robot arm requires coordination of three motors simultaneously to create a smooth movement. We need a mechanism to create different combinations of motor movement for the robot to test. We could just use random numbers, but that is inefficient, and could take thousands and thousands of trials to get the level of training we want. What if we had a way of trying different combinations of motor movement, and then competing them against one another to pick the best one. It would be some sort of Darwinian *survival of the fittest* for arm movement scripts.

Here is our process. We do a trial run to go from position 1 (neutral carry) to position 2 (pickup). The robot moves the arm 100 times before getting the hand into the right position. We score each movement based on the percentage of goal accomplishment, indicating how much did this movement contribute to the goal. We take the 10 best moves and put them in a database. We run the test again and do the same thing – now we have 10 more *best moves* and 20 moves in the database. We take the five best from the first set and cross them with the five best from the second set – plus five moves chosen at random *and* five more made up of totally random moves. We run that sequence of moves, and then take the 10 best individual moves and continue on. We should quickly, through selection, get down to a sequence that performs the task. It may not be optimum, but it will work. We are managing our *gene pool* to create a solution to a problem by successive approximation.

We want to keep a good mix of possibilities that can be combined in different ways to solve moving our arm to its goal:

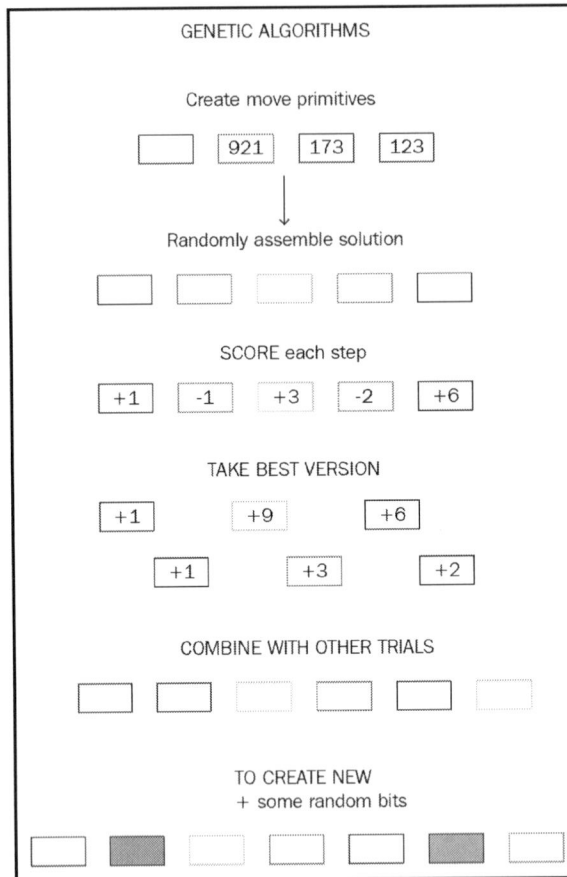

```
                    GENETIC ALGORITHMS

                    Create move primitives
              [      ]  [921]  [173]  [123]
                           |
                           v
                 Randomly assemble solution
          [    ]  [    ]  [    ]  [    ]  [    ]

                    SCORE each step
          [ +1 ]  [ -1 ]  [ +3 ]  [ -2 ]  [ +6 ]

                    TAKE BEST VERSION
          [ +1 ]      [ +9 ]      [ +6 ]
             [ +1 ]      [ +3 ]      [ +2 ]

                 COMBINE WITH OTHER TRIALS
        [   ]  [   ]  [   ]  [   ]  [   ]  [   ]

                    TO CREATE NEW
                   + some random bits
       [   ]  [▓▓]  [   ]  [   ]  [   ]  [▓▓]  [   ]
```

We can actually use several methods of **cross breeding** our movement sequences. What I described is a simple cross – half the **male** genetic material and half the **female** material (if you will pardon the biological metaphor). We could take this by quarters – ¼ male, ¼ female, ¼ male, ¼ female to have two crosses. We could also randomly grab bits from one or the other. We will stick with the half/half strategy for now, but you are free to experiment to your hearts content.

You are about to issue an objection: what if the movement takes less than 10 steps? Easy –when we get to the goal, we stop, and discard the remaining steps.

We are not looking for a perfect or optimum task execution, but something just good enough to get the job done. For a lot of real-time robotics, we don't have the luxury of the time to create a perfect solution, so any solution that gets the job done is adequate.

Why did we add the five additional random sample moves, and five totally random moves? This mimics natural selection also – the power of mutation. Our genetic codes are not perfect, and sometimes inferior material gets passed along. We also experience random mutations from bad copies of genes, cosmic rays, or virus diseases. We are introducing some random factors to "bump" the tuning of or algorithm – the natural selection – in case we converge on a local minimum or miss some simple path because it has not occurred yet to our previous movements.

Why on Earth are we going to all this trouble? The generic algorithm process can do something very difficult for a piece of software– it can **innovate**, or evolve a new process out of primitive actions by basically trying stuff until it finds what works and what does not. We have provided another machine learning process to add to our toolbox, but one that can create solutions we, the programmers, have not pre-conceived.

Let's dive into the genetic algorithm process.

We'll be building our own tools in this version, but there are some pre-built tool sets that will help you to create genetic algorithms, such as DEAP (Distributed Evolutionary Algorithms in Python), which can be found at `https://github.com/DEAP` and installed by typing in `pip install deap`.

In the interest of transparency, we are going to build our own genetic algorithm process from scratch. You have heard of *survival of the fittest*? This is how we decide which plans are the fittest and get to survive and propagate. I'm giving you a sandbox to play genetic engineer in where you have access to all of the parts and nothing is hidden behind the curtain. You will find that for our problem the code is not all that complex.

We'll start by creating the `computefitness` function, the one that scores our genetic material. Fitness is our criteria for grading our algorithm. We can change fitness to our heart's content to tailor our output to our needs. In this case, we are making a path in space for the robot arm from the starting location to the ending goal location. We judge our path by how close any point of the path comes to our goal. Just like in our previous programs, we make up the movement of the robot as 27 combinations of the three motors going clockwise, counterclockwise, or not moving. We divide the movement into small steps, each three motor units (1.8 degrees) of so of motion. We string together a whole group of these steps to make a path. The fitness function steps along the path and computes the hand position at each step.

The `predictReward` function makes a trial computation of where the robot hand has moved as a result of that step. Let's say we move motor 1 clockwise three steps, leave motor 2 alone, and move motor 3 counterclockwise three steps. This causes the hand to move slightly up and out. We score each step individually by how close it comes to the goal. Our score is computed out of 100; 100 is exactly at the goal, and we take away one point for each 1/100 distance away from the goal, up to a maximum of 340 mm. Why 340? That is the total length of the arm. We score the total movement a bit differently than you might think. Totaling up the rewards make no difference, as we want the point of closest approach to the goal. So we pick the single step with the highest reward and save that value. We throw away any steps after that, since they will only take us away. Thus we are automatically pruning our paths to end at the goal.

I used the term `allele` to indicate a single step out of the total path, which I called a `chrom`, short for chromosome:

```
def computeFitness(population, goal, learningRate, initialPos):
  fitness = []
  gamma = 0.6
  state=initialPos
  index = 0
  for chrom in population:
  value=0
  for allele in chrom:
  action = ACTIONMAT[allele]
  indivFit, state = predictReward(state,goal,action,learningRate)
  value += indivFit
  if indivFit > 95:
  # we are at the goal - snip the DNA here
  break
  fitness.append([value,index])
  index += 1
  return fitness
```

How do we make our paths to start with? The `make_new_individual` function builds our initial population of chromosomes, or paths, out of random numbers. Each contains a path made up of a number from 0 to 26 that represent all the valid combinations of motor commands. We set the path length to be a random number from 10 to 60:

```
def make_new_individual():
  # individual length of steps
  lenInd = random.randint(10,60)
  chrom = []  # chromosome description
  for ii in range(lenInd):
  chrom.append(randint(26))
  return chrom
```

We use the `roulette` function to pick a portion of our population to continue. Each generation, we select from the top 50% of scoring individuals to donate their DNA to create the next generation. We want the reward value of the path, or chromosome, to weigh the selection process; the higher the reward score, the better chance of having children. This is part of our selection process:

```
# select an individual in purportion to its value
# i.e. the higher the value, the better the odds of getting picked
def roulette(items):
total_weight = sum(item[0] for item in items)
weight_to_target = random.uniform(0, total_weight)
for item in items:
weight_to_target -= item[0]
if weight_to_target <= 0:
return item
# main Program
INITIAL_POS = [127,127,127]
GOAL=[-107.39209423, -35.18324771]
robotArm=RobotArm()
robotArm.setGoal(GOAL)
population = 300
learningRate = 3
crossover_chance = .50
mutate_chance = .001
pop = []
```

We start by building our initial population out of random parts. Their original fitness will be very low: about 13% or less. We will maintain a pool of 300 individual paths, which we call chromosomes:

```
for i in range(population):
  pop.append(make_new_individual())
trainingData=[]
epochs = 100
```

Here we set up the loop to go through 100 generations of our natural selection process. We begin by computing the fitness of each individual and adding that score to a fitness list with an index pointing back to the chromosome:

```
for jj in range(epochs):
# evaluate the population
fitnessList = computeFitness(pop,GOAL,learningRate, INITIAL_POS)
```

We sort the fitness to get the best individuals. We sort in inverse order. The largest number should be first:

```
fitnessList.sort(reverse=True)
```

We keep the top 50 % of the population and discard the bottom 50%. The bottom half is out of the gene pool as being unfit:

```
fitLen = 150
fitnessList = fitnessList[0:fitLen]
# survival of the fittest...
```

We pull out the top performer from the whole list and put it into the **hall of fame** (or **HOF**). This will eventually be the output of our process. In the meantime, we use the **HOF** (or **HOFF**) value as a measure of the fitness of this generation:

```
hoff = pop[fitnessList[0][1]]
print("HOF = ",fitnessList[0])
```

We store the HOFF value to a `trainingData` list so we can graph the results at the end of the program:

```
trainingData.append(fitnessList[0][0])
newPop = []
for ddex in fitnessList:
newPop.append(pop[ddex[1]])
print ("Survivors: ",len(newPop))
```

At this phase, we have deleted the bottom 50% of our population, removing the worst performers. Now we need to replace them with the children of the best performers of this generation. We are going to use crossover as our mating technique. There are several types of genetic mating that can produce successful offspring. Crossover is popular and a good place to start, as well as being easy to code. All we are doing is picking a spot in the genome, and taking the first half from one parent, and the second half from the other. We pick our parents to "mate" randomly from the remaining population, weighted proportionally to their fitness. This is referred to as "roulette wheel selection". The better individuals are weighted more heavily and are more likely to be selected for breeding. We create 140 new individuals as children of this generation:

```
# crossover
# pick to individuals at random
# on the basis of fitness
numCross = population-len(newPop)-10
print ("New Pop Crossovers",numCross)
# #
# add 5 new random individuals
for kk in range(10):
newPop.append(make_new_individual())
for kk in range(int(numCross)):
p1 = roulette(fitnessList)[1]
p2 = roulette(fitnessList)[1]
chrom1 = pop[p1]
chrom2 = pop[p2]
lenChrom = min(len(chrom1),len(chrom2))
xover = randint(lenChrom)
# xover is the point where the chromosomes cross over
newChrom = chrom1[0:xover]+chrom2[xover:]
```

Our next step is mutation. In real natural selection, there is a small chance that DNA will get corrupted, changed by cosmic rays, mis-copying of the sequence, or other factors. Some mutations are beneficial, and some are not. We create our version of this process by having a small chance (1/100 or so) that one gene in our new child path is randomly changed into some other value:

```
# now we do mutation
bitDex = 0
for kk in range(len(newChrom)-1):
mutDraw = random.random()
if mutDraw < mutate_chance:
# a mutation has occured!
bit = randint(26)
newChrom[kk]=bit
#print ("mutation")
newPop.append(newChrom)
```

Now that we have done all our processing, we add this new child path to our population, and get ready for the next generation to be evaluated. We record some data and loop back to the start:

```
# welcome the new baby from parent 1 (p1) and parent 2 (p2)
print("Generation: ",jj,"New population = ",len(newPop))
pop=newPop
mp.plot(trainingData)
mp.show()
```

So, how did we do with our mad genetic experiment? The following output chart speaks for itself:

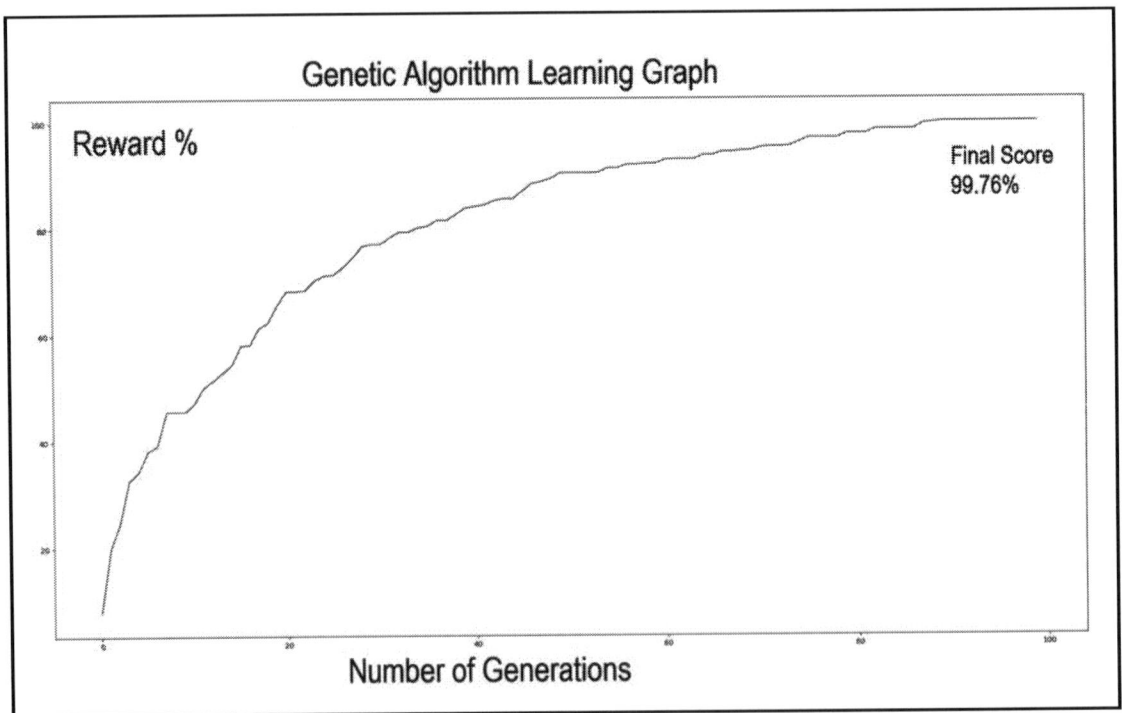

The genetic algorithm, for all it seems like a bit of voodoo programming, works quite well as a machine learning tool for this specific case of training our robot arm. Our solution peaked at 99.76% of the goal (about 2 mm) after just 90 generations or so, which is quite fast for an AI learning process. You can see the smooth nature of the learning that shows that this approach can be used to solve problems in path planning for our robot arm. I have to admit that I was quite skeptical about this process, but it seems to work quite well for this particular problem domain.

The programming really was not too hard, and you can spend some time improving the process by tweaking the parameters of the genetic algorithm. What if we had a smaller population? What if we changed the fitness criteria? Get in there and muck about and see what you can learn.

Other robot arm machine-learning approaches

The realm of robot arm control via machine learning is really just getting started. There are a couple of research avenues I wanted to bring to your attention as you look for further study. One way to approach our understanding of robot movement is to consider the balance between exploitation and exploration. Exploitation is getting the robot to its goal as quickly as possible. Exploration is using the space around the robot to try new things. The path planning program may have been stuck on a local minimum, and there are better solutions available that had not been considered.

There is also more than one way to teach a robot. We have been using a sort of self-exploration in our training. What if we could show the robot what to do and have it learn by example? We could let the robot observe a human doing the same task, and have it try to emulate the results.

Google's SAC-X

Google is trying a slightly different approach to the robot arm problem. In their **SAC-X** program, which stands for **Scheduled Auxiliary Control**, they surmise that it can be quite difficult to assign reward points to individual movements of the robot arm. They break down a complex task into smaller auxiliary tasks, and give reward points for those supporting tasks to let the robot build up to a complicated challenge. If we were stacking blocks with a robot arm, we might separate picking up the block as one task, moving with the block in hand as another, and so on. Google referred to this as a "sparse reward" problem if they only did reinforcement on the main task, stacking a block on on top of another. You can imagine in the process of teaching a robot to stack blocks that there would be thousands of failed attempts before a successful move resulted in a reward.

Amazon Robotics Challenge

Amazon has a lot of stuff. Millions and millions of boxes, parts, bits, and things fill their shelves. They want to get the stuff from the shelves into small boxes so they can ship the stuff to you as fast as possible when you order it. For the last few years, Amazon has sponsored the Amazon Robotics Challenge, where they invited teams from universities in to use robot arms to pick up items off a shelf and, you guessed it, put them into a box. When you consider that Amazon sells almost everything imaginable, this is a real challenge. In 2017, a team from Queensland, Australia won the challenge with a low-cost arm and a really good hand tracking system.

Summary

Our task for this chapter was to use machine learning to teach the robot how to use its robot arm. We used two techniques with some variations. We used a variety of **reinforcement learning**, called **Q-learning**, to develop a movement path by selecting individual actions based on the robot's arm state. Each motion was scored individually as a **reward**, and as part of the overall path as a **value**. The process stored the results of learning into a Q-matrix that could be used to generate a path. We improved our first cut at the reinforcement learning program by indexing, or encoding, the motions from a 27-element array of possible combinations of motors to a number from 0 to 26, and likewise indexing the robot state to a state lookup table. This resulted in a 40x speedup of the learning process. Our Q-learning approach struggled with the large number of states that the robot arm could be in.

Our second technique was a **genetic algorithm**. We created individual random paths to make a **population**. We created a **fitness function** to score each path against our goal, and kept the top performers from each generation. We then **crossed** genetic material from two somewhat randomly selected individuals to create a new child path. The genetic algorithm also simulates **mutation** by having a slight chance of random changes in steps in the path. The results for the genetic algorithm had no problem with the state space complexity of our robot arm, and generated a valid path after just a few generations.

Questions

1. In Q-learning, what does the Q stand for (you will have to research this on the internet).
2. What could we do to limit the number of states that the Q-learning algorithm has to search through?
3. What effect does changing the learning rate have on the learning process?
4. What function or parameter serves to penalize longer paths in the Q-learning equation? What effect does increasing or decreasing this function have?
5. In the genetic algorithm, how would you go about penalizing longer paths so that shorter paths (fewer number of steps) would be preferred?
6. Look up the SARSA variation of Q-learning. How would you implement the SARSA technique into program 2.
7. What effect does changing the learning rate in the genetic algorithm change? What is the upper and lower bound of the learning rate?
8. In the genetic algorithm, what effect does lowering the population cause?

Further reading

- Zocca, Spacagna, Slater, Roelants. *Python Deep Learning,* Packt Publishing, April 2017.
- Joshi, Prateek. *Artificial Intelligence with Python,* Packt Publishing, January 2017.
- *AI Junkie: Genetic Algorithm- A Brief Overview.* Retrieved at `http://www.ai-junkie.com/ga/intro/gat2.html`.
- *Basic Reinforcement Learning Tutorial 2: SARSA,* `https://github.com/vmayoral/basic_reinforcement_learning/tree/master/tutorial2`.
- *Google DeepMind Blog: Learning by Playing (Robot Arm (SAC-X)),* `https://deepmind.com/blog/learning-playing/`.
- *Amazon Robotics Challenge Competition,* `https://blog.aboutamazon.com/amazon-robotics-challenge-winners-announced`.

6
Teaching a Robot to Listen

Teaching a robot to listen to spoken instructions is a whole discipline in itself. It is not sufficient for the robot to just recognize individual words, or some canned phrase. We want the robot to respond to normal spoken commands with a normal variety of phrasing. We might say, *Pick up the toys*, or *Please pick up all the toys*, or *Clean this mess up!*, any of which would be a valid command to instruct the robot to begin searching the room for toys to pick up and put away. We will be using a variety of techniques and processes for this chapter. We are going to be building on an open source *verbal assistant* called **Mycroft**. This is an AI-based speech recognition and natural language processing engine that can be programmed and extended by us. We will be adding some additional capability to Mycroft – we will use a technique I call the *fill in the blank* method of command processing to extract the intent of the user's voice instructions, so that the robot does what you want it to do, even if that is not exactly what you said. We will complete this chapter by teaching the robot to both tell and respond to a specific form of human communication – knock-knock jokes.

The following topics will be covered in the chapter:

- Natural language processing
- Reasoning from context
- Understanding intent
- Speech recognition (speech to text)
- Text to speech
- Call and response dialog for knock-knock jokes

Technical requirements

This chapter using the following tools:

- Mycroft Open Source Voice Assistant (`http://mycroft.ai`) – I had to build it from source from the GitHub repository, so expect to do the same to keep it compatible with the ROS (Robotics Operating System) we run the robot with.
- Python 3.2 (but you should be able to make 2.7 work as well).
- You will need a Git account at `https://github.com/`.
- I used the Google DIY Voice Kit (`https://aiyprojects.withgoogle.com/voice`), which provided a very nice set of speaker and stereo microphones for the Raspberry Pi. We will be using the hardware only.

Check out the following video to see the Code in Action:
`http://bit.ly/2MXj2HS`

Robot speech recognition

This is going to be a rather involved chapter, but all of the concepts are fairly easy to understand and I was very happy with the results I achieved when I developed this chapter. We will end up with a lot of collateral abilities for our robot that we are getting *for free*, and will end up with a very strong framework to build voice recognition and commands upon. Let's get right to it.

What are we doing?

We set several goals for our robot in Chapter 2, which included being able to give voice commands to the robot, since we may be using the robot without a base station. I also wanted the robot to be able to interact with my grandchildren, and specifically to be able to tell and respond to knock-knock jokes, a favorite activity of my grandson, William.

We can break this process down into several steps, which we will be handling independently. We need the robot to be able to *hear*, or have the ability to convert sound into a digital form. We need to process sounds into words, which is to say, turn sounds into text.

We need to not just recognize individual words, but to combine those words into sentences and from those sentences, infer the intent of the speaker to understand what the robot is to do. We do not want to use canned or memorized speech commands, but rather have the robot be able to do some **natural language processing** (NLP) to create a form of robot understanding of the spoken word.

For example, if we want to have a command for *pick up a toy*, we humans could phrase that several ways: *grab a toy, grasp a toy, pick up that toy car*, or even *get that*. We want the robot to understand or at least respond to all of those utterances with the same action, to drive to the nearest toy and pick it up with the robot arm.

The other half of the interface is that the robot needs to respond back by speaking. Text-to-speech systems are fairly commonplace today, but we would like to have some natural variations in the robot's speech patterns to help make the illusion that the robot is smarter than it really is.

Our steps for this chapter are as follows:

1. Receive audio (sound) inputs.
2. Convert those sounds into text that the robot can process.
3. Use processing on those text words to understand the intent of the speaker.
4. Use that intent as a command to perform some task.
5. Provide verbal responses in the form of spoken words (text to speech) back to the operator to confirm the robot heard and understood the command.
6. Create a custom verbal interface that both tells and responds to knock-knock jokes.

Speech to text

In the rest of this chapter, we will be implementing an AI-based voice recognition and response system in the robot and creating our own custom voice interface. We will be using Mycroft, an open source voice activated *digital assistant* that is adept at understanding speech and is easily extended for new functions and custom interfaces.

The process we will use for voice interaction with the robot follows this script:

1. **Wake word** (Hey, Albert)
2. Pause for the robot to make a **beep** sound to show it is listening
3. Command or query from human (*move forward one step*)
4. Robot responds verbally (*moving forward six inches*)

There are two forms of text-to-speech involved in this process that greatly simplify matters for the robot. First, the robot is listening continuously for only one sound – the *wake word*. This is a specific sound that just means one thing – get ready to process the next sound into a command. Why is this necessary?

Since the robot has only a very small processor – the Raspberry Pi – it really does not have the sort of onboard compute power to run a robust speech-to-text (STT) engine. But it can run a simple sound recognizer that can listen for just one thing – the *wake word*. You are familiar with this from other voice command systems, such as Alexa or Siri, that also either use a special wake word or a button to have the interface pay attention.

Once the wake word is received, the Raspberry Pi switches into record mode, and records the next thing we say. It then transfers that information to an online system, the Google Cloud Speed to Text system (the same thing that runs the Google Assistant).

How does the robot recognize the wake word? The speech system we will be using, the open source system **Mycroft**, uses one of two methods. The first is a **phoneme recognition** system called Sphynx. What the heck is a **phoneme**? You can understand that words are made up out of individual sounds, which we roughly assign to letters of the alphabet. An example would be the *p* sound in the word *pet* or *pick*. We make the *pppp* sound by putting our lips together. The burst of sound we make is identifiable as a *P* sound – this is a phoneme. The word Albert has several phonemes – the *A* sound, (*ah*), the *L* sound, the *B*, the *ER* together (*errrr*), and finally, the *T*. The letters we associate with the sounds – the *ch* in *cherry*, the *er* in Albert, are called graphemes, as they graphically represent these sounds. We could say that the speech-to -text problem is one of mapping these phonemes to graphemes, but we know that this is too easy – English has all sorts of borrowed words and phrases where the pronunciation and the spelling are far apart.

The frontend of the Mycroft speech recognition process uses phonemes to recognize the wake word. You will find that it is quite sensitive. I had no problem getting the speech processor to receive the wake word from eight feet away. When we get to the setup section, we will change the default Mycroft wake word from *Hey, Mycroft,* to *Hey, Albert*.

What is the other method for receiving the wake word? Mycroft can also use a trained neural network that has been taught to recognize entire words all at once by their spectral power graph. What is a spectral graph? Your voice sound is not one frequency of sound energy – it is a complex congregation of different frequencies produced by our mouths and vocal cords. If we spoke in pure frequencies, we would sound like a flute- pure tones at mostly one frequency. We can use a process called a fast **fourier** transform to convert a selection of speech into a graph that shows the amount of energy (volume) at each frequency. This is called a **spectral plot** or **spectral graph**. The low frequencies are at the left, and higher frequencies at the right. Most of human speech energy is concentrated between frequencies between 300 Hz and 4,000 Hz. Each word has a unique distribution of sound energy amounts in these frequencies, and can be recognized by a neural network in this manner:

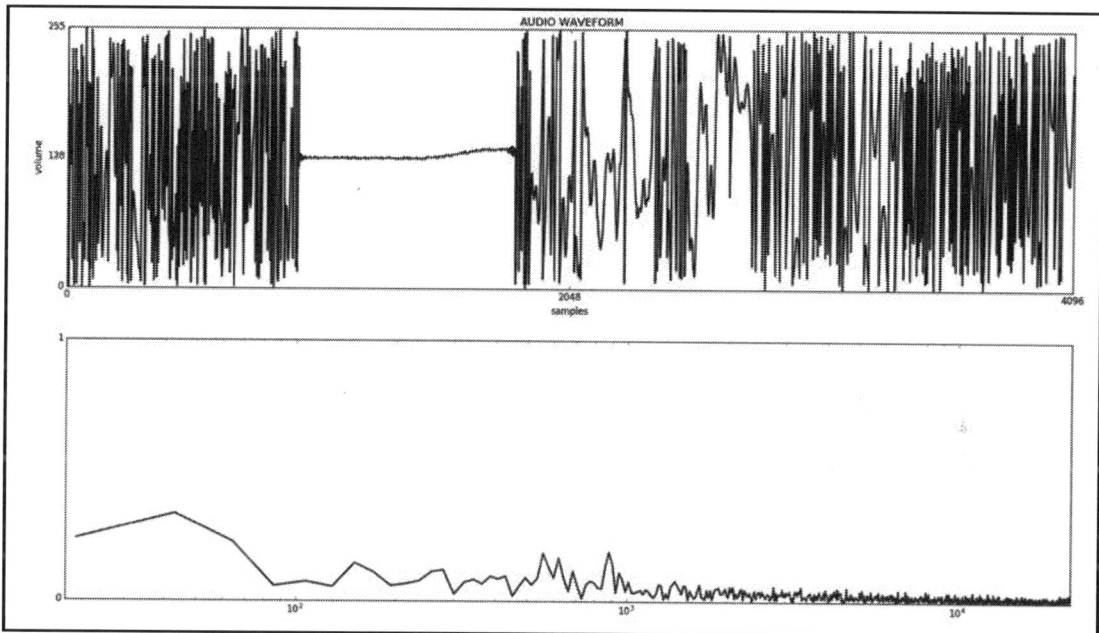

This preceding diagram shows both the audio wave form (top graph) in the time domain, and the spectral plot in the frequency domain for the phrase *Hey, Albert.*

Both the phoneme method and the neural network method use spectral plots to recognize sounds as words, but the phoneme process divides words into individual sounds, and the neural network listens and recognizes the entire word all at once. Why does this make a big difference? The phoneme system can be developed to recognize any word in English without reprogramming or retraining, while the neural network has to be trained on each word individually, and hopefully by a lot of different speakers with a lot of different accents.

You can remember from the neural networks chapter that we needed labeled data to train a neural network. You recall we had pictures in categories and trained on each category. Training ANNs for sound is the same: we need sounds and the associated words. Can you think of a place to get samples of lots of different voices where you also have the exact written script to match? Ever listened to a book On tape?

Our next step after receiving the wake word is to record the next sounds that the robot hears. The Mycroft system then transfers that audio data over the internet to the Google online speech-to-text engine (`https://cloud.google.com/speech-to-text/`). This is a quick way to resolve the problem of our little Raspberry Pi not having enough processing power or storage to have a robust speech recognition capability.

What goes on the in the Google Cloud? The STT engine breaks the speech down into phonemes (sounds) and uses a neural network to assign the most probable graphemes (letters) to those sounds. The output would be spelled out more phonetically than want to receive. For example, the sentence *How many ounces in a gallon?* will come out *HH AW . M EH N IY . AW N S AH Z . IH N . AH . G AE L AH N.* (source: *CMU Pronouncing Dictionary*) How is this the case? What happened? These are the phonemes that make up that sentence. The periods indicate spaces between words. Now the system has to convert this into the words we are expecting. The STT system uses word rules and dictionaries to come up with the most likely conversion into regular words. This includes both expert systems (word rules) as well as trained neural networks that predict output words based on phonemes. We can call this step the *language model*. Our STT outputs the sentence *How many ounces in a gallon?* and sends it back to the robot, all in less than 2 seconds.

So the robot receives the text *How many ounces in a gallon?* What do we do with it? Lets look at the sentence and break it down into its component parts, just like we did in grade school. The type of sentence is a question, as it starts with *How*. The subject of the sentence is *How Many*. The verb is *are*, which is implied in the form of the question (How many ounces **are** in a gallon). The object is *ounces* and the modifier (or adjective) is *in a gallon*.

Intent

The natural language processing we are doing has one aim, or goal. We are giving commands to our robot using a voice interface. Commands in English normally follow a sentence pattern, something like *You – do this*. Often the *you* subject of the sentence is implied or understood, and left out. We are left with statements like *Clean this room*, or *Pick up those toys*. The intent of these commands to to have the robot initiate a program that results in the robot picking up toys and putting them away. The robot and its processor have to divine or derive the intent of the user from the words that are spoken. What we want is for any reasonable sentence to have as it's meaning, *You, robot, start your pick up toys process*.

Think of how many ways we can say that command to the robot. Here are some examples:

- Let's clean up this room
- Put away the toys
- Pick up the toys
- Pick up all the toys
- Clean up this room
- Put those away
- Put this away
- Time to clean up

What do these phrases have in common? They all imply the subject who is doing the action is the robot. There are no words like *You, robot, Tinman* to indicate to whom the command in intended. The word *toys* appears a lot, as does *pick, clean*, and *put away*. It is possible that we can just pay attention to those keywords to understand this command. If we get rid of all the common conjunction and pronoun words, what does the list look like?

- Clean room
- Put toys
- Pick toys
- Pick toys
- Clean room
- Put away
- Put away
- Time clean

An important concept for this chapter is to understand that we are not trying to understand all speech, but only that subset of speech that are commands that the robot can execute. That list is fairly short. The robot can only be told to pick up toys, drive around, move its arm, and stop. That is about it.

A general solution to this voice recognition problem would be to have some ability to predict from the command given to the robot, the likelihood that intent of the user points to one command more than any of the others. You can see that in the case of the word *clean,* none of our other commands (drive around, move arm, or stop) relate to *clean* at all. Thus a sentence with *clean* in it most probably is associated with the pick up toys command.

This process of deciding intent will be used later in this chapter to send commands to the robot. We will use an open source AI engine called Mycroft to accomplish this.

Now we are going to jump right into programming the TinMan robot to listen and understand commands using a open source artificial intelligence package called Mycroft. Mycroft is a version of a digital assistant similar to Siri from Apple or Alexa from Amazon, in that it can listen to voice commands in a mostly normal fashion and interface those commands to a computer. We are using it because it has an interface that runs on a Raspberry Pi 3.   Here we go.

Mycroft

Installing Mycroft on Rapsberry Pi 3.

Hardware

One of the few things that the Raspberry Pi did not come with is audio capability. It has no speakers or microphones. I found a quick and effective way to add that capability was to use an existing hardware kit that provided both a very high quality speaker and an excellent set of stereo microphones in a robot-friendly form factor. Note that this works only with the Raspberry Pi 3 board – it will not work with earlier Raspberry Pis.

The kit is the Google AIY Voice Kit. The website is `http://aiyprojects.withgoogle.com:`

The original kit contains a **hat** or accessory board for the Raspberry Pi 3 that sits on top of the main board and has interfaces for a speaker and a set of stereo microphones. If you want, you can use the Google Assistant API that goes with this kit, but I could not make it work with the ROS, which is critical for our robot to move.

I decided to use the Mycroft open source voice assistant software instead, which offered much of the same functionality but in a more user-friendly arrangement. We'll cover Mycroft in the next section after we get the hardware installed.

You will not need any of the cardboard that came with the kit. Turn off the Pi, and install the Voice Hat to the top of the Raspberry Pi 3 circuit board. Be careful to line up the pins.

The next step is to connect the speakers with the screw terminals. Connect the microphones via the JST connector. This is the connector on the top that has the five wires. That ends the hardware part of the setup.

Turn on your Raspberry Pi 3 with the new speaker and microphone.

Now we can dive into the software.

We are going to get the software drivers for the Google AIY Voice Kit from the GiHhub site for the project. We will just be using the drivers, but we have to download the whole thing.

Go to the Google AIY project Raspian GitHub site: `https://github.com/google/` `aiyprojects-raspbian`, and input the following code:.

```
Sudo apt-get update
Cd
```

Start the Pulse Audio daemon. You may need to reboot after this step:

```
pulseaudio -D
```

Go back to the `home` directory:

```
cd
```

Now we download the AIY project source code to our RasPi:

```
git clone https://github.com/google/aiyprojects-raspbian.git voice-
recognizer-raspi
cd ~/voice-recognizer-raspi
```

These scripts will install the audio drivers:

```
sudo scripts/configure-driver.sh
sudo scripts/install-alsa-config.sh
```

Now we must reboot the Pi:

```
sudo reboot
```

After rebooting, we can test the sound set up by playing some sound:

```
speaker-test -c2
```

This will play some white noise from the speakers. You can also try the following:

```
speaker-test -c2 --test=wav -w /usr/share/sounds/alsa/Front_Center.wav
```

This will say the phrase `Front-Center`. If you don't hear the sounds, try re-installing the drivers and rebooting, and also check your wires.

Mycroft software

While there are several ways to install Mycroft, we have to put Mycroft on top of the other software we have already. Since Mycroft has to get along with the ROS, and all of the artificial intelligence packages we installed, such as TensorFlow, Theano, and Keras, it is better that we use the `git clone` method to download the source code and build Mycroft on the Raspberry Pi:

```
git clone https://github.com/MycroftAI/mycroft-core.git
cd Mycroft-core
bash dev_setup.sh
```

Mycroft will create a virtual environment it needs to run. It also isolates the Mycroft package from the rest of the packages on the Raspberry PI.

> *Note*: Please do not install Mycroft as the root user (or super user). This will cause permissions problems with the configuration files. You may correctly guess that I tried this and did not like the results.

In order to get the Mycroft system to work in this manner, I also had to do one more step. The Mycroft system kept failing when I first tried to get it to run. It would quit or get stuck when I tried to start the debugger. In order to correct this problem, I had to recompile the entire system using the following steps:

```
sudo rm -R ~/.virtualenvs/Mycroft
cd ~/mycroft-core
./dev_setup.sh
```

Once that is done (and it took quite a while – as in several hours), you should be able to run the Mycroft system with the startup commands:

```
./start-mycroft.sh debug
```

You can start in debug mode or:

```
./start-mycroft.sh all
```

You can start in normal mode.

You will probably be using debug mode quite a bit when you are developing your speech commands.

Now test that Mycroft is working properly. When you first get Mycroft to run, it will want to be paired with your login account on the Mycroft web server. You need to set up a services account on the Mycroft website at `http://home.mycroft.ai`. Then the Raspberry Pi will give you a six-letter code to put into the website under **Devices** (on the **Hamburger** menu on the far right hand side of the website).

Once the robot is paired with the Mycroft server, it can transfer data back and forth. The wake word will start out being the default *Hey, Mycroft*. You can test that everything is working by first asking *Hey, Mycroft, what time is it?*.

Mycroft divides its capabilities into *skills* that are each controlled by a separate script. The Time skill is totally self-contained inside the Raspberry Pi. The robot should give you a voice response that is replicated on the debug console.

Next you can ask Mycroft a more advanced skill, like looking up information on the internet. Ask "Hey, Mycroft, how many ounces in a gallon?" Mycroft will use the internet to look up the answer and reply.

For the next step, you can change the wake word on the Mycroft website to something more appropriate – we did not name this robot Mycroft. We have been calling this robot *Tinman*, but you can choose to call the robot anything you want. You may find that a very short name like *Bob* is too quick to be a good wake word, so pick a name with at least two syllables. Go to the Mycroft web page (`http://home.mycroft.ai`) and log in to your account. If you have not yet created an account, now is your chance.

Click on your name in the upper right corner and select **Settings** from the menu. You can select several settings on this page, such as the type of voice you want, the units of measurement, and time and date formats. What we want to do is change the wake word from the default (*Hey, Mycroft*) to the name of our robot (*Hey, Tinman* or *Hey, Albert*). Select the small text **Advanced Settings** in the third paragraph of the page. This will take you to the page where we can change the wake word.

We change the first field **Wake word** to **Custom**. We change the next line to put in our custom wake word – *Hey, albert*. We also need to look up the phonemes for this wake word. Click on the **this tool** hyperlink to be taken to the **CMU Pronouncing Dictionary** at Carnegie Mellon University. Put in our phrase and you will get out the phoneme phrase **HH EY . AE L B ER T** . The phoneme syntax puts periods to show the spaces between words. Copy and paste this phrase and go back to the Mycroft page to paste the phoneme phrase into the **Phonemes** field. You are done – don't change any of the other settings. Hit **Save** at the top of the page before you navigate away.

You can test your new wake word back on the Rapsberry Pi. Start Mycroft up again in debug mode and wait for it to come up. Say your new wake phrase and enjoy the response. I have a standard test set of phrases to show Mycroft's skill at being the voice of our robot. Try the following:

- *Hey, Albert. What time is it?*
- *Hey, Albert. What is the weather for tomorrow?*
- *Hey, Albert. How many ounces in a gallon?*
- *Hey, Albert. Who is the queen of England?*

You should get the appropriate answers to these questions. Mycroft has many other skills that we can take advantage of, such as setting a timer, setting an alarm at a clock time, listening to music on Pandora, or playing the news.

What we will be doing next is adding to these skills by creating our own that are specific to our room-cleaning robot. Then we can do the knock-knock jokes.

Skills

The first skill we will create is a command to pick up toys. We are going to connect this command to the ROS to control the robot.

Dialogs

Our first step is to design our dialog on how we will talk to the robot. Start by making a list of what ways you might tell the robot to pick up the toys in the playroom. Here is my list:

- Let's clean up this room
- Put away the toys
- Pick up the toys
- Pick up all the toys
- Clean up this room
- Put those away
- Put this away
- Time to clean up
- Who made this mess?

You will note that there are several key words that are specific to the command to clean up the room. We have the word *clean*, of course. We have the phrase *pick up*, and *away*. We also have the words *toys* or *toy*, and finally *mess*. These key words will cue in the natural language processor, and allow some variation in the exact words used.

Next, we write down what we want the robot to say back. We don't want the same canned response each time; it would be good to have some natural variation in the robot's responses. Here is my list of responses, with a variety of robot attitudes represented:

- Command received – picking up toys.
- I am glad to hear the grandchildren came for a visit. I will pick up now.
- Picking up toys.
- Message understood – toy pickup commencing.
- Toy pick up mode initiated.
- Time to pick up toys.
- Mary Poppins does not live here, so do not start singing.
- This is my job – picking up toys is what I do.
- Toy pick operation start. Scanning for toys. Wow, there are a lot of toys!
- Toys again? OK, I have got this.

You can use as many of these as you want. The Mycroft system will grab a random phrase from this list. This gives us some room for creativity, and gives the illusion that the robot is more intelligent than it really is. This type of response system does work quickly for us to develop our dialogs.

We have to now create a skill, and fit it into the standard skills framework Mycroft uses. We will have to create a GitHub repository to put our skill into, and use Python to create a programming framework around the skill. Make sure you have a GitHub repository to put your skill into. Create a GitHub account if necessary (it's free). We start by forking the Mycroft Skill repository into our GitHub account.

Go to the Mycroft skills GitHub web page at `https://github.com/MycroftAI/mycroft-skills/`.

At the upper right, you will see three buttons: **Watch**, **Star**, and **Fork**. Hit the **Fork** button to create a copy of all the skills in your repository. We are going to use the skill template to make a new skill. Now we need to clone this repository so we can edit it. Log onto your Pi (or your development machine) and clone your repository. For me, it looked like this:

```
git clone https://github.com/FGovers/mycroft-skills-1
```

We need to create a new skill set of directories. This has to follow a specific pattern in order to work. We are going to copy the skill template (`00__skill_template`) to do this.

```
cp -R 00_skill_template skill__pickup_toys
```

What we end up with looks like this:

```
ls -l
 4 drwxrwxr-x 3 ubuntu ubuntu 4096 Jun 20 04:06 dialog
 4 -rw-rw-r-- 1 ubuntu ubuntu 2829 Jun 20 04:06 __init__.py
52 -rw-rw-r-- 1 ubuntu ubuntu 49360 Jun 20 04:06 LICENSE
 4 -rw-rw-r-- 1 ubuntu ubuntu 412 Jun 20 04:06 README.md
 4 -rw-rw-r-- 1 ubuntu ubuntu 164 Jun 20 04:06 requirements.sh
 4 -rw-rw-r-- 1 ubuntu ubuntu 79 Jun 20 04:06 requirements.txt
 4 drwxrwxr-x 3 ubuntu ubuntu 4096 Jun 20 04:06 vocab
```

The dialog directory contains subdirectories for each language you want the robot to speak, and contains the responses to our commands. We will use the `en-us` directory to put our US English responses, since that is what my speech system is set to. You may use `it-it` for Italian, and so on. The directories use the **IETF Language Tag** (Internet Engineering Task Force), which you can look up at `https://en.wikipedia.org/wiki/IETF_language_tag`. Other examples are `de-de` for German, and `en-au` for Australian English.

We will create a file called `pickup.toys.dialog` and put our responses in it, one phrase per line. We can put multiple dialogs and multiple skills into a single skill category, but we will just put the `pickup toys` command in this example.

We also have the `vocab` directory. This directory contains our intent phrases. These are identified by a `.intent` file. We need to create a `PickupToys.intent` file in the `vocab/en-us` directory and put our command phrases we wrote in it:

```
~/Mycroft-skills-1/skill_pickup_toys/vocab/en-us/PickupToys.intent
Lets clean up this room
Put Away the toys
Pick up the toys
Pick up all the toys
Clean up
Put those away
Put this away
Time to clean up
Who made this mess
mess
toys
clean
```

You will also need to clear out the old .voc files that you got by copying the template. We can insert just the key words rather than the entire sentence, and the Mycroft Intent Engine will still activate this skill.

Now we can populate the Python code that will activate the command to the robot. We need to edit the __init__.py file in the skill_pickup_toys directory that we copied from the template.

We are going to import our parts from Mycroft (IntentBuilder, Mycroft Skill, getLogger, and intent_handler). We also import rospy, the ROS Python interface, and the ROS standard message String, which we use to send commands to the robot by publishing on the syscommand topic:

```
from adapt.intent import IntentBuilder
from mycroft.skills.core import MycroftSkill
from mycroft.util.log import getLogger
from mycroft import intent_handler
import rospy # ROS = Robotic Operating System
from std_msgs.msg import String # ROS string format for messages
__author__ = 'fxgovers'
```

This is the logger for Mycroft so that we can log our responses. Anything we put out to stdout, such as print statements, will end up in the log, or on the screen if you are in debug mode:

```
LOGGER = getLogger(__name__)
```

We set up the publisher for our syscommand topic in the ROS. This is how we send commands to the robot control program via the ROS publish/subscribe system. We will be publishing commands only, and the only message format we need is **String**:

```
pub = rospy.Publisher('/syscommand', String, queue_size=1000)
# define our service for publishing commands to the robot control system
# all our robot commands go out on the topic syscommand
def pubMessage(str):
 pub.publish(str)
```

Our Mycroft skill is created as a child object of the MycroftSkill object. We rename our skill object class to CleanRoomSkill:

```
class CleanRoomSkill(MycroftSkill):
def __init__(self):
super(CleanRoomSkill, self).__init__(name="PickupToys")
```

I can't explain why Mycroft has both an `init` method and an `initialize` method, but we need to follow the template. These commands set up the intent in the Intent Builder part of Mycroft and register our handler when any of our phrases are spoken. We refer to the dialogs we built earlier with `require("CleanRoomKeyword")`, so be careful that all the spelling is correct.

```
def initialize(self):
  clean_room_intent = IntentBuilder("PickupToys"). \
  require("PickupToys").build()
  self.register_intent(clean_room_intent, self.handle_clean_room_intent)
```

This section creates our handler for when the system has recognized one of our phrases, and we want to perform the action for this command. This is where we kick off the publish command to the robot's control program via the ROS using the `pubMessage` function we defined earlier:

```
def handle_clean_room_intent(self, message):
  self.speak_dialog("clean.up.room")
  pubMessage("PICK_UP_TOYS")
```

The rest of the program is just housekeeping. We need to define a stop handler and finally define a function to create the instance of our skill:

```
def stop(self):
  pass

def create_skill():
  return CleanRoomSkill()
```

In order for our skill to work, we need to copy our directory to `/opt/mycroft/skills`. From there, we can test it in debug mode. Remember to start the ROS Core service (**roscore**) first to receive the ROS messages.

Telling jokes – knock, knock

Our next section comes at the request of my grandson, William, who just adores knock-knock jokes. William is seven, so he is just the right age for this.

As you probably know, knock-knock jokes are a pun-based joke that always takes the same form.
(person 1) Knock, knock
(person 2) Who's there?
(person 1) Wooden
(person 2) Wooden Who?
(person 1) Wooden you like to know!

So the dialog is very simple. Several parts of it are automatic, such as the first two lines – *Knock, knock* and *Who's there?*. We can create a generic knock-knock joke in the following form:

1. *Knock, knock.*
2. *Who's there?*
3. *<word 1>*
4. *<word 1> who?*
5. *<punchline phrase>*

In defining our joke, you can see we just have two variable elements – the word in step 3, and the punchline phrase in step 5. Our word is repeated in step 4.

We begin by creating a joke database of literally one-line jokes, which we will put in a text file. Since we just have two elements, we can separate them by a slash /:

```
tarzan / tarzan stripes forever
orange / orange you glad I can tell jokes?
```

And so on. I'm providing you a database of about 10 jokes in the files section of the repository for this chapter. Please feel free to add all of your favorites, or send them to me and I'll add them.

In this first section, we will handle the case where the robot is telling the joke. We will start, like any skill, with the **wake word**, *Hey, Albert*. Then we need a phrase to indicate we want to hear a joke, so we will use variations on *Tell me a knock-knock joke*, such as *I want to hear a knock-knock joke*.

This will trigger our skill program to look up a joke. We will create several intents, or response capabilities, to respond to the user (or child) talking to the robot. We will start with the *who's there* **dialog intent**. That will let the robot know to proceed to the next part of the joke, which is to say our word. Then we disable the *who's there* dialog and enable a dialog for listening for *<word>* and the phrase *who*. Then we can deliver the final part of the joke by reciting the punch line phrase, and we are done.

We can start by creating our vocabulary files, of which we will need three. These are the things that the user will be saying to the robot. We have our first *tell me a knock, knock joke* phrase – so let's call that knockknock.voc and put the following in it:

```
Tell me a knock-knock joke
Can I have a knock-knock joke
Give me a knock-knock joke
Play me a knock-knock joke
```

Please note that the Mycroft speech-to-text system interprets the phrase *knock, knock* as *knock-knock* with a hyphen, so it is important to put that into our script.

That should be sufficient for our purposes. Feel free to elaborate on your end if you feel that more is needed. Now our second vocabulary is just *who's there*, so we can create this as a second `.voc` file, `whosthere.voc`, which contains the one line *Whos there*. Our final line is a bit trickier. We really only care about the keyword *who* to trigger the punchline, so we can look only for that in our third intent. Make a file called *who.voc* and put the one word *who* in it. Remember these all go in the `dialog/en-us` folder in our skill directory.

Now for our responses. We have one canned response, which is to reply to *tell me a knock-knock joke* with the phrase *knock, knock*. We don't need any sophisticated dialog system, we just have the robot say the knock-knock phrase.

We start by importing our libaries we need to call in this program, which are the `MycroftSkill` class and the `intent_file_handler` function:

```
from mycroft import MycroftSkill, intent_file_handler
```

We define our class skill as a child object of the `MycroftSkill` object – this is standard object-oriented design. We are inheriting all of the functions and data of the parent `MycroftSkill` and adding our own functionality to it. We create an `initialize` function and then call the parent `init` to execute the code of the parent class as well. We are augmenting the functionality of the parent `init` function. Without this call, we would be replacing the `init` function with our own, and might have to duplicate a considerable amount of work:

```
class Knockknock(MycroftSkill):
def __init__(self):
MycroftSkill.__init__(self)
```

The next step is to create our intent handler. The intent handler is called when the Intent Engine sees the key words that indicate that this is what we want. Whenever the user asks, *Do you know any knock-knock jokes*, or phrases with that meaning, this code will be invoked. We put our phrases into the `knockknock.intent` file and place that file in the `voc` directory:

```
@intent_file_handler('knockknock.intent')
  def handle_knockknock(self, message):
```

We now need to pick a joke from our database of wonderful, witty KKJs (knock-knock jokes). We will define our `pick_joke` function lower in the program. We get two parts from the joke database: the name to say after *who's there* and the punchline that ends the joke:

```
name,punchline = self.pick_joke()
```

We use the `get_response` function from `MycroftSkill` to have the robot make a statement and then wait for a reply, which will get turned into a text string and stored in the response variable:

```
response=self.get_response(announcement="knock, knock")
 # response will always be "who's there"
response=self.get_response(announcement=name)
```

Now we are at the part where the robot says the name, after replying to *who's there*. For example, the user says *who's there* and the robot replies *Harold*. What we are expecting next is for the user to say *Harold (or whatever name) who?*. We will check our response, and see if the word *who* is included. If it is not, we can prompt the user to follow along with the joke. We will only do this one time to keep from getting stuck in a loop. If they are not playing along, the robot will just continue:

```
response will be "name who"
# if end of respose is not the word who, we can re-prompt
if "who" not in response:
prompt = "You are supposed to say "+name+" who"
response=self.get_response(announcement=prompt)
```

We have moved through the joke, so now we get to say the punchline, such as *Harold you like a hug (How would you like a hug?)*. The robot is finished and we exit the routine; both the comedy routine and the program routine:

```
self.speak(punchline)
```

We need a function to read our joke database we defined earlier. The database has KKJs one per line, with a forward slash (/) between the name and the punchline. We read in all of the jokes, put them in a list, and then choose one at random using the (wait for it) `random.choice` function. We return the name and the punchline separately. We should only call this routine once per instance of the joke:

```
def pick_joke():
jokeFile="knockknock.jokes"
jfile = open(jokeFile,"r")
jokes = []
for jokeline in jfile:
jokes.append(jokeline)
```

```
joke = choice(jokes)
jokeParts = joke.split("/")
name = jokeParts[0]
punchline = jokeParts[1]
return name, punchline
```

We finish the program by defining our instance of the `Knockknock` class and returning that object to the calling program, `Mycroft`:

```
def create_skill():
  return Knockknock()
```

Receiving jokes – who's there?

The other end of the knock-knock joke concept is to receive a joke – where the child wants to tell the robot a joke. If you know any seven-year-olds, then you know that this is a requirement also – the child will want to tell the robot a joke as well.

The receiving dialog is pretty simple as well. The user will say *knock, knock,* which is the cue to the robot to go into the *receive knock-knock joke mode.* The robot then has only one response – *who's there.* We could also add *who is there?* if we want to keep to the common sci-fi concept that robots do not use contractions.

Note: Data, the android from *Star Trek: The Next Generation,* stated many times he was not able to use contractions, although the writers slipped up from time to time.

In order to create our schema for our new Mycroft skill, we will be using the Mycroft Skill Kit, or MSK. You can install MSK by typing `pip3 install msk`. MSK provides a dialog-driven approach to building skills that will make a framework, including all of the subdirectories for dialog files and vocabulary. This saves a lot of time, so let's try it out. The following is the dialog for creating the `receive knock-knock joke` code.

```
$ msk create
  Enter a short unique skill name (ie. "siren alarm" or "pizza orderer"):
recieveKnock
Class name: NockSkill
  Repo name: nock-skill

Looks good? (Y/n) n
  Enter a short unique skill name (ie. "siren alarm" or "pizza orderer"):
recieve Knock

Class name: RecieveKnockSkill
```

```
     Repo name: recieve-knock-skill

Looks good? (Y/n) y
 Enter some example phrases to trigger your skill:
 - knock knock
 -

 Enter what your skill should say to respond:
 - who's there
 -

 Enter a one line description for your skill (ie. Orders fresh pizzas from
the store): This skill recieves a knock knock joke from the user
 Enter a long description:
 > THis is the other half of the Knock Knock joke continuum - we are giving
the robot the ability to recieve knock knock jokes. The user says knock
knock, the robot responds whos there and so on
 >
 Enter author: Francis Govers
 Would you like to create a GitHub repo for it? (Y/n) Y
 === GitHub Credentials ===
 Username: **********
 Password:*********
 Counting objects: 12, done.
 Delta compression using up to 4 threads.
 Compressing objects: 100% (5/5), done.
 Writing objects: 100% (12/12), 1.35 KiB | 0 bytes/s, done.
 Total 12 (delta 0), reused 0 (delta 0)
 To https://github.com/FGovers/recieve-knock-skill
 * [new branch] master -> master
 Branch master set up to track remote branch master from origin.
 Created GitHub repo: https://github.com/FGovers/recieve-knock-skill
 Created skill at: /opt/mycroft/skills/recieve-knock-skill
```

We can then either log into the GitHub repository and edit the program, or edit the source code at /opt/Mycroft/skills/receive-knock-skill. The program is still the __init__.py file.

A Mycroft skill is a function that is called when one of its phrases is recognized by the Mycroft Intent Engine. As such, it has no body or main function, just a function definition for the create skill that instantiates a MycroftSkill object. The __init__ function does most of the work of setting up the various dialogs, intent handlers, and vocabulary for the skill. This arrangement works very well in our limited environment of giving the robot commands or telling jokes. We start with our imports, which are MycroftSkill and the intent_file_handler. We will also need the Time library to do some pauses:

```
from mycroft import MycroftSkill, intent_file_handler
 import time
```

Here is our class definition for our `RecieveKnock` class, which is a child class of the `MycroftSkill` object we imported. We start the `init` function by passing an `init` command back up to the parent class (`MycroftSkill`) and have it do its initialization. Then we add our custom functionality on top of that:

```
class RecieveKnock(MycroftSkill):
def __init__(self):
MycroftSkill.__init__(self)
```

This section is our intent handler for receiving a knock- knock joke (is it OK to make an acronym of this like KKJ?). We use the @ decorator to extend the intent handler, in this case, reading the parameters of the intent from a file called `knock.recieve.intent`. The intent handler just has our two key words, the immortal phrase: `knock, knock`. We are fortunate that all KKJs start exactly the same way, so we only have these two words.

After the `handle_knock_recieve` function has been activated by the Intent Engine seeing the phrase *knock, knock*, we then get control passed to our handler. What is our next step? We reply with the single answer *Who is there*. You will remember we said robots do not use contractions.

We use a different function next. We don't want to use another intent handler, but fortunately Mycroft provides a free-form interface called `get_response`. You need to look up the documentation for this versatile function, but it makes our joke routine a lot simpler. The `get response` function both lets us speak our reply (`who is there`) and then receive whatever the user says next, and store it as a string into the variable `response`:

```
@intent_file_handler('knock.recieve.intent')
def handle_knock_recieve(self, message):
response =self.get_response('who.is.there')
```

Now that we have our response, we can just repeat it back with the robot's voice, with the additional word *who?*. So if the child says, *Howard*, the robot responds *Howard who?*.

We use `get_response` again to have the robot speak and then record whatever the child or adult says next. We don't need it, but we want to have the robot's speech system listen to whatever is said next. We toss away the response, but insert our own comment to the joke, from our dialog `veryfunny.dialog`, which is a file in the dialog directory. I added a sleep timer to allow everything to settle down before returning control. We include the standard `Stop` function required of all `MycroftSkills`, and make our `create_skill` function make a `RecieveCall` object and return it:

```
response2= response + " who?"

response3 =self.get_response(announcement=response2)
```

```
self.speak_dialog('veryfunny')
time.sleep(3)

def stop(self):
pass
def create_skill():
return RecieveKnock()
```

I created a `veryfunny.dialog` file to hold responses to our jokes from the robot. I tried to make some responses that the grandchildren would find funny. I guess I can add `robot joke writer` to my resume, as I seem to have done this a lot in my career.

You can get as creative as you want, but here are my suggestions:

```
That was very funny!
Ha ha ha
very good joke
I like that one. Thank you!
Ho HO! ho
that was cute!
I do not have a sound for a groan
ththththppppp!
```

Here is our directory structure and files for our *receive knock-knock jokes* skill:

```
receive-knock-skill directory:
init__.py
README.md
settingsmeta.json
./dialog/en-us:
knock.recieve.dialog
veryfunny.dialog
./vocab/en-us:
knock.recieve.intent
```

Remember the local version of the skill goes in the `/opt/mycroft/skills/recieve-knock-skill` directory. Now test to your heart's content – how many knock-knock jokes can you tell the robot?

Summary

This chapter introduced natural language processing for robotics, and concentrated on developing a natural language interface for the robot that accomplished three tasks: starting the "pick up toys" process, telling knock-knock jokes, and listening to knock-knock jokes. The concepts introduced included recognizing words by phonemes, turning phonemes to graphemes and graphemes to words, parsing intent from sentences, and executing computer programs with a voice interface. We introduced the open source AI engine, Mycroft, which is an AI-based voice assistant program that runs on the Raspberry Pi. We also wrote a joke database to entertain small children with some very simple dialog.

Questions

1. Do some internet research on why the AI engine was named Mycroft. How many different stories did you turn up, and which one did you like?

2. In the discussion of intent, how would you design a neural network to predict command intent from natural language sentences?

3. Rewrite the "Receive knock-knock jokes" to remember the jokes told to the robot by adding them to the joke database used by the "tell Knock Knock jokes" program. Is this machine learning?

4. Modify the "tell Jokes" program to play sounds from a wave file, such as a music clip, as well as doing text to speech.

5. The sentence structure used in this chapter is all based on English grammar. Other languages, such as French and Japanese, have different structures. How does that change the parsing of sentences? Would our program we wrote be able to understand Yoda?

6. Do you think that Mycroft's Intent Engine is actually understanding intent, or just pulling out key words?

7. Describe the voice commands necessary to instruct the robot to drive to an object and pick it up without the robot being able to recognize the object. How many commands to you need?

8. From step 7, work to minimize the number of commands. How many can you eliminate or combine?

9. Also from step 7, how many unique keywords are involved? How many non-unique keywords?

Further reading

- Thanaki, Jalaj. Python Natural Language Processing. 2017, Packt Publishing.
- Joshi, Prateek. Artificial Intelligence with Python. 2017. Packt Publishing.
- Mycroft tutorial for developing skills is located at: `https://mycroft.ai/documentation/skills/introduction-developing-skills/`.
- Additional documentation for using Mycroft is located at `https://media.readthedocs.org/pdf/mycroft-core/stable/mycroft-core.pdf`.

7
Avoiding the Stairs

This chapter covers path planning and navigation for our toy-grabbing robot helper. You have to admit that one of the most difficult problems in any ground robot is navigation. There are two parts to the task – figuring out where you are (localization), and then figuring out where you want to go (path planning). Most robots at this point would be using some sort of Simultaneous Localization and Mapping (SLAM) algorithm that would first map the room, and then figure out where the robot is within it. But is this really necessary? First of all, SLAM generally requires some sort of 3D sensor, which we don't have, and a lot of processing, which we don't want to do. We can also add that it does not use machine learning.

Is it possible to perform our task without making maps or ranging sensors? Can you think of any other robot that cleans rooms but does not do mapping? Of course you can. You probably even have a Roomba, as I do, and most models (with the exception of the 900 series) do not do any mapping at all – they navigate by means of a pseudo-random statistical cleaning routine.

Our task in this chapter is to create a reliable navigation system for our robot that is adaptable to our mission of cleaning a single room or floor of toys, and that uses the sensors we already have.

The following topics will be covered in this chapter:

- Mobile robot navigation concepts
- Vision processing
- The Floorfinder algorithm
- Vision-based navigation using neural networks
- Object recognition and navigation with neural networks
- Decision tree-based logic
- Goal-oriented behaviors
- Robot command and control

Technical requirements

We require the Robot Operating System (ROS) for this chapter. This book uses the Kinetic Kame release: `http://wiki.ros.org/kinetic/Installation`

This chapter assumes that you have completed chapter six, where we gave the robot a voice and the ability to receive voice commands. We will be using the Mycroft interface and voice text-to-speech system, which is called Mimic: `https://mycroft.ai/documentation/mimic/`

Check out the following video to see the Code in Action:
`http://bit.ly/2N6A06V`

Task analysis

As we do for each chapter, let's review what we are going to accomplish in this section. We will be driving the robot around the house, looking for toys. Once we have a toy, we will take that toy to the toy box and put it away by dropping it into the toy box. Then, the robot will go look for more toys. Along the way, we need to avoid obstacles and hazards, which include a set of stairs going down that would definitely damage the robot.

> I used a baby gate to cover the stairs for the first part of testing – and put pillows on the stairs for the second part. There is no need to bounce the robot down the stairs while it is still learning.

We are going to start with the assumption that nothing in this task list requires the robot to know where it is. Is that true? We need to find the toy box – that is important. Can we find the toy box without knowing where it is? The answer is, of course, that the robot can just search for the toy box until it locates it. We developed a technique for recognizing the toy box in an earlier chapter with a neural network.

Now, if the robot was doing a bigger job, like cleaning a 1,000,000 square foot warehouse, then we would need a map. But our task is to clean a single 16 x 16 room. The time lost searching for the toy box is not all that significant, considering we can't get too far away, and we have to drive to the toy box anyway.

We will set this as a challenge, then, to accomplish our task without making a map. What else do we need to do?

- Navigate the room avoiding obstacles (toys and furniture) and hazards (stairs)
- Find a toy
- Pick up the toy with the robot arm
- Carry the toy to the toy box
- Put the toy in the toy box
- Go and find another toy
- If there are no more toys, then stop

We've covered finding the toy and picking it up in other chapters. In this chapter, we will discuss driving up to the toy in order to pick it up.

I'm a big fan of the movie *The Princess Bride*. It has sword fights, cliffs, two battles of wits, and **Rodents of Unusual Size (ROUS)**. It also has a lesson in planning that we can emulate. When our heroes, Fezzik the Giant, Inigo Montoya, and Westley, plan on storming the castle to rescue the princess, the first things Wesley asks are *What are our liabilities? What are our assets?*

- **Our liabilities:** We have a small robot with a very limited sensor and compute capability. We have a room full of misplaced toys and a set of deadly stairs the robot can fall down.
- **Our assets:** We have a robot with tracks that can drive around, a voice, one camera, and a robot arm. The robot has a datalink via Wi-Fi to a control computer. We have this book. We have a toy box that is a distinctive color. And lots of **Toys of Usual Size (TOUS)**.

The appropriate next step, whether we are designing robots or invading castles, is to do some brainstorming. How would you go about solving this problem?

We could use SLAM and make a map, then locate the robot on the map, and use that to navigate. But to really do SLAM, we need more sensors.

What is SLAM?

SLAM is a common methodology for navigating indoor robots. The first problem we have in indoor robot driving is that we don't have a map. The second problem we have is that we have no frame of reference to locate ourselves – GPS does not work indoors. That is two problems – we need a map, and then we need a way to locate ourselves on that map. While SLAM starts with the letter "S" for Simultaneous, in truth, most robots make a map, store it away, and then drive on it later. Of course, while maps are being made, the robot has to make the map and then locate itself on the map–usually in the center.

How does SLAM work? The sensor usually associated with SLAM is the spinning LIDAR. You can think of **LIDAR** as a **laser radar** – it uses a laser to measure the distance to objects, and spins in a circle to collect data all around the robot. You can actually get a very small robot LIDAR, called the Rplidar, for around $100.00, and use it to make maps. There is an excellent ROS package called Hector Mapping that makes using this LIDAR fairly straightforward. You will find that SLAM is not a reliable process, and will require several fits and starts to come up with a map that is usable. Once the map is created, you have to keep it updated if anything in the room changes (such as, for instance, grandchildren leaving toys everywhere).

The SLAM process is actually very interesting, not for what happens in an individual scan, but in how scans are stitched together.
(There is an excellent video that the authors of Hector SLAM at the University Of Darmstadt, Germany, put together illustrating map making available at `https://www.youtube.com/watch?v=F8pdObV_df4list=PL0E462904E5D35E29` – Handheld Mapping in the Robocup 2011 Rescue Arena).

What we have to do in the SLAM process is to first take a sweep that measures the distance from the robot to all of the objects in the room. Then we move the robot some distance – for example, three inches forward. Then we take another sweep and measure the distances again. We now need to come up with a transformation that converts the data in the second sweep to line up with the data in the first sweep. To do this, there has to be information in the two sweeps that can be correlated – corners, doorways, edges, furniture. It can be difficult or impossible for SLAM to work in long, featureless hallways, for instance, as it simply has no information to work with – one lidar sweep looks just like the next. To help with this problem, many SLAM systems require the addition of other sensors to the robot, that measure wheel odometry or use optical flow to measure movement in order to provide additional data for the position estimate:

An illustration of a SLAM Map. The robot uses 500 particles for each LIDAR sample to estimate which changes in robot position best line up the lidar data with the data in the rest of the map. This is one of my earlier robot projects.

We can summarize SLAM as follows: The robot takes a measurement of the room by sweeping a laser rangefinder in a circle. The data returned is a list of distance measurements, where the angular measure is a function of the position in the list. If we have a list of 360 measurements in a circle, then the first number in our list is 0 degrees, the next is 1 degree, and so on. We can extract features in the LIDAR data by looking for corners, edges, jumps, and discontinuities. We look at the angle and distance to each feature from succeeding measurements, and create a function that gives the best estimate of how much the robot moved. We use that information to transform the LIDAR data from the sensor-centric coordinate system to some sort of room coordinate system, usually by assuming that the starting position of the robot is coordinate *0,0*. Our transform, or mathematical transformation, will be a combination of translation (movement) and rotation of the robot's body frame.

One way of estimating this transform is to use **particles**. We create samples of the robot's movement space of every point possible that the robot could have moved, and randomly place dots along all points. We compute the transform for each of these samples, and then test to see which sample best fits the data collected. This process is called a **particle filter**.

I wanted to give you a quick heads-up on SLAM so that we could discuss why we are not going to use it. SLAM is an important topic, and is widely used for navigation, but it is not the only way to solve our problem by any means.

The weaknesses of SLAM for our purposes include the following:

- The need for some sort of sweeping sensor such as LIDAR, which are expensive, mechanically complicated, and generate a lot of data. We want to keep our robot cheap, reliable, and simple.
- SLAM works better if the robot has wheel odometers, which don't work on tracked vehicles such as our TinMan. Tracked robots can also be referred to as **Skid steered** vehicles, because the tracks slide or skid over the surface in order to turn – we don't have Ackerman steering, like a car with wheels that point. When the track skids, it is moving over the surface without turning, which invalidates any sort of wheel odometry, which assumes that the wheels are always turning in contact with a surface.
- SLAM does not deal with floorplans that are changing. The TinMan robot has to deal with toys being distributed around the room, which would interfere with LIDAR and change the floorplan that SLAM uses to estimate position. The robot is also changing the floorplan as it picks up toys and puts them away.
- SLAM is somewhat computationally expensive.
- SLAM has problems if data is ambiguous, or if there are not enough features for the robot to estimate changes on. I've had problems with featureless hallways as well as rooms that where highly symmetrical.

Alternatives for navigation

We could do a process called **structure from motion** to get depth information out of our single camera, and use that to make a map. Structure from motion requires a lot of textures and edges, which houses may not have. It also leaves lots of voids (holes) that have to be filled in the map. Structure from motion uses parallax in the video images to estimate the distance to the object in the camera's field of view. There has been a lot of interesting work in this area, and I have seen some promising results. The video image has to have a lot of detail in it so that the process can match points from one video image to the next.

Here is a survey article on various approaches to Structure from Motion, if you are interested you can refer: `https://pdfs.semanticscholar.org/2ec3/` `32a1d0e73101eaecb0e066961a5e048464a1.pdf`.

We could just drive around randomly, looking for toys. When we find a toy, the robot picks it up, and then drives around randomly looking for the toy box. When it sees the toy box, it drives up to it and deposits the toy. We still need a method to avoid running over obstacles.

We could point the camera at the ceiling and use landmarks on the ceiling to determine our position. But the ceiling is mostly flat, and only has a few landmarks – a ceiling fan and a box with a movie screen hidden inside. But it does have lots of nice corners, and it is far enough away to get a good view. And this still does not handle obstacles.

You may not have heard about a technique called **floor finding** that is used in other robots – and self-driving cars. I learned about it from the DARPA Grand Challenge when this process was used by the winning car, Stanley, from Stanford University. I also learned a great deal about floor finding from the sophisticated algorithm written by Stephen Gentner in the software package RoboRealm, which is an excellent tool for prototyping robot vision systems. You can find it at `http://www.roborealm.com`.

What I will be presenting in this chapter is my version of a floor finder technique that is different from RoboRealm or Stanley, but that accomplishes the same results.

The concept is pretty simple. We know that the floor directly in front of the robot is free from obstacles. We use the video image pixels of the area just in front of the robot as an example, and look for the same texture to be repeated farther away. We are matching the texture of the part of the image we know is the floor with pixels farther away. If the textures map, we mark that area **green** to show that it is drivable and free of obstacles. We will be using bits of this technique in this chapter. By the way, did you notice that I said **texture**, and not **color**? We are not matching the color of the floor, because the floor is not all one color. I have a brown carpet in my upstairs game room, which still has considerable variation in coloring. Using color matching, which is simple, just won't cut it. We have to match the texture, which can be described in terms of color, intensity (brightness), hue, and texture roughness (a measure of how smooth the surface is).

Let's try some quick experiments in this area with our image of the floor in my game room. There are several steps involved when doing this **for real**. We start with the image we get from the camera. In order to accelerate processing and make the most efficient use of bandwidth, we set the native resolution of our camera – which has a full resolution of *1900 x 1200* – down to a mere *320 x 240*. We are using a small computer, after all. We move that to our image processing program, using OpenCV. Our first step is to blur the image using the Gaussian blur function. The Gaussian blur uses a parabolic function to reduce the amount of high frequency information in the image – it makes the image fuzzier by reducing the differences between neighboring pixels. To get a sufficient amount of **blurring,** I had to apply the blur function three times with a *5 x 5* convolution kernel. We discussed convolution kernels in the chapter on neural networks. This smoothing makes the colors more uniform, making the next steps easier.

We designate an area in front of the robot to be an area with a clear view of the floor. I used a triangular area, but a square area works as well. I picked each of the colors found in the triangle and grabbed all of the pixels that had a value with 15 units of that color. What does 15 units mean? Each color is encoded with an RGB value from 0 to 255. Our carpet color brown is around 162, 127, 22 in red, green, and blue units. We select all the colors that are within 15 units of that color, which, for red, is from 147 to 177. This selects the areas of the image similar in color to our floor. Our wall is a very similar brown or beige, but fortunately, there is a white baseboard that we can isolate so that the robot does not try to climb the walls.

Color is not the only way to match pixels in our floor. We can also look for pixels with a similar hue (shade of color, regardless of how bright or dark it is), pixels with the same saturation (darkness or lightness of color), and colors with the same value, or luminosity (which is the same result as matching colors in a monochrome image or grayscale image).

I compiled a chart illustrating this principle:

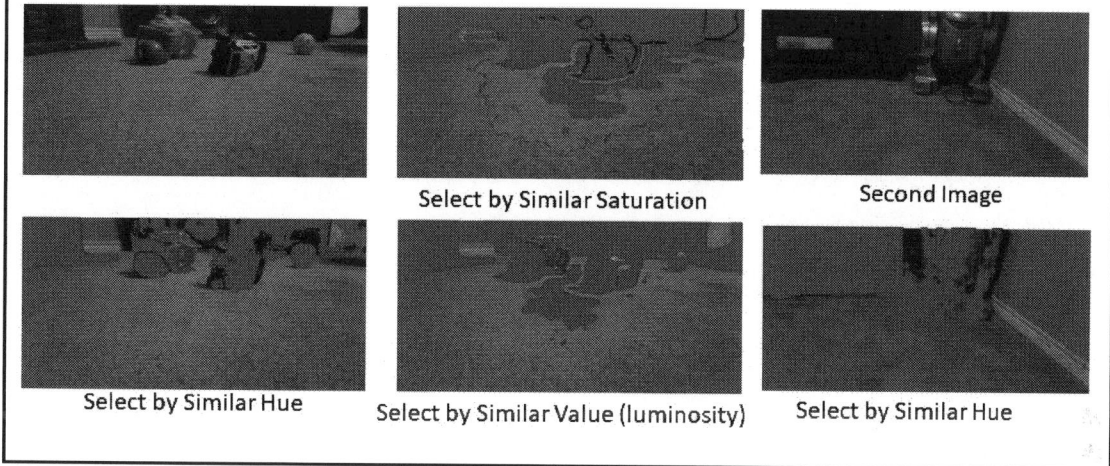

Selection by Different Attributes:

Select by Similar Saturation

Second Image

Select by Similar Hue

Select by Similar Value (luminosity)

Select by Similar Hue

The following diagram shows the ability of various selection attributes (color, hue, saturation, and luminosity) as a tool to perform floor finding for our robot. The Hue attribute seems to provide the best results in this test. I tested it on another image to be sure it was working. It seems to be missing the baseboards.

We select all of the pixels that match our floor colors and paint them green – or, to be more correct, we create a mask region in a copy of the image that has all of the pixels we want designated somehow. We can use the number 10, for instance. We make a blank buffer the size of our image, and turn all of the pixels in that buffer to 10 that would be the floor in the other image.

Performing an `erode` function on the masked data can help in this regard. There may be small holes or noise where one or two pixels did not match our carpet colors exactly – say there is a spot where someone dropped a cookie. The Erode function reduces the level of detail in the mask by selecting a small region – for example, *3 x 3*, and setting the mask pixel to 10 only if all of the surrounding pixels are also 10. This reduces the border of the mask by one pixel and removes any small **speckles** or dots that may be one or two pixels big. You can see from my diagram that I was quite successful in isolating the floor area with a very solid mask, which I painted green for you.

Given that we now know where the floor is, we paint the other pixels in our mask **red**, or some number signifying that it is unsafe to travel there. Let's use 255:

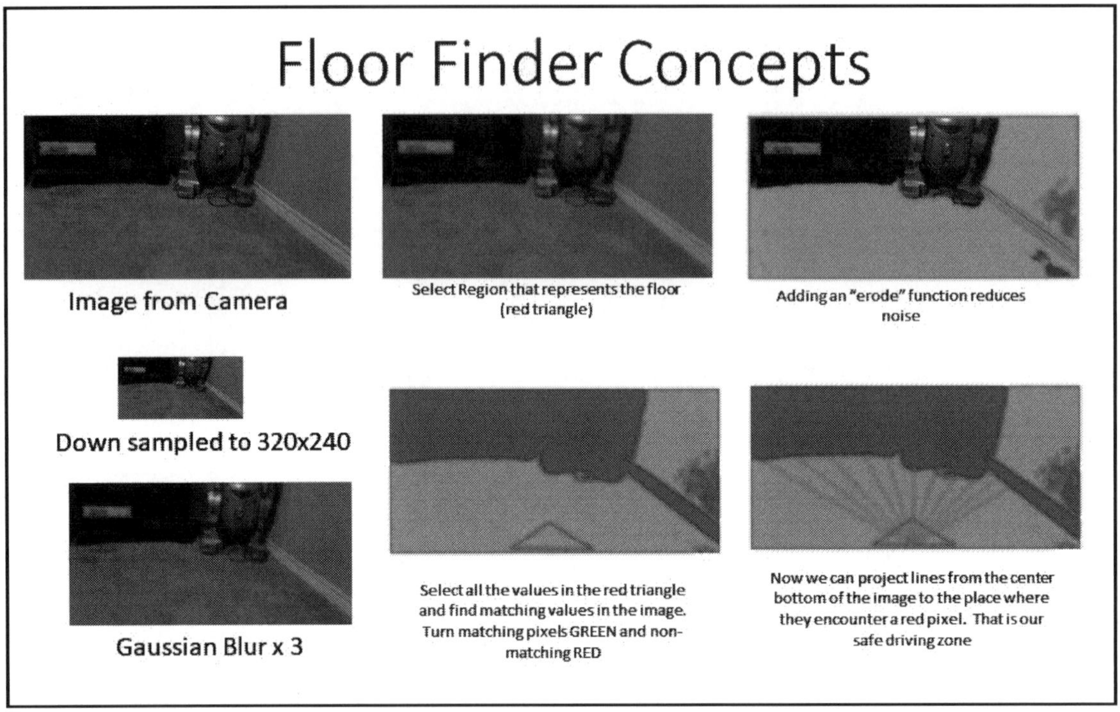

Floor Finder Concepts

Image from Camera

Select Region that represents the floor (red triangle)

Adding an "erode" function reduces noise

Down sampled to 320x240

Gaussian Blur x 3

Select all the values in the red triangle and find matching values in the image. Turn matching pixels GREEN and non-matching RED

Now we can project lines from the center bottom of the image to the place where they encounter a red pixel. That is our safe driving zone

My version of the floor finder algorithm has the steps illustrated here. Note that it does a very good job in this case of identifying where it is safe to drive. The projected paths are required to prevent the robot from trying to drive up the wall. You get bonus points if you can identify the robot in the corner.

Our next step may take some thought on your part. We need to identify the areas that are safe to drive. There are two cases in using this process that may cause us problems. We may have an object in the middle of the floor by itself – like a toy – that has green pixels on either side of it. We may also have a concave region that the robot can get into but not out of. In the preceding diagram, you can see that the algorithm painted the wall pixels green, since they match the color of the floor. There is a strong red band of no-go pixels where the baseboard is. To detect these two cases, we project lines from the robot's position up from the floor and identify the first red pixel we hit. That sets the boundary for where the robot can drive. You can get a similar result if you trace upward from the bottom of the image straight up until you hit a red pixel, and stop at the first one.

Let's try this process again, but add some toys to the image so that we can be sure we are getting the result we want:

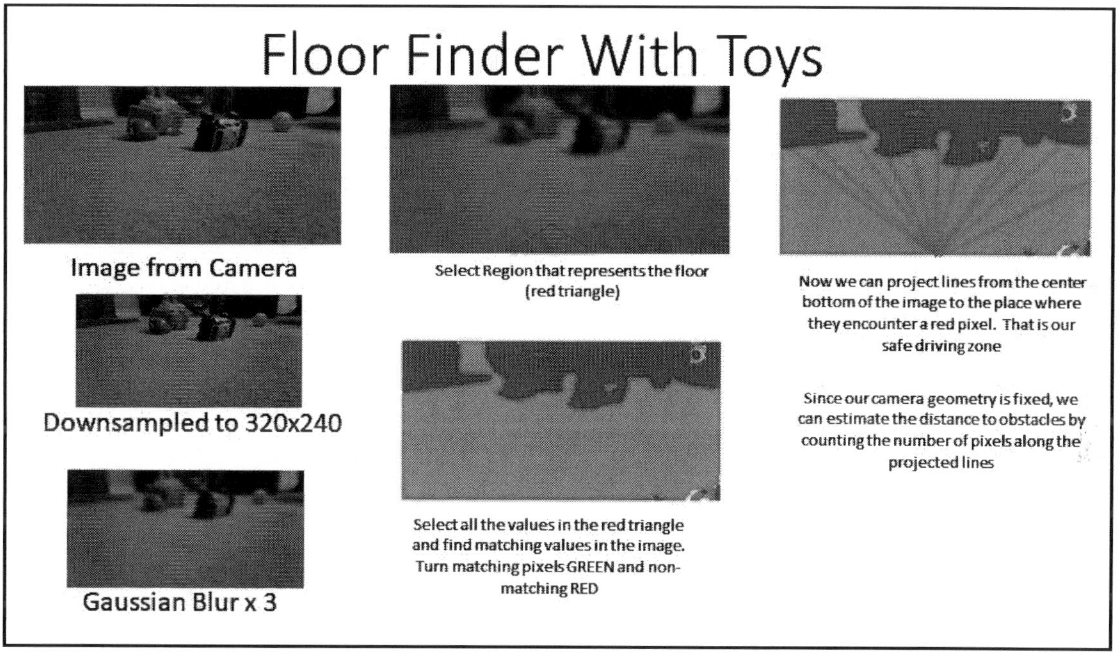

Floor Finder With Toys

Image from Camera

Downsampled to 320x240

Gaussian Blur x 3

Select Region that represents the floor (red triangle)

Select all the values in the red triangle and find matching values in the image. Turn matching pixels GREEN and non-matching RED

Now we can project lines from the center bottom of the image to the place where they encounter a red pixel. That is our safe driving zone

Since our camera geometry is fixed, we can estimate the distance to obstacles by counting the number of pixels along the projected lines

That seems to be working well. We are able to find a good path to drive on. Keep in mind that we are constantly updating the obstacle view with the Floor Finder and updating our path as we drive.

Another trick we can use with this process is to use the fixed camera geometry to do distance and size estimates. We have a "locked down" camera – it is fixed in position on the robot, a set height from the floor, and, therefore, distance along the floor can be measured from the y value of the pixels. We would need to carefully calibrate the camera by using a tape measure and a box to match pixel values to distance along the same path line we drew from the robot base to the obstacle. The distances will be non-linear and only valid out to the distance the pixels continue to change.

Since the camera is perpendicular to the floor, we get a certain amount of perspective effect that diminishes to zero about 20 feet from the camera. My calibration resulted in the following table:

Measurement in inches	Distance from top	Distance from bottom
0	1080	0
12	715	365
24	627	453
36	598.3	481.7
48	581.5	498.5
60	571.8	508.2
72	565	515

The image shows the technique for measuring distance in the robot camera field of view. The object is located four feet away from the robot base along the tape measure. Note that the robot easily sees its own treads in the foreground. TinMan uses a 180-degree fisheye lens on an HD-capable web camera.

One thing to watch out for are narrow passages that the robot will not fit into. We can estimate widths based on distance and pixels. One technique used by ROS is to put a border around all the obstacles equal to 1/2 the width of the robot. If there are obstacles on both sides, then the two borders will meet and the robot will know it does not fit.

Neural networks

How about this? We use a neural network to classify the images from our camera. We drive the robot around, and take a picture about four times a second. We record what the robot is doing at each picture – going forward, turning right, turning left, or backing up. We use that information to predict the robot's motion path given the image. We make a convolutional neural network, with the camera image as the input and four outputs – go forward, go left, go right, and back up. This has the advantage of avoiding obstacles and hazards automatically. When we get to the stairs (remember I have stairs going down in my game room that would damage the robot), the robot will know to turn around, because that is what we did in training. We are teaching the robot to navigate the room by example.

You may be yelling at the book at this moment (and you should be) saying *What about the toys?* Unless, of course, you are following my thought process and thinking to yourself, *Oh, that is why we just spent all that time talking about floor finder!*. The neural network approach will get us around the room, and avoid the hazards and furniture, but will not help the robot to avoid toys, which are not in the training set. We can't put them in this training set because the toys are never in the same place twice. We will use the floor finder to help avoid the toys. How do we combine the two? The neural network provides the longer range goal to the robot, and the floor finder modifies that goal to avoid local, short-range objects. In our program, we evaluate the neural network first and then then floor finder to pick a clear route.

On that theme, we are also going to pull another trick for training our robot. Since our floor surface is subject to change, and may be covered with toys, we will leave that part out of the training images. Before sending the image to the neural network, we'll cut the image in half and only use the top half.

Since our camera is fixed and level with the floor, that gives us only the upper half of the room to use for navigation. Our image is a 180-degree wide angle, so we have a lot of information to work with. This should give us the resiliency to navigate under any conditions:

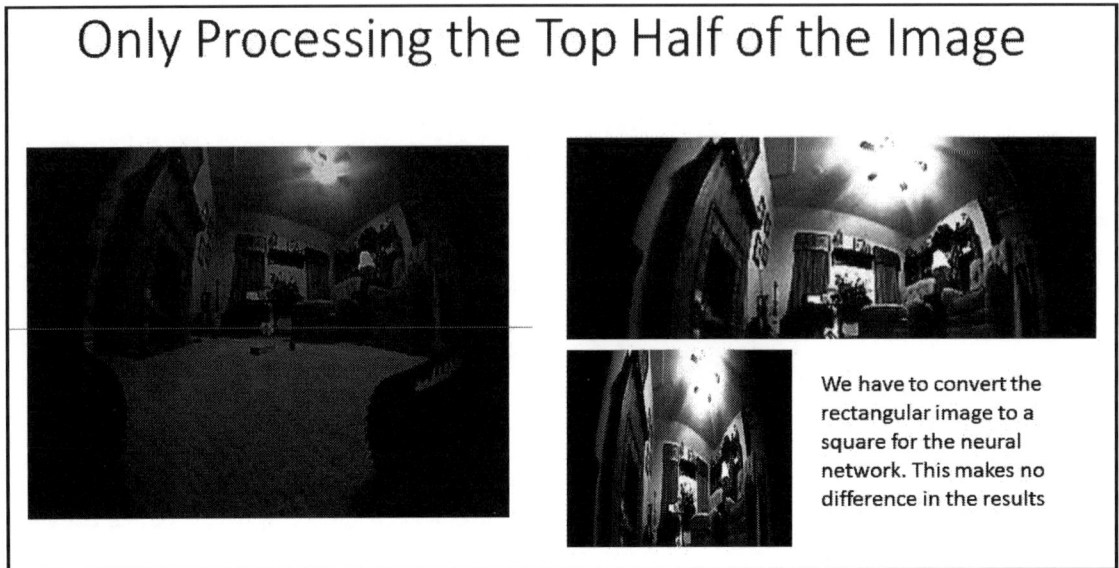

Only Processing the Top Half of the Image

We have to convert the rectangular image to a square for the neural network. This makes no difference in the results

Our second problem is locating the toy box. For that, we create a new training set of images. We start the robot in various random locations, and then simply drive to the toy box. We use exactly the same process we used before for navigation – we are creating a training set that tells the robot how to get to the toy box. The trick is to get a good sample of every possible starting location. We do have a bit of a break – if a point is already on one path, we don't need to cover it again. In other words, all points that are included in another path don't need to be repeated. We still want to have at least 1,000 images to train from both sets of images – the one that explores the room, and the set that drives to the toy box.

I created a simple program that just lets the operator drive the robot with a joystick, and takes a snapshot once a second. Each frame is labeled by simply looking at the value for the cmd_vel topic. If the angular velocity Z term (angular.z) is positive, we are turning right. If it is negative, we are turning left, and if the term is zero (you guessed it), we are driving straight ahead. I created an independent program that works with the camera and stores a snapshot whenever it receives a TAKE PIC LEFT/RIGHT/CENTER command on the ROS topic syscommand. These programs will be on the GitHub site for the book – I'm not going to include them here due to space limitations. We put each category of picture it its own subdirectory.

You can think of the neural network as working like this: We present an image to the neural network. It selects features from that image, and then selects the images that are most like the features in the image provided. It takes the matching labels from those training images, and produces a number of possible outputs – right, left, straight – that matched with the most features.

Processing the image

Now we have several steps to take before we can present our data to the neural network for training. Our camera on the robot has way too much resolution for what we need for the network, and we want to use the minimum amount of data in the neural network we can get away with:

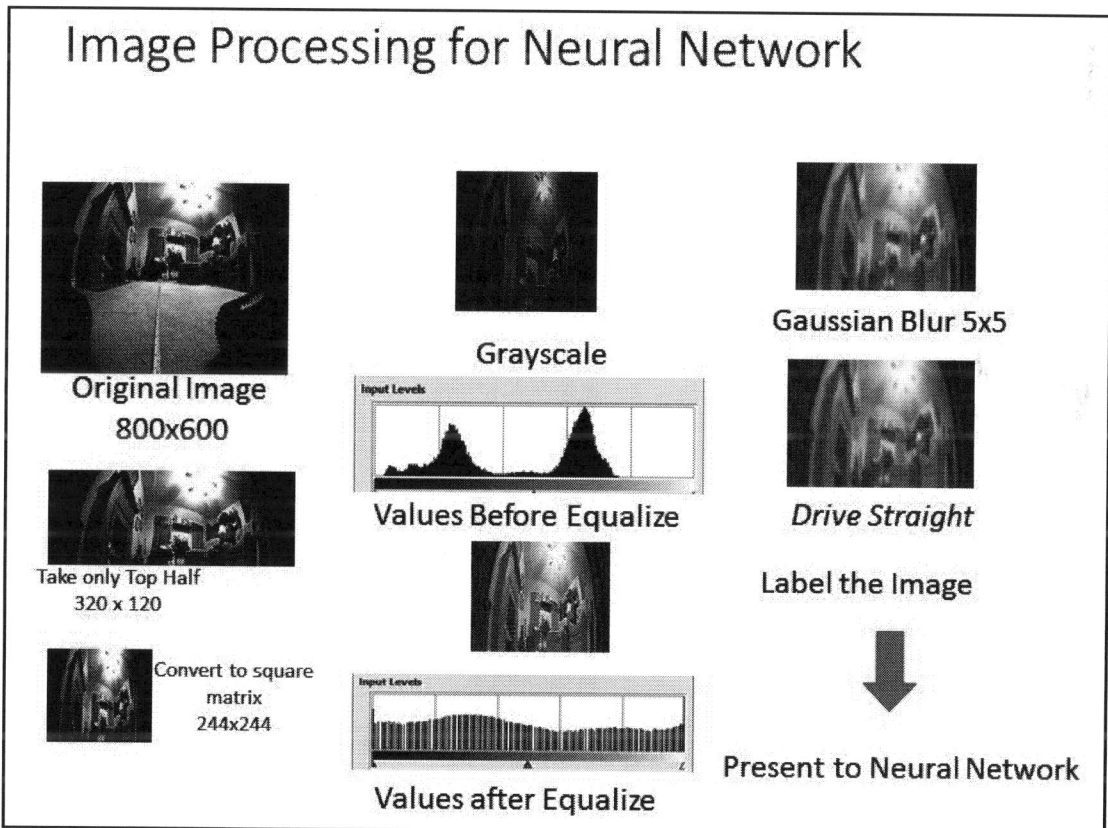

Image Processing for Neural Network

Original Image
800x600

Take only Top Half
320 x 120

Convert to square matrix
244x244

Grayscale

Values Before Equalize

Values after Equalize

Gaussian Blur 5x5

Drive Straight

Label the Image

Present to Neural Network

Our first step is to downsample the image to 320 x 200. We cut the image in half, and keep only the top half, which eliminates the floor from our consideration. We resize the rectangular image to 244 x 244, which is an appropriate size for our neural network to process. We convert the image to black and white, so that we only have one channel to process.

Our next step is to **equalize** the image, to take the entire range of possible values. The raw output of the camera contains neither pure white (255) nor pure black (0). The lowest value may be 53 and the highest, 180, for a range of 127. We scale the grayscale values by subtracting the low (53) and multiplying by the scale factor (127/255). This expands the range of the image to the full scale, and eliminates a lot of the variation in lighting and illumination that may exist. We are trying to present consistent data to the neural network.

The next step is to perform a Gaussian blur function on the data. We want to reduce some of the high frequency data in the image, to smooth out some of the edges. This is an optional step, and may not be necessary for your environment. I have a lot of detail in the robot's field of view, and I feel that the blur will give us better results. It also fills in some of the gaps in the grayscale histogram left by the equalization process in our previous step, which you can see in the diagram.

We also have to normalize the data to reduce the scale from 0-255 to 0-1. This is to satisfy the artificial neural network's input requirements. To perform this operation, we just divide each pixel by 255. We also convert the data from the OpenCV image format to a NumPy array.

Our neural network is a nine-layer **convolutional neural network** very similar to the toy/not toy detector we made before. However, in our final step, rather than being a binary output determined by a binary classifier, we will use a Softmax classifier with three outputs – forward, left, or right turns. We can actually make more categories if we want to, and have *easy right* and *hard right* turns rather than just one level of turns. We could even add a "back up" category, but let's try with the simple model first, and have three outputs. Remember that the number of output categories must match our training set labels exactly.

Our CNN has nine layers. The first six are pairs of convolution networks with max pooling layers in between. This lets the network deal with incrementally larger detail in the image. The final two layers are fully connected with ReLU (Rectifier Linear Units) activations. Remember, that ReLU only takes the positive values from the other layers. Our final layer is a Softmax classifier with three outputs:

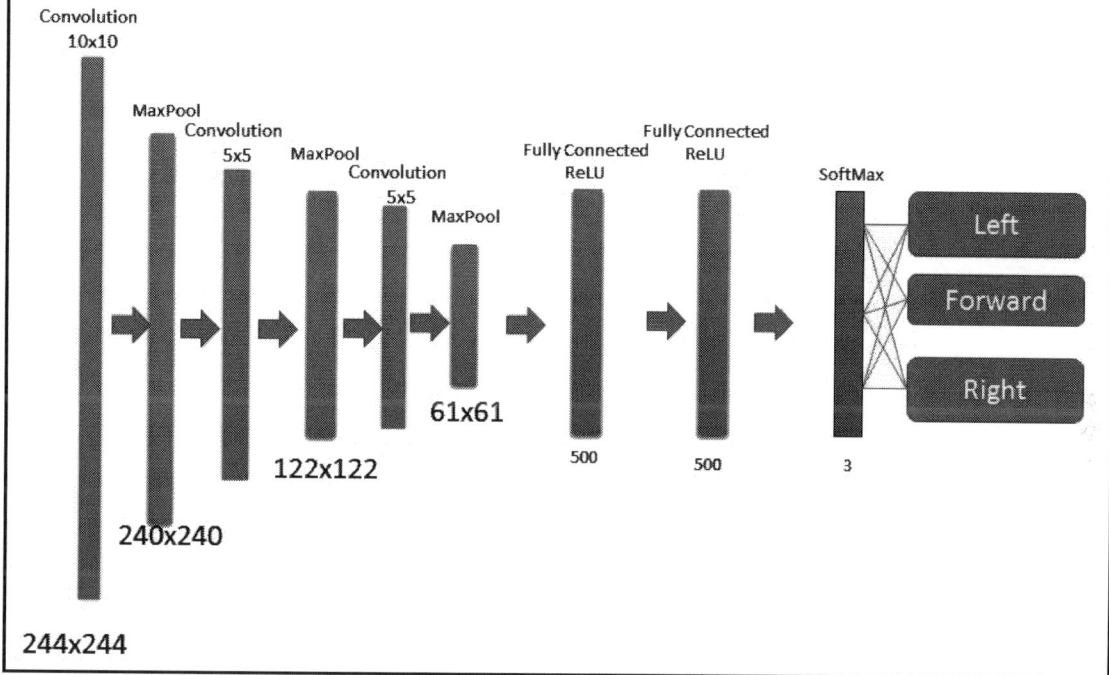

Like any other neural network training tasks, we have to split the input data into training sets and validation sets. We'll use 80% of our data on training and 20% on validation. We really can't use a process that **sweetens** the data by duplicating images with random rotations – as we did with the toy recognition program, since we are not just recognizing images, but using them for direction. Changing rotations would mess up our directions.

Training the neural network for navigation

Let's put our training program together here. We need to have collected our training data, by driving the robot around and recording our driving movements. This separated our data into three sets – left turn, right turn, and go straight. We have our training images in three subfolders to match our labels. We read in our data, associate it with the labels, and pre-process the data to present it to the neural network:

> I'm doing the training runs on my desktop computer, not on the Raspberry Pi. We'll deploy on the Raspberry Pi later with our fully trained networks.

```
# -*- coding: utf-8 -*-
"""
CNN based robot navigation - TRAINING program
@author: Francis Govers
"""
```

This program was partially inspired by Adrian Rosebrock's pyImageSearch blog and by the paper *Deep Obstacle Avoidance* by Sullivan and Lawson at the Naval Research Lab. Here are the imports that we need for this program – there are quite a few:

```
# import the necessary packages
from keras.preprocessing.image import ImageDataGenerator
from keras.optimizers import Adam
from sklearn.model_selection import train_test_split
from keras.preprocessing.image import img_to_array
from keras.utils import to_categorical
import matplotlib.pyplot as plt
import numpy as np
import cv2
import os

from keras.models import Sequential
from keras.layers.convolutional import Conv2D
from keras.layers.convolutional import MaxPooling2D
from keras.layers.core import Activation
from keras.layers.core import Flatten
from keras.layers.core import Dense
from keras import backend as K
```

Here is the setup for the convolutional neural network. We have three convolution layers, each followed by a maxpooling layer. Remember that each maxpooling layer will reduce the resolution of the image considered by the network by half, which is ¼ the data, because we halve the width and the height.

The convolution layers use the ReLU activation function, since we don't want any negative pixel values.

After the convolution layers, we have two fully connected layers with 500 neurons each. The final layer is our three neuron output layers, with a Softmax classifier that will output the percentage of each classification (left, right, center). The output will look like (0.8, 0.15, 0.05), with three numbers that add up to 1.

This is a generic convolution network class that can be reused for other things, as it is a general multi-class image classification CNN:

```
class ConvNet():
 @staticmethod
 def create(width, height, depth, classes):
 # initialize the network
 network = Sequential()
 inputShape = (height, width, depth)

 # first set of CONV => RELU => POOL layers
 network.add(Conv2D(50, (10, 10), padding="same",
 input_shape=inputShape))
 network.add(Activation("relu"))
 network.add(MaxPooling2D(pool_size=(2, 2), strides=(2, 2)))

 # second set of CONV => RELU => POOL layers
 network.add(Conv2D(50, (5, 5), padding="same"))
 network.add(Activation("relu"))
 network.add(MaxPooling2D(pool_size=(2, 2), strides=(2, 2)))

 # third set of CONV => RELU => POOL layers
 network.add(Conv2D(50, (5, 5), padding="same"))
 network.add(Activation("relu"))
 network.add(MaxPooling2D(pool_size=(2, 2), strides=(2, 2)))

 # Fully connected ReLU layers
 network.add(Flatten())
 network.add(Dense(500))
 network.add(Activation("relu"))

 network.add(Dense(500))
 network.add(Activation("relu"))
```

```
# softmax classifier
 network.add(Dense(classes))
 network.add(Activation("softmax"))

# return the constructed network architecture
 return network
```

Now we setup our learning regime. We will run 25 training runs, with a learning rate of 0.001. We set a batch size of 32 images per batch, which we can reduce if we end up running out of memory.

```
EPOCHS = 25
LEARN_RATE = 1e-3
BATCH = 32 # batch size - modify if you run out of memory
```

This section loads all of our images. We set the path here where the images reside. We put the three types of training images in folders called left, right and center. We will put all the images into a list called Images and likewise put the labels in an eponymous list:

```
print ("Loading Images")
 images=[]
 labels=[]
#location of your images
 imgPath = "c:\users\fxgovers\documents\book\chapter7\train\"
 imageDirs=["left","right","center"]

for imgDir in imageDirs:
 fullPath = imgPath + imgDir
 # find all the images in this directory
 allFileNames = os.listdir(fullPath)
 ifiles=[]
 label = imgDirs.index(imgDir) # use the integer version of the label
 # 0= left, 1 = right, 2 = center
 for fname in allFileNames:
 if ".jpg" in fname:
 ifiles.append(fname)
```

Now you can refer back to my diagram of the process we will go through to pre-process the images. We will cut the image in half and just process the upper half of the picture. Then, we reduce the image to 244 x 244 to fit into the neural network, which needs square images. We will convert the image to grayscale (black and white) since we don't need to consider color, just shapes. This cuts our data down further. We will equalize the image, which rescales the range of gray colors to fill the whole area from 0 to 255. This evens out the illumination and sets the contrast:

```
# process all of the images
for ifname in ifiles:
# load the image, pre-process it, and store it in the data list
image = cv2.imread(ifname)
# let's get the image to a known size regardless of what was collected
image = cv2.resize(image, (800, 600))
halfImage = 800*300 # half the pixels
# cut the image in half -we take the top half
image = image[0:halfimage]
#size the image to what we want to put into the neural network
image=cv2.resize(image,(224,224))
# convert to grayscale
image = cv2.cvtColor(image, cv2.COLOR_BGR2GRAY)
#equalize the image to use the full range from 0 to 255
# this gets rid of a lot of illumination variation
image = cv2.equalizeHist(image)
```

This is the Gaussian blur. This is an optional item – you may want to remove it if your room does not have a lot of detail. My game room has lots of furniture, so I think reducing the noise will improve performance:

```
# gaussian blur the image to remove high freqency noise
# we use a 5x kernel
image = cv2.GaussianBlur(img,(5,5),0)
```

We convert the image to a NumPy array of floats scaled from 0 to 1, instead of a set of integers from 0 to 255. We also put the number associated with the labels (left = 0, right=1, center = 3) into the matching label NumPy array:

```
# convert to a numpy array
image = img_to_array(image)
# normalize the data to be from 0 to 1
image2 = np.array(image, dtype="float") / 255.0
images=images.append(image)
labels.append(label)
labels = np.array(labels) # convert to array
```

We split the data into two parts – a training set that we use to train the neural network, and the testing set that we validate the training set with. We'll use 80% of the image samples for training and 20% for testing:

```
# split data into testing data and training data 80/20
(trainData, testData, trainLabel, testLabel) = train_test_split(data,
labels, test_size=0.20, random_state=42)
```

We have to convert the labels to be a tensor, which is just a particular data format:

```
# convert the labels from integers to vectors
trainLabel = to_categorical(trainLabel, num_classes=3)
testLabel = to_categorical(testLabel, num_classes=3)
```

Now, we build our actual neural network by instantiating the ConvNet object that actually builds our CNN in Keras. We set up the optimizer, which is ADAM, a type of adaptive gradient descent. **ADAM** stands for **Adaptive Moment Estimation**. ADAM acts against the error gradient like a heavy ball with friction – it has some momentum, but does not pick up speed quickly:

```
# initialize the artificial neural network
print("compiling CNN...")
cnn = ConvNet.build(width=224, height=224, depth=1, classes=3)
opt = Adam(lr=LEARN_RATE, decay=LEARN_RATE / EPOCHS)
model.compile(loss="categorical_crossentropy", optimizer=opt,
metrics=["accuracy"])
```

We train the network in this step. This will take quite some time to complete. We want the training to come out somewhere above 80%. If not, add some epochs to see where the learning curve levels off. If that still does not do the trick, you need more training images. I'm aiming for 1,000 images in each set, which is roughly 50 minutes of driving the robot around:

```
# train the network
print("Training network. This will take a while")
trainedNetwork = model.fit_generator(aug.flow(trainImage, trainLabel,
batch_size=BATCH),
validation_data=(testImage, testLable), steps_per_epoch=len(trainImage) //
BATCH,
epochs=EPOCHS, verbose=1)
# save the model to disk
print("Writing network to disk")
cnn.save("nav_model")
```

We are all done, so we save the model we created to disk so that we can transfer it to the Raspberry Pi.

Now make your second training set of driving from random locations to the toy box. Pick random spots and use the joystick to drive the robot to the toy box from each. Keep going until you have 1,000 images or so. Run these through the training program and label this model `toy box_model` by changing the last line of the program:

```
cnn.save ("toybox_model")
```

Convolutional neural network robot control implementation

This is great – we have built and trained our neural network. Now we need to put it to use to drive the robot around. We need to combine a program that sends out ROS commands with our neural network classification process. I added some commands through the ROS syscommand topic, which I use for non-periodic commands to my robots. Syscommand just publishes a string, so you can use it for just about anything:

```
# -*- coding: utf-8 -*-
"""
ROS Neural Network based Navigation Program
@author: Francis Govers
"""
# navigation program
# using neural network with ROS interface
```

We start with our imports from ROS, from OpenCV2, and from Keras, as we will be combining functions from all three libraries:

```
import roslib
import sys
import rospy
import cv2
from std_msgs.msg import String
from sensor_msgs.msg import Image
from geometry_msgs.msg import Twist
from cv_bridge import CvBridge, CvBridgeErrorfrom keras.preprocessing.image
import img_to_array
from keras.models import load_model
import numpy as np
```

This first section is the ROS interface. I like to encapsulate the ROS interface this way, with all of the publish and subscribe in one place. We have several topics to set up – we need to be able to send and receive commands on the `syscommand` topic. We will be publishing commands to the robot's motors on the `cmd_vel` topic. We receive images from the camera on the `image_topic`. We use callbacks to handle the event when a topic is published elsewhere on the robot. These can be called at any time. We have more control when we publish to a topic, which is handled using the `pubTwist` and `pubCmd` methods. I added flags to received commands and images so that we don't accidentally process the same image or command twice:

```python
class ROSIF():
 def __init__(self):
 self.bridge = CvBridge()
 self.image_sub = rospy.Subscriber("image_topic",Image,self.callback)
 self.cmd_sub = rospy.Subscriber("syscommand",String,self.cmdCallback)
 self.cmd_pub = rospy.Publisher("syscommand",String,queue_size=10)
 self.twist_pub = rospy.Publisher("cmd_vel",Twist,queue_size=10)
 self.newImage = False
 self.cmdReceived=""

 def callback(self):
 try:
 self.image = self.bridge.imgmsg_to_cv2(data, "bgr8")
 self.newImage = True
 except CvBridgeError as e:
 print(e)
 def cmdCallback(self,data):
 # receieve a message on syscommand
 self.cmdReceived = data.data


 def getCmd(self):
 cmd = self.cmdReceived
 self.cmdReceived = "" # clear the command so we dont do it twice
 return cmd
```

This function is the means for the rest of the program to get the latest image from the camera system, which is published on ROS on the `image_topic`. We grab the latest image and set the `newImage` variable to `False`, so that we know next time whether we are trying to process the same image twice in a row. Each time we get a new image, we set `newImage` to `True`, and each time we use an image, we set `newImage` to `False`.

```python
 def getImage(self):
 if self.newImage=True:
 self.newImage = False # reset the flag so we don't process twice
 return self.image
```

```
self.newImage = False
# we send back a list with zero elements
img = []
return img
```

This section sends speed commands to the robot to match what the CNN output predicts for us to do. The output of the CNN is one of three values: left, right, or straight ahead. These come out of the neural network as one of three enumerated values – 1, 2, or 3. We convert these back to left, right, and center values, and then use that information to send a motion command to the robot. The robot uses the Twist message to send motor commands. The Twist data message is designed to accommodate very complex robots, quadcopters, and omni wheel drive systems that can move in any direction, so it has a lot of extra values. We send a Twist.linear.x command to set the speed of the robot forward and backward, and a Twist.angular.z value to set the rotation, or turning of the base. In our case, a positive angular.z rotation value goes to the right, and a negative value to the left. Our last statement publishes the data values on the cmd_vel topic as a Twist message.

```
# publishing commands back to the robot
def pubCmd(self,cmdstr):
self.cmd_pub.publish(String(cmdstr)):

def pubTwist(self,cmd):
if cmd == 0: # turn left
turn = -2
speed = 1
if cmd==1:
turn = 2
speed = 1
if cmd ==3:
turn=0
speed = 1
# all stop
if cmd==4:
turn = 0
speed = 0
cmdTwist = Twist()
cmdTwist.linear.x = speed
cmdTwist.angular.z = turn
self.twist_pub.publish(cmdTwist)
```

We create a function to do all of our image processing with one command. This is the exact replica of how we pre-processed the images for the training program – just as you might think. You may think it a bit strange that I scale the image up, only to then scale it down again. The reason for this is to have detail for the vertical part of the image. If I scaled it down to 240 x 240 and then cut it in half, I would be stretching pixels afterward to get it square again. I like having extra pixels when scaling down. The big advantage of this technique is that it does not matter what resolution the incoming image is at – we will end up with the correctly sized and cropped image.

The other steps involve converting the image to grayscale, performing an equalization on the contrast range, which expands our color values to fill the available space, and performing a Gaussian blur to reduce noise. We normalize the image for the neural network by converting our integer 0-255 grayscale values to be floating point values from 0 to 1:

```
def processImage(img):
  # need to process the image
  image = cv2.resize(image, (640, 480))
  halfImage = 640*240 # half the pixels
  # cut the image in half -we take the top half
  image = image[0:halfimage]
  #size the image to what we want to put into the neural network
  image=cv2.resize(image,(224,224))
  # convert to grayscale
  image = cv2.cvtColor(image, cv2.COLOR_BGR2GRAY)
  #equalize the image to use the full range from 0 to 255
  # this gets rid of a lot of illumination variation
  image = cv2.equalizeHist(image)
  # gaussian blur the image to remove high freqency noise
  # we use a 5x kernel
  image = cv2.GaussianBlur(img,(5,5),0)
  # convert to a numpy array
  image = img_to_array(image)
  # normalize the data to be from 0 to 1
  image2 = np.array(image, dtype="float") / 255.0
  return image2
```

That is all of the setup. Now we go into the main program. We have to initialize our ROS node so that we can talk to the ROS publish/subscribe system. We create a variable, mode, that we use to control what branch of processing to go down. We make an interface to allow the operator to turn the navigation function on and off, and to select between normal navigation and our toy box seeking mode.

In this first section, we will load both neural network models that we trained before:

```
# MAIN PROGRAM
ic = image_converter()
rosif = ROSIF()
rospy.init_node('ROS_cnn_nav')
mode = "OFF"
# load the model for regular navigation
navModel = load_model("nav_model")
toyboxModel = load_model("toybox_model")
```

This section begins the processing loop that runs while the program is active. Running `rospy.spin()` tells the ROS system to process any message that may be waiting for us. Our final step is to pause the program for 0.02 seconds to allow the Raspberry Pi to process other data and run other programs:

```
while not rospy.is_shutdown():
  rospy.spin()
  time.sleep(0.02)
```

Summary

This chapter introduced some concepts for robot navigation in an unstructured environment, which is to say, in the real world, where the designers of the robot don't have control over the content of the space. We started by introducing SLAM, along with some of the strengths and weaknesses of map-based navigation. We talked about how Roomba navigate, by random interaction and statistical models. The method selected for our toy-gathering robot project, TinMan, combined two algorithms that both relied mostly on vision sensors.

The first was the floor finder, a technique used by the winning entry in the DARPA Grand Challenge. The FFA (Floor Finder Algorithm) uses the near vision (next to the robot) to teach the far vision (away from the robot) what the texture of the floor is. We can then divide the room into things that are safe to drive on, and things that are not safe. This deals with our obstacle avoidance. Our navigation technique used a trained neural network to identify the path around the room by associating images of the room from the horizon up (the top half of the room) with directions to travel. This also served to teach the robot to stay away from the stairs. We discarded the bottom half of the room from the image for the neural network because that is where the toys are. We used the same process to train another neural network to find the toy box.

This process was the same as before, but the training images were all labeled with the path from that spot to the toy box. This combination gave us the ability to teach the robot to find its way around by vision, and without a map, just like you do.

Questions

1. Regarding SLAM, what sensor is most commonly used to create the data that SLAM needs to make a map?
2. Why does SLAM work better with wheel odometer data available?
3. In the Floor Finder algorithm, what does the Gaussian blur function do to improve the results?
4. The final step in the floor finder is to trace upward from the robot position to the first red pixel. In what other way can this step be accomplished?
5. Why did we cut the image in half horizontally before doing our neural network processing?
6. What advantages does using the neural network approach provide that a technique such as SLAM does not?
7. If we used just a random driving function instead of the neural network, what new program or function would we have to add to the robot to achieve the same results?
8. How did we end up avoiding the stairs in the approach presented in the chapter? Do you feel this is adequate? Would you suggest any other means for accomplishing this task?

Further reading

- Sullivan and Lawson. "Deep Obstacle Avoidance" Naval Research Labs
- Rosebrock, Adrian. PyImageSearch Blog. Retrieved at https://www.pyimagesearch.com
- Bakker, Indra den. Python Deep Learning Cookbook. Packt Publishing, 2017
- Joshi, Prateek. Artificial Intelligence with Python. Packt Publishing, 2017.
- Zocca, V, Spacagna, G, Slater, D, and Roelants, P. Python Deep Learning. Packt Publishing, 2017

8
Putting Things Away

Imagine that you have to get to Grandma's house, which, according to legend, is *over the hills and through the woods*, and two states away. That would be two countries away if you live in Europe. To plan your trip, you can start in one of two ways. Ignoring the fact that Google has taken away most map reading and navigation skills from today's youth, you would get out a map and either:

- Start at your house and try to find the roads that are closest to a straight line to Grandma's house
- Start at Grandma's house and try to find roads leading to your home

From either direction, you will find that the road or path you seek forks, intersects, changes, meanders, and may even come to a dead end. Also, all roads are not created equally – some are bigger, with higher speed limits, and some are smaller, with more stop signs. In the end, you pick your route by the combination of decisions that results in the lowest cost. This cost may be in time – how long to get there. It may be in distance – how many miles to cover. Or it may be in monetary terms – there is a toll road that charges an extra fee.

We will be discussing several ways to solve problems involving choosing a chain of multiple decisions where there is some metric – such as cost – to help us select which combination is somehow the best.

There is a lot of information here that is widely used in robotics, and we will be expanding our horizons a bit beyond our toy-grabbing robot to look at robot path planning and decision making in general. These are critical skills for any robotics practitioner, so they are included here.

This chapter covers the basics of decision-making processes for artificial intelligence where the problem can be described in terms of either a classification problem (determining if this situation belongs to one or more groups of similar situations) or a regression problem (fitting or approximating a function that can be a curve or a path).

We will be applying the following machine learning or artificial intelligence techniques:

- Decision trees and random forests
- Path planning, grid searches, and the A* (A-Star) algorithm
- Dynamic planning with the D* (D-Star) technique
- Expert systems and knowledge bases

Finally, we will be applying two approaches to our robot problem – an expert system and random forests.

At first glance, the concepts we will cover in this section, namely path planning, decision trees, random forests, grid searches, and GPS route finders, don't have much in common, other than all being part of artificial intelligence computer algorithms. From my point of view, they are all basically the same concept and approach problems in the same way.

Technical requirements

We will be using PyKE – the Python Knowledge Engine – as our expert system. It can be installed from:

```
https://sourceforge.net/projects/pyke/?source=directory
```

The other tool you should have already installed from earlier chapters – Scikit_Learn:

```
http://scikit-learn.org/stable/developers/advanced_installation.html
```

Or if you have the pip installer in Python:

```
pip install —U scikit-learn
```

Check out the following video to see the Code in Action:
```
http://bit.ly/2PN1soo
```

Task analysis

Our task in this chapter is one that you may have been waiting for, if you have been keeping score since Chapter 3, where we discussed our storyboards. We need to choose a way to pick up the toys with the robot arm. This involves picking a proper orientation for the wrist joint. Since our toys are randomly placed, by those experts at random, my grandkids, the toy may be in any orientation relative to the floor, and at any angle relative to the robot. We need some method for observing the toy with the robot and appropriately orienting the robot's hand to grasp the toy.

Decision trees

The concept of a decision tree is fairly simple. You are walking down the sidewalk, and come to a corner. Here you can go right, turn left, or go straight ahead. That is your decision. After making the decision – turn left – you now have different decisions ahead of you than if you turned right. Each decision creates paths that lead to other decisions:

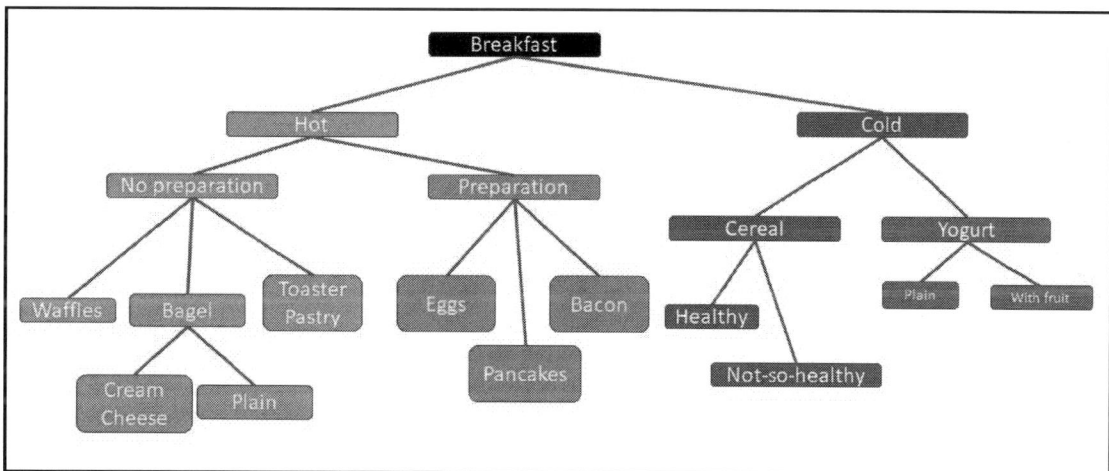

In this decision tree, I decide what to have for breakfast on any given morning. Should I make something, or get a prepared food out of the pantry? Hot or cold? Healthy or not?

Now as we are walking down the sidewalk, we have a goal in mind. We are not just wandering around aimlessly; we are trying to get to some goal. One or more combinations of decisions will get us to the goal. Let's say the goal is to get to the grocery store to buy bread. There may be four or five paths down sidewalks that will get you to the store, but each path may be different in length, or may have different paths. If one path goes up a hill, that may be harder than going the level path. Another path may have you wait at a traffic light, which costs time. We assign a value to each of these attributes, and generally want to pick the path with the lowest cost, or the highest reward, depending on the problem.

The general problem with decision tree type problems is one of exponential growth. Let's consider a chess game, a favorite problem set for artificial intelligence. We have 20 choices for an opening move (eight pawns and two knights, each with two possible moves). Each of these 20 moves has 20 possible next moves, and so on. So the first move has 20 choices, the second moves has 400 choices. The third move is 197,281 choices! We soon have a very, very large decision tree as we try to plan ahead. We can call each of these possible decisions a **branch**, the state we are in after making the decision is a **leaf**, and the entire conceptual structure is a **decision tree**.

Let me emphasize one very important concept for this chapter.

The secret to working with decision trees is to ruthlessly prune the branches so you consider as few decisions as possible

There are two ways to deal with a decision tree (actually, there are three – see if you can guess the third before I explain it…).

The first way is to start at the beginning, and work outwards towards your goal. You may come to a dead end, which means back-tracking or possibly starting over. We are going to call this **forward chaining** (chain, as we are making a path of links from leaf to leaf in the tree).

The other way is to start with the goal and work down the tree towards the start. This is **backward chaining**. The cool thing about backward chaining is that there are lot few branches to traverse. You can guess that a major problem with backward chaining is you have to know what all the leaves are in advance before you can use it. In many problems, such as a grid search or a path planner, this is possible. It does not work in chess, with an exponentially massive tree.

The third technique? No one says we can't do both – we could combine both forward and backward chaining and meet somewhere in the middle.

The choice of decision tree shapes, chaining techniques, and construction are based on:

- What data is available?
- What information is known or unknown?
- How is the path scored or graded?

There are also different kinds of solutions for path planning and decision trees. If you were given unlimited resources, the biggest computer, perfect knowledge in advance, and are willing to wait, then you can generate an **optimal path** or solution.

One of my lessons learned from years of developing practical AI-based robots and unmanned vehicles, is that any solution that meets all of the criteria or goals is an acceptable and usable solution, and you don't have to wait and continue to compute the perfect or optimal solution. Often then, a "good enough" solution is found in 1/10 or even 1/100 the time of an optimal solution, because an optimal solution requires an exhaustive search that may have to consider all possible paths and combinations.

What do we mean by pruning?

Sometime in the computer business, we have to make metaphors to help explain to people how something works. You may remember the "desktop metaphor" that Apple and later Windows adopted to help explain operating systems. Sometimes we just run those metaphors into the ground, such as the trash can to delete files, or "Clippy", the paper clip assistant.

You may feel that I've gone off the metaphorical deep end when I discuss **pruning** your decision trees. What's next, fertilizer and tree spikes? Actually, pruning is a critical concept in decision tree type systems. Each branch in your tree can lead to hundreds or thousands of sub-branches. If you can decide early that that branch is not useful, you can cut it out and you don't have to process any of the branches or leaves in that branch. The quicker you can discover that a path is not getting you to your goal, you reduce the time and effort involved in creating a solution, which is a real-time system like a robot, or a self-driving car, or autonomous aircraft, which can spell the difference between usable and worthless.

Let's run through a quick example. One great use for a decision tree process is **FDIR – Fault Detection, Isolation, and Recovery**. This is a typical function of a robot. Let's make a decision tree for FDIR in the case of our Tinman robot not moving. What automated steps could we take to detect the fault, isolate the problem, and then recover?

One technique we can use is root cause analysis, where we try to figure out our problem by systematically listing and then eliminating (pruning) causing factors and see if the symptoms match.

We will use a special form of decision tree called a **Fishbone diagram, or Ishikawa diagram**. This diagram is named after its inventor, Professor Kaoru Ishikawa from the University of Tokyo. In his 1968 paper, *Guide to Quality Control*, the Fishbone diagram is named because of its shape, which has a central spine and ribs jutting off on either side. I know, the metaphors are getting deep when we have a decision "tree" in the shape of a "fish".

Now we begin to have a problem. Remember that in a robot, a problem is a symptom, not a cause. Our problem is: the robot is not moving. What can cause this problem? Let's make a list:

- The drive system
- The software
- The communications system
- The battery and wiring
- The sensors
- Operator error

Now for each of these, we subdivide our branches into smaller branches. What parts of the drive system can cause the robot to not be able to move? The wheels could be stuck. The motors could not be getting power. The tracks could have fallen off. The motor driver could have overheated.

Here is my Fishbone diagram for the problem of the robot not moving:

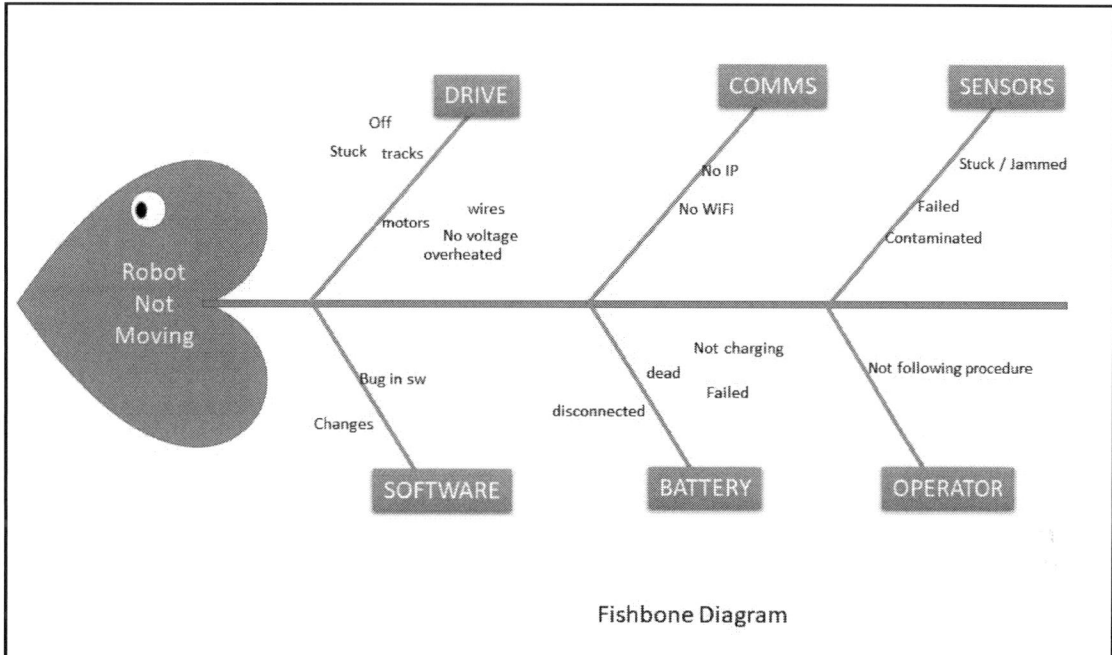

Fishbone Diagram

For each of these, you can consider what would be the symptoms of that problem being the cause? If the tracks have fallen off, the drive wheels would still be turning, but the tracks would not be moving. For the robot not to move, both tracks would have to be affected. If we can check any of these facts out, we can prune or eliminate the tracks from our diagram or decision tree. We check the tracks, and the drive wheels are not moving, so the tracks are not the cause. We prune that branch.

How about the battery? The battery can be in need of charging (dead battery), the battery could be disconnected, or a power wire could be loose. We check the battery voltage – that is OK, prune that leaf off the tree. We check the wiring – nothing loose. The battery branch gets pruned.

And so we go on until we have something that either matches all our symptoms, or is the last one left. Let's say the last branch was communications. Now what? We ask, "What things in communications would cause us not to move?" Our first answer is, motor command messages not getting through to our robot over the network. We check the log, and see indeed, no motor messages are present (cmd_vel, in our case). There is our problem, what caused the problem? The network could be broken (checked- no, network is OK), the IP address could be wrong (no, that's OK). We look to see if any recent changes were made to the control software, and indeed there were. We revert to the previous version, and see the robot moves. There is our problem and we used decision trees to find it.

So in this case, we solved our problem almost entirely by **pruning** branches and leaves off our tree until only one path was left, or we arrived at our goal.

How can we prune branches in software? We can look for dead ends. Dead ends are leaves – parts of the tree that end and have no future branches. When we reach a dead end, we can not only prune that leaf, but the parts of the path that exclusively lead to that branch. This would be a backward-chaining approach to pruning, as we start at the end and work backward.

We can also see sections of the tree that are unused, or never referenced or called. We can remove entire sections in this manner. This is forward pruning, because we are traversing the tree in the forward direction, from the front to the back.

Self-classifying decision trees and AI tools

Up to this point we, the humans in the story, have been making these decision trees by hand. We have not even discussed how we write a program to allow the robot to use trees to make decisions. Wouldn't it be a lot nicer if the computer was doing all the hard part of making the tree, deciding the branches, and labeling the nodes instead of us? That is exactly what we will do in this section.

Let's consider the problem of classifying toys. We may want to come up with a more efficient robot, which sorts toys in some manner instead of just dumping them in a box. In an ideal world, out of a population of 20 toys, we would have some characteristic that divided the group evenly in half – 10 and 10. Let's say it is length – half of the toys are under six inches long and half are over. Then it would also be ideal if some other characteristic divided each of those groups of 10 in half – to four groups of five. Let's say its color – we have five red toys, five blue toys, five green toys, and five yellow toys. Very nice and organized. You may recognize that we are doing what biologists do in classifying new species – we are creating a taxonomy. Now we pick another attribute that separates the toys into even smaller groups – it might be what kind of toy it is, or what size wheels it has. I think you get the picture

Let's look at an example.

Now what would be great is if we could list all the toys, and all the attributes in a table, and let the computer figure out how many groups and what kinds there are. We could create a table like this one:

Type	Length	Width	Weight	Color	Number of wheels	Noise	Soft	Material	Eyes	Toy Name
car	3	1	35	red	4	0	hard	metal	0	HotWheels
car	3	1	35	orange	4	0	hard	metal	0	HotWheels
car	3	1	35	blue	4	0	hard	metal	0	HotWheels
car	3	1	35	blue	4	0	hard	metal	0	HotWheels
car	3	1	35	white	4	0	hard	metal	0	HotWheels
stuffed	5	5	50	white	0	0	verysoft	fur	2	Plush
stuffed	7	5	55	brown	0	0	verysoft	fur	3	Plush
action	2	4	80	grey	0	0	hard	metal	0	slinky
build	2	2	125	wood	0	0	hard	wood	0	wood block 2x2
build	2	2	75	wood	0	0	hard	wood	0	wood block triangle
build	4	2	250	wood	0	0	hard	wood	0	wood block 4x2
dish	3	3	79	blue	0	0	hard	ceramic	0	teapot
aircraft	7	5	65	white	4	1	hard	plastic	0	space shuttle
aircraft	13	7	500	green	8	1	hard	plastic	0	Thunderbird 2

car	5	1	333	yellow	6	1	hard	metal	0	school bus
music	12	4	130	wood	0	2	hard	wood	0	toy guitar
music	5	2	100	yellow	0	1	hard	plastic	0	play microphone
music	4	4	189	white	0	2	hard	wood	0	toy drum

We have a problem we have to solve. We will be using a decision tree classifier that is provided with the Scikit-Learn Python package, called `DecisionTreeClassifier`. This program cannot use strings as input data. We will have to convert all of our string data into some sort of numeric figure. Fortunately, the Scikit library people have provided us with a function just for this purpose. Actually, they have provided several encoding functions that convert strings into numbers. The function we will use is called the `LabelEncoder`. This function takes an array of strings and converts it into an enumerated set of integers.

We can take our first column, which has the type of the toy. My nomenclature is toy = toy car, stuffed = stuffed animal, aircraft = toy aircraft, and music = toy musical instrument. Action is for action toys, and build stands for building toy (that is, blocks, Legos™, and so on). We'll have to turn these into some sort of numbers.

The `LabelEncoder` will convert a column in our data table that is populated with strings.

The toy type column from data is shown in the following code:

```
['car' 'car' 'car
' 'car' 'car' 'stuffed' 'stuffed' 'action' 'build' 'build' 'build' 'dish'
'aircraft' 'aircraft' 'car' 'music' 'music' 'music']
```

It converts it to the label encoded toy type:

```
[3 3 3 3 3 6 6 0 2 2 2 4 1 1 3 5 5 5]
```

You can see that everywhere where it said `car`, we now have the number 3. 6 = stuffed, 0=action and so on. Why the odd numbering? The encoder first sorts the strings in alphabetical order.

We are going to just dive right in from here to create a classification program. I'll explain things along the way, so at least follow along with the code.

Here is our decision tree classifier program:

```
# decision tree classifier
# author: Francis X Govers III
#
# example from book "Artificial Intelligence for Robotics"
#
```

We can import our libraries we will be using. There is an extra library called graphviz that is useful for drawing pictures of decision trees. You can install it with pip install graphviz. We are going to be using the **Pandas** package, which provides a lot of data table handling tools:

```
from sklearn import tree
import numpy as np
import pandas as pd
import sklearn.preprocessing as preproc
import graphviz
```

Our first step is to read in our data. I created my table in Microsoft Excel, and exported it as a CSV (comma separated values) format. This allows us to read in the data file directly with the column headers. I print out the shape and size of the data file for reference. My version of the file has 18 rows and 11 columns. The last column is just a note to myself on the actual name of each toy. We will not be using the last column for anything. We are building a classifier that will separate the toys by type:

```
toyData = pd.read_csv("toy_classifier_tree.csv")
print ("Data length ",len(toyData))
print ("Data Shape ",toyData.shape)
```

Now we can start building our decision tree classifier. We first build an instantiation of the DecisionTreeClassifer object. There are two different types of DTC (decision tree classification) algorithms to chose from. We are going to use Gini. What is Gini? It took quite a bit of digging, but the Gini coefficient was developed in 1912 by the Italian statistician Corrado Gini in his paper, *Variabilita e Mutabilita*. This coefficient, or index, measures the amount of inequality in a group of numbers. A zero value means all the members of the group are the same. For example, if we had a group of toy cars that were all the same size and all red, then the Gini index of the group would be 0. If the members of the group are all different, then the Gini number is closer to 1. The Gini Index is 1 minus the sum of the squares of the probability of an item being in that class. We have four toy cars out of 18 toys, so the probability of a toy car being in a group is 4/18 or 0.222. The decision tree will continue to subdivide classes until the Gini Index of the group is 0:

```
dTree = tree.DecisionTreeClassifier(criterion ="gini")
```

We need to separate out the values in our data table. The data in the first column, which is called column 0 (zero) in Python, are our classification labels. We need to pull those out separately, as they are used to separate the toys into classes. From our previous work with neural networks, these would be our outputs or the label data we have used in other machine learning processes. We will be training our classifier to predict the class of the toy based on the attributes in the table (size, weight, color, and so on). We use slicing to pull the data out of the Pandas table. Our Pandas data table is called `toyData`. If we want the entries in the table, we need to ask for `toyData.values`, which will be returned as a 2D array:

```
dataValues=toyData.values[:,1:10]
classValues = toyData.values[:,0]
```

This is our label encoder that we talked about – it will be converting the strings in our data into numbers. For example, colors like "red", "green", and "blue" will be converted to numbers like 0,1, and 2. The first item to be encoded is the list of class values that we use to label the data. We use the `LableEncoder.fit()` function to come up with the formula for converting strings to numbers, and then the `LabelEncoder.transform()` function to apply it. Note that `fit()` does not produce an output. Finally, we need to make the string text and the list of encoded numbers match up.

What the `LabelEncoder` will do is sort the strings alphabetically and start numbering them from "A", ignoring any duplicates. If we put in "car, car, car, block, stuffed, airplane" we will get out "2,2,2,1,3,0" as the encoding, and we will have to know that airplane = 0, block = 1, car = 2, and stuffed = 3. We need to generate a "decoder ring" to match up the numbers and text descriptions that looks like "airplane, block, car, stuffed". We duplicate the `LabelEncoder` function by using two functions on our list of string-formatted class names. We use the `set()` function to eliminate duplicates and the `sorted()` function to sort in the correct order. Now our class name table and the enumerations generated by `LabelEncoder` match. We'll need this later:

```
lencoder = preproc.LabelEncoder()
lencoder.fit(classValues)
classes = lencoder.transform(classValues)
classValues = list(sorted(set(classValues)))
```

To make it easy on ourselves, I created a function to automatically find out which columns in our data are composed of strings, and to convert those columns into numbers. We start by building an empty list to hold our data. We will iterate through the columns in our data and look to see if the first data value is a string. If it is, we will convert that whole column into numbers using the label encoder object (`lecoder`) we created. The label encoding process has two parts. We call `lecoder.fit()` to see how many unique strings we have in our column and to create a number for each one. Then we use `lecoder.transpose` to insert those numbers into a list:

```
newData = []
for ii in range(len(dataValues[0]))
line = dataValues[:,ii]
    if type(line[0])==str:
        lencoder.fit(line)
        line = lencoder.transform(line)
```

Now we put all of the data back into the `newData` list but there is a problem – we have turned all our columns into rows! We use the `transpose` function from numpy to correct this problem. But wait! We don't have an array anymore, as we turned it into a list so we could take it apart and put it back together again. (You can't do that with a numpy array – believe me, I tried):

```
    newData.append(line)
newDataArray = np.asarray(newData)
newDataArray = np.transpose(newDataArray)
```

Now all of our preprocessing is done, so we can finally call the real `DecisionTreeClassifer`. It takes two arguments: first the array of our data values, and then the array of class types that we want the decision tree to divide our groups into. The `DecisionTreeClassifier` will determine what specific data from the table is useful for predicting what class one of our toys fits into:

```
dTree = dTree.fit(newDataArray,classes)
```

That's it – one line. But wait –we want to see the results. If we just try and print out the decision tree, we get the following:

```
DecisionTreeClassifier(class_weight=None, criterion='gini', max_depth=None,
            max_features=None, max_leaf_nodes=None,
            min_impurity_split=1e-07, min_samples_leaf=1,
            min_samples_split=2, min_weight_fraction_leaf=0.0,
            presort=False, random_state=None, splitter='best')
```

That does not tell us anything; that is a description of the `DecisionTreeClassifier` object. (It does show us all of the parameters we can set, which is why I put it here.) So, there is a package called `graphviz` that is very good at printing decision trees. Let's use that. We can even pass our column names and class names into the graph. The final two lines output the graph as a `.pdf` file and stores it on the hard drive:

```
c_data=tree.export_graphviz(dTree,out_file=None,feature_names=toyData.colum
ns,                                 class_names=classValues, filled = True,
                            rounded=True,special_characters=True)
graph = graphviz.Source(c_data)
graph.render("toy_graph_gini")
```

And here is the result:

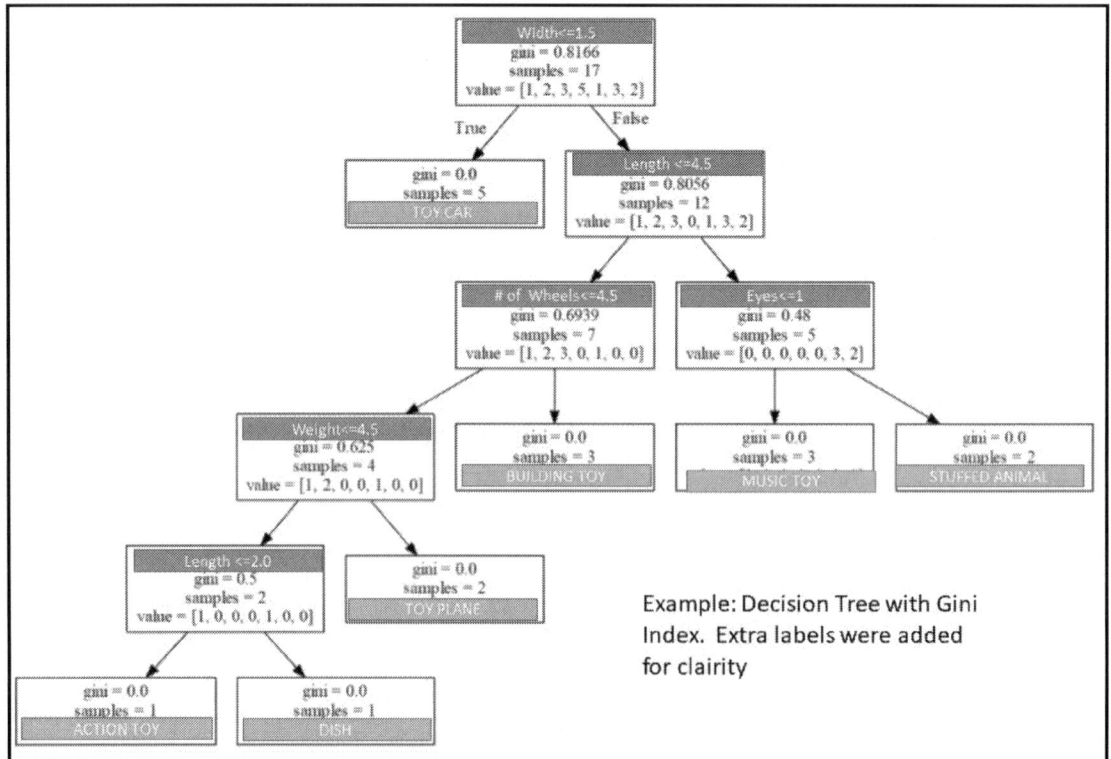

Example: Decision Tree with Gini Index. Extra labels were added for clairity

We can quickly check our solution by looking at our input table and seeing if the numbers line up. We should see:

- Six toy cars
- Three building blocks
- One dish
- One action toy
- Two stuffed animals
- Three musical instruments
- Two toy airplanes

And that is indeed the case.

The other number to look at is the Gini Index. The top-level box shows that the Index for the entire group has an overall value of .8166, which is close to 1 and shows a high degree of heterogeneity. As we progress down the tree, the Gini numbers get smaller and smaller until reaching 0 at each of the identified groups, which shows that the items in those groups share all of the same attributes.

What does this graph tell us? First of all, we can separate out the toy cars by only one attribute – width. Only the toy cars are less than 1.5 inches wide (38 mm). We don't need to look at color, or weight, or anything other than width to separate out all the toy cars from everything else. We see we have five toy cars out of our 17 toys, so we have 12 left to classify. Our next division comes in length. We have seven toys less than 4.5 inches long (11 cm) and five that are longer. Of the group of five, two have eyes and three do not. The toys with eyes are the two stuffed animals. If you follow the tree, the branches that lead to the toy music instruments are: width > 1.5 inches, length > 4.5 inches, and no eyes, and they are indeed larger than the other toys in length and width, and don't have eyes.

None of the other bits matter in terms of classifying. That means that an attribute like color is a poor predictor of what class a toy belongs to – which make sense. Our other useful criteria are the number of wheels, the weight, and the length. That data is sufficient to classify all our toys into groups. You can see that the Gini Index of each leaf node is indeed zero. I will confess that I added some additional labeling to the graph to make the illustration clearer.

So, that exercise was satisfactory – we were able to create an automatic decision tree from our toy data that classified our toys. We can even use that data to classify a new toy, and predict which class it might belong to. If we found that that new toy violated the classification somehow, then we would need to re-rerun the classification process and make a new decision table.

Entropy

There is another type of process for creating decision trees and subdividing data into categories. That is called the **Entropy model,** or information gain. Entropy is a measurement of the amount of disorder in the sample of data provided. We can also call this process information gain, since we are measuring how much each criteria contributed to our knowledge of which class it belongs to.

The formula for entropy is a negative log base 2 function, that is still primarily looking at the probability of a class belonging to a population, which is just the number of individuals belonging to each class divided by the total number in the sample:

```
Entropy = ∑_(i=1)^c█[-p_i*log2(p_i)]
```

To substitute entropy as our group criteria in our program, we only have to change one line:

```
dTree = tree.DecisionTreeClassifier(criterion ="entropy")
```

The results are shown in the following diagram:

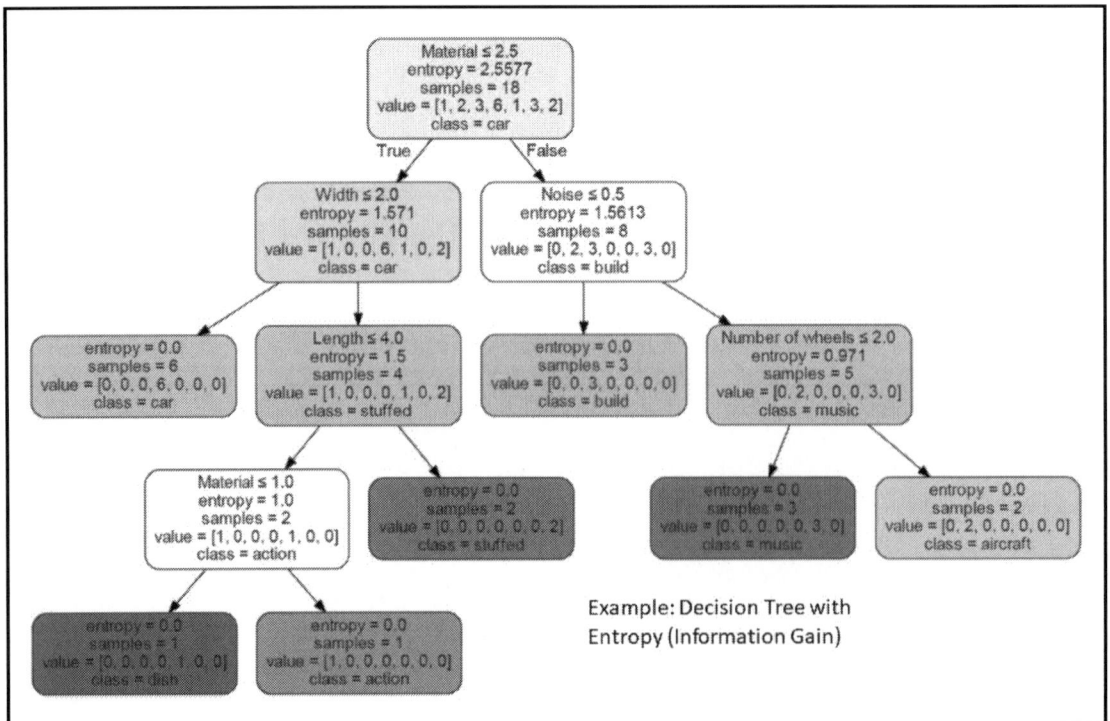

Example: Decision Tree with Entropy (Information Gain)

You can note that entropy starts at 2.55 for our whole group, and decreases to 0 at the leaf nodes (ends of the branches). We can check that we have seven classifications, but you can see that the entropy method selected different criteria than the Gini method. For example, the Gini classifier started with Length, and the entropy classifier started with Material. The entropy method also chose Noise (whether the toy makes a noise or not) and correctly selected that the only toys that make a noise were the toy musical instruments, and the toy airplanes, which both have electronic sound boxes that make airplane sounds.

There is one item that causes some concern, however. There are two blocks that are show Material, dividing the toy's values in material less than 2.5. Material is a discrete value. We can generate a list of materials and run this through our `sorted(set(list))` process to get the unique values in sorted order:

```
['ceramic', 'fur', 'metal', 'plastic', 'wood']
```

So, a material value of 2.5 or less would be either ceramic or fur. Fur and ceramic have nothing in common, other than where they are found in the alphabet. This is a rather troubling relationship, which is an artifact of how we encoded our data as a sequential set of numbers. This is implying relationships and grouping that don't really exist. How can we correct for this?

As a matter of fact, there is a process for handling just this sort of problem. This technique is widely used in AI programs, and is a "must have" tool for working with classification, either here in the decision tree section, or with neural networks. This tool has the strange name of "one hot encoding".

One hot encoding

The concept is pretty simple. Instead of replacing a category with an enumeration, we add one column to our data for each value, and set it to be a 1 or 0 based on that value. The name comes from the fact that only one column in the set is "hot" or selected.

We can apply this principle to our example. We can replace the one column, "Material", with four columns for each material type in our database. So our column, "Material", becomes "ceramic", "fur", "metal", "plastic", and "wood":

Material	ceramic	fur	metal	plastic	wood
metal	0	0	1	0	0
metal	0	0	1	0	0
metal	0	0	1	0	0
metal	0	0	1	0	0
metal	0	0	1	0	0
fur	0	1	0	0	0
fur	0	1	0	0	0
metal	0	0	1	0	0
wood	0	0	0	0	1
wood	0	0	0	0	1
wood	0	0	0	0	1
ceramic	1	0	0	0	0
plastic	0	0	0	1	0
plastic	0	0	0	1	0
metal	0	0	1	0	0
wood	0	0	0	0	1
plastic	0	0	0	1	0
wood	0	0	0	0	1

This does cause some structural complications to our program. We have to insert columns for each of our types, which replaces three columns with 14 new columns.

I've found two functions that we can use to convert text categories into one hot encoded multiple columns. One is the OneHotEncoder that is part of Scikit-learn. It is used like the LabelEncoder – in fact, you have to use both functions at the same time. You will have to convert the string data to numeric form with LabelEncoder and then apply the OneHotEncoder to convert that to the one-bit-per-value form that we want.

The simpler way is with a Pandas function called `get_dummies()`. The name is apparently because we are creating dummy values to replace a string with numbers. It does perform the same function. The steps involved are a quite a bit simpler than using the `OneHotEncoder` process, so that will be the one in our example.

The top header section is the same as before – we have the same imports:

```
# decision tree classifier
# with One Hot Encoding and Gini criteria
#
# Author: Francis X Govers III
#
# Example from book "Artificial Intelligece for Robotics"
#
from sklearn import tree
import numpy as np
import pandas as pd
import sklearn.preprocessing as preproc
import graphviz
```

We will begin by reading in our table as before. I added an extra column for myself called `toy name` so I could keep track of which toy is which. We don't need this column for the decision tree, so we can take it out with the Pandas `del` function by specifying the name of the column to remove:

```
toyData = pd.read_csv("toy_classifier_tree.csv")
del toyData["Toy Name"]    # we don't need this for now
```

Now we are going to create a list of the columns we are going to remove and replace from the Pandas `dataTable`. These are the columns "Color", "Soft", and "Material". I used the term "Soft" to identify toys that were soft and squished easily, because that is a separate criteria for using our robot hand. We generate the "dummy" values and replace the three columns with 18 new columns. Pandas automatically names the columns with a combination of the old column name and the value. For example, the single Color column is replace by `Color_white`, `Color_blue`, `Color_green`, and so on:

```
textCols = ['Color','Soft','Material']
toyData = pd.get_dummies(toyData, columns=textCols)
```

I put a print statement here just to check that everything got assembled correctly. It is optional. I've been really impressed with Pandas for data tables – there is a lot of capability there to do database-type functions and data analysis:

```
print toyData
```

Now we are ready to generate our decision tree. We instantiate the object and call it dTree, setting the classification criteria to Gini. We then extract the data values from our toyData dataframe, and put the class values in the first (0th) column into the classValues variable, using array slicing operators:

```
dTree = tree.DecisionTreeClassifier(criterion ="gini")
dataValues=toyData.values[:,1:]
classValues = toyData.values[:,0]
```

We still need to convert the class names into an enumerate type using the LabelEncoder, just as we did in the previous two examples. We don't need to one hot encode. Each class represents an end state for our classification example –the leaves on our decision tree. If we were doing a neural network classifier, these would be our output neurons. One big difference – when using a decision tree, the computer tells you what the criteria were that it used to classify and segregate items. With a neural network, it will do the classification but you have no way of knowing what criteria were used:

```
lencoder = preproc.LabelEncoder()
lencoder.fit(classValues)
classes = lencoder.transform(classValues)
```

As we said, to use the class value names in the final output, we have to eliminate any duplicate names and sort them alphabetically. This pair of nested functions do that.

```
classValues = list(sorted(set(classValues)))
```

This is the conclusion of our program. Actually creating the decision tree only takes one line of code, now that we have set up all the data. We use the same steps as before, and then create the graphic with graphviz and save the image as a PDF. That was not hard at all—now that we have had all that practice setting this up:

```
print ""
dTree = dTree.fit(dataValues,classes)


c_data=tree.export_graphviz(dTree,out_file=None,feature_names=toyData.colum
ns,
                            class_names=classValues, filled = True,
                            rounded=True,special_characters=True)
graph = graphviz.Source(c_data)
graph.render("toy_decision_tree_graph_oneHot_gini ")
```

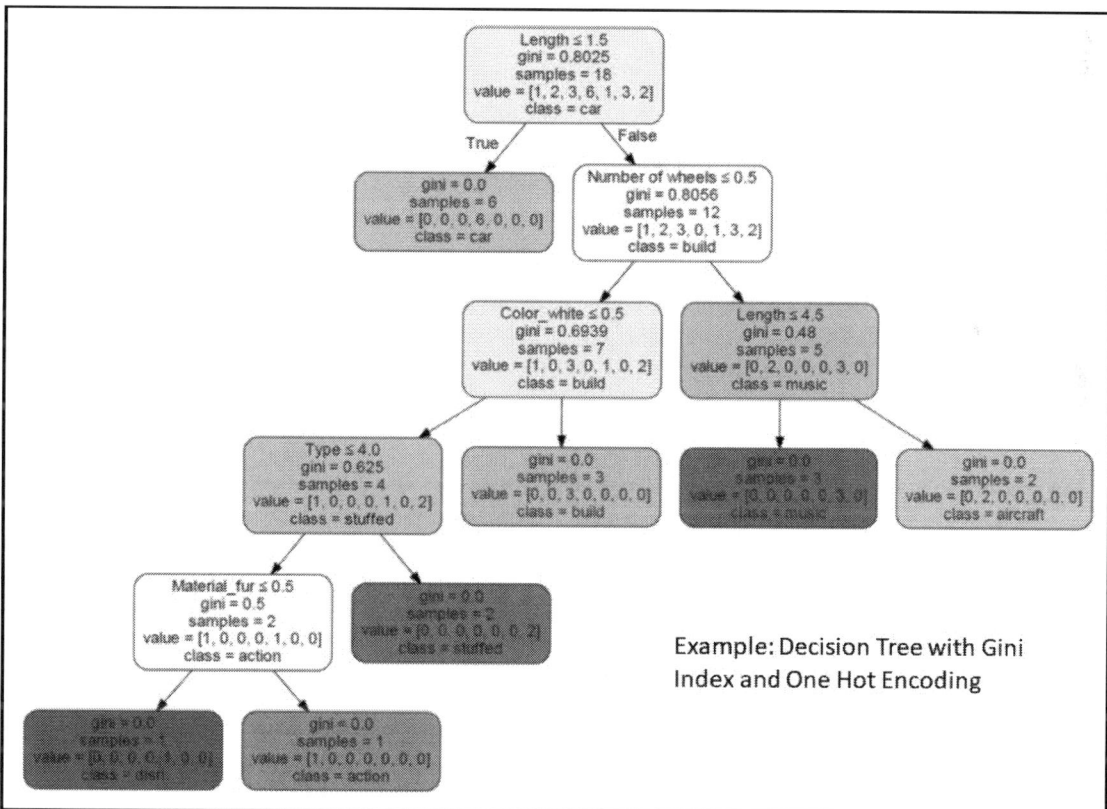

Example: Decision Tree with Gini Index and One Hot Encoding

Random forests

I really wanted to add this section on **random forest** classifiers, just because the name sounds so darn cool. There has even been talk of extreme random forests. While I may have been accused of stretching metaphors to the breaking point, this time the name may have inspired the software. We learned how to make decision trees, and we have learned that they have some weak points. It is best if the data really belongs in distinct and differentiated groups. It is not very tolerant of noise in the data. And it really gets unwieldy if you want to scale it up – you can imagine how big a graph would get with 200 classes rather than the six or seven we were dealing with.

If you wanted to take advantage of the simplicity and utility of decision trees, but wanted to handle more data, more uncertainty, and more classes, you can use a **random forest**, which, just as the name indicates, is just a whole batch of randomly generated decision trees. Let's step through the process.

We collect our database of information, but instead of 18 rows in our database, we have 10,000 records, or 1 million records. We subdivide this data into random sets – we generate 100 sets of data each randomly chosen from all of our data- and we put them in random order. We also pull out one set of data to use as a test set, just as we did for the neural networks.

Now for each set of random data, we make a decision tree using the same process we have already learned.

Now we have this collection of 100 classification engines, each generated from a different, randomly generated subset of data. We now test our random forest by taking data from the test set and running through all 100 of the trees in our forest. Each tree will provide an estimate of the classification of the data in our test record. If we are still classifying toys, then one of the trees would estimate that we are describing a toy car. Another may think it's a musical instrument. We take each estimate and treat it as a vote. Then the majority rules – the class that the majority of the trees selected is the winner. And that is all there is to it.

The setup and program is just the same as what we did before, but you can't draw a decision tree from a random forest, or just create a tree as an end in itself, because that is not what a random forest does – if you just need a decision tree, you know how to do that. What you can do is to use a random forest like a neural network, as either a classification engine (to what class does this data belong?) or a regression engine that approximates a non-linear curve.

Grid searching and A* (A-Star)

We are going to take what we have learned so far and press on to a problem related to classification, and that is grid searching and path finding. We will be learning about the famous and widely used A* (pronounced A-Star) algorithm. This will start with grid navigation methods, topological path finding, such as GPS route finding, and finally, expert systems. You will see that these are all versions and variations on the topic of decision trees that we have already learned.

Some problems and datasets, particularly in robotics, lend themselves to a grid-based solution as a simplification of the navigation problem. It makes a lot of sense if we were trying to plot a path around a house or through a field for a robot, that we would divide the ground into some sort of checkerboard grid and use that to plot coordinates that the robot can drive to. We could use latitude and longitude, or we could pick some reference point as zero – like our starting position – and measure off some rectangular grid relative to the robot. The grid serves the same purpose in chess, limiting the number of positions under consideration for potential future movement and limiting and delineating our possible paths through the space.

While this section deals with gridded path finding, regardless of whether maps are involved or not, there are robot navigation paradigms that don't use maps, and even some that don't use grids, or use grids with uneven spacing. I've designed robot navigation systems with multiple layer maps where some layers were mutable – changeable – and some were not. This is a rich and fertile ground for imagination and experimentation, and I recommend further research if you find this topic interesting.

Let's get back to the topic at hand. We have a robot and room that is roughly rectangular, and within that rectangle are some also roughly rectangular obstacles in the form of furniture, chairs, bookcases, a fireplace, and so on. It is a simple concept to consider that we mark off a grid to represent this space and create an array of numbers that matches the physical room with a virtual room. We set our grid spacing at 1 cm – each grid square is 1 cm x 1 cm, giving us a grid with 580 x 490 squares or 284,200 squares. We represent each square by an unsigned integer in a 2D array in the robot's memory.

Now we are going to need some other data. We have a starting location and a goal location, specified as grid coordinates. We'll put 0,0 for the grid in the nearest and leftmost corner of the room, so that all our directions and angles will be positive. In the way I've drawn the room map for you, that corner will always be the lower left corner of our map. In standard "right hand rule" notation, left turns are positive angles and right turns are negative. The x direction is horizontal and the y direction is vertical on the page. For the robot, the x axis is out the right side and the y axis is the direction of motion.

You may think it odd that I'm giving these details, but setting up the proper coordinate system is the first step in doing grid searches and path planning. We are using Cartesian coordinates indoors. We would use different rules outdoors with latitude and longitude. There we might want to use "north-east-down" (north is positive, south is negative, east is positive, west is negative, the z axis is down, and the x axis is aligned on the robot with the direction of travel):

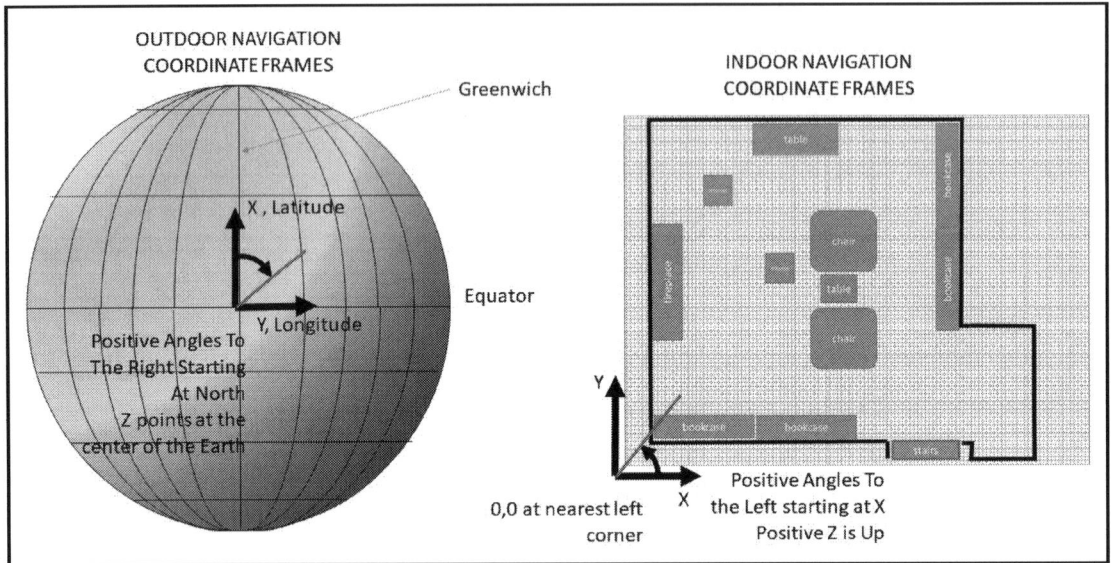

So, we have our grid and a coordinate system that we agree upon, or at least agree that we both understand. We also have a starting location and an ending location. Our objective is to determine the best path for the robot from the start to the finish point. And in between, we have to plan a path around any obstacles that may be in the way.

Now we have to start talking about knowledge. There are basically two kinds of grid search and path finding routines: the one where you know where everything is on the map – we call this a priori knowledge – and the one where you don't know where the obstacles are – this is called a posteriori knowledge. We will start in the easier position where we can do our path planning with perfect knowledge of the layout of the room – we have a map.

We really have three goals we are trying to achieve simultaneously with path planning. We are trying to reach our goal, avoid obstacles, and take the shortest path we can get away with.

We can talk about how we might go about this. We can start with our pencil at the start point and draw an imaginary line from our start to the goal. If there are no obstacles in the way, we are done – that is it. But wait – our pencil is a tiny line on paper. Our robot is somewhat chubbier – it has a significant width as it drives around. How do we judge if the robot is not going down some narrow passage that it won't fit into? We need to modify our map!

We have our grid, or a piece of paper that represents the grid. We can draw on that grid the outlines of all the obstacles, to scale. We have two chairs, an end table, a fireplace, a toy box (that's important), two footstools, and four bookcases. We color in all the obstacles in the darkest black we can. Now we get a lighter colored pencil – say a blue color – and draw an outline around all of the furniture that is half the width of the robot. Our robot is 32 cm wide, so half of that is 16 cm, a nice even number. Our grid is 1 cm per square, so we make a 16-square border around everything. It looks like this:

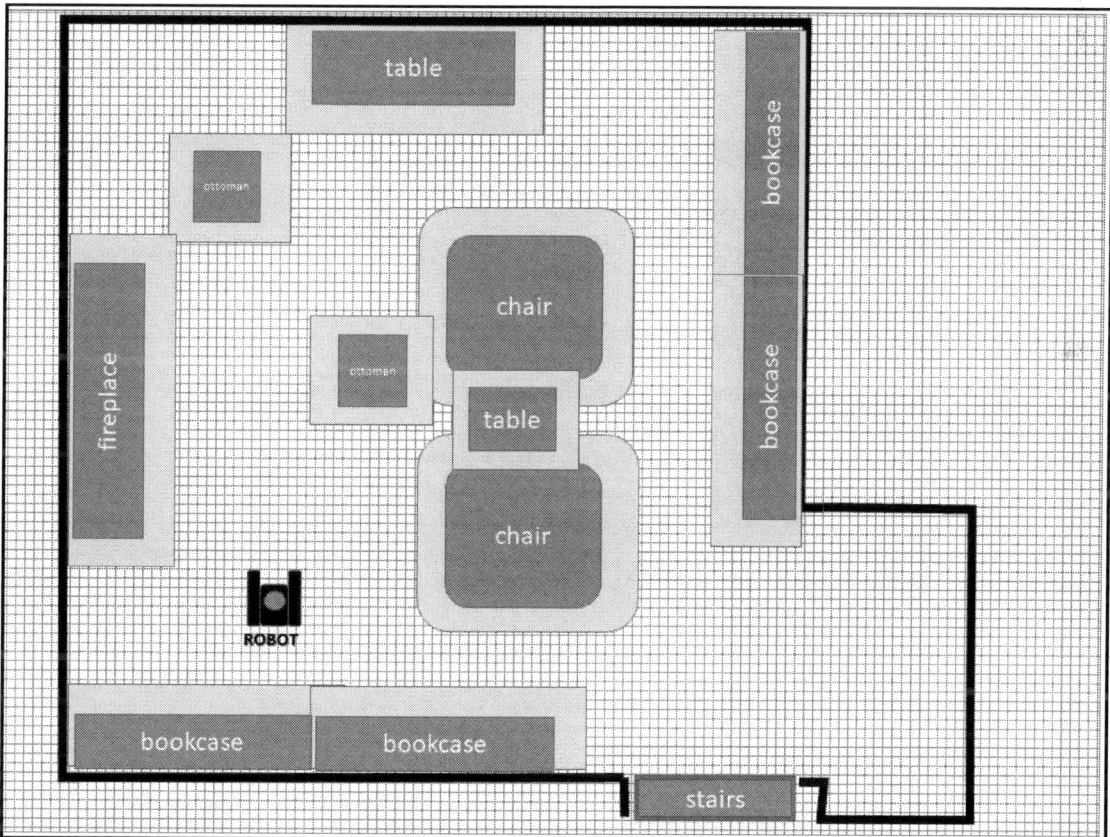

So, now our map has two colors – obstacles and a "keep out" border. We are going to keep the center of the robot out of the "keep out" zone, and then we will not hit anything. This should make sense. As for judging passages and doorways, if the keep out zones touch on either side, so if there are no white squares left in the middle, then the robot is too big to pass. You can see this around the ottoman in the upper left corner of the illustration.

We look at our line now. We need a way to write a computer algorithm that determines the white squares that the robot can pass through that gets us from the start point to the finish point.

Since we have the goal in Cartesian coordinates, and we have our start spot, we can express the distance in a straight line from the start to the finish. If the start point is *x1,y1*, and the finish point is *x2, y2*, then the distance is the square root of the sums of the difference between the points:

```
distance = sqrt(x2-x1)^2 + (y2-y1)^2)
```

One approach is to use a wavefront method. We know where the start is. We go out in every direction, to the eight squares adjacent to the start point. If any of those hit an obstacle or keep out zone, we throw it out as a possible path. We keep track of how we got to each square, which in my illustration is indicated by the arrows. We use the information on how we came to the square because we don't yet know where we are going next. Now we take all the new squares and do the same thing again – grabbing one square, seeing which of its eight neighbors is a legal move, and then putting an arrow (or a pointer to the location of the previous square) in it to keep track of how we got there. We continue to do this until we get to our goal. We keep a record of the order of the squares we examined, and follow the arrows backward to our starting point.

If more than one square has a path leading to the current square, then we take the closet one, which is to say the shortest path. We follow these predecessors all the way back to the starting point, and that is our path:

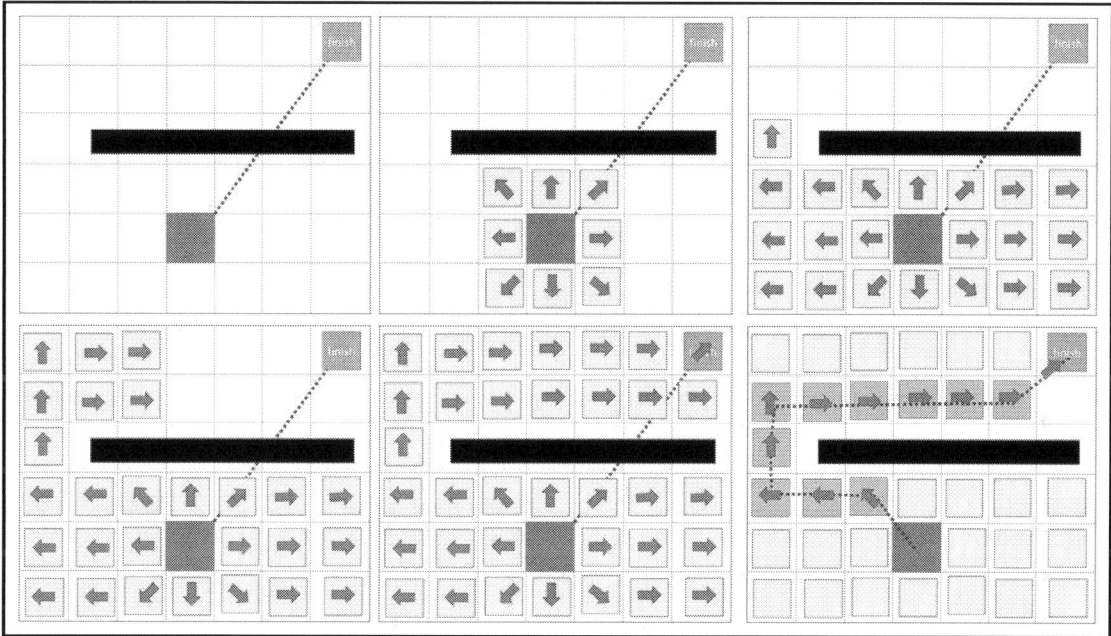

You will notice in this example that I allowed the robot to make diagonal turns to get from one square to another. I could have also specified that only right angle turns are allowed, but that is not very efficient and hard on the robot's drive system. Only allowing right angle turns simplifies the processing somewhat, since you only have to consider four neighbors around a square instead of eight.

Another approach that would look promising we can call the Greedy Best First approach. Instead of keeping record and checking all of the grid points like we did in the wavefront method, we just keep the single best path square out of the eight we just tested. The measure we use to decide which square to keep is by the one that is closest to our straight line path. Another way of saying this is to say it's the square that is closest to the goal. We remove squares that are blocked by obstacles, of course. The net result is we are considering a lot (really a lot!) fewer squares than the wavefront method of path planning:

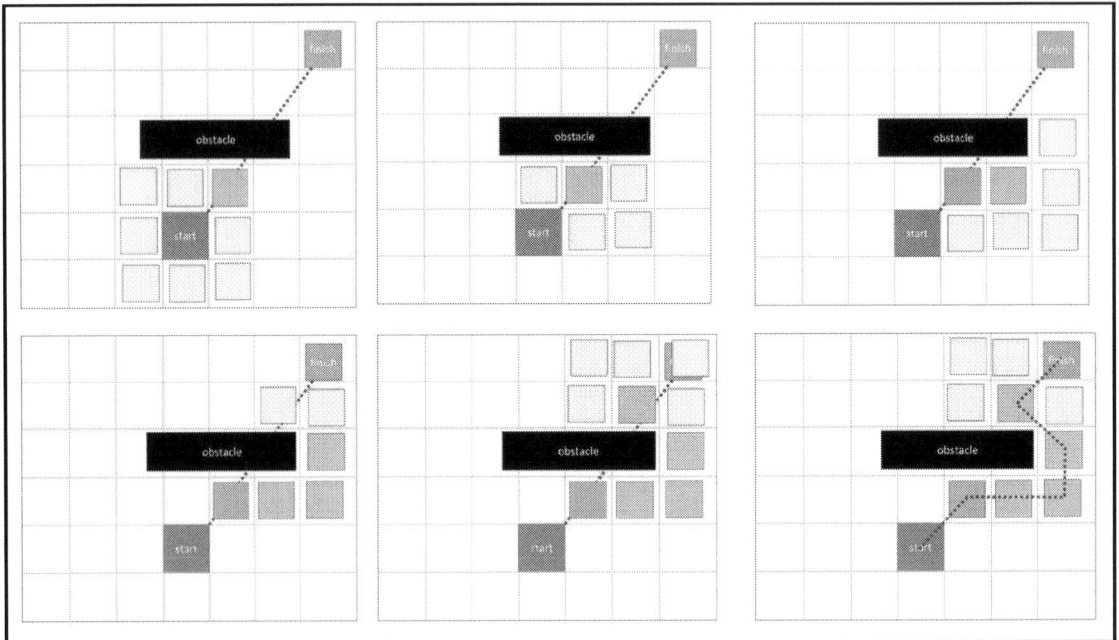

Does the greedy technique work for all cases? Not really.

Why not? That seems a simple algorithm, and we are only considering legal moves. The problem is it can't deal with a local minima. What the heck is a local minima? It is a place on the map where the robot would have to go backward in order to find a good path. The easiest type of minima to visualize is a U-shaped area where the robot can get in but not back out. The Greedy Best First algorithm is also not trying to find the shortest path, just a valid path. If we want to find the shortest path, we need to do some more math:

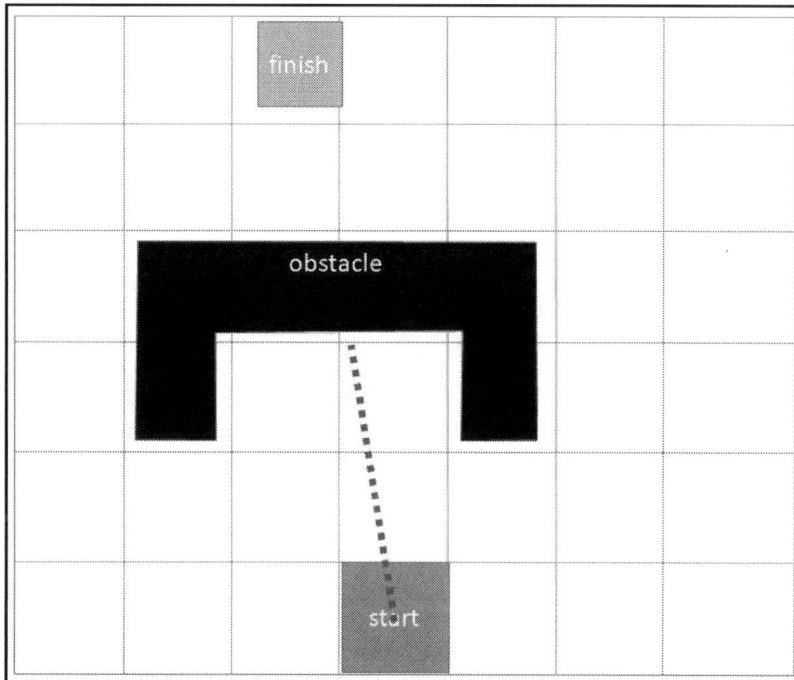

The A* algorithm

Honestly, you can't really write a book about robotics without mentioning the A* algorithm. A* has its origins with Shakey the Robot at Stanford University back in 1968. This was one of the first map navigating robots. Nils Nilsson and his team were trying to find a method to navigate Shakey around the hallways at Stanford, and started trying different algorthms. The first was called "A1", and so forth. After several iterations, the team decided that a combination of techniques worked best. In computer science, A* means the letter A followed by anything else, and thus the A-Star was named.

The concept of the A-Star process is very much like what we have already been doing with our other path planners. Like the wavefront planner, we start by considering the neighbors around our starting location. We will compute a heuristic, or estimate, for each square based on two factors: the distance from the starting location and the distance in a straight line to the goal. We are going to use these factors to find the path with the lowest cumulative cost. We calculate that cost by adding up the heuristic value for each grid square that is part of the path. The formula is:

```
F(n) = g(n) + h(n)
```

where: F = contribution of this square to the path cost, g(n) = distance from this square to the start position along the path chosen (that is, the sum of the path cost), and h(n) is the straight line distance from this square to the goal.

This value represents the cost or contribution of this square if it were a part of the final path. We will select the square to be part of the path which has the lowest combined cost. As with the wavefront planner ,we keep track of the predecessor square, or the square that was traversed before this one to reconstruct our path:

		finish				
	obstacle				G=5 H=3.6	G=6 H=5
		G=2.4 H=3	G=2 H=4.2	inf	G=4 H=5	G=5 H=6
G=2.4 H=4	G=1.4 H=4	G=1 H=4.5	G=2 H=5	G=3 H=5.3	G=4 H=7	
G=2 H=4	G=1 H=5	start	G=1 H=5.8	G=2 H=4	G=3 H=8	

The preceding diagram illustrates the A* (A Star) algorithm. Each square is evaluated based on the sum of the distance along a path back to the start(G), and an estimate of the remaining distance to the goal (H). The yellow squares represent the path selected so far.

Here is some Python code to illustrate how the A* algorithm works.

We keep a set of all the grid squares on the map we have computed values for. We'll call this the `exploredMap`.

Our map grid square object looks like this:

```
# globals
mapLength = 1280
mapWidth = 1200
mapSize = mapLength*mapWidth
map = []
for ii in range(0, mapWidth):
                for jj in range(0,mapLength):
                                mapSq = mapGridSquare()
                                mapSq.position = [ii,jj]
                                mapSq.sType =EMPTY
# create obstacles
obstacles = [[1,1],[1,2],[1,3],[45,18],[32,15] …..[1000,233]]
# iterate through obstacles and mark on the map
for pos in obstacles:
                map[pos]. sType = OBSTACLE
pathGrid = []
START = [322, 128]
GOAL = [938,523]

def mapGridSquare():
                def __init__(self):
                                self.F_value = 0.0   #total of G and H
                                self.G_value = 0.0   # distance to start
                                self.H_value = 0.0   # distance to goal
                                self.position=[0,0]    # grid location x and
y
                                self. predecessor =None    # pointer to
previous square
                                self.sType = PATH

                def compute(self, goal, start):
                                self.G_value = sum(pathGrid.distance)
                                self.H_value =
distance(goal.position,self.position
                                self.F_value = self.G_value + self.H_value
                                return self.F_value

def reconstructPath(current):
                totalPath=[current]
                done=False
                while not done:
                                a_square = current.predecessor
                                if a_square == None:  # at start position?
                                                done = True
                                totalPath.append(a_square)
                                current = a_square
                return totalPath
```

```
def A_Star_navigation(start, goal, exploredMap, map):
while len(exploredMap>0):
            current = findMin(exploredMap)  # the findMin function
returns the grid block data with
the lowest "F" score
            if current.position == goal.position:
                            # we are done - we are at the goal
                            return reconstructPath(current)
            neighbors = getNeighbors(current)
# returns all the neighbors of the current square that are not marked as
obstacles
            for a_square in neighbors:
                            if a_square.predecessor == None:
                                            # square has not been
previously evaluated
                                            old_score =
a_square.F_value
score = a_square.compute(GOAL, START)
exploredMap.append(a_square)  # add this to the map
# we are looking for a square that is closer to the goal than our current
position
if a_square.G_value < current.G_value:
            a_square.predecessor = current
            current = a_square
```

D* (D-Star or Dynamic A*)

Earlier in the chapter, I talked about a priori knowledge. The A Star algorithm, for all its usefulness, requires that obstacles in the entire map be known in advance. What do we do if we are planning movement into an unknown space, where we will creating the map as we go along? If we have a robot with sensors, such as sonar or lidar, then the robot will be detecting and identifying obstacles as it drives along. It also has to continually replan its route based on increasing information.

The A* process is only run one time to plan a route for a robot, before it begins to move. D*, a dynamic replanning process, is constantly updating the robot's path as new information becomes available.

The D* algorithm allows for replanning by adding some additional information to each grid square. You will remember that in A*, we had the G-Value (distance to the start along the path), and the H-Value (straight line distance to the goal). D Star adds a tag to the square that can have several possible values. The square's tag could be NEW, for a new square that had never been explored before. It could be OPEN, for tags that have been evaluated and are being considered as part of the path. CLOSED is for squares that have been dropped from consideration. The next two tags are RAISED and LOWERED. The RAISED flag is set if a sensor reading or additional information caused the cost of that square to increase, and LOWERED is the opposite. For LOWERED squares, we need to propagate the new path cost to the neighbors of the now lower cost square, so that they can be re-evaluated. This may cause tags to change on the neighboring squares. Raised squares have increased cost, and so may be dropped from the path, and Lowered squares have reduced cost, and may be added into the path. Keep in mind that changes in cost values ripple through the D* evaluation of paths like a wave as each square's new values are propagated onto its neighbors.

Another major difference between D* and A* is that D* starts at the goal and works backward toward the start. This allows D* to know the exact cost to the target – it is using the actual path distance to the goal from the current position and not a heuristic or estimate of the distance to go, like A* did.

This is a good time to remind you that all of these grid-searching techniques we just covered are still variations of decision trees. We are going from leaf to leaf – which we have been calling squares, but they are still leaves of a decision tree. We set some criteria for choosing which of several paths to take, which make branching paths. We are working toward some goal or endpoint in each case. I bring this up because in the next section we will combine decision trees and the type of path planning we did in the A* and D* sections to find a path through streets with a GPS.

GPS path finding does not use a map!

I wanted to have the opportunity, since we have come this far, to talk just for a little bit about topological path planners. This is an alternative method to the grid-based techniques we used in the preceding sections. There are types of problems and types of navigation where a grid-based approach is not appropriate or would require astronomical amounts of detailed data that may not be available or practical in a small robot.

As an example, I wanted to talk about how your GPS in your car finds a route along streets to reach your destination. You must have wondered about how that box has enough information in its tiny brain to provide turn-by-turn directions from one place to another. You may have imagined, if you stopped to think about it, that the GPS was using the same map you were viewing on the LCD-screen to determine where you need to go. And you would also think that some sort of grid-based search took place like the A* algorithm we discussed in such detail. And you would be wrong.

The data that the GPS uses to plan a route does not look like a map at all.

Instead, it is a topological network that shows how streets are interconnected. In format, it looks more like a database of vectors, rather than a raster map with pixels and colors. The database format also takes up a lot less room in the GPS internal storage. The streets are divided by nodes, or points where things intersect or change. Each node shows which streets are connected together. The nodes are connected by links, which allow you to traverse the data from node to node. The links represent the roads, and have a length, along with cost data about the quality of the road. The cost data is used to compute the desirability of the route. A limited access highway with a high-speed limit would have a low cost, and a small side street or dirt road with a lot of stop signs would have a high cost, since that link is both less desirable, and slower.

We use exactly the same procedures with the GPS road network database as we would working the A-Star process on a grid map. We evaluate at each node, and progress outward from our start node, choosing the path that takes us closest in the direction of our destination. Many GPS systems also simultaneously try to backward chain from the endpoint – the goal or destination – and try to meet somewhere in the middle. An amazing amount of work has gone into making our current crop of GPS systems small, lightweight, and reliable. Of course, they are dependent on up-to-date information in the database:

Road Network Database has a list of nodes (circles) and links (lines).

Each node has a list of which links intersect at the node

Each link has a length and a cost (type of road), as well as a pointer to the node at each end

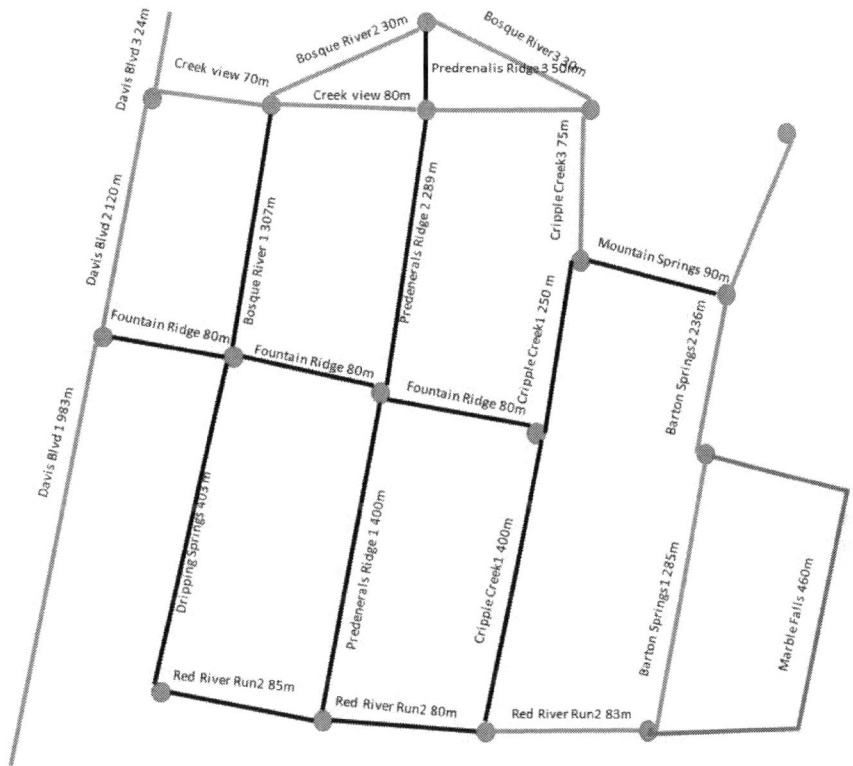

Davis Blvd 3 24m

Creek view 70m

Bosque River2 30m

Bosque River3 30m

Predrenalis Ridge 3 50m

Creek view 80m

Cripple Creek3 75m

Davis Blvd 2 120 m

Bosque River 1 307m

Predenerals Ridge 2 289 m

Mountain Springs 90m

Cripple Creek1 250 m

Davis Blvd 1 983m

Fountain Ridge 80m

Fountain Ridge 80m

Fountain Ridge 80m

Barton Springs2 236m

Dripping Springs 403m

Predenerals Ridge 1 400m

Cripple Creek1 400m

Cripple Creek1 400m

Barton Springs1 285m

Marble Falls 460m

Red River Run2 85m

Red River Run2 80m

Red River Run2 83m

Summary

Well, this has been a very busy chapter. We covered the various uses of decision trees for a variety of applications. The garden variety decision tree has leaves (nodes) and links, or branches, that each represent a decision or a change in a path. We learned about Fishbone diagrams and root cause analysis, a special type of decision tree. We showed a method using Scikit-Learn to have the computer build a classification decision tree for us and create a usable graph. We discussed the concept of random forests, which are just an evolved form of using groups of decision trees to perform prediction or regression. Then we got into graph search algorithms and path planners, spending some time on the A* or A-Star algorithm, which is widely used for making routes and paths. For times when we do not have a map created in advance, the D* or Dynamic A-Star process can use dynamic replanning to continually adjust the robot's path to reach its goal. Finally, we introduced topological graph path planning and discussed how GPS systems find a route for you to the coffee shop.

Questions

1. What are the three ways to traverse a decision tree?
2. In the Fishbone diagram example, how does one go about pruning the branches of the decision tree?
3. What is the role of the Gini evaluator in creating a classification?
4. In the toy classifier example using Gini indexing, which attributes of the toy were not used by the decision tree? Why not?
5. Which color for the toys was used as a criteria by one of the classification techniques we tried?
6. Give an example of label encoding and one hot encoding for menu items at a restaurant.
7. In the A* algorithm, discuss the different ways that G() and H() are computed.
8. In the A* algorithm, why is H() considered a heuristic and G() is not. Also, in the D* algorithm, heuristics are not used. Why not?
9. In the D* algorithm, why is there a RAISED and a LOWERED tag and not just a CHANGED flag?

Further reading

- *Introduction to A-Star.* https://www.redblobgames.com/pathfinding/a-star/introduction.html
- Murphy, Robin R. *Introduction to AI Robotics.* MIT Press, Cambridge MA 2000
- *How Decision Tree Algorthms Work.* https://dataaspirant.com/2017/01/30/how-decision-tree-algorithm-works/
- *Game Programming Heuristics.* http://theory.stanford.edu/~amitp/GameProgramming/Heuristics.html
- Koening, Sven. *D*Lite Algorithm Blog* (Project Fast Replanning) http://idm-lab.org/project-a.html
- Wooden, David, *Graph-Based Path Planning for Mobile Robots,* Dissertation, School of Electrical and Computer Engineering, Georgia Institute of Technology, December 2006
- Stentz, Anthony. *Real Time Re-planning in Dynamic and Unknown Environments (D*).* http://www.frc.ri.cmu.edu/~axs/dynamic_plan.html

Giving the Robot an Artificial Personality

9

When a person thinks of a robot with AI, what many consider AI is a robot that has emotions, feelings, a state of mind, and some sort of model or concept of how humans think or feel. We can call this form of AI an **artificial personality**. While giving a robot feelings is definitely way beyond the scope of this book (or current technology), what we can do is create a simulation of a personality for the robot using standard computer modeling techniques, such as Monte-Carlo analysis, and finite state machines.

In this chapter, we will cover the following topics:

- Transaction-based conversation
- Designing a chatbot
- Natural language processing (advanced)
- Simulation tools
- Monte Carlo modeling

Technical requirements

- We will not be introducing any new programming libraries in this chapter. We will be building on the voice system we constructed previously.
- All you will need is imagination and some writing skills

Check out the following video to see the Code in Action:
http://bit.ly/2wmar8i

What is an artificial personality?

Hollywood and the movie industry have turned out some very memorable robots. You can think of R2D2 and C3PO, the Laurel and Hardy of science fiction. What do you like most about these two? Could it be their personalities? Think about this a bit. Even though R2D2 is mostly a wastebasket shape with a dome head and no face, he has a definite personality. You describe him as *feisty*, or *stubborn*. The website Robots and Androids (`http://www.robots-and-androids.com/R2D2.html`) described him this way:

> *"The droid is shown as being highly courageous, unwavering in loyalty, and a little bit stubborn. He never backs down from a mission, even when the odds appear to be stacked against him. His personality is often contrasted against that of [C3PO], who is fussy and timid."*

This is pretty impressive for a robot who never says a word and communicates with beeps and whistles.

What were other movie robots that made an impression on you? Certainly WALL-E, the lovable trash compacting robot from the eponymous movie is a favorite. WALL-E also had a small vocabulary, consisting of only his name, much like a Pokemon. WALL-E displayed a lot of emotion, and even developed hobbies, collecting and repairing old trash. You may also remember M-O, the tiny, obsessive cleaning robot that gets frustrated with all of the dirt WALL-E brings in.

So one thing that we might do as robotics creators and designers is to imbue our robot with some sort of personality. This has an advantage of letting humans relate to the robot better. It also gives the false impression that the robot is much smarter and is capable of more than it really is. This does give the advantage of the robot being more engaging and interesting.

We can also infer from the examples given to us by R2D2 and WALL-E that less can be more when it comes to communication – we need to not just have words, but also body language and sound.

What we are going to do in this section is develop an artificial personality for our robots. While it is impossible for us to give a robot actual emotions or feelings, however you might define that, we can create a simulation of personality that will provide a convincing illusion. I think this is a meaningful exercise because the current state of the art in robotics demands some sort of personality and consistent demeanor from robotics that interact with humans.

There is a lot of work going on in this area right now with digital personal assistance, such as Apple's Siri and Google's Alexa. Note that these robots, or artificial intelligence, have distinct names and voices. I would feel that they are very similar in personality and capability. There is some distinction when you ask Siri or Alexa a personal question, such as how old they are (Siri is considerably older than Alexa).

In this chapter, we are going to take tools from the science of simulation – specifically, state machines and Monte Carlo analysis – and use them to form a model of a personality for Tinman, the robot. We already have a fairly powerful tool, in the Mycroft speech system we used to tell knock-knock jokes. We will be extending Mycroft with some new skills and capabilities, as well as developing cybernetic emotions, both for our robot, and for the robot's opinion of what we, the humans, are feeling.

I want to emphasize that we are simulating emotions, not creating an emotional robot. Our simulation bears the same resemblance to real emotions as a flight simulator bears to the space shuttle – both provide the same information, but the space shuttle flies around the Earth in 90 minutes, and the flight simulator never moves.

The Turing test

Alan Turing proposed his famous test, which he called *The Imitation Game* in a paper titled *Computing Machinery and Intelligence,* published in 1950 in the journal *Mind – A Quarterly Review of Psychology and Philosophy* (see `https://www.abelard.org/turpap/turpap.php#the_imitation_game`). In the original text, Turing imagined a game where a player would have to guess the sex – male or female – of a hidden person by typing questions on a teletype. Then he suggested that a truly intelligent machine would be one where you would not be able to distinguish if the hidden personality on the other end of the teletype was a human or a computer software program.

> The movie called *The Imitation Game* stars Benedict Cumberbatch as Alan Turing but features his role in breaking German code in WWII as part of the mathematicians of Bletchley Park. The title refers to Turing's original name of the famous test that bears his name.

These days, you may talk to computer software many times a day and not realize that you are not speaking to a human. *Robocalls* and *chatbots* may call you on the telephone, or engage you in a fake political conversation on Twitter. The Turing test has been won by the machines—but have we developed intelligence in computers? Not at all – we have just become very clever at simulating conversation.

Recently, robotics experts have suggested replacing the Turing test with a more demanding and difficult assignment – assembling a piece of furniture from Ikea using the directions provided (`https://motherboard.vice.com/en_us/article/vvbqma/the-plan-to-replace-the-turing-test-with-a-turing-olympics`).

We are going to use another tool that Alan Turing mentioned in his paper –state machines. We will use state machines to define and model the emotions of our robot.

Let's go back to the concept of a chatbot. A working definition may be a software program designed to engage a human in conversation, or to interact with a person via voice or text. While most chatbots are up-front about being computer generated, there are a lot of chatbots that are not – including Twitter chatbots that seek to influence elections or public option. Many chatbots are gainfully employed answering tech support phone calls, making marketing calls, and entertaining users as the dialog of **Non-Player Characters** (**NPCs**) in games.

According to `chatbotslife.com,` in their article *Ultimate Guide to Leveraging NLP [Natural Language Processing] and Machine Learning for Your Chatbot* (Stefan Kojouharov, September, 2016), chatbots come in two flavors: retrieval based and generative based.

Retrieva-based chatbots rely on stored phrases and words, and use the software decision making to select which reply is most appropriate. There may be some keyword recognition and noun-subject insertion involved, but the main action is to select the most appropriate phrase.

Generative-based chatbots are making up new sentences based on parts of speech and the robot's divination of your intent. They can be thought of as machine translation engines that translate the input (your text or speech) into an output (the robot's reply). As you might imagine, the generative type chatbot is far more difficult to achieve, which is why we will be using a retrieval-based approach.

There are two other details we need to attend to. Chatbots can be designed to handle either short conversations, or long conversations. The vast majority of chatbots, and that includes digital assistants, such as Siri, Alexa, and Mycroft, are designed for very short conversations. *Siri, what is the weather? There is a 20% chance of rain. The high is 88 degrees.* That's it – the whole conversation in three sentences and two interactions. If you ask another question, it starts a new conversation with little reference to the previous one.

A more difficult task is to have a longer conversation with several interactions, and even a selection of topics. This requires the computer to keep track of context, or what information has been discussed and might be referred to again.

We will be attempting to teach our robot to be able to have medium-length conversations on a seven-year-old level. I'll define medium length to be between two and six interactions.

The art and science of simulation

What is simulation? A **simulator** is a computer model of the physical world. You are probably familiar with flight simulators, which provide the sensations and interactions of flight without leaving the ground. There are also a lot of other types of simulations and simulators. We could have a medical simulator that mimics diseases or responds to treatments. It could be a financial simulation that models returns on the stock market based on trends. There are structural simulations that model the loads on bridges and buildings to see whether the materials are adequate.

The most common way of creating a simulation is by building a physics model of the item under test. For a flight simulator, this means plugging in formulas for the four forces on an airplane or helicopter – lift, gravity, thrust and drag. Each factor has parameters that affect its performance – for instance, lift is a function of the speed through the air, the weight of the aircraft, the size of the wing, and the angle of attack, or the angle between the wing and the wind. Vary any of those, and the lift changes. If the amount of lift exceeds the force due to gravity (that is, the weight of the aircraft) then the aircraft flies. The simulation sets up a time step interval, just like our control loop for the robot, and computes the forces on the aircraft for each time step. We can then apply controls and see how our model performs. Models just like this are used to predict performance in advance of building a prototype or test airplane.

Another type of simulation is called a Monte Carlo model. The Monte Carlo method uses probability theory to replace sophisticated physical models with a variation of random numbers that approximates the same result. If you wanted to create a computer model of flipping a coin, you wouldn't spend a lot of time determining the physical properties of a nickel, or modeling the number of flips in the air based on force. You would just pick a random number from 1 to 100, and say the result is heads if the number drawn is less than 50 and tails if it is greater than 50. That, in essence, is the Monte Carlo method. There are a lot of physical processes that can be approximated and studied using this technique.

We can apply Monte Carlo analysis to model people going through security at an airport. If you had a copy of a typical schedule for the airlines, and the average number of passengers per flight, you would know the daily traffic at the airport. The difficult bit was modeling when people would arrive for their flight. Let's imagine that we commissioned a study, and determined roughly that 50% of people arrive 1 hour early, 25% arrive 2 hours early, and the rest are evenly distributed between 2.5 hours and 30 minutes, with one passenger out of every 200 missing their flight by being late. This information allows us to create samples sizes of passenger arrivals and thus an estimate length of lines at security.

Passenger Arrival Times

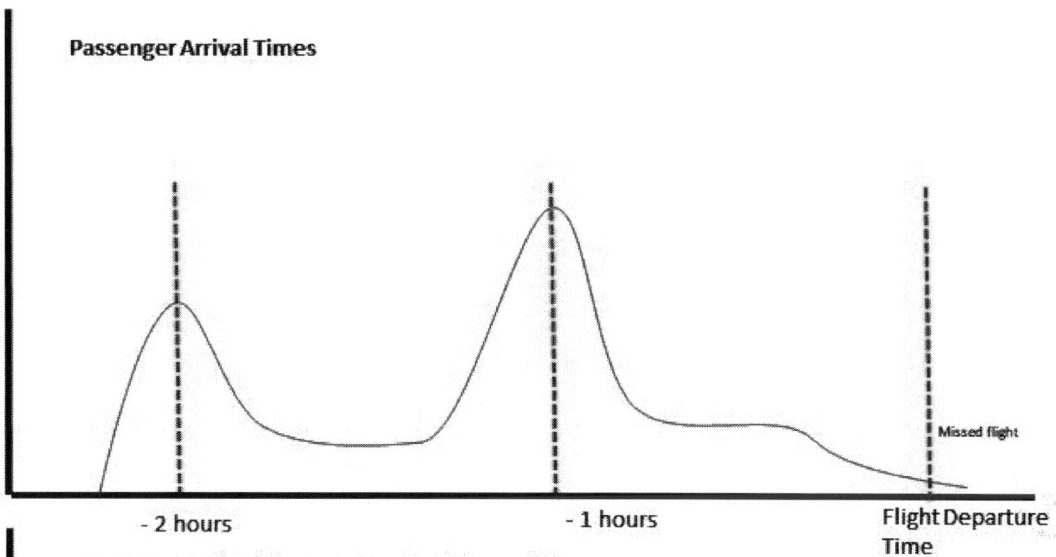

- 2 hours   - 1 hours   Flight Departure Time

Missed flight

Passenger Arrival Times Approximation Model

We can approximate the arrival function with two standard distributions (bell curves) and two uniform distributions (boxes)

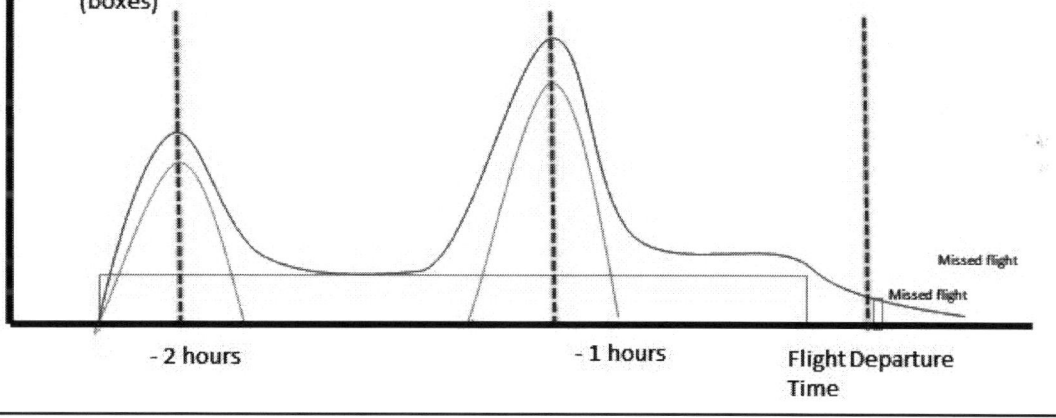

- 2 hours   - 1 hours   Flight Departure Time

Missed flight

Missed flight

We would add some distribution of values of how long it took to get through security, and we would have our model. We have a list of flights, and for each flight we generate a distribution of passenger arrival times based on the study by assigning random numbers to each passenger and separating them out into groups based on arrival time. Let's assign random numbers from 1 to 100 to our 212 passengers arriving for the 08:00 flight from Dallas to Washington DC. Now we assign an arrival time based on that number – if the number is from 1 to 25, the passenger arrives two hours earlier than the flight (06:00). If the number is from 26 to 75 (the next 50%) then they arrive one hour early (07:00). The rest of the passengers, having numbers from 76 to 100, are assigned random times between 2.5 hours early to 30 minutes early. And we pick one unlucky passenger out of our 200 to miss the flight completely by arriving late. Since there is some variability to people who intend to arrive at exactly two hours ahead, but are delayed or advanced slightly, we can **dither** or add a small random factor to each arrival time of plus or minus 10 minutes. Now we have a statistically correct distribution of people arriving for a flight. Now repeat this process for the other 1,849 flights leaving today from this airport.

You can see from this model that we can still put a great deal of science into picking random numbers.

As you might have guessed from my example, the true secret of making this technique work is picking the correct distribution of random numbers. You may think, *Hey, random numbers are random numbers, right?* but this is not correct at all. You have heard of the standard distribution, or the bell-shaped curve. Most of the values are in the center, with fewer and fewer as you go away from the center. Many natural processes follow this bell-shaped curve, including grades on a test, how tall people are, or how many grapes grow in a bunch. When you do Monte Carlo analysis, most often we use some form of normal or standard distribution.

Can you think of other types of random numbers? The second most common type of random numbers are a uniform distribution. Each number has the exact same probability of being selected, which make for a flat distribution curve. Another name for this uniform distribution is white noise. Uniform distributions do occur in analysis, and if we want to add noise to an image, for example, we would use a uniform distribution. But in modeling emotions and people, normal or standard distributions are the rule.

You may have heard of pink noise – this is a distribution where the probability decreases with the increase in value of the number. Another way of saying this is the probability is equal to 1/value.

You may find that in using Monte Carlo modeling that a standard distribution or uniform distribution just won't work. Then you can create a custom distribution like I did in the airport example, where we used re-sampling to change a uniform distribution to a custom distribution fitting our passenger arrival model:

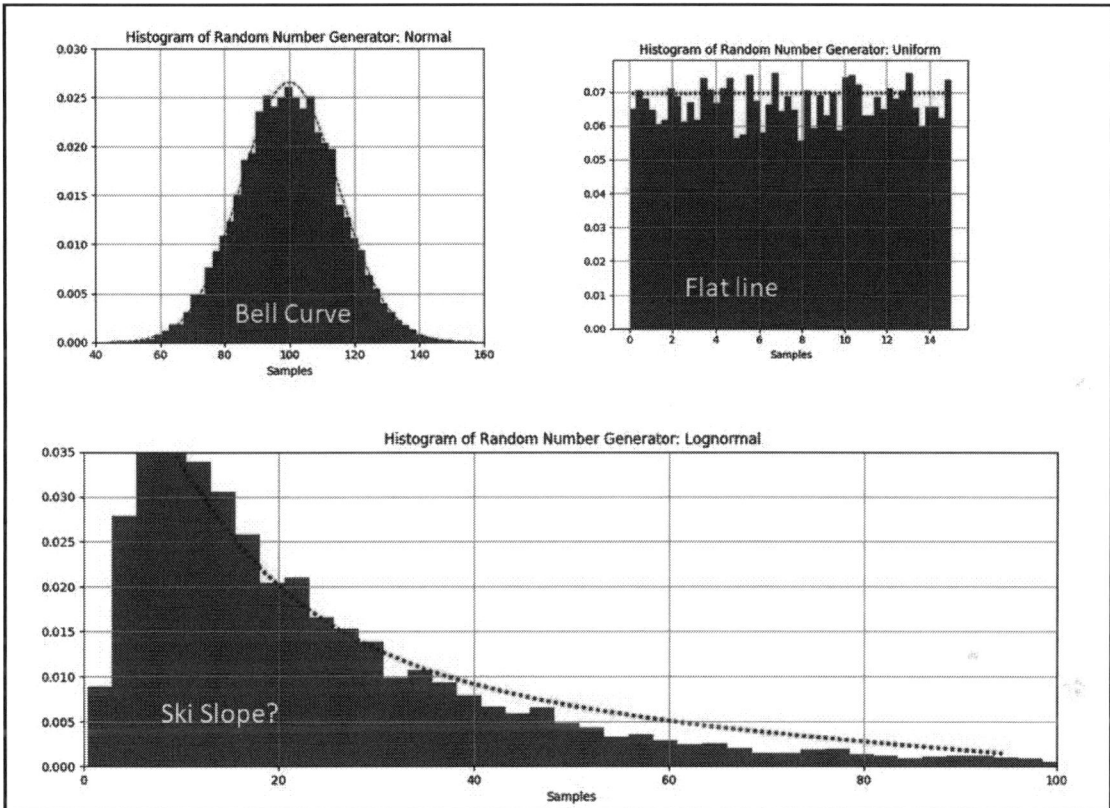

We are going to be making a personality simulation for our robot, and we will be using Monte Carlo modeling plus a state machine.

An emotion state machine

What is a state machine? We covered state machines in the section on systems engineering – state machines are a technique for understanding or modeling automation or computer programs. A state is a set of conditions that exist at the present. I like to think of a state as being a set of functions that are constrained by limits. The machine (our robot) changes from state to state based on some event that causes the state to change.

Let's work through a quick refresher example. Let's take a slice of bread. When we get it, it is already baked and sliced, so it's initial state is as a slice of bread. If we subject the bread to infrared radiation (that is, heat), then the surface becomes caramelized and we call that **toast**. The state of the bread has changed, along with its taste and texture, from baked bread to toast. The event that caused that transition was the act of putting the bread in a toaster. This is pretty simple stuff, and I'm sure you have encountered state machines before.

Now let's think about our model of robot emotions. We can start by listing what emotions we want our robot to have:

- Happy
- Welcoming
- Friendly
- Curious
- Fresh

And the opposites of those emotions:

- Sad
- Distant
- Stranger
- Frustrated
- Tired

These are the list of emotions I wanted to simulate in our robot. I looked at the different interactions the robot might have, and how a human version of the robot would react. This line of development was partially inspired by the work at the MIT Media lab with Kismet, a facial expression robot that was used to model social interactions, much like what we are trying to accomplish here. (See Breazeal and Scassellati: *How to Build Robots that Make Friends and Influence People*, MIT, 2000.):

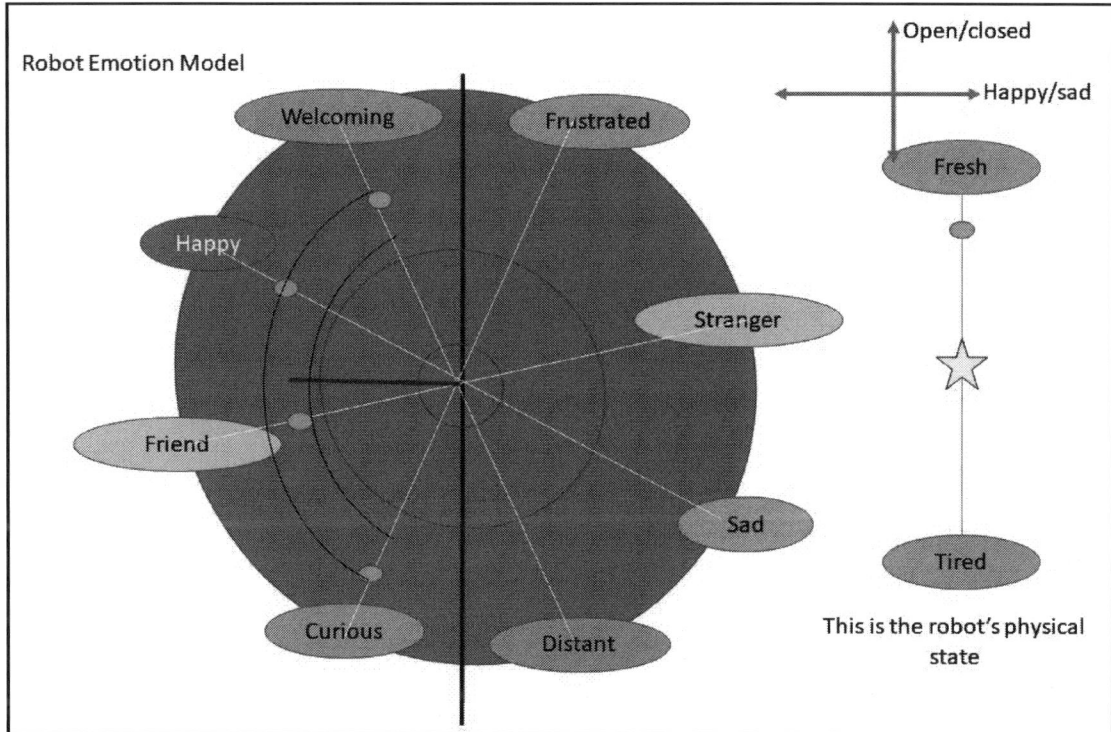

Robot Emotion Model

Open/closed

Happy/sad

Welcoming

Frustrated

Fresh

Happy

Stranger

Friend

Sad

Tired

Curious

Distant

This is the robot's physical state

In the preceding diagram, we model the overall emotive state of the robot by plotting the various emotional components or states on a polar plot. Each emotional element has a vector or direction. The left side of the plot are the happy, friendly, open feelings, and the right side are the sad, closed, distant feelings. We take the area made up by the four components, and find the center of that area and that is the overall state of the robot. In this example, the predominant emotion is **Friendly**. Since the robot's physical state determines whether it feels **tired** or not, that data is computed separately –this lets the robot feel tired but friendly, or refreshed but sad.

The robot starts in the state of happy, distant, curious, and fresh. That is to say, it feels happy, it is not in an interaction, so there is no-one to be friendly to, and it will be curious about its surroundings. As the environment changes, the robot's state will change. For example, we have about a two-hour run time on Tinman's current battery. It starts off in the **fresh** state, and will get more and more tired as it approaches the two-hour mark. We are going to use a simple timer to create this state, but you could also have a voltage sensor in the Arduino provide information about how fresh the robot's power supply is at. Each emotion exists along an axis that all cross a central or neutral point.

We will drive the **happy-sad** axis based on how many conversation **points** the robot is earning. We'll cover this in detail in a few paragraphs. We will also be describing an empathy function for our robot that simulates the robot sharing feelings with you. The distant-welcoming aspect is controlled by how the human interacts with the robot. If you are acting friendly to the robot, then it will be welcoming. If you are new, the robot will start off cautiously in asking questions or interacting. If you are not answering questions, then the robot will become more distant. Likewise, the friend-stranger aspect is based on how much the robot knows about the person it is talking to. Finally, the curious-frustrated axis is based on how hard the robot has to work to get information or to accomplish a task. If it keeps failing at a task, or not getting rewards, it will become frustrated in its expressions and vocabulary.

How does a robot with no face express emotions? Remember we started talking about Hollywood robots, many of whom have distinct personalities without having faces or even heads. We will use body language with the robot arm and changes in vocabulary to express our simulation of emotions. And we will have the robot be open about how it is feeling and why.

Our goal for this part of the robot development is to provide a human interaction framework that invites people to talk to the robot and feel welcome or wanted. I'm modeling this interaction from watching my grandchildren. I wanted a robot that they would enjoy and find interesting.

Playing the emotion game

What we want to do is develop the ability for the robot to convey intent, or to provide a simulation that the robot has needs and desires. We are going to do this by creating a game that the robot will play with humans. The robot will be trying to score points by getting the human to interact socially. The robot will gain points by getting information from the person so that it can *get to know them better*. The trick for us is, we need the robot to keep this information and remember it.

So, what is this game? What we want the robot to do is ask questions of another person and to use conversation to get personal information out of them, so that the robot then can use that information in replies. We will be saving all this information and using it to modify the actual code the robot is running, thus implementing machine learning in the conversation. The robot will be using the same type of point-reward system we used in training the robot arm back in a previous chapter. Once the robot has **scored** by learning a fact, it will no longer get rewarded for that fact, and will go on to get other facts. Once it has learned all the facts, it will end the conversation. In practice, I think most users will want fairly short conversations, so we are setting our goal to have between two and six interactions per conversation.

The game will be played like this: the user will always initiate a conversation by saying the robot's wake phrase, which right now is *Hey, Albert*. The robot will respond using the Mycroft speech engine with a beep. The user will initiate a conversation by saying some version of *hello.* The robot will then try to earn rewards by getting points, which it does by asking questions. The emotion engine will respond to the human answers by modifying the robot's emotions. We will rank questions by importance – let's say the robot gets 10 points for learning your name, nine points for learning your age, and so on. Once a fact is learned, no more points are earned, so the robot won't repeat the questions.

The facts we want the robot to know about each person are:

- Your name
- Your age
- How are you feeling today?
- What is your favorite food?
- What is your favorite book?
- Do you go to school?
- If so, what is your favorite subject?
- When is your birthday?
- What is your favorite song?
- Do you like (the color pink/singing/dancing/dinosaurs/race cars/building things/robots/airplanes/spaceships)
- Do you brush your teeth?
- Do you like knock-knock jokes?

As part of the learning game for the robot, we will adjust the robot's emotions as it learns and interacts, by adjusting the levels of the eight emotions (or four emotion types) we provided to the robot. We will particularly pay attention to the place where the eight emotions balance – are they on the happy/friendly/curious side of the graph, or more on the sad/frustrated/distant side?

Our robot will also have a backstory or a biography that it will use to answer questions about itself. We'll give the robot a little narrative. His name is Albert, he is a Tinman Robot, he is eight months old, he was made by Grandad, and he was born on January 28, 2018. He likes the color green, his favorite food is electricity, and his favorite author is Isaac Asimov. He does not go to school but loves to learn. His job and his hobby and his passion is picking up toys. If you ask him how he feels, he will tell you which emotional state is highest, plus how fresh or tired his battery is. We want him to occasionally interject how he is feeling into conversation without being asked. We will also be using the emotional state to set the robot's body language, which is primarily how he is carrying his robot arm. If he is happy, the arm will be extended with the hand pointed upwards. If he is sad, the arm will be close to his body and his hand will point down. We will store all this information to give the robot a consistent set of answers to personal questions.

I've been addressing this robot as *he* and *him* all through the book. This is just an anthropomorphic projection on my part and is implying features that a robot just does not have. The primary reason for Tinman's identity is his voice – I used a male voice for his synthesizer, mostly because I wanted it to stand out from all the female GPS and personal assistant computer voices around. Please feel free to create any voice you like – there are a lot of female voices available, and you can create whatever persona you like in your robot and give him/her/it any form of address. It is interesting that we tend to do this even with non-humanoid robots. According to Colin Angle, CEO of iRobot(1), over 80% of Roomba owners have given their robot a name, including him. You don't see people naming their toaster ovens, or stand mixers, no matter how attached they are to them. Albert the Tinman robot may very well be getting a sex-change operation, or get a sister, as my granddaughter gets a bit older. (1) Biever, Celeste. *My Roomba's Name is Roswell*, www.slate.com., March 23, 2014.

Creating a model of human behavior

For the robot to support conducting a conversation, we have to also have a model of how the human it is talking to is feeling. You may have had a friend or relation who went on talking about themselves and were oblivious to how you were feeling or reacting to their conversation. We don't want that type of robot personality. Therefore, the robot has to have some internal representation of how it thinks you are feeling. We will not be using vision for this function, so the only way the robot knows how you are doing is by asking questions and evaluating the use of language.

We will give the robot a human model similar to our state machine, but with just four emotions on two axis: happy/sad, and friendly/distant. The robot will assume that everyone is somewhere in the middle when conversation begins. The robot can use clues in language to understand how you might be feeling, so we will assign *colors* or shades of emotions to words to help drive the robot's human model. Different emotion from the person will drive different responses from the robot. We particularly want the robot to pay attention to clues that the human is becoming frustrated due to the robot not understanding or responding in a way the person wants.

Integrating artificial personality into our robot

This brings us to actually selecting and designing an artificial personality for our robot. We need to set some guidelines and parameters that will determine what kind of personality the robot has.

We can start by listing some types of personality that a robot might have, and what kind of role they might be playing. This is particularly important because this robot will primarily be interacting with children. Let's try a few out and see what fits:

- **Teacher/professor**: The robot is attempting to convey information and to teach or cause the person to change behavior in some way. The robot presents itself as an authority and provides facts and information about itself. "I'm a robot. Do you know what a robot is?"
- **Hyper-friendly:** The robot is playful and excited about talking with humans, and aggressively engages people in conversation and asks lots of questions. The robot expresses a lot of enthusiasm and encouragement. "I love my job. Don't you love your job? It's so great! I just love talking to people! Do you want to hear a joke?"

- **Chummy and friendly**. The robot is trying to make friends and be helpful. *Hi! Nice to see you! What is your name?*
- **Friendly but neutral**: The robot is not quick to share information, but does want to talk to you. *Hello, I am Albert. How are you today?*
- **Feisty**: The robot is supportive, friendly, and wants interaction. It keeps prompting for more information. It will repeat questions if necessary. *Hi! Nice to meet you. What is your name? How old are you?*
- **Somber and staid**. The robot is stuffy and authoritative. Think of having a conversation with a British butler. The robot uses formal English. (This is apparently the default non-personality of many digital assistants.) *Greetings. How may I help you? May I ask you your name?*
- **Very neutral (robotic)**: The robot expresses no opinions, and gives no information about itself. It expresses no emotions or interjections. *Hello. I am a robot. State a command.*
- **Annoyed and grumpy**. The robot is not very happy about having to pick up toys and does not mind saying so clearly and distinctly. This personality is aiming for comedy, not anger. *So you are back again. I guess this means more toys to pick up.*

We can see from this list, the sort of gamut of personalities we can chose for simulation. I'm going to choose the *chummy and friendly* type personality, since that is what I feel will go over best with my grandchildren. You, of course, may choose any of these you please, or add some more.

Personality construction – building blocks

In a quick review, what parts do we have so far for our robot with an artificial personality? We have simulation tools to model emotions. We have a state machine with six types of emotions that we can mix together. We have a backstory or biography of robot personal information. We have picked a personality to emulate. We have the concept of a game engine where the robot is trying to score points for collecting information by engaging in small talk, or phatic communication. The robot will change emotions based on conversations. Emotions will be expressed either by asking the robot how he is feeling, or by body language of the robot arm.

Now we need some sort of framework to put all of these pieces together, which can roughly carry on a conversation that we can adjust and manipulate. For that, we are going to revisit an old, old friend. I want you to meet **ELIZA**.

ELIZA is probably the original conversation engine software program. It was invented back in 1964 by Joseph Weizenbaum, professor at MIT, a Jewish German refugee from WWII, and considered one of the fathers of artificial intelligence.

ELIZA was named after Eliza Doolittle, the main character in George Bernard Shaw's book *Pygmalion.* In Greek mythology, Pygmalion was a sculptor who fell in love with one of his statues. He prayed to Aphrodite, who granted his wish for the statue to come to life. This is very apt for what we are doing – bringing our robot to simulated life via this weird chain of events, titles, and Greek mythology.

ELIZA was a simulation of a Rogerian therapist. What the heck is a Rogerian therapist? According to *Psychology Today* (`https://www.psychologytoday.com/us/blog/what-doesnt-kill-us/201210/unconditional-positive-regard`), Carl Rogers is the founder of "Client-Centered Therapy", which believes in UPR – Unconditional Positive Regard. Which is to say that the therapist keeps their own opinions out of the therapy sessions, and primarily mirrors the patient's words back at them. If the patient says, *I've always hated cats,* the therapist may respond, *Why do you think you hate cats,* rather than saying, *I have a cat and they are lovable creatures.* So ELIZA, the computer program, reflects back at you what you are saying without interjecting anything else. You have a conversation with ELIZA via what we now call texting, and what we used to call typing. Here is an actual ELIZA interaction between me and an open source version of ELIZA by Wade Brainerd, which can be found at `https://github.com/wadetb/eliza`. The user is typing at the > prompt. By the way, `I love cats` – this is just an example. Please don't tell my cat about this example:

```
ELIZA: How do you do. Please tell me your problem.
 > I hate cats.
You say you hate cats?
 > Yes.
You seem to be quite positive.
 > I hate cats.
Can you elaborate on that?
 > I don't like cats because they smell bad.
Don't you really like cats because they smell bad?
 > No. Don't like cats.
Are you saying no just to be negative?
 > No.
You are being a bit negative.
 > I am
Is it because you are that you came to me?
 > No
Why not?
 > I am afraid of cats
How long have you been afraid of cats?
 > About a year
I'm not sure I understand you fully.
```

```
> 1 year
Please go on.
> I have been afraid of cats since the cat jumped on my head.
Your head ?
> yes
```

So you can see that ELIZA repeats back phrases to the user, reflecting what the user is talking about. When I said *I am afraid of cats*, the program replied, *How long have you been afraid of cats?*.

ELIZA goes through several steps in recognizing and responding to sentences. Most of the program is not hardcoded, and it works from a series of scripts that you can edit and replace to basically reprogram the personality of the program – which is why we are talking about ELIZA right now:

1. The first step is to divide the sentence into words separated by spaces. The program also replaces all capital letters with lower case.

2. The program replaces words with several versions with a standard word. For example, the program replaces *cant* with *can't* in case you left out the apostrophe. This is called **preprocessing**.

3. The program looks for **keywords** that it knows about. A simple keyword is *sorry*. Any sentence with *sorry* gets a response like *please don't apologize*. Keywords are collected and prioritized by the order they appear in the script file.

4. The program looks for **decomposition** patterns for that keyword. This collects the sentences into common groups. For example, one pattern is: * i was *, which can be read *any word phrase – I was - any word phrase*.

5. ELIZA picks a **reassembly** pattern to form the reply. If the program has several options for responses, it picks one at random. In our * I was * pattern, one response is *Perhaps I already know you were (2)*. The number (2) in parentheses tells the program to substitute the word phrase that comes after *I was* in the sentence. If you typed in *Then I was left at a bus station*, the reply in this pattern could be, *Perhaps I already know you were left at a bus station*. You might also get a more pragmatic, *Oh, really*. It is important to know that ELIZA has no idea about the contents of phrases – it is just manipulating words to create sentences based on patterns.

6. ELIZA performs **post-processing** substitutions of words. For example, it replaces the word *I* with *you*. If you type *I went to sleep*, the program replies with, *You say you went to sleep ?*, which is the final reply rule after all the others are exhausted.

The data that controls ELIZA's personality is called a **script**. This gives the program all of the rules for forming replies. The script for the Rogerian therapist is called the DOCTOR script. It contains some greeting words, some final words when the program exits, a list of pre-subsitution rules, a list of post-processing substitution words, a list of synonyms, and a list of key words with decomposition and re-assembly rules.

Here is a sample rule for the key words *I am*:

```
decomp: * i am *
reasmb: Is it because you are (2) that you came to me ?
reasmb: How long have you been (2) ?
reasmb: Do you believe it is normal to be (2) ?
reasmb: Do you enjoy being (2) ?
```

The program selects a random phrase out of the four provided. If I said, *I am afraid of cats*, then this rule will be triggered, and one of these four phrases would be generated. It might say, *Do you enjoy being afraid of cats?*, or *How long have you been afraid of cats?*.

Almost all of the dialog created by ELIZA comes from the script file, making ELIZA a form of rule-based expert system, and also gives an open framework for creating new applications of conversational engines.

As all computer programs do, ELIZA's concepts for generating conversation were extended and amplified into a general purpose (that is, not just a therapist) software program called ALICE, which is a retronym for Artificial Linguist Internet Computer Entity. The simple script data file used by ELIZA became AIML, the Artificial Intelligence Markup Language. ALICE was extended to be far more useful than ELIZA ever was, and to cover far more subjects and capabilities. However, ALICE retains the same concepts of pre- and post-substitution, keywords, and response patterns. There is a Mycroft plugin engine that allows Mycroft to use AIML files to design conversations. This tool makes a great alternative construction kit for your robot personality.
https://github.com/forslund/fallback-aiml

AIML looks like this:

```
<category>
<pattern>I PLAY *</pattern>
<template>Is <set_it><person/></set_it> a game or a musical
instrument?</template>
</category>
<category>
<pattern>I PLAY THE *</pattern>
<template>I wish I played an instrument. My parents could not afford the
lessons.
<think><set_it><set_does><settopic>play the
```

```
<person/></settopic></set_does></set_it></think></template>
</category>
<category>
<pattern>I PRIDE MYSELF *</pattern>
<template>It seems you have good self esteem.</template>
</category>
<category>
<pattern>I QUIT MY JOB *</pattern>
<template>Where did you work and why did you quit?</template>
</category>
<category>
<pattern>I READ *</pattern>
<template>I don't think I've read that. Can you give me a reference?
<think><set_it><set_does><settopic>read
<person/></settopic></set_does></set_it></think></template>
</category>
<category>
<pattern>I READ * BOOKS</pattern>
<template>Name some books in that genre.
<think><set_it><set_does><settopic>read <person/>
books</settopic></set_does></set_it></think>
<think><set_personality>critical</set_personality></think></template>
</category>
```

Source: http://www.digitalanywhere.com/projects/dany/index.html. **ALICE** is open source software released under the GNU public license.

Context

One of the most important shortcomings of ELIZA is a total lack of memory. ELIZA only remembers the previous statement. You can't talk about your father and then say, *He was a good man.* ELIZA will have no idea whom you are talking about. ELIZA has no concept of context beyond the previous sentence.

What is context? In the course of a conversation, we often shorten nouns into pronouns. We might say, *I like my dog,* and in the next sentence say, *He is well behaved.* Who does the *he* refer to? We know it is the dog, but how does the computer know? We are going to add some ability to reason from context to our program.

We are going to create a storage object we will call the **context memory**. In that object, we will be able to keep up with several parts of our conversation, including the person we are talking to currently, the last subject we talked about, if we had asked any questions we still don't have the answer to, and the answers to any previous questions, in case we need them again. The computer will assume that a pronoun other than *I* will refer to the last subject, whatever that was. If I was talking about a dog, and then say, *He is so cute*, then the robot will assume I mean the dog.

Previously, we discussed playing a game to get information from our person. The robot will be collecting and remembering this information, even after it is turned off, so that the next time that person is talking to the robot, it remembers the information it learned the last time – just as you do with a new friend. If you want to continue to expand this AI chatbot concept, you can use this information to create additional conversation. For example, if the human tells you they like baseball, the robot could ask what their favorite team is, and then look up from the internet when the next baseball game is scheduled.

That is the end of our list of parts we are going to use to build our robot personality. We can now dive in and use our personality construction kit. I'm going to use the bones of the ELIZA Python open source program from Wade Brainerd to build Albert the Tinman's personality.

In the interest of time and space, I'm only going to put the parts here that I added to the base program. The entire code will be in the GitHub repository. You can get the original program at `https://github.com/wadetb/eliza` if you want to follow along from the book.

Under construction

Let's review all the parts we have to put together to make our robot personality:

- Simulation
- Monte Carlo (stochastic, or random based) modeling
- Our robot emotion state machine
- Perception of human emotion state machine
- Our robot biography (list of internal facts about the robot)
- A conversation engine framework called ELIZA
- Context – the ability to remember and return facts and "fill in the blanks"

In the next few sections, I will be presenting the code that I added to Albert to facilitate his artificial personality. A lot of it will be contained in script files that provide rules and patterns for Tinman's speech. There will also be code functions for his emotion engine, human emotion model, and game engine.

Let's get started.

I needed to add some new functions to the script language used by ELIZA. First, I added the context of our robot, who takes the place of ELIZA, the therapist.

First, we have the opening words when we initiate the interactive conversation mode of Tinman by saying *Hey, Albert* (or whatever you decided to call it), the wake word for Mycroft, and then just *Hello*.

Albert the robot gets his name from Albert, the Prince Consort to Queen Victoria, since he was famous for taking wonderful care of his children. All nine of his children survived to adulthood, a rarity in the Victorian age, and he had 42 grandchildren. He went by his middle name – his actual first name was Francis.

The robot responds with the "initial" phrase, as noted by the tag before the colon. We also have our closing phrase here. You can actually put as many phrases as you like and the computer will randomly choose one. These rules go into the file I named `AlbertPersonality.txt`, which started as a copy of the original `doctor.txt` script file that came with ELIZA:

```
initial: Hello. My name is Albert the Tinman Robot.
initial: Hello. I am Tinman the Robot, but you can call me Albert.
initial: Hello. Nice to meet you. Call me Albert.
final: Goodbye. Thank you for talking to me.
final: Goodbye. It was nice to talk to you.
final: Goodbye. I need to get back to my tasks.
quit: bye
quit: goodbye
```

I added some word substitutes in case the user calls the robot by name rather than *you*. This just substitutes *you* for anything you might call the robot. I also set synonyms for various versions of the robot's name so you can call it *robot* or *bot*, as well as *Albert*, *Bert*, or even *Bertie*.

A rule with `pre:` in front of it is substituted before any other processing takes place. From the first rule, if the word *robot* appears in a sentence, as in *Robot, how old are you?*, the program removes *robot* and substitutes *you* to make the parsing consistent. We also change all uppercase letters to lowercase, so there are no capital letters in the rules. The `synon:` rule replaces any of the listed words with the first word given:

```
pre: robot you
pre: albert you
...
synon: you robot albert bert bertie bot
synon: belief feel think believe wish
```

The next thing we needed to was create the questions that we want the robot to ask in order to gain information. The program will automatically *harvest* this data in any of the keywords we define to appear in a sentence. Here is the definition for the rules about asking questions:

```
questions:
  reasmb: What is your name? <assert name>
  reasmb: What can I call you? <assert name>
  reasmb: How old are you? <assert old>
  reasmb: How are you feeling today <assert feeling>
```

We create a new flag for questions to add to our script file. Each line represents one question, but we can ask in different ways or forms. The program will select one version at random, and decides which question to ask based on the relative priority we will set on the questions. The `assert` keyword with the <> symbols around it are another new flag I added to cue the context memory that we have created a context of asking some question, and the next statement is probably an answer:

```
datum: name
  decomp * my name is *
  decomp I am *
  decomp call me *
  decomp <name> * # we are in the name context
  reasmb: Hello (1). Nice to meet you
  reasmb: Hi (1).
  reasmb: Your name is (1), right?
  reasmb: Thank you for telling me your name, (1)
  store: <name> (1)
  decomp * my name is *
  reasmb: Hello (2). Nice to meet you.[welcome][happy]
  store:<name> (2)
```

I created a new data structure I called `datum`, the singular of **data**. This represents some information we want the robot to ask about. We give the datum a name – `name` in this case, as we want the robot to ask the name of who it is talking to. The `decomp` (for decomposition) tags are the patterns of the sentences where the user might say his or her name. The * represents any phrase. So if the human says *Hello. My name is Fred Rodgers*, then the robot will call him Fred Rodgers from then on. If the human says *Call me Ishmael* for some unknown reason, then the robot will use that. We have to reassemble the response phrase with the reasmb rules. The (1) refers to the first * phrase that appears. If the user says, *I am John*, then when we use the reassemble rules, (1) will be replaced by *John*. The robot will pick one of the phrases provided at random, such as: *Your name is John, right?*.

I added another new tag to allow the robot to use the context memory area to perform two functions. We can declare a context subject when we ask a question, which we will do in a later section. For example, when we ask the user, *What is your name?*, then we want the robot to know that the next answer will be in the context of that question. It's perfectly reasonable for the robot to say *Who are you?* and the user to immediately answer *Julia* with no other words in that sentence. How is the program to know what to do with Julia? The answer is the context flag, noted by being bracketed by <>. We read the decomposition rule `decomp <name> *` as if you are in the context of asking for a name, and you get a reply with no keywords, take whatever you get as the answer.

Emotion tags are noted by a bracket like `[happy]` or `[sad]`. This will move ether the robot's emotions or the robot's perception of the human emotions, depending on if it is a statement received from a human or a sentence uttered by the robot. There can be more than one emotion tag associated with a statement.

Here are the rules for listening for the answer to the `age` question:

```
datum: age
decomp <age> * I am * years old
decomp <age> * I am % # integer
reasmb: You are (2) years old?
reasmb: (2) years old!
decomp <age> *
reasmb: You are (1) years old?
reasmb: (1) years old!
store: <age> (1)
```

The final line `store:` is the command to tell the computer that this is the answer to the question and to store that away in the dictionary with the title provided.

Next, let's use an example of an interaction with some emotions tied to it, so we can see how we will use the emotion engine to control what the robot says. This set of rules are enacted when the user says *How are you?* to the robot:

```
key: feeling
    decomp: how are you feeling
    decomp: how are you
    decomp: hows it hanging
    decomp: how are you today
    reasmb: <happy> I'm doing well. How are you? <assert feeling>
    reasmb: <sad> I am feeling sad. How are you? <assert feeling>
    reasmb: <curious> I am curious about my surroundings
    reasmb: <friend> I am feeling friendly today
    reasmb: <welcome> I am in a welcoming mood today, my friend
    reasmb: <frust> I am a bit frustrated, to tell you the truth
    reasmb: <frust> I am feeling a bit frustrated
    reasmb: <strange> I am having relationship problems
    reasmb: <distant> None of my friends have come to visit
    reasmb: <tired> goto tired
```

We will be putting the robot's emotions into the context memory so that the script processing program can have access to it. We treat an emotion – for dialog purposes- as part of the context that we are speaking about, which I think is a reasonable approach to working with emotions. Each emotion has a tag or name in the context memory dictionary. If the predominant emotion in the robot is *happy,* then the robot sets the *happy* context in the context memory. Then the rule base will use the context tag to determine which phrase to use to reply to *how are you feeling?*. We can also ask a follow-up question. Look at the rule for <happy>. The robot replies, *I'm doing well. How are you?* and then sets the feeling context to let the engine know that we asked a question about feeling. Finally, the last line relates to the tired emotion. If the robot is feeling tired, then we jump to a separate section for the robot to talk about being tired. We make it a separate routine because we need to call if from several places, which illustrates the utility of this rule-based approach to speech. I don't want to imagine how many C or C++ SLOC (source lines of code) it would take to create all of these rules for each line of dialog.

We continue to modify the scripts using these guidelines until we have completed all our questions and have patterns for all of the answers.

Now we are going to switch back to Python code for the rest of this example. Our next section describes how we are going to simulate emotions.

The robot emotion engine

Now we are going to put together the robot's emotion model. This is the heart of the artificial personality as it computes, updates, and remembers the emotional state of the robot. The robot starts in a generally neutral state, and performs updates based on the combination of eight emotional traits: happy/sad, welcoming/ distant, friendly/ stranger, curious/frustrated, and fresh/tired. As events happen in the experience of the robot, it gets cues that cause its emotional state to change. For example, if the user said *That is stupid* to something the robot said, then the robot would add to the sad axis of its emotion.

We compute the overall emotional state using a polar coordinates, just like you saw in the diagram we drew. The current emotional state is determined by computing the center of mass of the other emotions. If the emotions are more or less balanced, the center of mass of the emotions, as plotted on our polar chart, would be near the center. If the robot is mostly happy and friendly, then the mass moves more over to that side of the graph. We pick the single emotional state that is closest to the center of the mass. This is intended to be the basis of creating a complex emotional character for the robot. The attribute of fresh/tired is unique, in that the value for that emotion is based on the elapsed runtime of the robot.

The primary expressions of emotion for the robot will be the position of the robot arm – happier robots carry their arms higher and more forward – and in the choice of vocabulary in conversation:

```python
class robotEmotionEngine():
    def __init__(self):
        self.emostate = [90,0]
        self.emoText = "neutral 50"
        self.emotions = {
            "happy" : 50, "sad": 50,
            "welcome" : 50, "distant":50,
            "friend" : 50,"strange" :50,
            "curious" : 50,"frustrated":50,
            "fresh" : 50, "tired",50}
        self.bio = {"name":"Albert Tinman", "lastname": "Tinman", "age":
"6 months",
            "maker": "granddad", "color":
"green","food","electricity","author":"Isaac Asimov, of course",
            "school": "I do not go to school but I love to
learn","hobby":"picking up toys", "job":"picking up toys"}
        # list of happy emotions and sad emotions
        self.emotBalance={"happy": "sad", "welcome":"distant",
            "friend": "strange", "curious": "frustrated","fresh": "tired"}
        self.emotionAxis{"happy":112, "welcome":
22,"friend":67,"curious":157,
            "sad":292,"distant":202,"strange":247,"frustrated",337}
```

```
        self.update()
def change(self,emot, val):
    self.emotions[emot]=val
    balance = 100 - val
    otherEmotion = self.emotBalance[emot]
    self.emotions[otherEmotion]=balance
```

This is the update function:

```
def update(self):
rmin = 100
rmax = 0
thetamin =360
thetamax=0
for emote in self.emotions:
theta = self.emotionAxis[emote]
thetamax = min(theta,thetamax)
thetamin = max(theta,thetamin)
r = self.emotions[emote]
rmin = max(rmin, r)
rmax = max(rmax,r)
stateR = (rmax-rmin)/ 2
stateTheta = (thetamax-thetamin) / 2
for emo in self.emotionAxis:
thisAngle = self.emotionAxis[emo]
if stateTheta > thisAngle
myEmotion = emo
break
self.emostate = [stateTheta, stateR]
if stateR < 55 and stateR > 45:
    myEmotion = "neutral"
self.emoText = myEmotion + " "+ str(stateR)
print "Current Emotional State" = myEmotion, stateR, stateTheta
return
```

The human emotion model

The robot also needs a model of the human it is talking to, so it can make different responses based on how the human is feeling. We are going to create a smaller version of the emotion model we used earlier. We model four emotions for our human interactions for the robot to use in formulating responses: happy/sad, and welcoming/distant. We can put emotion tags into our patterns in the script file with [happy] , [sad],[welcome] or [distant] to mark the emotions of responses. For example, if we are not getting answers to our questions, we can mark that response with [distant] to note that our subject is not being cooperative:

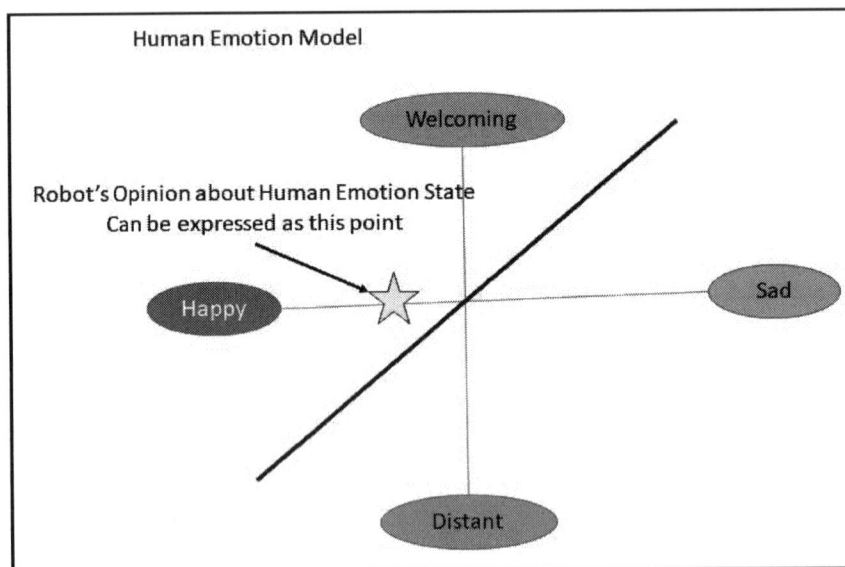

Our human emotion model makes use of a Python dictionary data structure to hold our model. We have two axes, the **Happy/Sad** axis and the **Welcome/Distant** axis. We move the **Happy/Sad** index up or down based on responses. If we think a response expresses happy thoughts (*Do you like school? Yes*), the program moves up the emotion index in the happy direction. We use the intersection of these to set the current emotional index. If the human is near the center, we note this as neutral, our starting point:

```
class HumanEmotionEngine():
    def __init__(self):
        self.emostate = [90,0]
        self.emoText = "neutral 50"
        self.emotions = {
            "happy" : 50, "sad": 50,
            "welcome" : 50, "distant":50}
```

```
# list of happy emotions and sad emotions
self.emotBalance={"happy": "sad", "welcome":"distant"}
self.emotionAxis = {'distant': 315, 'welcome': 135, 'sad': 225,
'happy': 45}
self.update()
```

Let's look at the `change` function. If *happy* goes up, *sad* goes down, so we balance this automatically when emotions change:

```
def change(self,emot, val):
    self.emotions[emot]=val
    balance = 100 - val
    otherEmotion = self.emotBalance[emot]
    self.emotions[otherEmotion]=balance
```

The `update` function gets the current emotional balance of the human model:

```
def update(self):
    stateR = self.emotion["happy"]
    stateS = self.emotion["welcome"]
    self.emostate = [stateR, stateS]
```

If the emotional state is near the middle, we call that `neutral`:

```
if stateR < 55 and stateR > 45 and stateS < 55 and stateS > 45:
    myEmotion = "neutral"
happySad = stateR-50
welcomDist = stateS-50
if abs(happySad) > abs(welcomDist):
    myEmotion = "sad"
    if happySad > 0:
        myEmotion = "happy"
else:
    myEmotion = "distant"
    if welcomDist> 0:
        myEmotion = "welcome"
self.emoText = myEmotion + " "+ str(stateR)
print "Current Human Emotional State" = myEmotion, stateR, stateTheta
return
```

Human information storage

This data structure stores the information we have collected about the human user, and lets the robot know what questions have yet to be answered. We use a Python dictionary to hold the data. This type of data structure let's us make a freeform version of a database-like table. I add values to the dictionary as we go to make extension easier.

I put a list of miscellaneous questions called **stuff** to throw some spice in the robot's information gathering, so that the questions don't seem too monotonous. The robot will ask if you like the color pink, singing, dancing, robots, airplanes, and so on.

We put the list in priority order by copying the dictionary, and replacing the data fields with relative point values from 20 to zero. Name is first with 20 points, age is second with 18, and so on. As each question is answered, we set this points value to zero. For example, if we get the answer for what is your favorite food as apple, we set self.info["food"] = apple, and set self.points["food"] = 0:

```
class HumanInformation():
 def __init__(self):
     self.info = {"name":"none"}
     self.info["age"]=0
     self.info["school"]="none"
     self.info["feeling"]="none"
     self.info["food"]="none"
     self.info["book"]="none"
     self.info["subject"]="none"
     self.info["song"]="none"
     self.info["teeth"]="none"
     self.info["jokes"]="none"
     # stuff is random information that we use to get more information and
have the human answer questions
     # these are aimed at 3-7 year olds
     self.info["stuff"]="none"
     self.stuff = ["the color pink", "singing", "dancing", "dinosaurs",
"race cars", "building things",
     "robots", "airplaines", "space ships", "unicorns", "princesses"]
     self.points = self.info
     # setup points scoring scheme
     points = 20
     for item in self.points:
         self.points[item]=points
         points -= 2
```

Context memory

This is our context memory. You can think of this as a pool of information that the robot can remember. We set up the robot's emotion and the model of human emotion to both be neutral". I created some data structure so that we can refer to multiple human users by pointing self.currentHuman to the HumanInformation data object we created previously.

We use the `inContext` function to retrieve data from the context pool. If no data is available, we return an integer of zero:

```
class ContextMemory():
    def __init__(self):
    self.currentContext = "None"
    self.currentHuman = None # pointer to the data file for the human we
are currentl talking to
    self.humanFile = []
    self.emotion = "neutral"
    self.humanEmotion = "neutral"
    self.contextDict={}
    self.contextDict['neutral']=True  # asserts that the robot is
currently at a neutral state of emotion
    self.contextDict['currentHuman'] = self.currentHuman
    self.contextDict['robotEmotion'] = self.emotion
    self.contextDict['humanEmotion'] = self.humanEmotion
  def inContext(self, datum):
    if datum in self.contextDict:
        return self.contextDict[datum]
    else:
    return 0
  def setHuman(self,human):
    self.currentHuman = human
    self.humanFile.append(human) # add this person to the database of
people we know
  def addHuman(self,human):
    self.humanFile.append(human) # add this person to the database
    # used at startup to recall humans we have met before
```

Questions

1. What is your favorite movie robot? How would you describe its personality?
2. What techniques did the movie-makers use to express that robot's personality (body language, sounds, and so on)?
3. What are the two types of chatbots? List some of the strengths and weaknesses of each.
4. In the diagram on modeling custom distributions (the airport example), the bottom picture shows two standard distributions and two uniform distributions. Why don't the curves go all the way to the top of the graph?
5. Design your own robot emotions. Pick six contrasting emotions that can express the entire range of your robot's personality. Why did you pick those?

6. If you were designing a robot to have the personality of an annoying little boy (think Bart Simpson, Cartman, or Dennis the Menace, if you are that old), what traits would it have?

7. Why is it important for the robot to have a backstory or biography?

For the next two questions, pick a persona from my list to model (from the *Integrating artificial personality* section)

8. Write six lines of dialog for the robot to ask a human where they last went on vacation.

9. . Write six ways for the robot to express that it is tired and needs to recharge, without sounding like a robot.

Further reading

- Janarthanam, Srini. *Hands-On Chatbots and Conversational UI Development Build Chatbots and Voice User Interfaces with Chatfuel, Dialogflow, Microsoft Bot Framework, Twilio, and Alexa Skills*. Birmingham: Packt Publishing, 2017.
- Rothman, Denis. *ARTIFICIAL INTELLIGENCE BY EXAMPLE: Develop Machine Intelligence from Scratch Using Real Artificial Intelligence Use Cases*. Birmingham: Packt Publishing, 2017.
- *How to Develop a Chatbot from Scratch*: https://chatbotsmagazine.com/how-to-develop-a-chatbot-from-scratch-62bed1adab8c
- *A Complete guide to Chatbot Frameworks*: https://www.marutitech.com/complete-guide-bot-frameworks/
- *The Ultimate Guide for Leveraging Your Natural Language Processing Machine Learning for Your Chatbot*: https://chatbotslife.com/ultimate-guide-to-leveraging-nlp-machine-learning-for-you-chatbot-531ff2dd870c
- *Design Guide for Chatbot Conversation*: https://www.marutitech.com/ebooks/guide-design-chatbot-conversation/
- *Phatic Posts: Even the Small Talk Can Be Big*: https://blogs.scientificamerican.com/guest-blog/phatic-posts-even-the-small-talk-can-be-big/
- *Kizmet: Sociable Robot with Facial Expressions, MIT Media Lab:* http://www.ai.mit.edu/projects/sociable/facial-expression.html
- Weizenbaum, Joseph. ELIZA – A Computer Program For the Study of Natural Language Communication Between Man And Machine *Communications of the ACM, Vol 9, No. 1, January 1966*

10
Conclusions and Reflections

We have been on quite a journey over the course of this book. I will tell you that I've learned a lot, and hope you have as well. I had the chance to revisit my love of robotics, and to spend a lot of time examining the state of the art of AI and robot design to try and find a way to explain the concepts to you in an easily digestible form. I tried to break through the jargon, the acronyms, and the equations to try to convince you that the science and art of AI robotics is something you can do and have a good time doing it.

I set out to give you a set of tools that I felt you needed to create artificial intelligence for robots. These are tools that I've collected over my many years designing robots.

I introduced you to my version of the subsumption architecture and how our robot can have several layers of goals at once. This type of approach has become a standard across unmanned vehicles and robotics, and I've used it a number of time as the overall architecture for my robots:

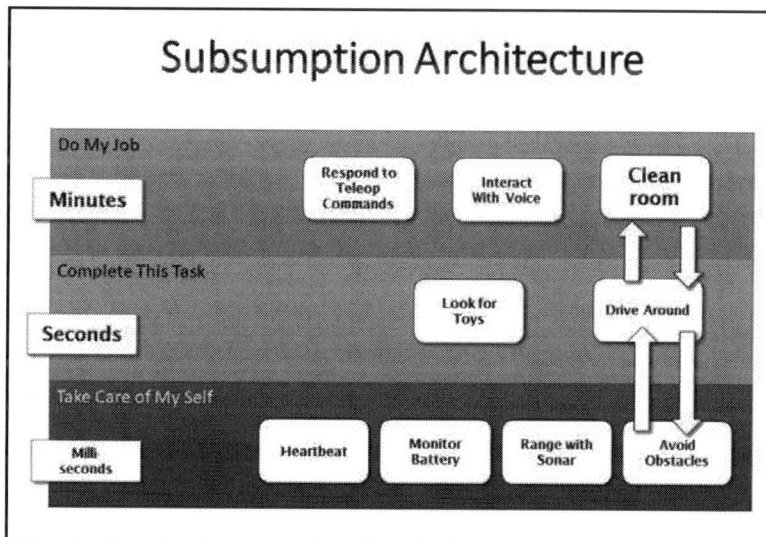

Subsumption Architecture

Do My Job — Minutes: Respond to Teleop Commands, Interact With Voice, Clean room

Complete This Task — Seconds: Look for Toys, Drive Around

Take Care of My Self — Milli-seconds: Heartbeat, Monitor Battery, Range with Sonar, Avoid Obstacles

I also introduced you to the other keystone of robot design, the OODA loop (Observe – Orient – Decide – Act), the key to both command/control and robot decision making. The second "O" – the orient part – is by far the most important, challenging, and time-consuming part of the OODA loop. This is the process of getting all of the robot's data into the same coordinate frame, or perspective. You may also hear this step called by the more impressive name of **data fusion**. It is very difficult to make decisions if all of the input data is not in some sort of consistent form:

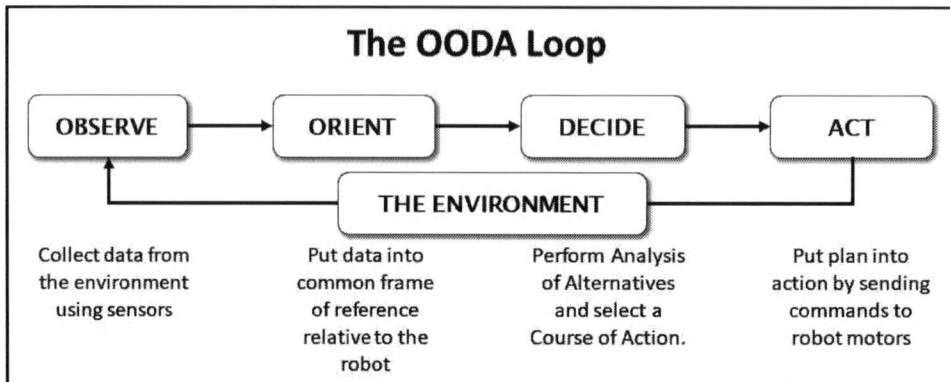

The OODA Loop

OBSERVE	ORIENT	DECIDE	ACT

THE ENVIRONMENT

| Collect data from the environment using sensors | Put data into common frame of reference relative to the robot | Perform Analysis of Alternatives and select a Course of Action. | Put plan into action by sending commands to robot motors |

We talked about soft-real-time control systems, and the importance of managing the time and update rate of a robot that has to deal with the real world. This type of frame-based system gives you a stable foundation to have your robot perform consistently and smoothly, and the controls we added corrected for jitters in the robot's timing that are unavoidable in soft real-time.

Chapter 2, set up the robot's hardware and software, and showed you how to build the frame of the Tinman robot, with its triangular tracks and robotic servo arm. If you end up getting this kit, my directions are the only ones you will have – I had to figure all of this out without any guidance, which was part of the fun.

I was really pleased with the chapter on *Systems Engineering and Design*. Very few robot books go into the design process, and the techniques I have shown you are stripped to the very bone, but still give you the proper foundation for approaching the design of your own robotic projects. I like the storyboard process, and found it kept me on track through the rest of the book. I think you will find it will do the same for you.

In the section on image recognition, I tried to give you a no-math (or almost no math) approach to understand how to put together a basic convolutional neural network. The Keras toolkit for Python really helps make the setup and training as simple as possible while still giving a lot of control.

Next, we tackled teaching the robot to use its servo-mechanical arm and hand. We used two different approaches. The first was reinforcement learning, or Q-learning, which did not match well with our arm state space, which was more continuous than discrete. Q-learning is good for situations where the robot's decision making only has a few different states, and the learning program can explore all possible states several times. We had much more success with the genetic algorithm, and I built you a custom GA sandbox where you can explore breeding algorithms, combinations, mutations, and learning rates in safety. I was very pleased that my GA approach trained the robot arm to a 99% score in just a 100 generations.

Of course, you remember that the next section was natural language processing, listening and divining intent from spoken commands using the Mycroft AI-based robot personal assistant software. We added a lot of capability to Tinman to give you weather reports, the news, look up items on the internet, and respond to commands. We also competed my grandson's special request to have the robot tell and understand knock-knock jokes. We were able to take advantage of Mycroft's wait-for-response command to make this task a lot easier that I thought it was going to be.

Here is an encore knock-knock joke I just made up:

> *Robot: Knock, Knock*
> *User: Who's there?*
> *Robot: Robot!*
> *User: Robot, who?*
> *Robot: Ro, Ro, Ro (your) bot, gently down the stream.*

Let's see – what came after that? We learned a new way to navigate using object recognition, neural networks, and image processing to memorize directions by looking at the upper half of the room. The lower half of the room was processed using the Floor Finder algorithm to detect and avoid obstacles using vision. This bit of work was entirely new for this book, and I don't think this combination of techniques have been used elsewhere. Neural networks are versatile functions that seem to be used for just about everything, these days.

Chapter 8 introduced decision trees and path planners, truly useful processes that are found in games, robots, medical equipment, spacecraft, and airliners. We used our decision tree to make object classifiers, and then tried out some path planning algorithms, with a very short bonus section on GPS path planning.

We finished with designing an artificial personality for our robot. This chapter had a lot more theory and processes, and provided you with more tools for using simulation and Monte Carlo models. These are skills that I use every day. We created an emotion engine for our robot, with a model for human interaction as well. We ended by connecting a very old chat bot called ELIZA and taught her a few new tricks. Even though the ELIZA concept is over 50 years old, the techniques pioneered with that program are still being used to create chatbots today. I believe that artificial personality creation will become its own career path in robotics, if it is not already.

Conclusions about our journey

I hope you have discovered the enjoyment, entertainment, education, and even some of the frustration of making an AI-based robot. I want to remind you that the primary goal of this book was always to teach you about artificial intelligence and robotics techniques. Making the Tinman robot perform was always just an example that we used to keep the story moving, and not an end in itself. I'm sure that you have not seen the last of Albert the Tinman robot or his sisters or cousins, and I will try to continue to develop code and to blog about the robot after this book is published. Please keep checking the GitHub site for the book at: `https://github.com/PacktPublishing/Artificial-Intelligence-for-Robotics`

I certainly learned a lot along the way, as I hope you have done. I think that we are about to see a big increase in the use in AI in robotics and unmanned systems of all kinds, and I hope that this book provides a seed for some people to seek out this area for a career, and join the ranks of those who make robots professionally.

Careers in robotics

I am often asked what sorts of skills, courses, or degrees do robot designers need to have, or to take. I meet a lot of young people at robot competitions, student events, conferences, and recruiting trips. A lot of the advice I give people I have put into this book already – especially now, artificial intelligence, neural networks, GPUs, expert systems, chatbots, navigation, and image processing are all important. You do have to understand that robotics is an umbrella term that covers a lot of industries and a lot of skill sets.

Who uses robotics? The range of applications are continuing to grow every day. In the medical field, there is robot assisted surgery, robotic prosthetic limbs, exoskeletons helping paraplegics to walk, and implantable devices to help people hear and see.

We have self-driving cars and self-flying airplanes and helicopters in transportation. We have robots delivering packages on the sidewalks in San Francisco, and a number of companies testing parcel delivery by aerial drone in Africa, Switzerland, and in other places.

Look at the world of robotics around you now. We have self-driving cars being tested in a number of states. Safety features that debuted in the DARPA Grand Challenge robot car race and were developed for autonomous cars – lane keeping, adaptive cruise control, driver assistance, and self-parking are now common feature on even base level automobiles. There are over 60 companies currently developing some sort of electric VTOL (vertical take off and landing) manned vehicle, every one of which uses advanced automation and autonomy as part of its control system. In far western Australia, Rio Tinto Mining has developed the "Mine of the Future" in Pilbara, where 80 autonomous trucks are remotely operated from Perth, 1,500 kilometers away.

The future of robotics is just being written, and you, reading this book, may play a part in determining the path it takes.

So, what skills are required to design and make robots like the ones I just described? The truth is, a modern robot company would employ just about every skill imaginable. Even the simplest robot takes mechanical designers to develop the parts, gears, and levers to make robots move and to package the electronics. Electrical engineers work with batteries and motors. RF engineers and technicians work with radios and datalinks. Cognitive specialists design artificial intelligence routines, develop robot emotions, and harness machine learning techniques. Writers and artists craft voice routines, write dialog, design user interfaces, write manuals and documentation, and add creative touches to the inside and outside of the robot. Managers and supervisors track budgets and schedules, while supply specialists work with suppliers, parts, build-to-print shops, electronics warehouses, and salesmen to get the parts to put together the assembly line. Industrial robots are managed by special types of programmers who use PLA (programmable logic arrays) and ladder logic to control robot arms that paint and assemble components. Bookkeepers and accountants make sure the bills are paid as well as the employees. Salespeople, marketing, and customer relations teams get the product sold and keep the customers happy.

All of these skills together have to be present in some form in the professional roboticist, particularly if you think you will run your own company. I've been part of every size of robot project, from one person to tens of thousands. Each has its own strengths and weaknesses, but you can be sure as a robot designer that you will be the center of the storm, making the magic happen, solving problems, and turning ideas into physical form.

To me, there is no more satisfying moment than seeing my creation driving or flying around, doing its job, and knowing that all of the hard work, sleepless nights, smashed fingers and toes, and skipped meals was worth this result.

Issues in AI – real and not real

There is really a lot of hype going on right now in the intersecting worlds of artificial intelligence and robotics. And a lot of is just hype and exaggeration.

One common myth is that robots are taking jobs away from people. In truth, robots and automation free up workers to do more productive tasks. The truth of this can be seen in job statistics – unemployment in the US is at a 20-year low, despite massive improvements in factory automation. The fact is that the improved productivity of robotics creates more jobs than it removes (source: *The Financial Review*, November 11, 2016. `https://www.afr.com/business/robots-not-taking-jobs-economist-busts-automation-myths-20161110-gsmo3j`)

I'm not here to say that individuals are not losing manufacturing jobs, but I do say that the overall level of employment has increased, not gone down as a result of automation and increased productivity.

I do recognize that the modern worker, even someone like myself, who works in technology, must be ready and willing – at any age – to retrain themselves and to learn and adapt to new ways of working, new economies, and new opportunities. I've had to completely retrain myself at least five times as new markets were invented and new technologies have emerged. Sometimes there is a "second wave" where some technology was invented but then disappeared when it was too expensive for the benefits it provided, or the proper hardware had not been invented yet. Neural networks fit into that category, as does virtual reality, which was a big deal in 1999, and has now re-emerged with very small high resolution screens that were developed for cell phones.

I'm quite interested in the long-term impact of what has been called the "sharing economy", where companies like Uber, Lyft, and AirBnB create value by connecting suppliers and consumers on a massive scale without owning any of the capital or resources to actually provide any services. All of this is enabled and made possible by the ubiquitous internet, which continues to grow and evolve at a rapid pace. I often use the term, "but that's a decade in internet years", referring to some idea that is maybe 24 months old, to indicate the rapid turnover in internet tech. This trend will continue. It will be interesting to see if anyone owns a car in 20 years, or only a subscription to a car service.

Another trend that has become very interesting is the lowering of barriers to entry in a lot of businesses. You used to have to have an enormous machine shop and giant machines to make plastic parts – before 3D printers came and put that capability on your desktop. Want to make movies? You can do it on an iPhone. Want to start your own recording studio? The parts for professional results (with a large amount of effort) are available for less than $200.

One item that definitely fits into that category are drones, or small unmanned aerial vehicles. When I started making unmanned aerial vehicles, or UAVs as we called them, a decent GPS and IMU (inertial measurement unit) – the things that make unstable quadcopters possible to control– cost tens of thousands to hundreds of thousands of dollars. The real breakthrough in drone technology did not come from aviation, but rather from your cell phone. The developments in cell phones enabled companies to make billions of dollars making the next cell phone or smartphone, or hand-held computer pacifier, or whatever you would want to call it. The convergence of very small radios, very small GPS, and very, very small accelerometers, enabled an entire world of unmanned flying things to emerge. That, along with higher density batteries that came from (you guessed it) cell phones and laptops, allowed people to discover that if you put enough power on it, you can make almost anything fly, including you.

The secret to the flying quadcopter's amazing success is that the tiny accelerometers (that measure changes in movement) and tiny gyroscopes (that measure changes in angles) became cheap and readily available. Without these sensors, and the robotics algorithms that control them, quadcopters are unstable and impossible to control. Another reason for the quadcopter's success is that it uses only the throttle setting – the speed of the motors – to control all of its aspects of flight, including stability. This compares with the very complicated collective controls and cyclic pitch controls that make a helicopter work. You can see the difference in an R/C helicopter, that is very expensive, and only a few people can fly, and a quadcopter, that is quite cheap and can be flown by anyone, with the help of a computer and some sensors.

Some very brief words about robots and AI phobia

You have been hearing blazing headlines on the internet from various very credible sources, saying some incredible (as in not credible) things:

Mark my words — A.I. is far more dangerous than nukes — Elon Musk (CNBC. March 13, 2018).

I am in the camp that is concerned about artificial intelligence. First the machines will do a lot of jobs for us and not be super intelligent. That should be positive if we manage it well. A few decades after that though the intelligence is strong enough to be a concern. I agree with Elon Musk and some others on this and don't understand why some people are not concerned. — Bill Gates, TechEmergence.com, March 9, 2018.

The development of full artificial intelligence could spell the end of the human race ... It would take off on its own, and re-design itself at an ever increasing rate. Humans, who are limited by slow biological evolution, couldn't compete, and would be superseded— Stephen Hawking, speaking to the BBC, from `https://www.forbes.com/sites/bernardmarr/2017/07/25/28-best-quotes-about-artificial-intelligence/#383649e24a6f`

Let me say I do not think I'm in the same league as these gentlemen. But what I am is someone who works every day at the leading edge of artificial intelligence, unmanned vehicles, and robotics, and who attends and speaks at a lot of AI conferences.

The source of this fear can be found in any bathroom, hanging on the wall – we are reflecting our own motivations and desires onto our creations.

The state of the art of AI today I would liken to a teenager who has managed to strap a V-8 engine to a skateboard – an enormous amount of power with no way to use it. While computers, hardware, and networks have advanced and scaled at an amazing rate, we are still building software exactly the same way today as we did 20 years ago, and many of the advances of AI were really invented 40 or 50 years ago. Neural networks were invented in the 1940s(1). Genetic algorithms were suggested by Alan Turing in the 1950a (2). We have been able to make some advancements on applying learning theory now that we have lots of data (thank you, internet) and lots of bandwidth, but we have not created any new concepts or capabilities that show any sort of breakthrough in AI. We are no closer to creating a general AI – a computer that learns any task without reprogramming – than we were in 1969.

While the hardware is advancing, the software is not, at least not at the same rate as the hardware. I simply don't see any path forward that leads to the type of problems that the esteemed Mr. Gates, Mr. Musk, or Dr. Hawking are suggesting. Why not?

It is because robots don't have needs. Humans have needs and ambitions in order to exist. We are encased in a frail flesh cell, what William Burroughs called "the Soft Machine". We must provide air, food, water, shelter and clothing to protect our fragile shell, and interact with other soft machines (people) to reproduce and make more of ourselves. You can argue, as Richard Dawkins did in his book, *The Selfish Gene*, that all of this is simply an evolved way for our DNA to perpetuate itself, and that we are simply the product of our biological programming. It is absolutely impossible to separate a human from his or her needs – if you don't, we die in a matter of minutes. It is our needs that drive us forward, to come out of the trees, to learn to farm, to build cities, and make civilizations.

Robots, on the other hand, do not have needs as a condition of their existence. They are just sets of instructions we have set down in electronics – golems with words in their heads that make them move (3). If we don't feed them – nothing happens. If we don't use them – nothing happens. If we forget them for a week and check on them later, they are still the same. Try that with a cat or dog.

Let's talk for a moment about what a set of robot needs might look like. I found this an interesting thought experiment – we make a baby robot that is fully capable of learning anything a baby human (or baby mouse, or baby cricket) can. What needs would it have? We can start with what our needs are. It has been a running joke between my wife and I that every textbook we ever read in college contained some reference to Abraham Maslow, and his Hierarchy of Needs. This was quite unusual since I studied math and engineering, and my wife's degree is in human resources. Mr. Maslow came up with this list of needs back in 1943, and he has been quoted ever since. (4) Maslow says that we not just have needs, but they form a hierarchy – the more important needs at the bottom, and more abstract needs at the top.

We only worry about the need at any given level when all of the needs below it are satisfied:

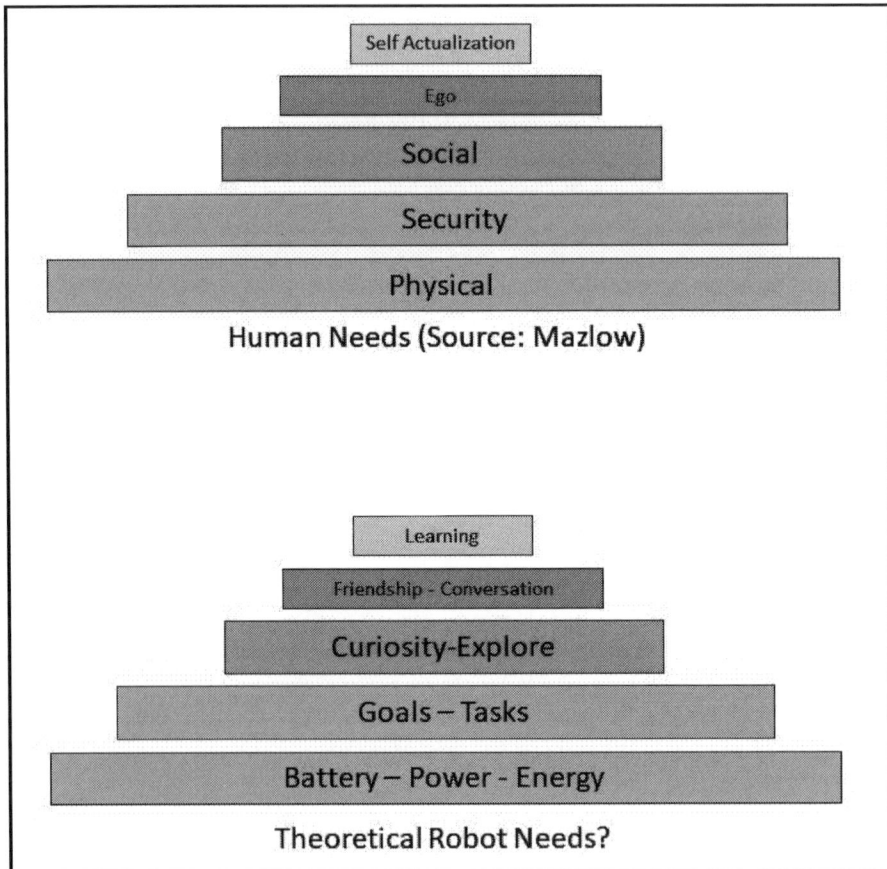

```
                    Self Actualization

                         Ego

                       Social

                      Security

                      Physical
              Human Needs (Source: Mazlow)




                       Learning

                Friendship - Conversation

                   Curiosity-Explore

                    Goals – Tasks

                Battery – Power - Energy
               Theoretical Robot Needs?
```

So at the bottom of the pyramid of needs are the physical needs – air, food, water, and clothing. The next level is security – we need to feel secure from predators or from other humans wanting to harm us. Above the security needs are social needs – to be in a group or part of a society. Humans want to belong to a family, a community, a nation. This drive is very strong, as our invention of war to protect our society attests. Next we have ego needs- the need to be recognized, to be special, to stand out from the crowd we fought so hard to be part of. Remember, we only get to express this once all the other needs are taken care of, so you only worry about recognition once you are part of a group. Our final need is called self-actualization by Maslow – we would call it self- improvement, or the drive to improve one's self. This is where we get athletes, artists, musicians, and people writing books.

Now let's look at a machine intelligence. For us, hunger is built into our biology. We, the creators, would need to build it into an AI system. That would equate, as we did in our artificial personality, with electrical power or battery life. The next level of needs would be the goals and tasks for which the AI was created. The next level up would be curiosity and the need to explore – our AI system would have a drive to acquire more data, or to get access to more resources. Once a robot has data that gives it the basis to get more data, and so on. The next level of needs we would endow to our AI would be the need for friendship or communication, either with other robots or with people. Finally, we could give our robot the need for learning, or to acquire and learn new skills and techniques – to grow as a robot.

You may notice that we did not cover these subjects in this book, nor in any other. We did not talk about giving the robot needs, only the simulation of emotions and some rules for conversation that make no sense to the robot at all. It gets no joy from telling a terrible joke to a 7-year-old, because it does not know what any of those concepts are. It just sends electrons down either one path or another because we tell it to. The only intelligence here is the reflection and imagination of us, the robot designers. Everything else is an illusion, a magician's trick.

That got a bit deep from a guy that started off this chapter telling you knock-knock jokes. I do get this sort of question quite a lot and felt that I could give you some of my answers, if that helps arm you against anti-artificial intelligence mobs with torches and pitchforks.

The bottom line is I simply do not worry about AI taking over the world. I don't say that there will never be a general AI, just I don't see one coming about in the foreseeable future.

Understanding risk in AI

One subject I talk about frequently at conferences and in print is the risk of artificial intelligence in terms of trust and control. I'm not talking here about AI running amok, but rather with AI being dependable.

It is quite interesting that the sort of AI we have been doing – specifically, artificial neural networks—does something very few other computer software do.

Given the exact same inputs and conditions, the output of an AI system is not always the same. Given the same inputs, the AI will sometimes come up with a different answer.

The formal name for this behavior is non-determinism.

There is a second corollary to this. Given the same inputs, the AI process will sometimes take a different amount of time to complete its task.

This is simply not normal behavior for a computer. We have gotten used to 2+2 = 4 on a pretty consistent basis from a computer. Indeed, we depend on it. Remember, computers are navigating your airliners, keeping you alive in a hospital, sending astronauts to the moon. How can we deal with a computer sometimes saying 2+2 = 2, and taking a different amount of time to do it?

You can verify this for yourself – look at the examples when we did training on neural networks. Did we ever achieve a 100% success from a training run, where we got all of the answers right? No, not once.

This is because artificial neural Networks are universal approximation functions that map inputs – which can be quite complex – to outputs. They do this by dealing in probabilities and averages, which were developed over time. You can think of an artificial neuron to be a probability engine that says, *45 out of the last 50 times I got this set of inputs, the output was supposed to be true. The odds are it will be true this time.* And it sets itself to true. We may have millions of little artificial neurons in our network, each of them making the same sort of calculation. The net result is making a very educated guess about the answer.

For most applications of our neural networks, this is OK behavior. We are classifying pictures, and it is OK if a few are wrong. We do a Google search for platypus, and we get one picture out of 100 of Platypus brand tennis shoes. That is OK for a Google search, but what if we were doing something more serious – like recognizing pedestrians in a self-driving car. Is it OK if we misidentify one pedestrian out of 100 and not avoid them? Of course not. That is why, right now, we don't allow AI system in such critical functions. But people want to use AI in this way – in fact, quite a lot. It would be great to have an AI function that recognized geese in flight and told your airliner how to avoid them. It would be great to have an AI recognize that a patient was misdiagnosed in the hospital and needed immediate attention. But we can't do that until we come up with processes for dealing with the non-deterministic and thus non-reliable nature of AI.

Now today, we deal with non-deterministic elements in automobiles all of the time. They are called drivers. We also know that 94% of car crashes (5) are caused by that human element behind the wheel, which is why we need self-driving cars with a better percentage. How do we deal with human drivers? We require them to be a certain age, which means they have gained experience. They have to pass a test, demonstrating competency in accomplishing tasks. They have to demonstrate compliance with rules and regulations by passing a knowledge test. And they have to get periodically re-certified by renewing their license. We also require seat belts and airbags to partially mitigate the risk of the human driver making mistakes by reducing some of the resulting injury.

We can apply these types of criteria to AI. We can require a certain amount of training cases. We can test and demonstrate a level of competency. We can predict in advance the level of errors or mistakes, and put measures in place to mitigate that risk. Perhaps we can have two AI systems, one that detects obstacles, and the other that is trained to recognize that the first AI has made a mistake. If we have a 90% chance of the first AI being right, and another 90% of the second AI being right, then we have a 90% + (90% of 10%) = 99% chance of avoidance.

I think the key to using AI in safety-critical applications is being able to predict risk in advance, and designing in advance to mitigate either the cause of the risk or the effect.

Final words

I want to thank you for coming on this journey with me. I hope you have learned something along the way, even if it is just to know more questions to ask. I encourage you to dive in and build your own robot, learn about artificial intelligence, and become part of the community of people who contribute to robotics as a hobby or a profession.

I have to acknowledge a debt of gratitude to all of the robotics and AI open source community for making all of this material, knowledge, and expertise available, and continuing to make AI the poster child for why open source, as a model for advancement of human knowledge, works and works well.

Summary

In this final chapter of our book, we summarized the journey through robotics and AI that is presented in the other chapters. We talked about robotics as a career, and discussed AI robotics as a profession. I brought up some issues regarding the future of AI, both real and imaginary. Drones and self-driving cars are real; robots taking jobs from humans or taking over the world is imaginary, at least in my opinion. I talked about robots and AI not having needs, and thus lacking the motivation or pressure, or even capability to evolve. Finally, we talked about risk in AI and how to recognize it.

Questions

1. Given that we started the chapter with knock-knock jokes and ended up taking about robot phobia and philosophical questions about existence, do you feel that AI is a threat, and why?

2. List five professions that would be necessary to turn our Tinman robot into a product company.

3. Why would our imaginary Tinman robot company need a psychologist?

4. What components found in cell phones or smartphones are also found in quadcopters?

5. Why are artificial intelligence systems, specifically artificial neural Networks, naturally non-deterministic in both result and in time?

6. What might be a practical application of an AI system that predictably makes mistakes?

7. If an AI system was picking stocks for you, and predicted a winning stock 43% of the time, and you had a second AI that was 80% accurate at determining when the first AI had *not* picked a good stock, what percent of the time would the AI combination pick a profitable stock?

Further reading

- Hebb, Donald (1949). *The Organization of Behavior*. New York: Wiley. ISBN 978-1-135-63190-1

- Turing, Alan M. *Computing machinery and intelligence*. Mind. LIX (238): 433–460

- Pratchett, Terry. *Feet of Clay*. HarperCollins, London 2009

- Maslow, A. H. (1943). *A Theory of Human Motivation*. Psychological Review, 50(4), 370-96.

- US Dept. of Transportation. *Critical Reasons for Crashes Investigated in the National Motor Vehicle Crash Causation Survey* (https://crashstats.nhtsa.dot.gov/Api/Public/ViewPublication/812115)

- Damer, T. Edward. 2013. *Attacking Faulty Reasoning: A Practical Guide to Fallacy-Free Arguments*. Boston, MA: Wadsworth, Cengage Learning

Assessments

Chapter 1, Foundation for Advanced Robotics and AI

1. PID stands for Proportional, Integral, Derivative, and is a type of closed loop controller which does not require a model to operate. PID is not an AI method because it doesn't involve learning and there is no simulation of decision making.

2. The Turing test, originally called "The Imitation Game" by Alan Turing, is an imaginary test, or thought experiment, in which a person is communicating with someone or something via a teletype (text message for you millennials). An AI would pass the Turing test if the person was unable to tell if the entity he/she was communicating with was a human or a robot. The Turing test has been pretty much smashed by modern AI-based chatbots, and a new test has been proposed – assembling IKEA furniture via the directions.

3. Because they cannot see them completely with a range sensor, such as a LIDAR. Also, most robot obstacle detection sensors are parallel to the floor and are not looking down.

4. In the Orient step, all of the data is put into the same reference frame, which is usually the robot's central point of view. This allows the robot to determine which data is relevant to decision making.

5. This is a bit of a rhetorical question. The correct answer is "a lot". Using Python as an interpreted language can save a lot of time for very complex builds, where a C / C++ compiler and link can take 20 minutes or more. The C program test cycle in the question would take 6.25 hours to complete while Python would take 2.5 minutes.

6. RTOS stands for Real-Time Operating System.

7. You need a number that all of the rates 10, 5, 50, 20 divide into evenly. The smallest number that fits is 100 Hz. I would also accept 50 Hz if the student assumed that the 20 Hz would update twice in one frame and three times in the next frame.

8. As given in the previous questions, there does not have to be the same number of samples in each frame in order to come out with a constant frame rate, as long as there is a multiple of the base frame rate every sample divides into. In this case, 20 x 7 = 140, so the 7 Hz can run in a 20 Hz base rate, and it will repeat patterns every 140 frames, or 7 seconds. 3.5 is half of seven and can run at the same base rate with a pattern that repeats every 70 frames or 3.5 seconds. Each update would be 5.7 frames apart, which gets rounded up to 6.

9. A blocking call suspends the execution of your program until some interrupt or event occurs, such as receiving a datagram or UDP packet. They are bad because you lose control of your program timing and cannot maintain a soft real-time execution. Use polling type calls instead for serial ports and network interfaces.

Chapter 2, Setting Up Your Robot

1. Sensors mentioned in the text include:
   - Sonar sensors
   - Cameras
   - Microphones
   - Buttons
   - Analog-to-digital voltage sensors
   - Temperature via thermistors

2. PWM stands for Pulse Width Modulation, a type of digital-to-analog control scheme where pulses are sent out that get longer based on the amount of control desired. It is commonly used to control DC motors.

3. As the name says, analog to digital conversion (A2D) takes in an analog value, typically a voltage, and converts it into a digital value or number that the digital part of the computer can understand.

4. As stated in the text, the subsumption architecture was originally described by Dr. Rodney Brooks, a professor at MIT who would later help found iRobot Corporation and invent the Baxter Robot. Rodney was trying to develop analogues of insect brains in order to understand how to program intelligent robots. Brooks, Rodney. Cambrian Intelligence: The Early History of the New AI. MIT Press, 1999. Boston, MA.

5. The three laws of robots from Isaac Asimov first of all are fictional, while the subsumption architecture is a real process that is used to make real robots.

    The three laws are:

- Robots will not harm a human being, or through inaction, allow a human to come to harm.
- Robots will obey orders from humans except when that violates the first law.
- Robots will protect themselves from harm, except when that violates the first two laws.

    The bottom layer of the SA (subsumption architecture) is the part that looks inside the robot and takes care of internal systems. I like to compare it to the autonomic nervous system. That protects the robot. The second layer is the short-term manager. It tells the robot where to go, which includes obeying orders from users. The top layer contains the strategic thinking and planning processes. The correlation is pretty weak, to be truthful.

    And, yes, readers, I am aware of the fourth, or Zeroth, law: the robot shall not harm humanity , or allow humanity to come to harm. That was a later addition.

6. This is a personal, subjective question for the reader. Why do we give robots names and not washing machines?
7. The most important variable in this set is the ROS_MASTER_URI, which tells all of the ROS parts where ROSCORE is located at. ROSCORE makes all of the connections in a ROS system.

Chapter 3, A Concept for a Practical Robot Design Process

1. A storyboard for a movie is used not just for advancing the plot, but showing what point of view will be used – in other words, it is used to plan camera angles, directions, and movements. The purpose of both storyboards is to "tell the story" of what happens, so they are different, and the same. The point of view of a computer software storyboard should be the user.
2. Who? What? When? Where? Why?. More relevant questions might be: How well? How often? How much?

3. Use cases are from the user's perspective and never include implementation details.

4. The robot has to: determine a route to the toybox; plan a path; avoid obstacles along the way; align itself with the front of the toybox; drive up to the toybox; and move the robot arm to clear the top.

5. It is to complement the teller of the joke – the robot should say "That is very funny", or "I am sorry, I am unable to groan".

6. The robot needs to send a video back to the operator so the operator can see where they are going.

7. The robot shall have a sensor capable of detecting negative obstacles in the floor (that is, stairs going downward, balconies) at a distance of at least six inches from the robot, along the robot's driving direction.

8. 30 degrees/320 pixels wide = 0.0937 deg/pixel.

   35 pixels* deg/pixel = 3.28 degrees.

   This makes an isosceles triangle; we need a right triangle to do the math.

   Divide the base in two to make a right triangle – base = 3 inches.

   We also divide the angle in half. 3.28 becomes 1.64 degrees.

   3" / tan(1.64) = 104 inches or 8.73 feet.

Chapter 4, Object Recognition Using Neural Networks and Supervised Learning

1. This is an exercise for the student. You should see different curves develop as the activation function is changed. Some will not produce an answer at all (which look like random results – the curve stays at the same level as no learning is taking place). Some will learn faster or slower.

2. Refer to Figure 3 in the chapter. The artificial neuron has a number of inputs, a set of weights, one for each input, a bias, an activation, and a set of outputs.

3. Both have multiple inputs and multiple outputs, and accept inputs, perform some processing, and then make an output. Both use some sort of activation to determine when to "fire" or produce an output.

4. The natural neuron is an analog device that can handle many levels or degrees of inputs, with no simple on/off binary representations like the computer neuron. Neurons use chemical paths that make pathways and connections easier the more they are used, which is the learning function of a neuron. This is simulated by the weights in an artificial neuron. The natural neuron has an axon, or connecting body that extends out to the outputs that can be a quite distance from the nerve inputs. Neurons are randomly connected to other neurons, while artificial neurons are connected in regular patterns.

5. The first layer contains the number of inputs to the network.

6. The last layer of an ANN is the output layer and has to have the same number of neurons as outputs.

7. Loss functions in ANNs are the error function. They compare the expected output of the neuron with the actual output.

- Mean square loss: The most commonly used loss function. Sum of the squares of the distances between the output and the expected output. MSL amplifies the error the farther away from the desired solution.

- Cross-entropy: Also called log loss. Used mostly for classification CNNs. As the predicted value approaches 1 (no error), XE (cross-entropy) slowly decreases. As the values diverge, the XE increases rapidly. Two types of cross-entropy are binary (on/off, used for yes/no questions) and sigmoid cross-entropy, which can handle multiple classes.

8. You are probably "overfitting" and have too small a sample size, or your network is not wide or deep enough.

Chapter 5, Picking up the Toys

1. The origin of the Q-learning title is the doctoral thesis of Christopher John Cornish Hellaby Watkins from King's College, London in May, 1989. Evidently, the Q just stands for "quantity".

2. Only pick the Q-states that are relevant and follow-ons to the current state. If one of the states is impossible to reach from the current position, or state, then don't consider it.

3. If the learning rate is too small, the training can take a very long time. If the learning rate is too large, the system does not learn a path, but instead "jumps around" and may miss the minimum or optimum solution. If the learning rate is too big, the solution may not converge, or suddenly drop off.

4. The discount factor works by decreases the reward as the path length gets longer. It is usually a value just short of 1.0 (for example, 0.93). Changing the discount factor higher may have the system reject valid longer paths and not find a solution. If the discount is too small, then paths may be very long.

5. You would adjust the fitness function to consider path length as a factor in the fitness.

6. You can implement the SARSA technique into program 2 ,as follows:

```
# SARSA = State, Action, Reward, State, Action
Q[lastStat,lastAction]=reward+gamma*Q[stat2,action]
#Q[stat,action]=reward + gamma * np.max(Q[stat2])
```

7. Generally, increasing the learning rate shortens the learning time in generations, up to a limit where the path jumps out of the valid range. For our example program, the lowest learning rate that returns a valid solution is 5, and the highest value is 15.

8. It causes the simulation to run much faster, but takes many more generations to find a solution.

Chapter 6, Teaching a Robot to Listen

1. I found at least three. My favorite is that Mycroft is Sherlock Holmes' older, and some say, smarter, brother. Sherlock Holmes is played on TV by Benedict Cumberbatch, who also played Alan Turing in *The Imitation Game*, the original name of the Turing test, a test of AI conversation, which is what Mycroft does.

2. One approach has been to gather a selection of commands, label the intent of the commands, use the commands as input to a neural network, and the label as the training output.

3. It is fairly simple to add a program to just write to the knock-knock joke program database. I'll post a version of this on the HitHub site. Is this machine learning? I would say, definitely! The machine has a capability that it did not have before.

4. `play_wav_cmdline: paplay %1 --stream-name=mycroft-voice`.

    You can use this to play the audio. You can also add a tag to the joke file that indicates a wave file, `<groan.wav>`. Then if you see this tag, call the play wave function.

5. In other languages, the object or the subject appear in a different order, just as in Yoda's speech patterns. "Backwards, talk I", Yoda would say.

> That does require us to change or add the new sentence patterns to our `.voc` files.

> You can follow Mycroft's instructions for changing the engine to understand French from this web page:

> ```
> https://mycroft.ai/documentation/language-support/french/
> #download-and-install-french-language-model
> ```

6. I do not place Mycroft in the category of construction AI chatbots, but it is rather a referential type that looks up answers in a database, which makes it more of an expert system than an AI program. It does use AI neural networks in the speech-to-text section.

7. The voice commands are:

   ```
   Hey Albert!
   Can you see any objects?
   Drive to closest object.
   ```

8. From step 7, work to minimize the number of commands. How many can you eliminate or combine?

```
Hey Albert.
Drive to the nearest object.
```

9. Also from step 7, how many unique keywords are involved? How many non-unique keywords?

```
Key words are: see, objects, drive, closest.
All of the words are unique except "object".
```

Chapter 7, Avoiding the Stairs

1. LIDAR, a type of laser radar, is the most common SLAM sensor used, by a wide margin. The 3D data that LIDAR provides is perfect for SLAM's mapping function.
2. The Wheel odometers reduce the search space that the SLAM algorithm needs to look for possible locations of the robot after moving. Thus, it increases information and reduces uncertainty in the map.

3. It reduces noise and gets rid of stray single pixels in the image, making for a smoother result.

4. Instead of using radial red lines, the program can just draw upwards from the bottom of the screen in a series of vertical lines.

5. We just want to use the upper half of the room to train the network because the lower half has the toys on it and are subject to change. The upper half of the room does not change with the addition of toys.

6. We don't have to have a map to successfully navigate the room. We are providing labeling of our training set by just driving the robot around and taking pictures at regular intervals. This approach is also far more resilient to changes in the room, like throwing toys all over the place.

7. We would need to have a navigation function that determined where in the room we were at – this would probably mean a SLAM algorithm. We would also need a something to detect the stairs.

8. We trained the robot to navigate by looking at the upper part of the room. We only drove the robot in safe areas, and used that information to allow the robot to predict its next driving command based on where it is in the room. Since we hopefully did not drive the robot down the stairs in this process, the robot will never get a command to drive towards the stairs. We have to be careful to get a good training result before letting the robot loose, however. I used a "baby gate" to block the stairs for early testing. We can add a lookdown sensor to detect stairs as an additional safety measure. I would use an IRPD (Infrared Proximity Detector) for this purpose.

Chapter 8, Putting Things Away

1. From the beginning to the end (start to goal); from goal to start; and from both ends at once and meeting in the middle.

2. By eliminating the effect of the item on the branch. For example, using our "robot does not move" fault, if the branch says, "Arduino- no power", if you check to see if the Arduino has power, and it does, you can prune that branch. If the branch is "Motor stuck", the effect of having a motor stuck is that the robot will drive in circles. As the robot is not driving in circles – it's not driving at all – you can prune that branch.

3. It determines the amount of "impurity" in the sample or pool. When the Gini impurity = 0, all of the members of the class have the same attributes, and no further subdivision is possible. Gini minimizes misclassification. The Gini Index is 1 minus the sum of the squares of the probability of an item being in that class.

4. Color, noise, soft, and material were not useful in dividing the categories by labels. The labels and the items did not correlate. It does make sense that color is not useful in subdividing toys by type.

5. The color white was used by the decision tree that used the Gini Index and One Hot Encoding to separate out the stuffed animals.

6. Let's have three types of menu items: appetizers, entrée, and dessert. Label encoding would substitute 0 for appetizers, 1 for entrée, and 2 for dessert. One Hot Encoding would use 1 0 0 for appetizers, 0 1 0 for entrees, and 0 0 1 for desserts.

7. The `G()` function is the distance along the path from the current position to the start. `H()` is the distance from the current position directly to the goal (Euclidean Distance). Note that `G()` follows the path, and `H()` is the straight line distance to the goal, since we have not computed a path to the goal yet.

8. A heuristic is an approach that is not guaranteed to be optimal, but instead is just sufficient for the task. Since `H()`, the direct line distance to the goal, is an estimate and ignores any obstacles, it can't be used directly, but is just a way to compare one position to another. A major difference between D* and A* is that D* starts at the goal and works backwards toward the start. This allows D* to know the exact cost to the target – it is using the actual path distance to the goal from the current position and not a heuristic or estimate of the distance to go, like A* did.

9. `RAISED` squares or points are eliminated from consideration. `LOWERED` squares may be added back into the queue for consideration to be a path. Keep in mind that lowering scores due to new sensor readings ripple through the path planner.

Chapter 9, Giving the Robot an Artificial Personality

1. This is of course, a subjective question. I'm a big R2D2 fan. R2 is feisty, determined, and stubborn, as well as being a faithful companion and helper. R2 will get you out of a jam, fix your star fighter, provide cover from hostile fire, and hack Imperial computers. He is a Swiss Army Knife with wheels.

2. R2 D2 owes his personality to a combination of his emotional beeps and squawks (provided by Ben Burtt), his body movements provided by having a person inside his chassis (Kenny Baker). They were stuck with the not-very versatile chassis designed for the first *Star Wars* movie, which only has a head that moves. Most of R2's persona comes through his sounds, including his famous scream.

3. The two types are retrieval based and generative. Retrieval-based chatbots look up responses in lists of scripts, and choose from a number of phrases that are written in advance by humans. Generative chatbots use the rules of grammar and models of sentences to create new sentences with the proper meaning. The strengths of the retrieval-based chatbots is that they are easy to program, with more control over the outputs, and much smaller and faster programs. Weaknesses include limited responses, and the use of keywords give them a small vocabulary. The generative chatbots are more flexible, and can handle a wider range of topics, but are much harder to program, and are complex and slow.

4. Because the two distributions will join together – the standard distributions sit "on top" of the uniform distributions and the two combined go to the top of the graph.

5. This is another subjective question. My answers are in the text. I picked emotions that represented the range of capability of my robot and the situations it would be in. I kept to a friendly-type robot, and the only negative emotion is sad. There is no anger, for instance.

6. A small boy would be mischievous, have a short attention span, constantly change the subject, keep trying to bring up the same topic over and over, and would repeat variations of the same questions.

7. In order to provide consistent answers to personal questions, such as "how old are you?".

> For the next two questions, pick a persona from my list to model (from the *"Integrating artificial personality"* section).

8. Write six lines of dialog for the robot to ask a human where they last went on vacation:

```
So, where did you go on vacation last?
Summertime is coming up. Where did you go on vacation last year?
Do you like to travel? Where have you been?
I never get to go on vacation. Where did you go last?
I have heard of this concept called vacation. Where do you like to
go?
Have you been to the beach?
```

9. Six ways for the robot to express that it is tired and needs to recharge, without sounding like a robot, are:

```
I'm tired – have you seen my recharger?
 Wow, it is getting late. I've been at this a long time.
 Well, my battery is getting low. Must be about quitting time.
 I am starting to feel a bit run down.
 Well, look at the time! My battery needs attending to.
 I'm getting hungry in here. Can I go charge now?
```

Chapter 10, Conclusions and Reflections

1. I do not feel that robots or AI are a threat in any way, because the necessary and sufficient conditions for robots to be a threat do not exist. Which is to say, the robots have to *want* to take over the world, and have a *need* to take over. Currently, robots and AI have no wants or needs.

2. We would need project managers, packaging designers, advertising and marketing, sales people, and support staff.

3. Psychologists study normal and abnormal mental states and cognitive processes, exactly what we are trying to simulate for artificial personality. We want the robot to not trigger bad responses in people. I once had a robot with flashing red eyes that caused small children to have panic attacks. Psychologists would help avoid such errors.

4. GPS receivers, radios, Wi-Fi, Bluetooth, accelerometers, gyroscopes, and these days, apps.

5. Because they are universal approximation systems that work in probabilities and averages, not in discrete numbers and logic. ANNs can take a different amount of time because a particular bit of data may take different paths at different times, going through a different number of neurons and thus not taking the same amount of time to process.

6. You can use a neural network based system to model a bad human operator for a driving simulation to help teach other drivers (and self-driving cars) how to avoid bad drivers. The desired state is an unpredictable driver, so just train the neural network to 60% or so.

7. So we have a group of 100 stocks picked by our AI program. Of that set, an indeterminate number are winners and losers. There is a 43% chance the stock is a winner, and a 57% chance it is a loser. We have no way of judging the stocks being winners or losers except by investing our money, which is what we are trying to avoid – investing in bad stocks. A 43% chance of winning is not good. The second AI has an 80% chance of telling you that the first AI chose a bad stock. So 80 times out of 100, you will know that the stock was not a winner. So you are left with an 80% chance of correctly identifying one of the 57 bad stocks, which eliminates 45 stocks. That leaves you with 55 stocks, of which 43 are winners (on average), which raises your odds to 78%.

Using Bayes Theorem, I recomputed the combined probabilities as 75.1% - so I'll take either answer:

Bayes theorem $p(x|c) = (px^* pc) / (px^*pc)+(1-px)(1-pc)$

Other Books You May Enjoy

If you enjoyed this book, you may be interested in these other books by Packt:

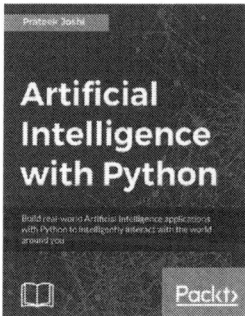

Artificial Intelligence with Python
Prateek Joshi

ISBN: 978-1-78646-439-2

- Realize different classification and regression techniques
- Understand the concept of clustering and how to use it to automatically segment data
- See how to build an intelligent recommender system
- Understand logic programming and how to use it
- Build automatic speech recognition systems
- Understand the basics of heuristic search and genetic programming
- Develop games using Artificial Intelligence
- Learn how reinforcement learning works
- Discover how to build intelligent applications centered on images, text, and time series data
- See how to use deep learning algorithms and build applications based on it

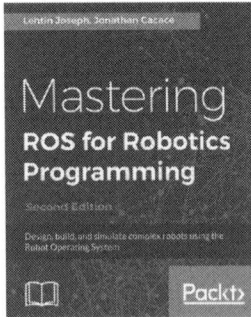

Mastering ROS for Robotics Programming - Second Edition
Lentin Joseph, Jonathan Cacace

ISBN: 978-1-78847-895-3

- Create a robot model with a seven-DOF robotic arm and a differential wheeled mobile robot
- Work with Gazebo and V-REP robotic simulator
- Implement autonomous navigation in differential drive robots using SLAM and AMCL packages
- Explore the ROS Pluginlib, ROS nodelets, and Gazebo plugins
- Interface I/O boards such as Arduino, robot sensors, and high-end actuators
- Simulate and motion plan an ABB and universal arm using ROS Industrial
- Explore the latest version of the ROS framework
- Work with the motion planning of a seven-DOF arm using MoveIt!

Leave a review - let other readers know what you think

Please share your thoughts on this book with others by leaving a review on the site that you bought it from. If you purchased the book from Amazon, please leave us an honest review on this book's Amazon page. This is vital so that other potential readers can see and use your unbiased opinion to make purchasing decisions, we can understand what our customers think about our products, and our authors can see your feedback on the title that they have worked with Packt to create. It will only take a few minutes of your time, but is valuable to other potential customers, our authors, and Packt. Thank you!

Index

task, defining 82, 83, 84, 85
use cases 75
toy/not toy detector
building 126, 127, 128, 129, 130, 132, 133, 134, 135
Toys of Usual Size (TOUS) 203
Turing test 10

U

Ubuntu
reference link 52
universal servo bracket 66
unsharp mask 111
unstructured environment 12
use cases, TinMan robot

pick up toys 75, 76, 77
user interaction 80
user interaction, use case
commands, receiving 81
distance, determining 82
robot, responding 82
verbally interacting, with children 81
with robot 80

V

version 1, robot arm
adaptive learning rate 153
Virtual Network Computing (VNC)
setting up 57
VirtualBox
reference link 52

Printed in Great Britain
by Amazon